THE OFFICIAL RED BOOK
OF UNITED STATES COINS®

—— *2003* ——

A GUIDE BOOK
of
UNITED STATES COINS

By R. S. YEOMAN

56th Edition

Edited by Kenneth Bressett

Best wishes Norm from
Ken Bressett
11-16-02

Fully Illustrated Catalog
and Retail Valuation List — 1616 to Date
With pricing analysis by Philip Bressett

A BRIEF HISTORY OF AMERICAN COINAGE
EARLY AMERICAN COINS AND TOKENS
EARLY MINT ISSUES   REGULAR MINT ISSUES   PROOFS
PRIVATE, STATE AND TERRITORIAL GOLD
SILVER AND GOLD COMMEMORATIVE ISSUES

WHITMAN and THE OFFICIAL RED BOOK OF UNITED STATES COINS are registered
trademarks of St. Martin's Press.
Library of Congress Catalog Card No.: 47-22284

ISBN: 1-58238-188-7   Printed in U.S.A.

The publisher of this book does not deal in coins; the values shown here are not offers to sell or buy but are included only as general information. Descriptions of coins are based on the most accurate data available, but could contain beliefs that may change with further research or discoveries.

 WHITMAN® COIN PRODUCTS

THE PURPOSE OF THIS BOOK

Coin values listed in the *Guide Book* are retail prices averaged from data supplied by contributors several months before publication. The coin market is so active in some categories that values can easily change during this period Prices are shown as a guide and are not intended to serve as a price-list for any dealer's stock. A dash appearing in a price column indicates the existence of coins in that grade, whose current values cannot be determined. It does not necessarily mean that such coins are excessively rare. Italicized prices indicate unsettled values. A number of listings of rare coins do not have prices or dashes in certain grades. This indicates that they are not available or known in those grades.

Prices rise when: 1. The economic trend is inflationary. The number of collectors increases, while coin supplies remain stationary or decrease through attrition or melting. 2. Dealers replace their stocks of coins only from collectors or other dealers, who expect a profit over what they originally paid. 3. Speculators buy in large quantities. 4. Bullion gold and silver prices rise sharply.

Prices decline when: 1. Changes in collecting habits alter demand for certain coins. 2. Speculators sell in large quantities. 3. Hoards or large holdings are suddenly released and cannot be quickly absorbed by the normal market. 4. Bullion gold and silver prices decline sharply.

Those who edit, contribute to, and publish this book advocate the collecting of coins for pleasure and educational benefits. A secondary consideration is that of investment, the profits from which are realized over the long term based on intelligent purchases.

The *Handbook of United States Coins* by R. S. Yeoman, St Martin's Press, New York, NY, containing average prices dealers will pay for these coins, is obtainable at most coin dealers, hobby shops and bookstores.

THE SPANISH MILLED DOLLAR

The Spanish Milled Dollar valued at 8 *reales*, otherwise known as the "pillar dollar" or "piece of eight," has been given a place in romantic fiction unequaled by any other coin.

This time-honored piece and its fractional parts of 1/2 and 1 *real*, 2 and 4 *reales* were the principal coins of the American colonists, and were the forerunners of our own silver dollar and its fractional divisions.

The coin shown above bears the M̄ mint mark for Mexico City. Similar pieces with other mint marks were struck in Bolivia, Chile, Colombia, Guatemala and Peru. Average value for an 8 *reales* of common date and mint is about $135.00 in Fine to Very Fine condition. Dates range from 1732 to 1772.

Note: Many modern copies of the 8 reales exist. These are produced mostly as souvenirs and have little or no value.

CONTRIBUTORS TO THE FIFTY-SIX EDITION

KERRY JASIN, Project Coordinator

*Gary Adkins, Philip E. Bressett, Leonard R. Saunders, and
William J. Spencer, Special Consultants.*

David Akers
Buddy Alleva
Dr. Richard S. Appel
Richard M. August
Richard A. Bagg, Ph.D.
Mitchell A. Battino
Lee J. Bellisario
Philip E. Benedetti
George H. Blenker
Mark R. Borckardt
Q. David Bowers
Donald E. Brigandi
J. H. Cline
Elizabeth W. Coggan
Alan R. Cohen
John West Dannreuther
Tom DeLorey
Kurt Eckstein
Col. Steven Ellsworth
Bob Entlich
Dennis J. Forgue
Mike Fuljenz
Henry G. Garrett
William G. Gay
Dennis M. Gillio
Ronald J. Gillio
Harry Gittelson
Ira M. Goldberg
Lawrence S. Goldberg
Kenneth M. Goldman
J. R. Grellman

Brian H. Hendelson
Gene L. Henry
John W. Highfill
Karl D. Hirtzinger
Jesse Iskowitz
Robert H. Jacobs
Floyd O. Janney
A. M. Kagin
Donald H. Kagin
Bradley S. Karoleff
Stanley Kesselman
Jack Klausen
Mike Kliman
Paul L. Koppenhaver
John J. Kraljevich, Jr.
Richard A. Lecce
Robert B. Lecce
Julian M. Leidman
David Leventhal
Denis W. Loring
Robert T. McIntire
Glenn E. Miller
Lee S. Minshull
Robert Mish
Scott P. Mitchell
Donald A. Mituzas
Michael C. Moline
Paul Nugget
Sid Nusbaum
John M. Pack

William S. Panitch
Robert M. Paul
William P. Paul
John C. Porter
Joel D. Rettew
Joel Rettew, Jr.
Robert J. Rhue
Tom Rinaldo
Mike Ringo
Maurice Rosen
Mary Sauvain
Gerald R. Scherer, Jr.
J. S. Schreiber
Richard J. Schwary
Hugh J. Sconyers
Robert R. Shaw
James A. Simek
Thomas J. Smith
Richard E. Snow
Paul Spiegel
Maurice A. Storck, Sr.
David M. Sundman
Charles Surasky
Anthony J. Swiatek
Anthony Terranova
Frank E. Van Valen
Russell P. Vaughn
Fred Weinberg
Douglas Winter
Mark S. Yaffe

Special credit is due to the following for service and data in this book:
Stewart Blay, Columbus-America Discovery Group, Mike Danish, Charles
Davis, Bill Fivaz, George Fuld, Tom Hallenbeck, James A. Haxby, Michael J.
Hodder, Charles Hoskins, Robert W. Julian, David W. Lange, G. J. Lawson,
Dwight Manley, Arnold Margolis, J. P. Martin, Eric P. Newman, Margaret
Olsen, Doug Plasencia, Len Roosmalen, P. Scott Rubin, Dr. Paul Rynearson,
Neil Shafer, Robert W. Shippee, Arlie Slabaugh, Mark R. Vitunic, Holland
Wallace, Weimar White, John Whitney, and John Wright.

Special credit is also due to the Museum of the American Numismatic
Association, The Smithsonian Institution, Douglas F. Bird, and to Bowers and
Merena Galleries, Inc. for allowing the use of numerous photos from their
files, Stacks® for permission to use color illustrations from various auction
catalogs, PHOTO PROOF and Dawn Hencinsky for photographs from the
NGC archives, and Anthony Swiatek for providing photos used in the modern
commemorative section. Special credit also goes to Bill Fivaz for the many
photos of overdates, double dies, and mint marks.

CONDITION OF COINS
Essential elements of the A.N.A. grading system

PROOF — A specially made coin distinguished by sharpness of detail and usually with a brilliant mirrorlike surface. Proof refers to the method of manufacture and is not a condition, but normally the term implies perfect mint state unless otherwise noted and graded as below. See pages 67 and 68 for details.

MINT STATE — The terms Mint State (MS) and Uncirculated (Unc.) are interchangeably used to describe coins showing no trace of wear. Such coins may vary to some degree because of blemishes, toning or slight imperfections as described in the following subdivisions.

PERFECT UNCIRCULATED (MS-70) — Perfect new condition, showing no trace of wear. The finest quality possible, with no evidence of scratches, handling or contact with other coins. Very few regular issue coins are ever found in this condition.

CHOICE UNCIRCULATED (MS-65) — An above average Uncirculated coin that may be brilliant or lightly toned and has very few contact marks on the surface or rim. MS-67 through MS-62 indicate a slightly higher or lower grade of preservation.

UNCIRCULATED (MS-60) — Has no trace of wear but may show a number of contact marks, and surface may be spotted or lack some luster.

CHOICE ABOUT UNCIRCULATED (AU-55) — Barest evidence of light wear on only the highest points of the design. Most of the mint luster remains.

ABOUT UNCIRCULATED (AU-50) — Has traces of light wear on many of the high points. At least half of the mint luster is still present.

CHOICE EXTREMELY FINE (EF-45) — Light overall wear shows on highest points. All design details are very sharp. Some of the mint luster is evident.

EXTREMELY FINE (EF-40) — Design is lightly worn throughout, but all features are sharp and well defined. Traces of luster may show.

CHOICE VERY FINE (VF-30) —Light even wear on the surface and highest parts of the design. All lettering and major features are sharp.

VERY FINE (VF-20) —Shows moderate wear on high points of design. All major details are clear.

FINE (F-12) —Moderate to considerable even wear. Entire design is bold with overall pleasing appearance.

VERY GOOD (VG-8) —Well worn with main features clear and bold although rather flat.

GOOD (G-4) —Heavily worn with design visible but faint in areas. Many details are flat.

ABOUT GOOD (AG-3) —Very heavily worn with portions of lettering, date and legends worn smooth. The date may be barely readable.

IMPORTANT: Damaged coins, such as those that are bent, corroded, scratched, holed, nicked, stained, or mutilated, are worth less than those without defects. *Flawless uncirculated coins are generally worth more than values quoted in this book.* Slightly worn coins ("sliders") that have been cleaned and conditioned ("whizzed") to simulate uncirculated luster are worth considerably less than perfect pieces.

Unlike damage inflicted after striking, manufacturing defects do not always lessen values. Examples are: Colonial coins with planchet flaws and weakly struck designs; early silver and gold with weight adjustment "file marks" (parallel cuts made prior to striking); and coins with "lint marks" (dust or other foreign matter which may mar the surface during striking).

Brief guides to grading are placed before each major coin type in this book. For those readers who desire more detailed descriptions of all coin grades, we recommend OFFICIAL A.N.A. GRADING STANDARDS FOR UNITED STATES COINS, by the American Numismatic Association.

RARE COINS AS AN INVESTMENT

Investing in rare coins can be a rewarding experience for anyone who approaches the calling armed with the right attitude and background knowledge about this exciting field. It can just as easily become a costly mistake for anyone who attempts to profit from coins without giving serious thought to the idiosyncrasies of this unique market.

The best advice given to anyone considering investing in rare coins is to use common sense. No thinking person would consider buying a diamond ring from a street peddler, or an art masterpiece at a garage sale. It is just the same with rare coins, and the more careful you are in selecting a qualified dealer and making an educated evaluation of the coins that you purchased, the greater will be your chance of making a profitable investment.

The opportunities for successful collecting and investing in quality numismatic items are as great today as at any time in the past. Inexperienced buyers can now purchase coins that have been graded and authenticated by third-party services to assure the quality of each item, and there is more written information available for beginners than ever before. The pricing of rare coins is also very competitive in today's open market where profit margins are often lower than in the past.

The shift in emphasis from collecting to investing has created a new market and demand for coins resulting in more stringent grading methods, and pricing geared to the perceived rarity of coins in various levels of uncirculated perfection. Coins in high grades of condition that have been certified and encapsulated (slabbed) may be valued at multiples of similar coins that have not been so graded. The "raw" (non-serviced) coins that are listed in this catalog are valued at what collectors normally pay for such items without encapsulation, and in many cases will be lower than what is charged for "investment" coins.

For hundreds of years rare coins and precious metals have proven themselves to be an excellent hedge against inflation and source of ready money in times of disaster. There is no reason to think that this will change in the future. Gone are the days when coin collecting was only a passive hobby for those who would study the history and artistry of these enjoyable objects. It has now grown into an activity where speculation on the future demand for rare coins has made them a part of many investment portfolios.

With this change in attitude about collecting has come a measure of concern for those who purchase coins without the background or experience necessary to avoid costly mistakes in accepting overpriced or overgraded coins that simply are not worth what is paid for them. Extreme caution is advised for anyone considering an investment in rare coins. Investigate the person or firm with whom you are dealing. Seek professional non-biased help with grading determinations. Satisfy yourself that the coins you select are not priced considerably higher than is being charged by other dealers.

Protecting valuable coins is an important part of investing. The best protection for keeping coins pristine is to store them in an inert, airtight plastic holder, away from paper products, cigarette smoke, wood, natural rubber, paint and textiles such as wool or felt. Humidity greater than 75% can also be harmful.

Collectors and investors alike can profit by investigating the background and history of the coins they buy. Coins are a mirror of history and art that tell the story of mankind over the past 2,600 years, reflecting economic struggles, wars, prosperity and creativity of every major nation on earth. We are but the custodians of these historical relics, and must appreciate and care for them while in our possession. Those who treat rare coins with the consideration and respect they deserve will profit in many ways, not the least of which can be in the form of a sound financial return on one's investment of time and money.

AN INTRODUCTION TO UNITED STATES COINS
Money of the Early Americans

The story of American money, which occupies a period of over three centuries, began when the early settlers in New England carried on their fur trade with the Indians through the use of wampum, which had been fashioned from mussel shells in the form of "beads." Beaver skins, wampum, and in Virginia, tobacco, soon became the commonly accepted media of exchange for all other available commodities. The immigrants, in fact, had little use for coined money at first, but when traders arrived from foreign lands, coins were usually demanded in payment for goods. Any foreign coins were usually accepted, such as French louis, English guineas, German thalers, Dutch ducats, and various Spanish coins, including doubloons and particularly the Spanish milled dollar, or piece of eight. The piece of eight continued to be a standard money unit throughout the entire colonial period. Even after the Revolutionary War, the Spanish dollar and its fractional parts circulated in this country with official sanction until 1857. One *real* equaled 12½ cents and was known as a "bit." A quarter of the dollar thus became known as "two bits," a term still in use.

England consistently ignored the plight of the colonists and made no effort to provide gold or silver coins, or a small-change currency for them. Although coins known as "Hogge Money" were provided for the Sommer Islands, now known as the Bermudas, about the year 1616, the first coins minted in America were minted by John Hull in the Massachusetts Bay Colony. The General Court of the colony granted him authority to begin coinage. Starting in 1652 the Boston mint provided the famous N.E., pine tree, and similar shillings, with their fractional parts, for the hardpressed colonists. Other colonies tried similar projects but failed.

As time went by, coins and tokens of many types were introduced and employed by the colonists in their daily course of business. Lord Baltimore in Maryland was responsible for a series of silver pieces, which were probably struck in England in 1659. Mark Newby introduced a piece known as St. Patrick's Halfpence into the province of New Jersey in 1682. Coins dated 1722 to 1724, known as Rosa Americana and Hibernia coppers, were produced by William Wood in England and were widely circulated in America. The Carolina and New England Elephant Tokens were passed in the years following 1694. There were also a few issues of uncertain date and origin, such as the New Yorke Token, which circulated among the early settlers.

Enterprising American individuals were responsible for some of the copper pieces that circulated during the eighteenth century. The Gloucester Token, about which little is known, was one of these. Samuel and John Higley of Granby, Connecticut, made an interesting series of threepence pieces during the period from 1737 to 1739. J. Chalmers, a silversmith in Annapolis, Maryland, issued silver shillings, sixpence, and threepence pieces in 1783. In 1787 Ephraim Brasher, a New York goldsmith, struck a gold piece of the value of a doubloon (about $15.00 in New York currency). Standish Barry of Baltimore, Maryland, made a curious silver token threepence in 1790.

Still other tokens, struck in England, reached our shores in Revolutionary times and were for the most part speculative ventures. These much-needed, small-denomination coppers were readily circulated because of the great scarcity of fractional coins. Included in this category were the Nova Constellatio and the Bar copper pieces.

During the period of confederation following the War of Independence, still more English tokens were added to the great variety of coins and tokens employed in the new nation. In 1787 the Nova Eboracs, known as New York Coppers, the Georgius Triumpho, and the Auctori Plebis tokens were introduced.

Another interesting series, historically important because of its close association with our early country and first president, consists of the Kentucky,

Myddelton and Franklin Press pieces, and those tokens bearing the portrait of Washington. Although most of these pieces are dated from 1783 to 1795, many of them were made in England around the turn of the century.

Coinage of the States

The Articles of Confederation, adopted March 1, 1781, provided that Congress should have the sole right to regulate the alloy and value of coin struck by its own authority or by that of the respective states.

Each state, therefore, had the right to coin money, but Congress served as a regulating authority. New Hampshire was the first state to consider coinage, but few if any coins were placed in circulation. The only specimens known bear the date 1776.

Vermont, Connecticut, and New Jersey granted coining privileges to companies or individuals. Massachusetts erected its own mint in which copper coins were produced. A number of interesting varieties of these state issues, most of which were struck in fairly large quantities, can still be acquired, and form the basis for many present day collections of early American coins.

The Beginnings of United States Coinage

Throughout the Colonial years, Americans had become accustomed to the use of the Spanish dollar and its fractional parts, the *real,* the medio (half-*real*), etc. It was only natural, therefore, that when a national coinage was under consideration the dollar was mentioned most frequently. In earlier years currency statutes in many of the colonies had given first consideration to the Spanish dollar. Connecticut, Massachusetts, and Virginia, particularly, passed laws making Spanish coins a legal tender. The first issue of Continental paper money May 10, 1775, offers further evidence that the dollar was to be our basic money unit, for it provided that the notes should be payable in "Spanish Milled Dollars or the value thereof in gold or silver."

The Assistant Financier of the Confederation, Gouverneur Morris, proposed a decimal coinage ratio, and his plan was incorporated in a report presented by Robert Morris, Superintendent of Finance, to the Congress, January 15, 1782. Plans for a mint were advanced, and a uniform national currency to relieve the confused money conditions was outlined. Morris's unit, 1/1440 of a dollar, was calculated to agree without a fraction with all the different valuations of the Spanish Milled Dollar in the various States. Although a government mint was approved February 21, 1782, no immediate action was taken. During 1784 Thomas Jefferson, then a member of the House of Representatives, brought in a report concerning the plan, and expressed disagreement with Morris' complicated money unit. He advocated the simple dollar unit because he believed the dollar was already as familiar and convenient a unit of value as the British pound. He favored the decimal system and remarked that, "The most easy ratio of multiplication and division is that of ten. George Washington referred to it as 'a measure, which in my opinion, has become indispensibly necessary.'"

The Grand Committee in May 1785 recommended a gold five-dollar piece; a dollar of silver with fractional coins, of the same metal, in denominations of half, quarter, tenth, and twentieth parts of a dollar; and copper pieces valued at one-hundredth and one two-hundredth of a dollar.

In 1783 Robert Morris submitted a series of pattern pieces in silver that were designed by Benjamin Dudley to carry out the decimal idea for United States money. These are known as the Nova Constellatio Patterns and consist of the "Mark" or 1,000 units, the "Quint" or 500 units, the "Bit" or 100 units, and a copper "five". The unit was to be a quarter grain of silver. This was not the first attempt at a dollar coin, for the Continental Currency piece of dollar size, dated 1776, had been struck in such metals as brass, pewter, and silver. The variety in silver possibly saw limited service as a dollar, although there is a theory that the Continental Congress considered circulating pewter pieces as an emergency coinage.

Congress gave formal approval to the basic dollar unit and decimal coinage ratio in its resolution of July 6, 1785, but other more pressing matters delayed further action. Not until the Constitutional Convention had placed the country on firm ground and the new nation had elected George Washington President, did the Congress again turn attention to the subject of currency, a mint, and a coinage system.

The Massachusetts cents and half cents struck in 1787 and 1788 were the first official coins to bear a stated value in terms of decimal parts of the dollar unit in this country. The cent represented a hundredth part of a Spanish dollar.

The first federally authorized coin was the Fugio Cent, sometimes called the Franklin Cent, as he was supposed to have supplied the design and composed the legends. This piece, similar in design to the Continental Currency dollar of 1776, was privately struck in 1787 by contract with the government.

Alexander Hamilton, then Secretary of the Treasury, reported his views on monetary matters January 21, 1791. He concurred in all essentials with the decimal subdivisions and multiples of the dollar contained in the earlier resolutions and urged the use of both gold and silver in our standard money.

Congress passed a resolution March 3, 1791, that a mint be established and authorized the President to engage artists and procure machinery for the making of coins. No immediate steps were taken, but when Washington delivered his third annual address, he recommended immediate establishment of a mint.

On April 2, 1792, a bill was finally passed providing "that the money of account of the United States should be expressed in dollars or units, dismes or tenths, cents or hundredths, and milles or thousandths; a disme being the tenth part of a dollar, a cent the hundredth part of a dollar, a mille the thousandth part of a dollar..."

Denominations specified in the act were as follows:

	Value of	Grains Pure	Grains Standard
Gold Eagle	$10.00	247 - 4/8	270
Gold Half Eagle	5.00	123 - 6/8	135
Gold Quarter Eagle	2.50	61 - 7/8	67 - 4/8
Silver Dollar	1.00	371 - 4/16	416
Silver Half Dollar	.50	185 - 10/16	208
Silver Quarter Dollar	.25	92 - 13/16	104
Silver Disme (dime)	.10	37 - 2/16	41 - 3/5
Silver Half Disme	.05	18 - 9/16	20 - 4/5
Copper Cent	.01	11 pennyweights	
Copper Half Cent	.005	5 1/2 pennyweights	

The word "pure" meant unalloyed metal; "standard" meant, in the case of gold, 11/12 fine or 11 parts pure metal to one part alloy, which was mixed with the pure metal to improve the wearing qualities of the coins. The fineness for silver coins was 1485/1664 or approximately 892.43 thousandths, in contrast with the gold coins of 22 karats, or 916 2/3 thousandths fine.

The law also provided for free coinage of gold and silver coins at the fixed ratio of 15 to one, and a token coinage of copper cents and half cents. Under the free coinage provision no charge was to be made for converting gold or silver bullion into coins "weight for weight." At the depositor's option, however, he could demand an immediate exchange of coins for his bullion, for which privilege a deduction of one-half of one percent was to be imposed.

Washington appointed David Rittenhouse, a well-known philosopher and scientist, as the first Director of the Mint. Construction began on a mint building nearly four months after the passage of the Act of April 2, 1792. The building was located on Seventh Street near Arch in Philadelphia.

The first coin struck by the government was the half disme. Fifteen hundred of these pieces were produced during the month of July 1792 before the mint was completed. Washington supplied some of his own silver to the value of about one hundred dollars for those first coins. Dismes also were probably struck at this time or a short while later. The portrait on these pieces may have been modeled by Martha Washington.

Copper for cents and half cents was covered in the Act of May 8, 1792 when the purchase of not over 150 tons was authorized. On September 11, 1792, six pounds of old copper were purchased, this being the first purchase of copper for coinage, which was probably used for the striking of patterns.

Planchets with upset rims for cents and half cents were purchased from Boulton of Birmingham, England from 1798 to 1838.

Several pattern coins were prepared in 1792 before regular mint operations commenced. These included the silver center cent by Henry Voigt, a smaller piece than that of regular issue. The small plug of silver, worth about three-quarters of a cent, was evidently intended to bring the intrinsic value of the coin up to the value of one cent and permit production of a coin of more convenient size. Alexander Hamilton had mentioned a year before that the proposed "intrinsic value" cent would be too large, and suggested that the amount of copper could be reduced and a trace of silver added. The pattern cent with a silver center may have been designed to conform to this recommendation.

The cents by Robert Birch are equally interesting. These patterns are identified by their legends which read "LIBERTY PARENT OF SCIENCE AND INDUSTRY" and "TO BE ESTEEMED BE USEFUL." The quarter with an eagle on the reverse side by Joseph Wright belongs among the early patterns devised before regular issues were struck.

The Bank of Maryland deposited the first silver, sending $80,715.73½ in French coins to the mint July 18, 1794. Moses Brown, a Boston merchant, deposited the first gold in the form of ingots, February 12, 1795, amounting to $2,276.22, receiving silver coin in payment. The first coins transferred to the Treasurer consisted of 11,178 cents on March 1, 1793. The first return of coined silver was made on October 15, 1794, and the first gold coins, 744 half eagles, were delivered July 31, 1795.

File marks on early U. S. coins are usually a result of the mint process of weight adjustment.

Regular Mint Issues

Cents and half-cents exclusively were coined during the year 1793, and by 1799 approximately $50,000 in these coins had been placed in circulation. This amount proved insufficient for the requirements of commerce, and small denomination coins of the states and of foreign countries continued in use during the first few years of the nineteenth century.

One of the most serious problems confronting the commercial interests during the early years was the failure of the government to provide a sufficient volume of circulating coins. The fault, contrary to popular opinion at the time, did not lie with any lack of effort on the part of the mint. Other circumstances tended to interfere with the expected steady flow of new coinage into the channels of trade.

Free circulation of United States gold and silver coins was greatly hindered by speculators. For example, worn Spanish dollars of reduced weight and value were easily exchanged for U. S. silver dollars, which meant the export of most of the new dollars as fast as they were minted, and a complete loss to American trade channels.

Gold coins failed to circulate for similar reasons. The ratio of 15 to 1 between gold and silver was close to the world ratio when Hamilton recommended it, but by 1799 the ratio in European commercial centers had reached 15¾ to 1. At this rate the undervalued gold coins tended to flow out of the country, or were reduced for bullion. After 1800, therefore, United States gold coins were rarely seen in general circulation. As no remedy could be found, coinage of the Eagle and the silver dollar was suspended by President Jefferson in 1804 and 1806 respectively. It is generally conceded that the silver dollar was discontinued in 1804, although the last coins minted for the period were dated 1803.

Lacking gold coins and silver dollars, the half dollar became the desirable coin for large transactions, bank reserves, and foreign payments. Until 1830, in fact, half dollars circulated very little as they were mainly transferred from bank to bank. This will account for the relatively good supply of half dollars of this period that is still available to collectors in better than average condition. A senate committee of 1830 reported that United States silver coins were considered so much bullion and were accordingly "lost to the community as coins."

There was only a negligible coinage of quarters, dimes, and half dimes from 1794 to 1834. It has been estimated that there was less than one piece for each person in the country in the year 1830. This period has been described as one of nondescript currency made up of banknotes, underweight foreign gold coins, foreign silver coins of many varieties, and domestic fractional silver coins. Notes of "wildcat banks" flooded the country before 1830 and were much more common than silver coins.

On June 28, 1834, a new law was passed reducing the weight of standard gold, which had the effect of placing our money on a gold standard. Trade and finance were greatly benefited by this act, which also proved a boon to the gold mines of Georgia and North Carolina. Branch mints in Dahlonega, Georgia, and Charlotte, North Carolina, were established in 1838 to handle the newly mined gold at the source. The Templeton Reid and Bechtler issues of private gold coins were struck in this area.

The law of January 18, 1837, completely revised and standardized the mint and coinage laws. Legal standards, mint charges, legal tender, mint procedure, tolerance in coin weights, accounting methods, a bullion fund, standardization of gold and silver coins to 900 thousandths fine, and other desirable regulations were covered by the new legislation. Results of importance to the collector were the changes in type for the various coin denominations and the resumption of coinage of the eagle in 1838 and larger quantities of silver dollars in 1840.

The political and financial elements underwent a crisis at about this time. The familiar "Jackson Tokens" and fractional notes of banks and commercial establishments completely eclipsed the circulation of metallic currency. This was the era of "shinplasters."

The California gold discovery in 1848 was responsible for an interesting series of private, state, and territorial gold issues in the Western states, culminating in the establishment of a branch mint at San Francisco in 1854.

Two new regular gold issues were adopted in 1849. In that year the double eagle and gold dollar joined our American family of coins. The California gold fields greatly influenced the world gold market, making the exportation of silver profitable. For example, the silver in two half dollars was worth $1.03 1/2 in gold. The newly introduced gold dollars soon took over the burden and hastened the disappearance of silver coins from trade channels. This was the situation when the new three cent postage rate brought about the bill authorizing the coinage of the silver three cent piece in 1851. This was our country's first subsidiary coin, for its value was intrinsically 86% of its face value, an expedient designed to prevent its withdrawal from circulation.

The three dollar gold piece was authorized by the act of February 21, 1853. Never a popular or necessary coin, it nevertheless was issued regularly from 1854 until 1889.

On February 21, 1853, fractional silver coins were made subsidiary by reducing the weights of all silver pieces, excepting the dollar. As the coins were now worth less than their face value, free coinage of silver was prohibited, and the mint was authorized to purchase its silver requirements on its own account using the bullion fund of the mint, and, according to law, "the profit of said coinage shall be...transferred to the account of the treasury of the United States."

Arrows were placed at the date on all silver coins except three cent pieces and dollars, and on the quarters and half dollars rays were added on the reverse side to denote the change of weight. In 1854 the rays were removed, and in 1856 the arrows disappeared. Production of silver coins in large quantities during this period greatly relieved the demands on gold dollars and three cent pieces. Consequently for the first time in our nation's history there was a sufficient supply of fractional coins in general circulation.

The law of 1857 was designed primarily to reform the copper coinage. No matter how interesting and valuable the large cents and half cents may have become in the eyes of the modern collector, they were very unpopular with the people and cost the mint too much to produce.

The new law abolished the half cent piece, and reduced the size and changed the design of the cent. The new Flying Eagle cent contained 88% copper and 12% nickel. Several hundred experimental cents were stamped from dies bearing the date 1856 although no authority for the issue existed before 1857. Other important effects of the law were the retirement of the Spanish silver coins from circulation, and dispersal of the new cents in such excessive quantities as to create a nuisance to business houses, particularly in the eastern cities. The Indian head device replaced the Flying Eagle in 1859, and in 1864 the weight of the cent was further reduced and its composition changed to a proportion of 95% copper and 5% tin and zinc. This bronze composition was the standard for our cent except for the years 1943, and 1944 to 1946. In 1962 the alloy was changed to 95% copper and 5% zinc. In 1982 the composition was changed to 97.5% zinc and 2.5% copper.

Both Jefferson and Hamilton had contended in their day that the currency of money of small value benefits society. The history of our cent and its daily use proves the soundness of this principle.

Abundance turned to scarcity following the outbreak of the Civil War. Anticipation of a scarcity and depreciation of the paper money was sufficient to induce hoarding. The large volume of greenbacks in circulation caused a premium on gold, and subsidiary silver as a result of the sudden depreciation quickly vanished in the North. Resort was soon made to postage stamps for small change. All types of fractional notes were put out at this time by municipalities and the government. "Postage currency" became widely used, and in 1863 a great variety of tokens appeared to help fill the vacuum. Like the tokens of 1837 they were of two general classes, tradesmen's coins and imitations of legal cents. Many of the latter were political or patriotic in character, carried slogans typical of the times, and were usually produced at a profit.

The Law of 1864, which effected changes in the cent, provided also for the new bronze two cent piece. The act, moreover, provided legal tender status for these two coins up to ten times their value. The two cent piece was the first coin to bear the motto IN GOD WE TRUST. The new coin was readily accepted by the people but proved an unnecessary denomination, going out of fashion and being discontinued only nine years later.

Secretary Chase had issued a great many currency notes of three cent denomination early in 1865. The nickel interests seized upon this circumstance to fight for a new three cent coin for redemption of the paper money. A law was quickly passed and signed by the president as of March 3, 1865, providing for a three cent coin of 75-25 copper-nickel composition. Our country now possessed two types of three cent pieces. The nickel three cent piece was struck continuously until 1889; the three cent silver until 1873.

The new copper-nickel alloy ratio was selected for the five cent coin, adopted May 16, 1866, to be thereafter known as a "nickel." Again the people had a coin value available in two forms. The silver half dime, like the three cent piece, was retired from service in 1873.

The Carson City Mint was established in 1870 as a convenient depository for the miners in that area and operated until 1893.

The Law of March 3, 1871, was a redemption measure and was passed to provide a means for the disposal to the United States Treasury of millions of minor coins which had accumulated in the hands of postmasters, newsdealers, and others. Small-denomination coins as a result of this new law were placed on an equal footing and could be redeemed when presented in lots of twenty dollars.

There was a general revision of the coinage laws in 1873. Several years of study and debate preceded the final enactment. The legislative history of the bill occupies hundreds of pages of the Congressional Globe, and the result was considered by many a clumsy attempt and a failure. The law has sometimes been referred to as the "Crime of '73." One consequence of the bill, which achieved final enactment February 12, 1873, was the elimination of the silver dollar. In its stead the Trade dollar of greater weight was provided for use in commerce with the Orient in competition with the Mexican dollar. The legal tender provision, which gave the Trade dollar currency within our borders, was repealed the following year.

The charge for converting standard gold bullion into coin was reduced by the act to one-fifth of one percent. The same rate was imposed on silver bullion for coining Trade dollars only.

It may be a surprise to some collectors to learn that the silver dollar had not circulated to any great extent in the United States after 1803. The coin had been turned out steadily since 1840, but for various reasons such as exportation, melting, and holding in bank vaults, the dollar was virtually an unknown coin. The Law of 1873 in effect demonetized silver and committed our country to a gold standard. The silver mining interests came to realize what had occurred a little later, and the ensuing quarter century of political and monetary history was filled with their voluble protests. There was a constant bitter struggle for the return to bimetallism.

From an economic point of view the inadequate supply of gold was responsible for a gradual decline in prices worldwide. This brought about a gradual business depression in our country, particularly in the South and Middle-West. Private silver interests influenced great sections of the West for bimetallism as a remedy for the failing price level. Authorities have concluded that a world-wide adoption of bimetallism would have improved economic conditions, but the United States alone proceeding to place its money on a double standard at the old 16 to 1 ratio would have led only to a worse situation.

Of particular importance to collectors, however, were those features of the Law of 1873 which affected the status and physical properties of the individual coins. The weight of the half-dollar, quarter, and dime, was slightly changed and arrows were placed at the date for the ensuing two years to indicate the difference in weight. Silver three-cent pieces, half-dimes, and two-cent pieces were abolished by the act, and the manufacture of minor coins was restricted to the Mint at Philadelphia.

The short-lived twenty-cent piece was authorized March 3, 1875. It was created for the Western states where the Spanish "bit" had become equivalent to a U. S. dime. The five-cent piece did not circulate there, so when a quarter was offered for a "bit" purchase, only a dime change was returned. However, it was confused with the quarter-dollar and was discontinued after 1878.

The Bland-Allison Act of February 28, 1878, gave the Secretary authority to purchase two to four million dollars worth of silver bullion each month to be coined into silver dollars. The coin, never popular, was produced in minimum quantities. This was not a bimetallic law, nor was it a free coinage act. Strictly speaking it was a subsidiary coinage law, called by some "a wretched compromise."

The North and East so disliked the silver dollars that they did not actively circulate there and eventually found their way back to the Treasury, mostly through tax payments. Secretary Manning transferred ownership to the people and removed them from Treasury holdings by the simple expedient of issuing silver certificates in small bills to effect a wide circulation.

The Bland-Allison Act was repealed in 1890 and the Sherman Act took its place. Under this new law 4,500,000 ounces of silver per month could be paid for with Treasury Notes that were to be legal tender, and redeemable in gold or silver dollars coined from the bullion purchased. Important in this case was the fact that the notes were constantly being redeemed for gold which was mainly exported. The measure was actually a government subsidy for the silver miners and as such it was marked for failure, and was hastily repealed. The Bland-Allison Act and the Sherman Act gave a total of 570 million silver dollars to our monetary stocks.

The "Gold Standard Act" of 1900 gave our country a single standard, but reaffirmed the fiction that the silver dollar was a standard coin. It still enjoyed unlimited legal tender, but was as much a subsidiary coin, practically speaking, as the dime, for its value in terms of standard gold, even before the gold surrender executive order, was far below its face value.

The lapse in coinage after 1904 and until 1921 was due to lack of demand. Legislation authorizing further metal supplies for silver dollars was not forthcoming until 1918 when the Pittman Act provided silver for the new dollars.

Before the first World War the value of gold was equal to the value of gold coined into money. In order to encourage a steady flow of gold to the mints, the government (with the exception of the period 1853-1873) had adopted a policy of gratuitous coinage. The cost of converting gold into coin had generally been considered an expense chargeable to the government.

In practice the mint made fine bars for commercial use or mint bars for coinage at its discretion. The bars in later years were stored in vaults and gold or silver certificates issued in place of the coins.

On April 5, 1933 President Roosevelt issued an order prohibiting banks from paying out gold and gold certificates without permission, and gold currency was thus kept for reserve purposes. Gold imports and newly mined domestic gold could be sold only to the government. Gold bullion and coins may now be collected and saved by anyone as all restrictions were removed in 1975.

Under the Coinage Act of 1965, the composition of dimes, quarters and half dollars was changed to eliminate or reduce the silver content of these coins. The "clad" dimes and quarters were composed of an outer layer of copper-nickel (75% copper and 25% nickel) bonded to an inner core of pure copper. Starting 1971 the half dollar and dollar composition was changed to that of the dime and quarter. All silver clad coins have an outer layer of 80% silver bonded to an inner core of 21% silver, with a total content of 40% silver.

By the Law of September 26, 1890, changes in designs of United States coins cannot be made more often than once every twenty-five years without Congressional approval. Since that date, there have been design changes in all denominations and there have been many gold and silver commemorative issues. These factors are largely responsible for the ever increasing interest in coin collecting.

QUANTITIES OF COINS STRUCK

Collectors are cautioned that mint reports are not always reliable for estimating the rarity of coins. In the early years of the mint, dies of previous years were often used until they became worn or broken.

It should also be emphasized that quantities reported, particularly for gold and silver, cover the number of coins struck and have no reference to the quantity reaching actual circulation. Many issues were deposited in the treasury as backing for paper currency and were later melted.

The rarity of gold pieces struck before 1834, particularly half eagles, can be traced to the fact that the gold content was reduced in 1834, making previous issues greater in value than face, causing melting and reminting.

The quantities reported by the mint of three dollar gold pieces from 1873 to 1877 and half cents from 1832 to 1836 are subject to doubt.

Coinage figures shown for 1964 through 1966 are for coins bearing those dates. Some of them were struck in more than one year and at various mints, both with and without mint marks.

Mint quantities are shown adjacent to each date throughout the book. Figures shown in *italic* are estimates based on the most accurate information available. PROOF TOTALS ARE SHOWN IN PARENTHESES.

A star (★) throughout the colonial section indicates that struck copies exist.

Copies of certain American issues were made after 1850 to provide facsimiles of rarer issues which would otherwise be unobtainable. A star has been placed adjacent to those pieces of which deceptive copies exist. Many crude imitations have also been made in recent years, as well as forgeries intended to deceive collectors. THE SPECIMENS ILLUSTRATED ARE GENUINE.

I. THE BRITISH COLONIES IN AMERICA
SOMMER ISLANDS (Bermuda)

This coinage, the first struck for the English colonies in America, was issued about 1616. The coins were known as "Hogge Money" or "Hoggies."

The pieces were made of copper lightly silvered, in four denominations: shilling, sixpence, threepence and twopence, indicated by Roman numerals. The hog is the main device and appears on the obverse side of each. SOMMER ISLANDS is inscribed within beaded circles. The reverse shows a full-rigged galleon with the flag of St. George on each of four masts.

The islands were named for Sir George Sommers who was shipwrecked there in 1609 while enroute to the Virginia Plantations. Shakespeare's *The Tempest* was possibly based on this incident.

The Bermuda Islands, as they are known today, were named for Juan Bermudez who is believed to have stopped there in 1515. A few hogs which he carried for delivery to the West Indies were left behind. When Sommers and his party arrived, the islands were overrun with the animals which served as a welcome source of food for the expedition.

Twopence   Threepence

Sixpence Large Portholes Small Portholes

Shilling ★ Small Sail Large Sail

	Good	V. Good	Fine	V. Fine
Twopence, large star between legs..	$2,250	$3,500	$7,200	$10,000
Twopence, small star between legs .	2,250	3,500	7,200	10,000
Threepence (V. Rare)	—	—	—	72,500
Sixpence, small portholes	2,100	3,250	5,250	10,000
Sixpence, large portholes	2,100	3,250	5,250	10,000
Shilling, small sail............................	2,800	4,000	6,000	14,000
Shilling, large sail	3,000	5,000	7,500	15,000

MASSACHUSETTS
"NEW ENGLAND" COINAGE (1652)

The earliest medium of exchange in the New England settlements was wampum. The General Court of Massachusetts in 1637 ordered "that wampamege should passe at 6 a penny for any sume under 12 d." Wampum consisted of shells of various colors ground to the size of a grain of corn. A hole was drilled through each piece so they could be strung on leather thongs for convenience and adornment.

Corn, pelts, and bullets were frequently used in lieu of coins, which were rarely available. Silver and gold coins brought over from England, Holland and other countries tended to flow back across the Atlantic to purchase needed supplies. The colonists thus left to their own resources dealt with the friendly Indians in kind. In 1661 the law making wampum legal tender was repealed.

Agitation for a standard coinage reached its height in 1651. England, with a civil war pending between the Puritans and Royalists, ignored the colonists, who took matters into their own hands in 1652.

The General Court in 1652 ordered the first metallic currency to be struck in the English Americas (the Spaniards had established a mint in Mexico City in 1535), the New England silver threepence, sixpence, and shilling. Silver bullion was procured principally from the West Indies. The mint was located in Boston, Massachusetts, and John Hull was appointed mintmaster; his assistant was Robert Sanderson (or Saunderson). At first, Hull received one shilling threepence for every twenty shillings coined as his compensation. This fee was adjusted several times during his term as mintmaster.

NE Threepence (1652)

NE Sixpence (1652) ★

Note: Early American coins are rare in conditions better than those listed and are consequently valued much higher.

NE Shilling (1652) ★

	V. Good	Fine	V. Fine
NE Threepence *(Unique)*	—	—	—
NE Sixpence *(8 known)*	—	$30,000	$75,000
NE Shilling	$20,000	35,000	80,000

[16]

MASSACHUSETTS
WILLOW TREE COINAGE (1653-1660)

The simplicity of the design on the N.E. coins invited counterfeiting and clipping of the edges. Therefore, they were soon replaced by the Willow, Oak and Pine Tree series. The Willow Tree coins were struck from 1653 to 1660, the Oak Trees 1660 to 1667, and the Pine Trees 1667 to 1682. All of them (with the exception of the Oak Tree twopence) bore the date 1652, which gives them the appearance of having been struck during the English civil war, when Cromwell was in power.

The coinage was abandoned in 1682; a proposal to renew coinage in 1686 was rejected by the General Court.

Early American coins were produced from handmade dies which are often individually distinctive. The great number of die varieties which can be found and identified are of interest to collectors who value each according to individual rarity. Values shown for type coins in this catalog are for the most common die variety.

Threepence

Sixpence

Shilling

	Fair	Good	V. Good	Fine	V. Fine
Willow Tree Threepence 1652 *(3 known)*.	—	—	—	—	—
Willow Tree Sixpence 1652 *(14 known)* ...	—	—	$15,000	$30,000	$60,000
Willow Tree Shilling 1652	$4,000	$10,000	15,000	30,000	60,000

OAK TREE COINAGE (1660-1667)

Twopence ★

Threepence

	Good	V. Good	Fine	V. Fine	E. Fine
Oak Tree Twopence 1662, small 2..........	$375.00	$750.00	$1,500	$2,800	$4,750
Oak Tree Twopence 1662, large 2	375.00	750.00	1,500	2,800	4,750
Oak Tree Threepence 1652, no IN on obv.	425.00	850.00	2,000	4,000	6,000
Oak Tree Threepence 1652, IN on obv.	425.00	850.00	2,100	4,100	7,250

[17]

MASSACHUSETTS

Sixpence **Shilling ★**

	Good	V. Good	Fine	V. Fine	E. Fine
Oak Tree Sixpence 1652, IN on rev........	$375.00	$850.00	$2,300	$4,750	$8,000
Oak Tree Sixpence 1652, IN on obv.	375.00	850.00	2,100	4,250	7,500
Oak Tree Shilling 1652, IN at left..........	425.00	875.00	2,400	4,500	7,750
Oak Tree Shilling 1652, IN at bottom....	425.00	875.00	2,100	4,000	7,250
Oak Tree Shilling 1652, ANDO..............	650.00	1,300	3,000	5,750	9,750
Oak Tree Shilling 1652, Spiny tree........	425.00	875.00	2,100	4,000	7,000

PINE TREE COINAGE (1667-1682)

The first pine tree coins were minted on the same size planchets as the Oak Tree pieces. Subsequent issues of the shilling were narrower and thicker to conform to the size of English coins.

Threepence ★ **Sixpence ★**

Shilling, Large Planchet (1667-1674) ★

Shilling, Small Planchet (1675-1682)

	Good	V. Good	Fine	V. Fine	E. Fine
Pine Tree Threepence 1652, pellets at trunk ..	$350.00	$625.00	$1,100	$2,500	$4,750
Pine Tree Threepence 1652, without pellets ...	350.00	625.00	1,100	2,500	4,750
Pine Tree Sixpence 1652, pellets at trunk.......	400.00	700.00	1,400	2,750	5,000
Pine Tree Sixpence 1652, without pellets	400.00	750.00	1,500	2,900	5,250
Pine Tree Shillings 1652—Large Planchet (27-31mm diameter)					
1652 Shilling, pellets at trunk..........................	475.00	825.00	1,600	3,500	6,250
1652 Shilling, without pellets at truck.............	475.00	825.00	1,600	3,500	6,250
1652 Shilling, no H in MASATUSETS	550.00	1,200	2,400	4,250	8,750
1652 Shilling, reversed N in ENGLAND.........	575.00	1,300	2,400	4,250	7,250
1652 Shilling, monogrammed NE in legend....	550.00	1,200	1,800	4,000	6,750
Pine Tree Shillings—Small Planchet (22-26mm diameter)					
1652 Shilling, small planchet...........................	400.00	750.00	1,500	3,000	5,500

MARYLAND

Cecil Calvert, the second Lord Baltimore, inherited from his father nearly absolute control over Maryland. Cecil believed he had the right to coin money for the colony and in 1659 he ordered shillings, sixpences and groats (four-penny pieces) from the Royal Mint in London and shipped samples to his brother Philip in Maryland, who was then his secretary for the colony. Cecil's right to strike coins was challenged but upheld by Cromwell's government. The whole issue was small, and while his coins circulated in Maryland at first, by 1700 they had largely disappeared.

Calvert's coins bear his portrait on the obverse, with a Latin legend calling him "Lord of Mary's Land." The reverses bear his family coat of arms and the denomination in Roman numerals. There are several die varieties of each. Many of these coins are found holed and repaired. The copper penny or denarium is the rarest denomination, with only five known specimens.

Penny (denarium) ★   Fourpence (groat)

Sixpence   Lord Baltimore Shilling

	Good	V. Good	Fine	V. Fine	E. Fine	A. Unc.
Penny (copper) (Ex. Rare).......	—	—	—	—	—	—
Fourpence	$1,300	$2,300	$4,800	$9,000	$13,500	$18,000
Sixpence..................................	1,200	1,850	3,800	5,500	10,000	13,500
Shilling...................................	1,400	2,500	5,250	9,000	13,000	16,000

NEW JERSEY
ST. PATRICK OR MARK NEWBY COINAGE

Mark Newby, who came to America from Dublin, Ireland, in November 1681, brought copper pieces believed by numismatists to have been struck in Dublin c. 1670-1675. These are called St. Patrick coppers.

The coinage was made legal tender by the General Assembly of New Jersey in May, 1682. The legislature did not specify which size piece could circulate, only that the coin was to be worth a halfpenny in trade. Most numismatists believe the larger size coin was intended. However, as many more farthing size pieces are known than halfpennies, some believe that the smaller size piece was meant. Copper coins often circulated in the colonies at twice what they would have been worth in England.

The obverses show a crowned king kneeling playing a harp. The legend FLOREAT REX (May the King prosper) is separated by a crown. The reverse side of the halfpenny shows St. Patrick with a crozier in his left hand and a trefoil in his right, surrounded by people. At his left is a shield. The legend is ECCE GREX (Behold the flock). The farthing reverse shows St. Patrick driving away

NEW JERSEY

reptiles and serpents, as he holds a Metropolitan cross in his left hand. The legend reads QUIESCAT PLEBS (May the people be at ease).

The large size piece, called a halfpenny, bears the arms of the City of Dublin on the shield on the reverse; the smaller size piece, called a farthing, does not.

The decorative brass insert found on the coinage, usually over the crown on the obverse, was put there to make counterfeiting more difficult. On some pieces this decoration has been removed or does not show. Numerous die variations exist.

St. Patrick "Farthing"

St. Patrick "Halfpenny"

	V. Good	Fine	V. Fine	E. Fine
St. Patrick "Farthing"	$125.00	$375.00	$1,000	$2,000
Similar, halo around saint's head	500.00	1,400	2,600	—
Similar, no C in QUIESCAT	600.00	1,500	2,900	—
St. Patrick "Farthing" — Silver	1,400	2,600	4,000	5,250
St. Patrick "Farthing" — Gold			(Unique)	
St. Patrick "Halfpenny"	275.00	700.00	1,500	3,s000

II. COINAGE AUTHORIZED BY ROYAL PATENT
AMERICAN PLANTATIONS TOKEN

These tokens struck in nearly pure tin were the first authorized coinage for the British colonies in America. They were made under a franchise granted in 1688 to Richard Holt. Bright, unblemished specimens are more valuable. Restrikes were made about 1828 from original dies.

	Fine	E. Fine	A. Unc.	Unc.
(1688) James II Plantation Token farthing,				
1/24 PART REAL — Tin	$325.00	$1,000	$1,250	$2,500
1/24 PART REAL — Tin ET. HB. REX	425.00	1,000	1,500	3,250
1/24 PART REAL — Tin. Sidewise 4 in 24	750.00	2,500	3,750	—
1/24 PART REAL — Tin. Arms transposed	900.00	3,250	—	—
Restrike	225.00	500.00	700.00	1,200

COINAGE OF WILLIAM WOOD
ROSA AMERICANA COINS

William Wood, an Englishman, obtained a patent from George I to make tokens for Ireland and the American Colonies.

The first pieces struck were undated; others bear the dates 1722, 1723, 1724 and 1733. The Rosa Americana pieces were issued in three denominations, halfpenny, penny and twopence, and were intended for America. This type had a full-blown rose on the reverse with the words ROSA AMERICANA UTILE DULCI (American Rose — useful and pleasant).

The obverse, common to both Rosa Americana and Hibernia pieces, shows the head of George I and the legend GEORGIUS D:G: MAG: BRI: FRA: ET. HIB: REX. (George, by the Grace of God, King of Great Britain, France and Ireland) or abbreviations thereof. Rosa Americana tokens, however, were rejected by the American colonists. The coins are made of a brass composition of 75% copper, 24.7% zinc and .3% silver, sometimes mistakenly referred to as Bath metal.

	V. Good	Fine	V. Fine	E. Fine	A. Unc.
Twopence (no date) (illustrated)	$125.00	$275.00	$525.00	$900.00	$1,800
Twopence (no date) motto without label (3 known)	—	—	—	—	—

	V. Good	Fine	V. Fine	E. Fine	A. Unc.
1722 Halfpenny VTILE DVLCI	725.00	2,000	3,000	—	—
1722 Halfpenny D. G. REX ROSA AMERI. UTILE DULCI	125.00	220.00	450.00	850.00	1,500
1722 Halfpenny DEI GRATIA REX UTILE DULCI	125.00	220.00	375.00	750.00	1,350

	V. Good	Fine	V. Fine	E. Fine	A. Unc.
1722 Penny GEORGIVS				—	—
1722 Penny VTILE DVLCI	125.00	220.00	400.00	800.00	1,750
1722 Penny UTILE DULCI	125.00	220.00	360.00	700.00	1,400

ROSA AMERICANA

	V. Good	Fine	V. Fine	E. Fine	A. Unc.
1722 Twopence, period after REX	$125.00	$250.00	$450.00	$850.00	$1,750
1722 Twopence, no period after REX	125.00	250.00	450.00	850.00	1,750

1723 Halfpenny, uncrowned rose	800.00	1,300	2,400	—	—
1723 Halfpenny	90.00	130.00	325.00	675.00	1,400

1723 Penny	85.00	125.00	275.00	550.00	1,000
1723 Twopence (illustrated)	125.00	250.00	400.00	850.00	1,500

1724, 4 over 3 Penny (Pattern) DEI GRATIA	5,250	7,750
1724, 4 over 3 Penny (Pattern) D GRATIA	6,250	10,500
1724 Penny (undated) ROSA: SINE: SPINA.(*3 known*)	8,000	13,000

ROSA AMERICANA

E. Fine

1724 Twopence (Pattern) $9,000

The 1733 twopence is a pattern piece and bears the bust of George II facing to the left. It was issued by the successors to the coinage patent, as William Wood had died in 1730.

1733 Twopence (Pattern) Proof... 20,000

WOOD'S HIBERNIA COINAGE

The type intended for Ireland had a seated figure with a harp on the reverse side and the word HIBERNIA. Denominations struck were halfpenny and farthing with dates 1722, 1723 and 1724. Hibernia coins were unpopular in Ireland, so many of them were sent to the American colonies.

	First Type		Second Type		1723 over 22	
	V. Good	Fine	V. Fine	E. Fine	Unc.	
1722 Farthing, D:G: REX	$140.00	$250.00	$500.00	$875.00	$1,500	
1722 Halfpenny, D:G: REX, rocks at right (Pattern)			1,500	3,500		
1722 Halfpenny, first type, harp at left ...	65.00	100.00	250.00	500.00	1,000	
1722 Halfpenny, second type, harp at right	60.00	90.00	175.00	325.00	750.00	
1722 Halfpenny, second type, DEII (blunder)	100.00	200.00	400.00	800.00	1,350	
1723 Farthing — D:G: REX.	90.00	120.00	200.00	475.00	775.00	
1723 Farthing — DEI. GRATIA. REX	50.00	70.00	125.00	240.00	575.00	
1723 Farthing — Silver pattern	1,000	1,500	2,500	3,400	5,500	

WOOD'S HIBERNIA COINAGE

1723 Hibernia Farthing   **1724 Hibernia Halfpenny**

	V. Good	Fine	V. Fine	E. Fine	Unc.
1723 over 22 Halfpenny	$65.00	$115.00	$250.00	$500.00	$1,000
1723 Halfpenny	32.00	60.00	100.00	230.00	575.00
1723 Halfpenny — Silver pattern	—	—	—	—	—
1724 Farthing	85.00	175.00	300.00	650.00	1,200
1724 Halfpenny	65.00	110.00	225.00	475.00	950.00
1724 Halfpenny, DEI above head	110.00	220.00	575.00	850.00	1,400

VIRGINIA HALFPENNY

In 1773 coinage of a copper halfpenny was authorized for Virginia by the Crown. The pattern in proof struck on a large planchet with wide milled border is often referred to as a penny.

The silver piece dated 1774 is referred to as a shilling, but may have been a pattern or trial for a halfpenny or a guinea.

Red uncirculated pieces without spots are worth considerably more.

	Fine	V. Fine	E. Fine	A. Unc.	Unc.
1773 Halfpenny, period after GEORGIVS	$85.00	$170.00	$300.00	$425.00	$725.00
1773 Halfpenny, no period after GEORGIVS	90.00	185.00	335.00	475.00	900.00

	Proof
1773 "Penny"	$7,750

Proof
1774 "Shilling" *(6 known)* $20,000

[24]

III. EARLY AMERICAN TOKENS

Struck in America or England for use by American Merchants

LONDON ELEPHANT TOKENS

The London Elephant tokens were struck circa 1672-1694. Although undated, two examples are known struck over 1672 British halfpennies. Most are struck in copper, but one is made of brass. The legend on this piece, GOD PRESERVE LONDON, is probably just a general plea for divine aid and not a specific reference to the outbreak of plague in 1665 or the Great Fire of 1666.

These pieces were not struck for the colonies, and probably did not circulate widely in America, although a few may have been carried here by colonists. They are associated with the 1694 Carolina and New England Elephant tokens, through a shared obverse die.

	V. Good	Fine	V. Fine	E. Fine	A. Unc.
(1694) Halfpenny GOD PRESERVE LONDON (Thick planchet)	$210.00	$375.00	$650.00	$1,250	$1,700
(1694) Halfpenny GOD PRESERVE LONDON (Thin planchet)	300.00	600.00	1,300	2,250	3,400
(1694) Halfpenny GOD PRESERVE LONDON (Diagonals in center of shield)	350.00	600.00	1,400	2,700	3,600
(1694) Halfpenny, similar. Variety with sword in second quarter of shield instead of first	—	—	—	—	—
(1694) Halfpenny LON DON	600.00	1,500	2,300	3,800	6,750

CAROLINA AND NEW ENGLAND ELEPHANT TOKENS

Although no law is known authorizing coinage for Carolina, two very interesting pieces known as Elephant Tokens were made with the date 1694. These copper tokens were of halfpenny denomination. The reverse reads GOD PRESERVE CAROLINA AND THE LORDS PROPRIETERS 1694.

The second and more common variety has the last word spelled PROPRIETORS. The correction was made on the original die, for the E shows plainly beneath the O. The elephant's tusks nearly touch the milling on the second variety.

CAROLINA ELEPHANT TOKENS

The Carolina pieces were probably struck in England and perhaps intended only as tokens, or possibly as advertising to heighten interest in the Carolina Plantation.

Like the Carolina Tokens, the New England Elephant Tokens were believed to have been struck in England as a promotional piece to increase interest in the American Colonies.

	V. Good	Fine	V. Fine
1694 PROPRIETERS	$3,800	$5,250	$8,800
1694 PROPRIETORS, O OVER E	3,400	4,650	7,000

NEW ENGLAND ELEPHANT TOKEN

1694 NEW ENGLAND	17,000	23,000	33,000

THE NEW YORKE IN AMERICA TOKEN

This is a farthing or halfpenny token intended for New York, issued by Francis Lovelace, who was governor from 1668 until 1673. The token uses the older spelling with a final "e", which predominated before 1710. The obverse shows Cupid pursuing the butterfly-winged Psyche, a rebus on the name Lovelace. The reverse shows an eagle, displayed, on a staff in fesse, raguly, which is identical to the crest of the Lovelace arms. In weight, fabric and die axis the tokens are similar to the 1670 farthing tokens of Bristol, England, where they may have been struck. There is no evidence that any of these pieces ever circulated in America.

	V. Good	Fine
Brass (undated)	$4,000	$7,750
Pewter (undated)	4,200	9,000

GLOUCESTER TOKENS

S. S. Crosby, in his book "The Early Coins of America" stated that this coin appears to have been intended as a pattern for a shilling; a private coinage by Richard Dawson of Gloucester (county), Virginia. The only specimens known are struck in brass, although the denomination XII indicates that a silver coinage (one shilling) may have been planned. The building may represent some public building, possibly the court house.

Although neither of the two known examples shows the full legends, combining the pieces shows GLOVCESTER COVRTHOVSE VIRGINIA / RIGHAVLT DAWSON- .ANNO.DOM. 1714. This recent discovery has provided a new interpretation of the legends, as a Righault family once owned land near the Gloucester Courthouse. A similar, but somewhat smaller piece dated 1715 exists. The condition of this unique piece is too poor for positive attribution.

	Fine
1714 Shilling (brass) *(2 known)*	$32,500

HIGLEY OR GRANBY COPPERS

Dr. Samuel Higley owned a private copper mine near Granby, Connecticut. He worked the mine as an individual, smelting his own ore and making his own dies for the coins that he issued. After his death in 1737 his brother John continued the coinage.

The Higley coppers were never officially authorized. All the tokens were made of pure copper. There were seven obverse and four reverse dies. The first issue, in 1737, bore the legend THE VALUE OF THREEPENCE. After a time the quantity exceeded the local demand, and a protest arose against the value of the piece. Higley, a resourceful individual, promptly created a new design, still with the Roman III, but with the inscription VALUE ME AS YOU PLEASE. On the reverse appeared the words I AM GOOD COPPER.

(Electrotypes and Casts Exist)

★

	Good	V. Good	Fine
1737 THE • VALVE • OF • THREE • PENCE. — 3 Hammers — CONNECTICVT.............................	$6,000	$9,000	$17,500
1737 THE • VALVE • OF • THREE • PENCE. — 3 Hammers — I • AM • GOOD • COPPER............	6,500	9,500	18,000
1737 VALUE • ME • AS • YOU • PLEASE — 3 Hammers — I • AM • GOOD • COPPER............	5,750	8,500	16,500

A star (★) throughout the colonial section indicates that struck copies exist. All specimens illustrated are genuine.

HIGLEY OR GRANBY COPPERS

	Good	V. Good	Fine
1737 VALUE • ME • AS • YOU • PLEASE —			
3 Hammers — I • AM • GOOD • COPPER..............	Ex. Rare		
(1737) VALUE • ME • AS • YOU • PLEASE —			
Broad Axe — J • CUT • MY • WAY • THROUGH	$6,250	$9,000	$18,000
(1737) THE • WHEELE • GOES • ROUND •, Rev.			
as above (*Unique*)			50,000
1739 VALUE • ME • AS • YOU • PLEASE —			
Broad Axe — J • CUT • MY • WAY • THROUGH	8,000	12,000	20,000

HIBERNIA-VOCE POPULI

These coins, struck in the year 1760, were prepared by Roche, of King Street, Dublin, who was at that period engaged in the manufacture of buttons for the army. Like other Irish tokens, some of these pieces found their way to Colonial America and possibly circulated in Colonies with numerous other counterfeit halfpence and "Bungtown Tokens."

There are two distinct issues. The first, with a "short bust" on the obverse, range in weight from 87 to 120 grains. The second, with a "long bust" on the obverse, range in weight from 129 to 154 grains. Most of the "long bust" varieties have the letter P on the obverse. None of the "short bust" varieties bear the letter P and judging from their weight may have been contemporary counterfeits.

Large Letter Variety
Farthing 1760

Halfpenny "P" before face

Halfpenny

VOOE POPULI

[28]

HIBERNIA-VOCE POPULI

	Good	V. Good	Fine	V. Fine	E. Fine	A. Unc.
1760 Farthing, large letters	$175.00	$250.00	$450.00	$900.00	$1,800	$3,200
1760 Farthing, small letters......	600.00	900.00	1,600	4,000	7,500	—
1760 Halfpenny	55.00	85.00	120.00	250.00	500.00	850.00
1760 Halfpenny VOOE POPULI	65.00	100.00	150.00	300.00	550.00	1,000
1760 Halfpenny, P below bust...	90.00	135.00	220.00	350.00	750.00	1,500
1760 Halfpenny, P in front of face	90.00	135.00	220.00	350.00	850.00	1,600

PITT TOKENS

William Pitt, who endeared himself to America, is the subject of these pieces, probably intended as commemorative medalets. The halfpenny served as currency during a shortage of regular coinage. The reverse legend refers to Pitt's efforts to have the Stamp Act repealed. The Pitt farthing-size tokens, struck in brass or copper on cast planchets, are rare.

	V. Good	Fine	V. Fine	E. Fine	A. Unc.
1766 Farthing		$3,000	$8,000	$15,000	—
1766 Halfpenny	$250.00	500.00	975.00	2,000	$3,500
1766 Halfpenny, silvered		750.00	1,600	3,200	4,750

RHODE ISLAND SHIP MEDAL

The obverse type shows the flagship of British Admiral Howe at anchor, while the reverse depicts the retreat of American forces from Rhode Island in 1778. The inscriptions show that it was meant for a Dutch speaking audience. It is believed the token was struck in England c. 1779-1780 for the Dutch market, as propaganda to pursuade the Dutch not to sign the Treaty of Armed Neutrality (December, 1780). Specimens are known in brass, copper, and pewter.

**1778-1779
Rhode Island
Ship Medal**

★

	V. Fine	E. Fine	A. Unc.	Unc.
VLUGTENDE (fleeing) below ship...............................		$13,000		
Wreath below ship..	$850.00	1,500	$2,200	$3,200
Without wreath below ship......................................	750.00	1,250	1,800	2,600

Values shown are for brass or copper pieces. Those struck in pewter are all rare and valued higher.

J. CHALMERS — Annapolis, Maryland

John Chalmers, a silversmith, struck a series of silver tokens at Annapolis in 1783. The shortage of change and the refusal of the people to use underweight cut Spanish coins, or "bits," prompted the issuance of these pieces.

On the Chalmers threepence and shilling obverses two clasped hands are shown, symbolizing unity of the several states; the reverse of the threepence has a branch encircled by a wreath. A star within a wreath is placed on the obverse of the sixpence, with hands clasped upon a cross utilized as the reverse type. On this denomination, the designer's initials TS (for Thomas Sparrow, a fellow silversmith of Chalmers) can be found in the crescents which terminate the horizontal arm of the cross. The reverse of the more common shilling varieties displays two doves competing for a worm underneath a hedge and a snake. There are only a few known examples of the shilling type with thirteen interlinked rings from which a liberty cap on pole arises.

	V. Good	Fine	V. Fine	E. Fine
1783 Threepence	$1,000	$2,200	$3,200	$6,000
1783 Sixpence, small date	1,400	2,800	4,700	9,000
1783 Sixpence, large date	1,300	2,700	4,500	8,250

1783 Shilling — Birds, long worm (illustrated) ...	850.00	1,850	3,400	6,250
1783 Shilling — Birds, short worm	850.00	1,850	3,200	6,000
1783 Shilling — Rings design	—	—	30,000	—

IV. THE FRENCH COLONIES

None of the coins of the French regime is strictly American. They were all general issues for the French colonies of the New World. The coinage of 1670 was authorized by an edict of Louis XIV dated February 19, 1670, for use in New France, Acadia, the French settlements in Newfoundland, and the French West Indies. The copper of 1717 to 1722 was authorized by edicts of 1716 and 1721 for use in New France, Louisiana, and the French West Indies.

ISSUE OF 1670

The coinage of 1670 consisted of silver 5 and 15 sols and copper 2 deniers or "double." A total of 200,000 of the 5 sols and 40,000 of the 15 sols, was struck at Paris. Nantes was to have coined the copper, but did not; the reasons for this may never be known, since the archives of the Nantes mint before 1700 were destroyed. The only known specimen is a pattern struck at Paris. The silver coins were raised in value by a third in 1672 to keep them circulating, but in vain. They rapidly disappeared, and by 1680 none was to be seen. Later they were restored to their original value. This rare issue should not be confused with the common 1670A 1/12 Ecu with reverse legend: SIT. NOMEN. DOMINI. BENEDICTUM.

The 1670-A Double de l'Amerique Françoise was struck in the Paris Mint along with the 5 and 15 Sols denominations of the same date. All three were

FRENCH COLONIES
ISSUE OF 1670

intended to circulate in France's North American colonies. Probably due to an engraving error, very few 1670-A Double's were actually struck. Today, only one specimen is known to survive.

	Copper Double		Silver 5 Sols		
	V. Good	Fine	V. Fine	E. Fine	Unc.
Copper Double 1670 (*Unique*)			—		
5 Sols 1670-A (200,000)	$350.00	$675.00	$1,500	$3,000	—
15 Sols 1670-A (40,000)	7,000	17,000	30,000	—	—

COINAGE OF 1717-1720

The copper 6 and 12 deniers of 1717 were authorized by an edict of Louis XV dated December 1716, to be struck at Perpignan (mintmark Q). The order could not be carried out, for the supply of copper was too brassy. A second attempt in 1720 also failed, probably for the same reason.

"COLONIES" and no crowned arms on reverse

Copper		
	Fine	E. Fine
6 Deniers 1717 Q......		Ex. Rare
12 Deniers 1717 Q......		$25,000
Crowned arms on reverse		
6 Deniers 1720-A.......$150.00		500.00
20 Sols, silver 1720-A....250.00		800.00

BILLON COINAGE

The piece of 30 deniers was called a *mousquetaire*, and was coined at Metz and Lyon. The 15 deniers was coined only at Metz. The sou marque and half were coined at almost every French mint, those of Paris being commonest. The half sou of 1740 is the only commonly available date. Specimens of the sou marque dated after 1760 were not used in North America. A unique specimen of the 1712AA 30 deniers is known in the size and weight of the 15 deniers coins.

	30 Deniers "Mousquetaire"		Sou Marque (24 Deniers)		
	V. Good	Fine	V. Fine	E. Fine	Unc.
15 Deniers 1711-1713AA	$110.00	$185.00	$375.00	$775.00	$1,500
30 Deniers 1709-1713AA	65.00	110.00	225.00	500.00	800.00
30 Deniers 1709-1713D................................	65.00	110.00	225.00	500.00	800.00
Half sou marque 1738-1748, various mints.	60.00	110.00	200.00	475.00	850.00
Sou marque 1738-1760, various mints.........	50.00	85.00	125.00	275.00	450.00

FRENCH COLONIES
COINAGE OF 1721-1722

The copper coinage of 1721-1722 was authorized by an edict of Louis XV dated June 1721. The coins were struck on copper blanks imported from Sweden. Rouen and La Rochelle struck pieces of 9 deniers in 1721 and 1722. New France received 534,000 pieces, mostly from the mint of La Rochelle, but only 8,180 were successfully put into circulation as the colonists disliked copper. In 1726 the rest of the issue was sent back to France.

COPPER SOU OR NINE DENIERS

	V. Good	Fine	V. Fine
1721-B (Rouen)	$135.00	$300.00	$600.00
1721-H			
(La Rochelle)..	60.00	135.00	300.00
1722-H	60.00	135.00	300.00
1722-H, 2 over 1...	100.00	220.00	400.00

FRENCH COLONIES IN GENERAL

Coined for use in the French colonies and only unofficially circulated in Louisiana along with other foreign coins and tokens. Most were counterstamped RF (République Française) for use in the West Indies. The mintmark A signifies the Paris Mint.

	V. Good	V. Fine	E. Fine	A. Unc.
1767 French Colonies, Sou...	$75.00	$225.00	$550.00	$1,150
1767 French Colonies, Sou. Counterstamped RF...	55.00	140.00	310.00	525.00

V. SPECULATIVE ISSUES, TOKENS & PATTERNS
THE CONTINENTAL CURRENCY

The Continental Currency pieces probably had some value at the time they were issued, but the exact nature of their monetary role is still unclear. They were the first silver dollar-sized coins ever proposed for the United States. One obverse die was engraved by someone whose initials were E.G. (undoubtedly Elisha Gallaudet) and is marked with his signature EG FECIT. Studies of the coinage show that there may have been two separate emissions made at different mints. The link design on the reverse was suggested by Benjamin Franklin.

Varieties result from differences in the spelling of the word CURRENCY and the addition of EG FECIT on the obverse. These coins were struck in pewter, brass and silver. The silver coins were intended to circulate as a dollar,

THE CONTINENTAL CURRENCY

while the brass pieces may have represented another denomination (although this is considered controversial). Pewter coins most likely had a token value only, if they were used in circulation. Pewter pieces in original bright Uncirculated condition are worth an additional premium.

Numerous copies and replicas of these coins have been made over the years. Authentication is recommended for all pieces.

"CURRENCY"   "CURENCY"

	Good	Fine	V. Fine	E. Fine	A. Unc.	Unc.
1776 CURENCY — Pewter (2 varieties)	$1,600	$3,750	$5,500	$8,500	$13,500	$22,000
1776 CURENCY — Brass (2 varieties)	6,500	13,000	18,000	24,000	—	—
1776 CURENCY — Silver		95,000				
1776 CURRENCY — Pewter	1,750	4,500	7,250	10,000	15,000	25,000
1776 CURRENCY — Pewter, EG FECIT	1,700	4,300	7,000	9,500	14,500	24,000
1776 CURRENCY — Silver, EG FECIT	—	—	—	—	—	—
1776 CURRENCEY — Pewter	—	—	—	—	—	—
1776 CURRENCY — Ornament after date		—	—	—		

A star (★) throughout the colonial section indicates that struck copies exist. The specimens illustrated are genuine.

NOVA CONSTELLATIO COPPERS

The Nova Constellatio coppers dated 1783 and 1785 and without denomination were struck in fairly large quantities in Birmingham, England beginning in 1785 and were shipped to New York where they entered circulation. Apparently they were a private coinage venture undertaken by Constable, Rucker & Co., a trading business formed by William Constable, John Rucker, Robert Morris and Gouverneur Morris as equal partners. The designs and legends were copied from the denominated patterns dated 1783 made in Philadelphia. A few additional coppers dated 1786 were made by an inferior die sinker.

NOVA CONSTELLATIO COPPERS

1783 "CONSTELLATIO"
Pointed Rays, Small U.S.

V. Good	$85.00
Fine............................	185.00
V. Fine	350.00
E. Fine	750.00
A. Unc.	1,500
Unc............................	2,750

1783 "CONSTELLATIO"
Pointed Rays, Large U.S.

V. Good	$90.00
Fine............................	200.00
V. Fine	425.00
E. Fine	925.00
A. Unc.	1,900
Unc............................	3,750

1783 "CONSTELATIO"
Blunt Rays

V. Good	$85.00
Fine............................	185.00
V. Fine	375.00
E. Fine	875.00
A. Unc.	1,700
Unc............................	2,900

1785 "CONSTELATIO"
Blunt Rays

V. Good	$90.00
Fine............................	200.00
V. Fine	425.00
E. Fine	950.00
A. Unc.	2,000
Unc............................	3,250

1785 "CONSTELLATIO"
Pointed Rays

V. Good	$85.00
Fine............................	185.00
V. Fine	375.00
E. Fine	850.00
A. Unc.	1,600
Unc............................	2,750

1785 Similar, small, close date...............V.Good $250.00, Fine $500.00, V. Fine $1,500
1786 Similar, small date.........................V.Rare

NOVA CONSTELLATIO PATTERNS

These Nova Constellatio pieces undoubtedly represent the first patterns for a coinage of the United States. They were designed by Benjamin Dudley for Gouverneur Morris to carry out his ideas for a decimal coinage system. The 1000 unit designation he called a "mark," the 500 a "quint." These denominations, together with the small 100 unit piece, were designed to standardize the many different coin values among the several states. These pattern pieces represent the first attempt at a decimal ratio, and were the forerunners of our present system of money values. Neither the proposed denominations nor the coins advanced beyond the pattern stage. These unique pieces are all dated 1783. There are two types of the "quint." The enigmatic copper "five" was first brought to the attention of collectors in 1980.

5 Units

BIT 100
Units

QUINT Type 1   Reverse   QUINT Type 2

★ Sets of
Electrotypes
Exist

MARK

1783 (Five) "5," Copper	*Unique*
1783 (Bit) "100," Silver, decorated edge — Garrett Sale, 1979	$97,500
1783 (Bit) "100," Silver plain edge	—
1783 (Quint) "500," Silver — Type 1 — Garrett Sale, 1979	165,000
1783 (Quint) "500," Silver — Type 2 — Garrett Sale, 1979	55,000
1783 (Mark) "1000," Silver — Garrett Sale, 1979	190,000

IMMUNE COLUMBIA PIECES

These are considered experimental or pattern pieces. No laws describing them are known. There are several types with the seated figure of Justice device. These dies were possibly the work of George Wyon. The Immune Columbia device with liberty cap and scale replaced the LIBERTAS and JUSTITIA on the Nova Constellatio coppers.

IMMUNE COLUMBIA PIECES

	V. Fine
1785 Copper, 13 stars........	$12,500
1785 Silver, 13 stars..........	18,000

1785 Ptd. Rays CONSTELLATIO
Copper. Extra star in reverse
legend ....V. Fine $12,500
1785 Blunt Rays CONSTELLATIO
Copper ....*2 known* $24,000
Gold ....*Unique*   —
A gold specimen in the National
Coin Collection was acquired from
Stickney in exchange for an 1804
dollar.

1785
George III Obverse
Good .....$2,500   Fine $5,000
1785
Vermon Auctori Obverse
Good .....$3,000   Fine $5,500

1787
IMMUNIS COLUMBIA
Eagle Reverse

V. Good..................................	$475.00
Fine	950.00
V. Fine...................................	2,400
E. Fine...................................	4,200

This piece is believed to be a prototype for Federal coinage. Evidence shows
that some of these pieces were coined sometime after 1787.

CONFEDERATIO COPPERS

The Confederatio Coppers are experimental or pattern pieces. This will
explain why the die with the CONFEDERATIO legend was combined with other
designs such as bust of George Washington, Libertas et Justitia of 1785,
Immunis Columbia of 1786, the New York "Excelsiors," Inimica Tyrannis
Americana and others. There were in all thirteen dies struck in fourteen combinations. Some of the dies may have been made by George Wyon of
Birmingham, England.

There are two types of the Confederatio reverse. In one instance the stars
are contained in a small circle; in the other larger stars are in a larger circle.

CONFEDERATIO COPPERS

Typical Obverse **Small Circle Reverse** **Large Circle Reverse**

★

	V. Fine
1785 Stars in small circle, various obverses	$18,000
1785 Stars in small circle, struck in silver	—
1785 Stars in large circle, various obverses	16,000

SPECULATIVE PATTERNS

The motto and shield design used on some of these patterns was later adopted for use on the New Jersey copper coins.

1786 IMMUNIS COLUMBIA **Eagle Reverse** **Shield Reverse**

1786 IMMUNIS COLUMBIA, eagle rev.	30,000
1786 IMMUNIS COLUMBIA, shield rev.	20,000

1786 (No date) Washington obv., shield reverse — Garrett Sale, 1980	50,000
1786 Eagle obverse, shield reverse — Garrett Sale, 1980	37,500
1786 Washington obverse, eagle reverse (*Unique*)	—

VI. COINAGE OF THE STATES
NEW HAMPSHIRE

New Hampshire was the first of the states to consider the subject of coinage following the Declaration of Independence.

William Moulton was empowered to make a limited quantity of coins of pure copper authorized by the State House of Representatives in 1776. Although cast patterns were prepared, it is believed that they were not approved. Little of the proposed coinage was ever actually circulated.

Other purported patterns are of doubtful origin. These include a unique engraved piece and a rare struck piece with large initials WM on the reverse.

	V. Good
1776 New Hampshire copper	$15,000

MASSACHUSETTS
MASSACHUSETTS UNOFFICIAL COPPERS

Nothing is known regarding the origin of the Pine Tree piece dated 1776. The obverse has a crude pine tree with the letters 1d LM at its base; Inscription, MASSACHUSETTS STATE. The reverse has a figure probably intended to represent the Goddess of Liberty, seated on a globe and holding a liberty cap and staff. A dog sits at her feet. The legend LIBERTY AND VIRTUE surrounds the figure.

1776 Pine Tree copper (*Unique*) ....   —

A similar piece, probably from the same source, has an Indian with bow on the obverse, and seated figure on the reverse.

1776 Indian copper (*Unique*)   —

MASSACHUSETTS UNOFFICIAL COPPERS

This piece is sometimes called the "Janus Copper." There are three heads facing left, front and right on the obverse with the inscription STATE OF MASSA. 1/2 D. The reverse shows the Goddess of Liberty facing right, resting against a globe inscribed GODDESS LIBERTY 1776.

  ★

1776 Halfpenny, 3 heads on obverse (*Unique*) — Garrett Sale, 1979 .... $40,000

MASSACHUSETTS AUTHORIZED ISSUES

An "Act for establishing a mint for the coinage of gold, silver and copper" was passed by the Massachusetts General Court October 17, 1786. The next year the Council directed that the design should incorporate "the figure of an Indian with a bow and arrow and a star at one side, with the word 'Commonwealth,' the reverse, a spread eagle with the words 'of Massachusetts A.D. 1787'."

The coinage of Massachusetts copper cents and half cents in 1787 and 1788 was under the direction of Joshua Witherle. These were the first coins bearing the denomination Cent as established by Congress. Many varieties exist, the most valuable being that with arrows in the eagle's right talon.

Most of the dies for these coppers were made by Joseph Callender. Jacob Perkins of Newburyport also engraved some of the dies.

The mint was abandoned early in 1789 in compliance with the newly ratified constitution.

Half Cent

Obverse	Arrows in Eagle's Right Talon			Arrows in Left Talon		
	Good	Fine	V. Fine	E. Fine	A. Unc.	Unc.
1787 Half Cent	$85.00	$210.00	$450.00	$975.00	$1,800	$3,000
1787 Cent, arrows in right talon........	3,500	9,000	—	—	—	—
1787 Cent, arrows in left talon...........	75.00	200.00	435.00	950.00	1,900	3,750
1787 Cent, "horn" (die break) from eagle's head.................................	75.00	200.00	435.00	950.00	2,000	4,250

MASSACHUSETTS

1788 Half Cent

Good	$100.00
Fine	250.00
Very Fine	500.00
E. Fine	1,000
A. Unc.	2,000
Unc.	3,200

1788 Cent
Period after Massachusetts

Good	80.00
Fine	220.00
V. Fine	450.00
E. Fine	1,000
A. Unc.	2,000
Unc.	3,800

No period after Massachusetts

Good	95.00
Fine	225.00
V. Fine	575.00
E. Fine	1,200
A. Unc.	2,200
Unc.	4,500

Early American coins were produced from handmade dies which are often individually distinctive. The great number of die varieties which can be found and identified are of interest to collectors who value each according to individual rarity. Values shown for type coins in this catalog are for the most common die variety.

CONNECTICUT

Authority for establishing a mint near New Haven was granted by the State to Samuel Bishop, Joseph Hopkins, James Hillhouse and John Goodrich in 1785.

Available records indicate that most of the Connecticut coppers were coined under a sub-contract by Samuel Broome and Jeremiah Platt, former New York merchants. Abel Buell and James Atlee were probably the principal die-sinkers.

1785 Copper
Bust Facing Right

Good	$55.00
V. Good	85.00
Fine	200.00
V. Fine	575.00
E. Fine	1,300

1785 Copper
African Head

Good	$70.00
V. Good	135.00
Fine	375.00
V. Fine	975.00
E. Fine	2,100

CONNECTICUT

1785 Copper
Bust Facing Left

Good	$200.00
V. Good..................	325.00
Fine	575.00
V. Fine..................	1,200
E. Fine..................	2,300

1786 Copper
ETLIB INDE

Good	$75.00
V. Good..................	150.00
Fine	300.00
V. Fine..................	700.00
E. Fine..................	1,500

1786 Copper
Large Head Facing Right

Good	$90.00
V. Good..................	225.00
Fine	550.00
V. Fine..................	1,500
E. Fine..................	3,500

1786 Copper
Mailed Bust Facing Left

Good	$55.00
V. Good..................	85.00
Fine	175.00
V. Fine..................	475.00
E. Fine..................	950.00

1786 Copper
Mailed Bust Facing Left
Hercules Head

Good	$100.00
V. Good..................	150.00
Fine	385.00
V. Fine..................	1,000
E. Fine..................	2,300

CONNECTICUT

1786 Copper
Draped Bust

Good	$85.00
V. Good.................	175.00
Fine	350.00
V. Fine..................	850.00
E. Fine..................	1,900

The Connecticut coppers, especially those dated 1787 and 1788, were usually crudely struck and on imperfect planchets.

1787 Copper
Small Head Facing Right
ETLIB INDE

Good	$100.00
V. Good	175.00
Fine	375.00
V. Fine	1,100
E. Fine	2,400

1787 Copper
Liberty Seated Right

2 known .... —

1787 Copper
Mailed Bust Facing Right
INDE ET LIB

Good	$110.00
V. Good.................	175.00
Fine	425.00
V. Fine..................	1,750

1787 Muttonhead Variety

Good	90.00
V. Good.................	150.00
Fine	350.00
V. Fine..................	1,200
E. Fine..................	2,400

	Good	V. Good	Fine	V. Fine	E. Fine
1787 Mailed bust facing left	$50.00	$85.00	$160.00	$440.00	$1,200
1787 Similar, laughing head variety.........	50.00	100.00	175.00	500.00	1,350
1787 Similar, Hercules head (see 1786)....	300.00	575.00	1,100	2,200	3,800
1787 Similar, dated 1787 over 1877..........	80.00	160.00	400.00	1,300	2,850
1787 Similar, dated 1787 over 1788..........	120.00	200.00	650.00	1,400	3,100

1787 Similar, horned bust variety	45.00	70.00	150.00	400.00	1,000
1787 Similar, CONNECT variety	50.00	110.00	230.00	600.00	1,300

CONNECTICUT

	Good	V. Good	Fine	V. Fine	E. Fine
1787 Draped bust facing left................	$45.00	$75.00	$125.00	$350.00	$775.00
1787 Similar, AUCIORI variety..............	45.00	75.00	150.00	400.00	850.00
1787 Similar, AUCTOPI variety..............	55.00	90.00	200.00	600.00	1,400
1787 Similar, AUCTOBI variety.............	55.00	90.00	200.00	550.00	1,300
1787 Similar, CONNFC variety	50.00	75.00	160.00	425.00	900.00
1787 Similar, CONNLC variety	75.00	175.00	350.00	725.00	1,500
1787 Similar, FNDE variety.................	55.00	85.00	175.00	425.00	1,000
1787 Similar, ETLIR variety	50.00	75.00	145.00	400.00	950.00
1787 Similar, ETIIB variety.................	55.00	80.00	150.00	475.00	1,000
1787 GEORGIVS III obv. Rev. as below ..	850.00	1,600	4,000	—	—

1788 Mailed bust facing right..............	45.00	75.00	180.00	500.00	1,100
1788 GEORGIVS III obv. Rev. as above ..	110.00	200.00	500.00	1,200	2,400
1788 Small head (see 1787 page 42)....	900.00	2,000	3,200	7,500	—

1788 Mailed bust facing left	45.00	70.00	150.00	425.00	850.00
1788 Mailed bust left CONNLC	50.00	100.00	235.00	550.00	1,350

CONNECTICUT

	Good	V. Good	Fine	V. Fine	E. Fine
1788 Draped bust facing left................	$50.00	$75.00	$200.00	$500.00	$950.00
1788 Similar, CONNLC variety	85.00	190.00	450.00	950.00	1,500
1788 Similar, INDL ET LIB variety.........	80.00	140.00	300.00	700.00	1,400

NEW YORK
THE BRASHER DOUBLOON

Perhaps the most famous pieces coined before establishment of the U.S. Mint at Philadelphia were those produced by the well-known goldsmith and jeweler, Ephraim Brasher, who was a neighbor and friend of George Washington, in New York.

The gold pieces Brasher made weighed about 408 grains and were valued at $15 in New York currency. They were approximately equal to the Spanish doubloon which was equal to 16 Spanish dollars.

Pieces known as "Lima Style" doubloons were dated 1742, but it is almost certain that they were produced in 1786, and were the first efforts of Brasher to make a circulating coin for local use. Neither of the two known specimens show the full legends, but weight, gold content and punch mark are all identical to the other Brasher coins.

An original design was used on the 1787 doubloon with an eagle on one side and the arms of New York on the other. In addition to his impressed hallmark, Brasher's name appears in small letters on each of his coins. The unique 1787 gold half doubloon is struck from doubloon dies on an undersized planchet that weighs half as much as the larger coins.

It is uncertain why Brasher produced these pieces. He was later commissioned to test and verify other gold coins then in circulation. His hallmark EB was punched on each coin as evidence of his testing and its value. In some cases the foreign coins have been weight-adjusted by clipping.

"1742" (1786) Lima style gold doubloon .... *2 known*

NEW YORK

★

1787 New York gold doubloon, punch on breast (*Unique*) Garrett Sale, 1981 .... $625,000
1787 New York gold doubloon, punch on wing. Garrett Sale, 1979 725,000
1787 New York gold half doubloon - Smithsonian Collection .... *Unique*
Various foreign gold coins with EB hallmark 2,750

COPPER COINAGE

Several individuals petitioned the New York legislature in early 1787 for the right to coin copper for the state, but a coinage was never authorized. Instead a law was passed to regulate the copper coins already in use. Nevertheless, various unauthorized copper coins were issued within the state, principally by two private mints.

One firm, known as Machin's Mills, was located at the mills of Thomas Machin near Newburgh. Shortly after this mint was formed, on April 18, 1787, it was merged with the Rupert, Vermont mint operated by Reuben Harmon, Jr. Harmon held a coinage grant from the Republic of Vermont. The combined partnership agreed to conduct their business in New York, Vermont, Connecticut, or elsewhere if they could benefit by it.

The operations at Machin's Mills were conducted in secret and were looked upon with suspicion by the local residents. They minted several varieties of imitation George III halfpence, and coppers of Connecticut, Vermont and New Jersey.

The other mints, located in or near New York City, were operated by John Bailey and Ephraim Brasher. They had petitioned the legislature on February 12, 1787 for a franchise to coin copper. The extent of their partnership, if any, and details of their operation are not known. Studies of the state coinages show that they produced primarily the EXCELSIOR and NOVA EBORAC pieces of New York, and the "running fox" New Jersey coppers.

★

(Believed to be the bust of Washington.)

	Good	Fine	V. Fine
1786 NON VI VIRTUTE VICI	$3,500	$7,250	$15,000

A star (★) throughout the colonial section indicates that struck copies exist. The specimens illustrated are genuine.

[45]

NEW YORK

	Good	Fine	V. Fine
1787 EXCELSIOR copper, eagle on globe facing right	$1,500	$4,000	$9,500
1787 EXCELSIOR copper, eagle on globe facing left..............	1,500	3,750	9,000

1787 Large Eagle on reverse—Arrows and branch
transposed —Garrett Sale, 1979.. $26,000

1787 George Clinton
Good...........................	$5,500
Fine...........................	13,000
V. Fine	23,000

1787
Indian and N.Y. Arms
Good...........................	$3,750
Fine...........................	8,500
V. Fine	15,000

NEW YORK

1787
Indian and Eagle
on Globe

Good	$6,250
Fine	16,000
V. Fine	26,000

★

1787 Indian and George III
Reverse (*3 known*)
V. Good $15,000

IMITATION BRITISH HALFPENCE
(Machin's Mills and other Coinage 1786-1789)

The most common coin used for small transactions in early America was the copper British halfpenny. Wide acceptance and the non-legal tender status of these copper coins made them a prime choice for unauthorized reproduction by private individuals. Many such counterfeits were made in this country by casting or other crude methods. Some were made in England and imported to this country. Pieces dated 1781 and 1785 seem to have been made specifically for this purpose, while others were circulated in both countries.

During the American state coinage era, James F. Atlee and/or others engraved dies used to mint unauthorized lightweight imitation British halfpence. These American-made British halfpence have the same devices, legends and in some cases the same dates as genuine regal halfpence. There are three distinct groups of these halfpence, all linked to the regular state coinages. The first group was probably struck in New York City prior to 1786. Group two was minted in New York City in association with John Bailey and Ephraim Brasher during the first half of 1787. The third group was struck at Machin's Mills during the second half of 1787 and into 1788. Pieces dated 1784 are believed to have been struck elsewhere in New England.

Dates used on these pieces were often evasive and are: 1771, 1772 and 1774-1776 for group one; 1747 and 1787 for group two; and 1776, 1778, 1787 and 1788 for group three. Pieces generally attributed to Atlee can be identified by a single outline in the crosses (British Union) of Britannia's shield and large triangular denticles along the coin's circumference. These pieces are not to be confused with the similar English made George III counterfeits, some of which have identical dates, or genuine British halfpence, dated 1770 to 1775.

NEW YORK

GROUP I   GROUP II   GROUP III

Machin's Mills Copper Halfpenny
GEORGIVS/BRITANNIA

	Good	V. Good	Fine	V. Fine	E. Fine
"1747" GEORGIVS II	$140.00	$250.00	$600.00	$1,800	$3,200
"1771" GEORGIVS III	75.00	125.00	325.00	750.00	2,200
"1772" GEORGIVS III	75.00	150.00	400.00	900.00	2,400
"1772" GEORGIVS III	185.00	350.00	800.00	2,000	3,500
"1774" GEORGIVS III	60.00	115.00	300.00	700.00	2,000
"1774" GEORGIVS III	75.00	150.00	350.00	900.00	2,400
"1775" GEORGIVS III	75.00	125.00	300.00	800.00	2,100
"1776" GEORGIVS III	150.00	250.00	600.00	1,200	2,700
"1776" Small date – CEORCVS	750.00	1,600	3,600	7,750	—
"1778" GEORGIVS III	60.00	115.00	300.00	675.00	2,300
"1784" GEORGIVS III	300.00	500.00	1,300	2,200	—
"1787" GEORGIVS III	60.00	100.00	250.00	600.00	1,900
"1788" GEORGIVS III	65.00	110.00	300.00	700.00	2,200

See related George III combinations under Connecticut, Vermont, and New York.

NOVA EBORAC COINAGE FOR NEW YORK

1787
NOVA EBORAC
Reverse Seated
Figure Facing Right

Fair	$45.00
Good	110.00
Fine	350.00
V. Fine	900.00
E. Fine	1,900

1787
NOVA EBORAC
Reverse Seated
Figure Facing Left

Fair	$35.00
Good	100.00
Fine	325.00
V. Fine	775.00
E. Fine	1,600

NEW YORK

1787
NOVA EBORAC
Small Head

Fair	$800.00
Good	2,200
Fine	6,000
V. Fine	12,000

1787
NOVA EBORAC
Large Head

Fair	$150.00
Good	475.00
Fine	1,400
V. Fine	3,900

NEW JERSEY

On June 1, 1786, the New Jersey Colonial legislature granted to Thomas Goadsby, Albion Cox and Walter Mould authority to coin some three million coppers weighing six pennyweight and six grains apiece, not later than June 1788, on condition that they delivered to the Treasurer of the State, "one-tenth part of the full sum they shall strike and coin," in quarterly installments. These coppers were to pass current at 15 to the shilling.

In an operation of this kind the contractors purchased the metal and assumed all expenses of coining. The difference between these expenses and the total face value of the coins issued represented the profit.

Later Goadsby and Cox asked authority to coin two-thirds of the total independently. Their petition was granted November 22, 1786. Mould was known to have produced his coins at Morristown, while Cox (and probably Goadsby) operated in Rahway. Coins were also minted in Elizabethtown and New York.

The series offers many varieties. The obverse shows a horse's head with plow and the legend NOVA CAESAREA (New Jersey). The reverse has a United States shield and legend E PLURIBUS UNUM (One composed of many).

1786 Date Under Draw Bar
No Coulter

1786 Date Under Plow
No Coulter

	Good	Fine	V. Fine
1786 Date under draw bar, no coulter..........................		$20,000	$40,000
1786 Date under plow, no coulter................................	$210.00	950.00	2,800

NEW JERSEY

Narrow Shield   **Wide Shield**

	Good	Fine	V. Fine	E. Fine
1786 Narrow shield, straight plow beam	$50.00	$200.00	$475.00	$1,000
1786 Narrow shield, curved plow beam	50.00	200.00	500.00	1,100
1786 Wide shield...	65.00	225.00	600.00	1,500
1786 Similar, bridle variety	65.00	225.00	600.00	1,500

Pluribs Variety, Lg. Planchet   Small Planchet   **Outlined Shield**

	Good	Fine	V. Fine	E. Fine
1787 Pronounced outline to shield...............	55.00	190.00	475.00	1,000
1787 Small planchet, plain shield................	55.00	190.00	450.00	950.00
1787 Large planchet, plain shield................	60.00	200.00	575.00	1,350
1787 Similar, PLURIBS variety	100.00	425.00	1,000	2,500
1787 Similar, second U over S in PLURIBUS .	175.00	400.00	900.00	2,500
1787 Similar, PLURIRUS variety	150.00	350.00	750.00	2,100
1787 Date over 1887	—			
1787 "Camel head" variety (snout in high relief)	65.00	200.00	600.00	1,200

   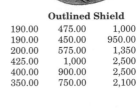

Camel Head   **Serpent Head**   **Fox Variety**

	Good	Fine	V. Fine	E. Fine
1787 Serpent head variety	80.00	300.00	1,000	2,400
1787 WM above plow		—		
1788 Horse's head facing right......................	55.00	185.00	500.00	1,100
1788 Similar, running fox before legend	95.00	375.00	1,400	3,200
1788 Similar, fox, indistinct coulter	400.00	1,700	4,500	9,500
1788 Horse's head facing left	240.00	1,000	2,600	5,000

Many varieties of these coins exist. Some have a sprig of three leaves above the plow.

VERMONT

Reuben Harmon, Jr., of Rupert, Vermont, was granted permission to coin copper pieces for a period of two years beginning July 1, 1785. The well-known Vermont plow coppers were first produced in that year. The franchise was extended for eight years in 1786.

Harmon's mint was located in the northeast corner of Rupert near a stream known as Millbrook. Col. William Coley, a New York goldsmith, made the first dies.

Some of the late issues were made near Newburgh, N.Y. by the Machin's Mills coiners.

1785 IMMUNE COLUMBIA

	Good	Fine	V. Fine	E. Fine
1785 IMMUNE COLUMBIA	$3,000	$5,500	—	—

1785 VERMONTS	200.00	900.00	$2,100	$5,000
1785 VERMONTIS	200.00	875.00	2,000	5,000

1786 VERMONTENSIUM

1786 VERMONTENSIUM	175.00	775.00	1,750	3,200

1786 Baby Head

1786 Baby head	250.00	1,000	3,250	6,000

VERMONT

1786 Bust Left   **1787 Bust Left**

	Good	Fine	V. Fine	E. Fine
1786 Bust left..	$135.00	$725.00	$1,900	$3,300
1787 Bust left..	3,200	11,000	20,000	–

1787 BRITANNIA

The reverse of this
coin is always weak.

| 1787 BRITANNIA .... | 85.00 | 235.00 | 500.00 | 1,400 |

1787, 1788 Bust Right (Several Varieties)

1787 Bust right (Several var.).......................	115.00	425.00	1,000	2,100
1788 (Several var.)...	95.00	350.00	800.00	1,350
1788 Backward C in AUCTORI.......................	2,500	8,000	–	–
1788 *ET LIB* *INDE	250.00	1,000	3,000	7,000

1788 GEORGIVS III REX

This piece should not be confused
with the common English halfpence
with similar design and reverse legend BRITANNIA.

| 1788 GEORGIVS III REX..................................... | 275.00 | 1,250 | 3,000 | 7,000 |

Most Vermont coppers are struck on poor and defective planchets. Well
struck coins on smooth full planchets command higher prices.

VII. PRIVATE TOKENS AFTER CONFEDERATION
NORTH AMERICAN TOKEN

This piece was struck in Dublin, Ireland. The obverse shows the seated figure of Hibernia facing left. The date of issue is believed to have been much later than that shown on the token.

Like many Irish tokens, this issue found its way to America in limited quantities and was accepted near the Canadian border.

1781 Copper or Brass

V. Good	Fine	V. Fine	E. Fine
$50.00	$110.00	$225.00	$600.00

BAR "COPPER"

The Bar "Copper" is undated and of uncertain origin. It has thirteen parallel and unconnected bars on one side. On the other side is the large roman letter USA monogram. The design was supposedly copied from a Continental button.

The significance of the design is clearly defined by its extreme simplicity. The separate thirteen states (bars) unite into a single entity as symbolized by the interlocking letters (USA).

This piece is believed to have first circulated in New York during November, 1785, and may have been made in England.

On the less valuable struck copy made by J. A. Bolen (c. 1862) the A passes under, instead of over, the S.

★

	V. Good	Fine	V. Fine	E. Fine	A. Unc.
Undated (about 1785) Bar "Copper"..	$700.00	$1,300	$2,400	$3,300	$4,500

AUCTORI PLEBIS TOKEN

This token is sometimes included with the coins of Connecticut as it greatly resembles issues of that state. It was struck in England by an unknown maker, possibly for use in America.

1787
AUCTORI PLEBIS

Good	$85.00
V. Good	150.00
Fine	250.00
V. Fine	550.00
E. Fine	950.00
A. Unc.	1,550

MOTT TOKEN

This item has long been considered as an early token because of its date 1789. Some scholars believe it was most likely produced c. 1809 as a commemorative of the founding of the Mott Company, and probably served as a business card. The firm, operated by Jordan Mott, was located at 240 Water Street, a fashionable section of New York at that time.

	Fine	V. Fine	E. Fine	A. Unc.
"1789" Mott Token, thick planchet...............	$250.00	$425.00	$850.00	$1,450
"1789" Mott Token, thin planchet	350.00	575.00	1,250	2,200
"1789" Mott Token, entire edge engrailed....	450.00	650.00	1,750	2,900

STANDISH BARRY, BALTIMORE, MARYLAND

Standish Barry, a Baltimore silversmith, circulated a silver threepence in 1790. He was a watch and clockmaker, engraver and later a silversmith. The tokens were believed to have been an advertising venture at a time when small change was scarce. The precise date, July 4, 90, on this piece may indicate that Barry intended to commemorate Independence Day, but there are no records to substantiate this belief. The head shown on the obverse is probably that of George Washington. The legend BALTIMORE TOWN JULY 4, 90 appears in the border. STANDISH BARRY THREE PENCE is on the reverse.

	Fine	V. Fine
1790 Threepence	$6,500	$12,000

ALBANY CHURCH PENNY

The First Presbyterian Church of Albany, New York authorized an issue of one thousand copper uniface tokens in 1790. These passed at twelve to a shilling and were used to stop contributions of worn and counterfeit coppers. Two varieties were made, one with the addition of a large D above the word CHURCH.

	V. Good	Fine
(1790) Without D	$4,500	$9,000
(1790) With D added....................	3,750	8,500

KENTUCKY TOKEN

These tokens were struck in England about 1792-94. Each star in the triangle represents a state, identified by its initial letter. These pieces are usually called Kentucky Cents because the letter K (for Kentucky) happens to be at the top. Some of the edges are plain; others are engrailed with an oblique reeding, and some have the edge lettered: "PAYABLE IN LANCASTER LONDON OR BRISTOL," or "PAYABLE AT BEDWORTH NUNEATON OR HINKLEY."

	V. Fine	E. Fine	A. Unc.	Unc.
Copper, (1792-94) plain edge	$200.00	$375.00	$525.00	$950.00
Copper, engrailed edge..................................	500.00	750.00	1,250	2,600
Copper, lettered edge PAYABLE AT BEDWORTH, etc.	—	—	—	—
Copper, lettered edge PAYABLE IN LANCASTER, etc.	225.00	425.00	600.00	1,000
Copper, lettered edge PAYABLE AT I. FIELDING, etc.	—	—	—	—

FRANKLIN PRESS

This piece is an English tradesman's token but, being associated with Benjamin Franklin, has accordingly been included in American collections.

	V. Fine	E. Fine	A. Unc.	Unc.
1794 Franklin Press Token............................	$225.00	$375.00	$575.00	$925.00
Similar edge: AN ASYLUM, etc.	Unique			
Similar edge: diagonally reeded	Unique			

TALBOT, ALLUM & LEE CENTS

Talbot, Allum & Lee, engaged in the India trade and located at 241 Pearl Street, New York, placed a large quantity of English-made coppers in circulation during 1794 and 1795. ONE CENT appears on the 1794 issue, and the legend PAYABLE AT THE STORE OF on the edge. The denomination is not found on the 1795 reverse but the edge legend was changed to read: WE PROMISE TO PAY THE

TALBOT, ALLUM & LEE CENTS

BEARER ONE CENT. Rare plain edge specimens of both dates exist. Exceptional pieces have edge ornamented or with lettering CAMBRIDGE BEDFORD AND HUNTINGDON.X.X.

1794 Cent with NEW YORK

V. Good	$80.00
V. Fine	250.00
E. Fine	415.00
A. Unc.	620.00
Unc.	1,200

1794 Cent Without NEW YORK

V. Good	425.00
V. Fine	1,300
E. Fine	3,000
A. Unc.	4,000
Unc.	6,000

1795 Cent

V. Good	$75.00
V. Fine	225.00
E. Fine	350.00
A. Unc.	550.00
Unc.	1,000

MYDDELTON TOKENS

These tokens were struck at the Soho Mint of Boulton and Watt near Birmingham, England, but they were never actually issued for circulation in Kentucky. They are unsurpassed in beauty and design by any piece of this period.

1796 Myddelton Token

	Proof
Copper	$8,500
Silver	8,000

COPPER COMPANY OF UPPER CANADA

The obverse of this piece is the same as the Myddleton token. The new reverse legend was apparently intended for Canadian circulation, or it was used to give the token credibility and display the designer's skill.

	Proof
1796 Copper	$4,500

CASTORLAND MEDAL

These medals or "jetons" are dated 1796 and allude to a proposed French settlement known as Castorland in Carthage, New York, at the time of the French Revolution. They were given to directors of the colonizing company for their attendance at board meetings.

Copy dies are still available and have been used at the Paris Mint for restriking throughout the years. Restrikes have a more modern look. Their metallic content (in French) is impressed on the edge: ARGENT (silver), CUIVRE (copper), and OR (gold).

	A. Unc.	Unc.
1796 Silver original. (Reeded edges, unbroken dies)	$3,600	$6,000
1796 Silver or bronze (original dies, reverse rusted and broken)	150.00	250.00
(1796) Silver restrike. (Paris Mint edge marks)	25.00	60.00
(1796) Bronze restrike. (Paris Mint edge marks)	12.00	30.00

NEW YORK THEATRE TOKEN

Token penny issued by Skidmore of London illustrating the Park Theatre, New York c. 1797.

	E. Fine	Proof
Penny, THE • THEATRE • AT • NEW YORK • AMERICA	$4,500	$8,750

NEW SPAIN (TEXAS) JOLA

These copper tokens were authorized by the military governor of San Antonio in 1818. Eight thousand pieces were coined by José Antonio de la Garza (JAG). Large and small planchet varieties exist, and all are very rare.

	Fine	V. Fine	E. Fine
1818, 1/2 Real	$3,500	$5,500	$12,000

NORTH WEST COMPANY TOKEN

These tokens were probably valued at one beaver and struck in Birmingham in 1820 by John Walker & Co. All but two known specimens are holed, and most have been found in the region of the lower Columbia River valley in Oregon.

1820 Copper or brass

Good	$400.00
V. Good	1,000
Fine	2,200
V. Fine	3,500

VIII. WASHINGTON PIECES

An interesting series of coins and tokens dated from 1783 to 1795 bear the portrait of George Washington. The likenesses in most instances were faithfully reproduced and were designed to honor Washington. Many of these pieces were of English origin and made later than the dates indicate.

The legends generally signify a strong unity among the states and a marked display of patriotism which pervaded the new nation during that period. We find among these tokens an employment of what were soon to become our official coin devices, namely, the American eagle, the United States shield and stars. The denomination One Cent is used in several instances, while on some of the English pieces Halfpenny will be found. Several of these pieces were private patterns for proposed coinage contracts.

GEORGIUS TRIUMPHO TOKEN

Although the head shown on this token bears a strong resemblance to that on some coins of George III, many collectors consider the Georgius Triumpho (Triumphant George) a token intended to commemorate the successful termination of the Revolutionary War.

The reverse side shows the Goddess of Liberty behind a framework of thirteen bars and fleur de lis. She holds an olive branch in her right hand and staff of liberty in her left. VOCE POPOLI (By the Voice of the People) 1783.

1783 GEORGIUS TRIUMPHO

V. Good	$85.00
Fine	200.00
V. Fine	525.00
E. Fine	950.00
A. Unc.	1,600

Military Bust
Large Military Bust
Point of Bust Close to W
(illustrated)

	Fine	V. Fine	E. Fine	A. Unc.
1783 Large military bust	$75.00	$160.00	$350.00	$850.00
1783 Small military bust, plain edge	80.00	170.00	425.00	950.00
1783 Small military bust, engrailed edge	110.00	250.00	550.00	1,400

1783 Draped bust, no button (illustrated)	80.00	175.00	375.00	750.00
1783 Draped bust, with button on drapery at neck	130.00	300.00	550.00	900.00

WASHINGTON PIECES

	Proof
1783 Draped bust. Copper restrike, plain edge	$725.00
1783 Draped bust. Copper restrike, engrailed edge	525.00
1783 Draped bust. Silver restrike, engrailed edge	1,250

1783
UNITY STATES

V. Good	$85.00
V. Fine	220.00
E. Fine	425.00
A. Unc.	850.00

Undated Double Head Cent

Fine	$85.00
V. Fine	200.00
E. Fine	425.00
A. Unc.	850.00

Satirical Medal presumably of American origin.
1784 Ugly head — Copper
  Roper Sale, 1983.......$14,850
1784 Ugly head — Pewter
Unique

1791 Cent
Edge Lettered: UNITED STATES OF AMERICA . ★ .

	Fine	*E. Fine*	*A. Unc.*	*Unc.*
1791 Cent, large eagle (date on obverse)	$275.00	$700.00	$1,300	$2,200
1791 Cent, small eagle (date on reverse)	300.00	750.00	1,450	2,400

1791 Liverpool
Halfpenny
Lettered Edge

Fine	$900.00
E. Fine	2,900
A. Unc.	5,200

WASHINGTON PIECES

1792 Eagle with Stars
Copper.................... —
Silver..................... —
Gold (*Unique*) .... —

Eagle reverse with "Washington Born Virginia" obverse (*3 known*)...... —

(1792) Undated Cent
"WASHINGTON BORN VIRGINIA"

	V. Good	Fine	V. Fine
Copper..............	$1,400	$2,700	$4,750
Silver................	—	—	—

1792 Cent
"WASHINGTON PRESIDENT"

	V. Good	Fine	V. Fine
Plain edge	$1,400	$4,500	$6,300
Lettered edge	—	—	—

Uniface restrike of obverse exists, made from transfer dies by Albert Collis, 1959.

GETZ PATTERNS

Dies engraved by Peter Getz of Lancaster, Pennsylvania were probably intended for the half dollar and cent, but were rejected by the president who did not want his portrait on the first United States coinage.

★

	V. Good	Fine	V. Fine
1792 Small eagle. Silver...	—	—	—
1792 Small eagle. Copper...	$3,750	$6,250	$12,000
1792 Same. Ornamented edge (circles and squares)	—	—	—
1792 Same. Silver..	—	—	—
1792 Lg. eagle. Silver — Garrett Sale, 1981 (E. F.).................	—	—	16,500

[60]

WASHINGTON PIECES

1792 Cent
Roman Head

Lettered Edge:
UNITED STATES OF
AMERICA

Proof........................... $18,000

1793 Ship
Halfpenny

Lettered Edge

Fine	$200.00
V. Fine.........................	350.00
E. Fine.........................	675.00
A. Unc..........................	950.00
Plain edge (Rare)	—

1795 Halfpenny
Grate Token

(Large coat buttons
variety illustrated.)

	V. Fine	E. Fine	A. Unc.	Unc.
1795 Large buttons, lettered edge	$350.00	$700.00	$1,200	$1,700
1795 Large buttons, reeded edge	175.00	335.00	475.00	775.00
1795 Small buttons, reeded edge	200.00	450.00	650.00	1,100

LIBERTY AND SECURITY TOKENS

	Fine	V. Fine	E. Fine	A. Unc.
1795 Halfpenny, plain edge................................	$125.00	$250.00	$525.00	$950.00
1795 Halfpenny, LONDON edge............................	125.00	225.00	500.00	900.00
1795 Halfpenny, BIRMINGHAM edge	125.00	275.00	575.00	1,100
1795 Halfpenny, ASYLUM edge	240.00	475.00	1,100	1,700
1795 Penny, ASYLUM edge	—	—		

WASHINGTON PIECES

Liberty and Security (1795)

	Fine	V. Fine	E. Fine	A. Unc.	Unc.
Undated Liberty and Security Penny.......	$225.00	$400.00	$800.00	$1,450	$2,500
Same, corded outer rims............................	500.00	800.00	1,800	2,900	—

SUCCESS MEDALS

	Fine	V. Fine	E. Fine	A. Unc.
SUCCESS medal, large. Plain or reeded edge	$200.00	$450.00	$800.00	$1,800
SUCCESS medal, small. Plain or reeded edge	250.00	525.00	1,000	1,900

These pieces are struck in copper or brass and are believed to have been made in the mid nineteenth century. Specimens with original silvering are rare and valued 20 to 50 percent higher. Varieties exist.

NORTH WALES HALFPENNY

	Good	Fine	V. Fine
1795 NORTH WALES Halfpenny	$100.00	$235.00	$500.00
Lettered edge	475.00	1,250	2,200
2 stars at each side of harp	975.00	3,500	—

IX. THE FUGIO CENTS

The first coins issued by authority of the United States were the "Fugio" cents. Entries in the Journal of Congress supply interesting information about proceedings relating to this coinage.

Saturday, April 21, 1787. ...

"That the board of treasury be authorized to contract for three hundred tons of copper coin of the federal standard, agreeable to the proposition of Mr. James Jarvis... That it be coined at the expense of the contractor, etc."

On Friday, July 6, 1787, there was "Resolved, that the board of treasury direct the contractor for the copper coinage to stamp on one side of each piece the following device, viz: thirteen circles linked together, a small circle in the middle, with the words 'United States,' around it; and in the centre, the words 'We are one'; on the other side of the same piece the following device, viz: a dial with the hours expressed on the face of it; a meridian sun above on one side of which is the word 'Fugio,' (The intended meaning is, 'time flies') and on the other the year in figures '1787', below the dial, the words 'Mind Your Business.'"

The legends have been credited to Benjamin Franklin, and the coin, as a consequence, has sometimes been referred to as the Franklin Cent.

These cents were coined in New Haven, Conn., and possibly elsewhere. Most of the copper used in this coinage came from military stores. It is believed to have been the copper bands which held together the powder kegs sent to us by the French. The dies were made by Abel Buell of New Haven.

1787 WITH POINTED RAYS

Cross after date **American Congress Pattern**

	V. Good	Fine	V. Fine	E. Fine	Unc.
Obv. no cinquefoils. Cross after date.					
Rev. Rays and AMERICAN CONGRESS Boston auction 2000 ...	—			$175,000	
Rev. label with raised rims..............			Ex. Rare		
Same obv., rev. STATES UNITED	$450.00	$850.00	$2,200	—	—
Same obv., rev. UNITED STATES	400.00	800.00	2,200	—	—

Cinquefoil after date

Note: The following types with pointed rays have regular obverses punctuated with four cinquefoils (five-leafed ornament.)

STATES UNITED at sides of circle.

Cinquefoils on label...........................	$175.00	$300.00	$575.00	$1,000	$2,200
STATES UNITED, 1 over horizontal 1	300.00	600.00	1,400	2,600	
UNITED STATES, 1 over horizontal 1	275.00	500.00	1,200	2,500	
UNITED STATES at sides of circle.............	185.00	325.00	600.00	1,100	2,600

THE FUGIO CENTS

	V. Good	Fine	V. Fine	E. Fine	Unc.
STATES UNITED. Label with raised rims (simply two concentric circles). Large letters in WE ARE ONE	$350.00	$575.00	$1,650	$3,900	—
STATES UNITED. 8-pointed stars on label	350.00	425.00	900.00	1,950	—
UNITED above, STATES below. (Rare)	—	—	—	—	—

1787 WITH CLUB RAYS

	V. Good	Fine	V. Fine	E. Fine
Club Rays. Rounded ends	$325.00	$625.00	$1,600	$3,000
Club Rays. Concave ends to rays:				
FUCIO (C instead of G). (Ex. Rare)	2,200	5,000	9,250	—
Club Rays. Concave ends. FUGIO, UNITED STATES	2,400	5,250	10,000	—
Club Rays. Similar, STATES UNITED Rev.	—	—		

New Haven "Restrike", note narrow rings

	E. Fine	Unc.
Gold (2 known)	—	—
Silver	$900.00	$1,900
Copper or brass	300.00	600.00

New Haven "restrikes" were supposedly struck from dies discovered by the fourteen-year-old C. Wyllys Betts in 1858 on the site of the Broome & Platt Store in New Haven, Conn., where the originals were made. Three pairs of dies were reportedly found and are still extant. Actually, the "restrikes" were made from copy dies c. 1860.

BIBLIOGRAPHY

Carlotto, Tony. *The Copper Coins of Vermont.* Chelsea, MI 1998.
Crosby, S. S. *The Early Coins of America.* Boston 1875 (reprinted 1945, 1965, 1974, 1983).
Dickeson, M. W. *The American Numismatic Manual.* Philadelphia 1859, 1860, 1865.
Kessler, Alan. *The Fugio Cents.* Newtonville, Massachusetts 1976.
Maris, Edward. *A Historic Sketch of the Coins of New Jersey.* Philadelphia 1881 (reprinted 1925, 1974, 1987).
Miller, Henry C. and Hillyer Ryder. *The State Coinages of New England.* New York 1920.
Nelson, Philip. *The Coinage of William Wood 1722-1733.* London 1903 (reprinted 1959).
Newman, Eric P. *Coinage for Colonial Virginia.* New York 1957.
    Studies on Money in Early America. American Numismatic Society. New York 1976.
Noe, Sydney P. *The New England and Willow Tree Coinage of Massachusetts.* New York 1943. *The Oak Tree Coinage of Massachusetts.* New York 1947, and *The Pine Tree Coinage of Massachusetts.* New York 1952. (all reprinted 1973).
Rulau, Russell and George Fuld. *Medallic Portraits of Washington.* Iola, Wisconsin 1999.
Wurtzbach, Carl. *Massachusetts Colonial Silver Money 1937.*

X. FIRST UNITED STATES MINT ISSUES

Many members of the House favored a representation of the President's head on the obverse of each coin; others considered the idea a monarchical practice. Washington is believed to have expressed disapproval of the use of his portrait on our coins.

The majority considered a figure emblematic of Liberty more appropriate and the Senate finally concurred in this opinion. Robert Birch was an engraver employed at designing proposed devices for our coins. He, perhaps together with others, engraved the dies for the disme and half disme. He has also been associated with a large copper cent of unusual design known as the Birch Cent.

1792 SILVER CENTER CENT

	V. Fine
Cent. Silver Center — (13 known. A unique specimen has no silver plug)	$90,000
Cent. No silver center (8 known)	60,000

1792 BIRCH CENT

Copper—Plain edge (Unique)
Copper—Lettered edge TO BE ESTEEMED * BE USEFUL * (8 known)
    Garrett Sale, 1981 (Unc.) 200,000
Copper—Lettered edge TO BE ESTEEMED BE USEFUL * (2 known)
White Metal—G*W.Pt. (George Washington President) below
    wreath. Garrett Sale, 1981 (Unique) 100,000

1792 HALF DISME

	Good	V. Good	Fine	V. Fine	E. Fine
Silver	$5,000	$10,000	$14,000	$18,500	$33,000
Copper (Unique)					

FIRST UNITED STATES MINT ISSUES

1792 DISME

	E. Fine	Unc.
Silver (*3 known*)	—	—
Copper (*about 15 known*)	$35,000	$75,000

1792 PATTERN QUARTER DOLLAR

Joseph Wright designed this attractive pattern quarter dollar intended for the original United States coins. He was George Washington's choice for the position of first Chief Engraver of the United States Mint, and designed the 1793 Liberty Cap Cent in that capacity, but died in 1793 before being confirmed by Congress. Unique uniface trials of the quarter dollar pattern obverse and reverse also exist.

Copper	*2 known*
White Metal	*2 known*

MINTS AND MINT MARKS

Mint marks are small letters designating where coins were made. Coins struck at Philadelphia before 1979 (except 1942-1945 five-cent pieces) do not have a mint mark. Starting in 1979 a letter P was used on the dollar, and thereafter on all other denominations except the cent. Mint mark position is on the reverse of nearly all coins prior to 1965 (the cent is an exception), and on the obverse after 1967. Letters used are as follows:

    C — Charlotte, North Carolina (gold coins only). 1838-1861.
    CC — Carson City, Nevada. 1870-1893.
    D — Dahlonega, Georgia (gold coins only). 1838-1861.
    D — Denver, Colorado. 1906 to date.
    O — New Orleans, Louisiana. 1838-1909.
    P — Philadelphia, Pennsylvania. 1793 to date.
    S — San Francisco, California. 1854 to date.
    W — West Point, New York. 1984 to date.

All dies for United States coins were made at the Philadelphia Mint prior to 1996. Some dies are now made at the Denver Mint. Dies for use at other mints are made with the appropriate mint mark before they are shipped to those mints. Because this was a hand operation prior to 1985, the exact positioning and size of the mint mark may vary slightly, depending on where and how deeply the punch was impressed. This also accounts for double-punched and superimposed mint marks such as the 1938 D over D, and D over S Buffalo nickels. Polishing of dies may also alter the apparent size of fine details. Occasionally the mint mark is inadvertently left off a die sent to a branch mint, as was the case with some of the recent proof dimes. Similarly, some 1982 dimes without mint mark, were made as business strikes. The mint mark "M" was used on coins made in Manila for the Philippines 1925-1941.

Prior to 1900, punches for mint marks varied greatly in size. This is particularly noticeable in the 1850 to 1880 period in which the letters range from very small to very large. An attempt to standardize sizes started in 1892 with the Barber series, but exceptions are seen in the 1892 O half dollar and 1905 O dime, both of which have normal and "microscopic" mint marks. A more or less standard size small mint mark was used on all minor coins starting in 1909, and on all dimes, quarters and halves after the Barber series was replaced in 1916. Slight variations in mint mark size occur through 1945 with notable differences in 1928, when small and large S mint marks were used.

In recent years a single D or S punch has been used to mark all branch mint dies. The change to the larger D for Denver coins occurred in 1933. Nickels, dimes, half dollars and dollars of 1934 exist with either the old, smaller size mint mark or the new, larger size D. All other denominations of 1934 and after are standard. The San Francisco mint mark was changed to larger size during 1941 and, with the exception of the half dollar, all 1941 S coins are known with either small or large size mint marks. Halves were not changed until 1942, and the 1942 S and 1943 S pieces exist both ways. The 1945 S dime with "microscopic" S is an unexplained use of a punch originally intended for Philippine coins 1907-1920. In 1979 the punches were replaced. Varieties of some 1979 coins appear with either the old or new shaped S or D. The S punch was again replaced in 1982 with a more distinct letter.

Mint mark application technique for proof coins was changed in 1985, and for business strike production in 1990-91, when the letter was applied directly to the production hub rather than being hand punched on each working die. At the same time all the mint mark letters were made much larger and clearer than those of previous years.

PROOF COINS

A "proof" is a specimen striking of coinage for presentation, souvenir, exhibition, or numismatic purposes. Pre-1968 proofs were made only at the Philadelphia Mint except in a few rare instances in which presentation pieces were struck at branch mints. Current proofs are made at San Francisco and West Point.

The term "proof" refers to the method of manufacture and not the condition of a coin. Regular production coins in mint state have coruscating, frosty luster, soft details, and minor imperfections. Proof coins can usually be distinguished by their sharpness of detail, high wire edge, and extremely brilliant, mirrorlike surface. All proofs are originally sold by the mint at a premium.

Very few proof coins were made prior to 1856. Because of their rarity and infrequent sales, they are not all listed in this catalog.

Frosted proofs were issued prior to 1936 and starting again in the late 1970's. These have a brilliant mirrorlike field with contrasting dull or frosted design.

Matte proofs have a granular "sandblast" surface instead of the mirror finish. Matte proof cents, nickels, and gold coins were issued from 1908 to 1916; a few 1921 and 1922 silver dollars were also struck in this manner.

Brilliant proofs have been issued from 1936 to date. These have a uniformly brilliant mirrorlike surface and sharp, high relief details.

"Prooflike" coins are occasionally seen. These are specimens from the first few impressions of regular coinage dies from any mint. They are not true proofs, but may have most of the characteristics of a proof coin and generally command a premium. Collectors should beware of coins that have been buffed to look like proofs; magnification will reveal polishing lines and lack of detail.

How A Proof Coin Is Made...

Selected dies are inspected for perfection and are highly polished and cleaned. They are again wiped clean or polished after every 15 to 25 impressions and are replaced frequently to avoid imperfections from worn dies. Coinage blanks are polished and cleaned to assure high quality in striking. They are then hand fed into the coinage press one at a time, each blank receiving two or more blows from the dies to bring up sharp, high relief details. The coinage operation is done at slow speed with extra pressure. Finished proofs are individually inspected and are handled by gloves or tongs. They also receive a final inspection by packers before being sonically sealed in special plastic cases.

After a lapse of twenty years, proof coins were struck at the Philadelphia Mint from 1936 to 1942 inclusive. In 1942, when the composition of the five-cent piece was changed, there were two types of this denomination available to collectors. The striking of proof coins was temporarily suspended from 1943 to 1949, and again from 1965 to 1967; during the latter period special mint sets were struck. Proof sets were resumed in 1968. They are available during the year of issue from: The United States Mint, Customer Service Center, 10003 Derekwood Lane, Lanham, MD 20706.

Sets from 1936 through 1972 include the cent, nickel, dime, quarter and half; from 1973 through 1981 the dollar was also included. Regular proof sets issued from 1982 to 1998 contain the cent through half dollar. Special sets containing commemorative coins were sold at an additional premium. Beginning in 1999 sets contain five different statehood quarters.

Figures in parentheses represent the total number of full sets minted. Values are for sets in average unspotted condition.

Year Minted	Sets Minted	Issue Price	Current Value
1936 ....(3,837)	$1.89	$5,000
1937 ....(5,542)	1.89	2,300
1938 ....(8,045)	1.89	950.00
1939 ....(8,795)	1.89	925.00
1940 ....(11,246)	1.89	725.00
1941 ....(15,287)	1.89	625.00
1942 Both nickels.............(21,120)	1.89	700.00
1942 One nickel ....Incl. above	1.89	650.00
1950 ....(51,386)	2.10	500.00
1951 ....(57,500)	2.10	500.00
1952 ....(81,980)	2.10	275.00
1953 ....(128,800)	2.10	250.00
1954 ....(233,300)	2.10	125.00
1955 Box pack ....(378,200)	2.10	90.00
1955 Flat pack ....Incl. above	2.10	100.00
1956 ....(669,384)	2.10	45.00

PROOF SETS

Year Minted	Sets Minted	Issue Price	Current Value
1957	(1,247,952)	$2.10	$18.00
1958	(875,652)	2.10	30.00
1959	(1,149,291)	2.10	25.00
1960 with lg. date 1¢	(1,691,602)	2.10	17.00
1960 with sm. date 1¢	Incl. above	2.10	30.00
1961	(3,028,244)	2.10	12.00
1962	(3,218,019)	2.10	12.00
1963	(3,075,645)	2.10	14.00
1964	(3,950,762)	2.10	12.00
1968S	(3,041,506)	5.00	6.00
1968S 10¢ w/o mint mark	Incl. above	5.00	7,500
1969S	(2,934,631)	5.00	6.00
1970S	(2,632,810)	5.00	12.50
1970S with sm. date 1¢	Incl. above	5.00	65.00
1970S 10¢ w/o mint mark (est 2,200)	Incl. above	5.00	500.00
1971S	(3,220,733)	5.00	5.50
1971S 5¢ w/o mint mark (est 1,655)	Incl. above	5.00	675.00
1972S	(3,260,996)	5.00	5.75
1973S	(2,760,339)	7.00	10.00
1974S	(2,612,568)	7.00	15.00
1975S (with 1976 25¢, 50¢, $1)	(2,845,450)	7.00	16.00
1975S 10¢ w/o mint mark	Incl. above	7.00	—
1976S	(4,149,730)	7.00	14.00
1976S 3 pc. set	(3,998,621)	15.00	20.00
1977S	(3,251,152)	9.00	9.00
1978S	(3,127,781)	9.00	10.00
1979S Filled S	(3,677,175)	9.00	10.00
1979S Clear S	Incl. above	9.00	120.00
1980S	(3,554,806)	10.00	12.00
1981S Filled S	(4,063,083)	11.00	10.00
1981S Clear S (all coins)	Inc. above	11.00	325.00
1982S	(3,857,479)	11.00	6.00
1983S	(3,138,765)	11.00	6.25
1983S 10¢ w/o mint mark	Incl. above	11.00	500.00
1983S Prestige Set (Olympic dollar)	(140,361)	59.00	80.00
1984S	(2,748,430)	11.00	7.25
1984S Prestige Set (Olympic dollar)	(316,680)	59.00	23.00
1985S	(3,362,821)	11.00	6.50
1986S	(2,411,180)	11.00	27.50
1986S Prestige Set (Statue 50¢, $1)	(599,317)	48.50	35.00
1987S	(3,792,233)	11.00	6.00
1987S Prestige Set (Constitution dollar)	(435,495)	45.00	23.00
1988S	(3,031,287)	11.00	16.00
1988S Prestige Set (Olympic dollar)	(231,661)	45.00	32.00
1989S	(3,009,107)	11.00	15.00
1989S Prestige Set (Congressional 50¢, $1)	(211,087)	45.00	36.00
1990S	(2,793,433)	11.00	20.00
1990S with no-S 1¢ proof set	(3,555)	11.00	3,000
1990S with no-S 1¢ Prestige set	Incl. above	45.00	3,200
1990S Prestige Set (Eisenhower dollar)	(506,126)	45.00	26.00
1991S	(2,610,833)	11.00	30.00
1991S Prestige Set (Mt. Rushmore 50¢, $1)	(256,954)	59.00	75.00
1992S	(2,675,618)	11.00	15.00
1992S Prestige Set (Olympic 50¢, $1)	(183,293)	56.00	44.00
1992S Silver	(1,009,586)	21.00	18.00
1992S Silver Premier Set	(308,055)	37.00	19.00
1993S	(2,409,394)	12.50	18.00
1993S Prestige Set (Madison 50¢, $1)	(224,045)	57.00	42.00
1993S Silver	(570,213)	21.00	32.00
1993S Silver Premier Set	(191,140)	37.50	32.00
1994S	(2,308,701)	12.50	15.00
1994S Prestige Set (World Cup 50¢, $1)	(175,893)	57.00	55.00
1994S Silver	(636,009)	21.00	40.00
1994S Silver Premier Set	(149,320)	37.50	42.00

PROOF SETS

Year Minted	Sets Minted	Issue Price	Current Value
1995S ....(2,010,384)		$12.50	$45.00
1995S Prestige Set (Civil War 50¢, $1) .....(107,112)		57.00	125.00
1995S Silver ....(549,878)		21.00	100.00
1995S Silver Premier Set ....(130,107)		37.50	100.00
1996S ....(1,695,244)		12.50	13.00
1996S Prestige Set (Olympic 50¢, $1)..........(55,000)		57.00	225.00
1996S Silver ....(623,655)		21.00	46.00
1996S Silver Premier Set ....(151,366)		37.50	50.00
1997S ....(1,975,000)		12.50	60.00
1997S Prestige Set (Botanic $1)..................(80,000)		48.00	200.00
1997S Silver ....(605,473)		21.00	95.00
1997S Silver Premier Set ....(136,205)		37.50	95.00
1998S		12.50	30.00
1998S Silver ....(638,134)		21.00	35.00
1998S Silver Premier Set ....(240,658)		37.50	36.00
1999S 9 piece set		19.95	55.00
1999S 5 piece quarter set............................		13.95	50.00
1999S Silver 9 piece set..............................(800,000)		31.95	100.00
2000S 10 piece set....................................(2,968,900)		19.95	25.00
2000S 5 piece quarter set ....(937,600)		13.95	20.00
2000S Silver 10 piece set............................(856,400)		31.95	35.00
2001S 10 piece set		19.95	25.00
2001S 5 piece quarter set............................		13.95	20.00
2001S Silver 10 piece set		31.95	35.00

Values shown are for sets in original government holders.

UNCIRCULATED MINT SETS

Official Mint Sets are specially packaged by the government for sale to collectors. They contain uncirculated specimens of each year's coins for every denomination issued from each mint. Unlike the proof sets, these are normal coins intended for circulation and are not minted with any special consideration for quality. Coins struck only as proofs are not included.

Uncirculated sets sold by the Treasury from 1947 through 1958 contained two examples of each regular-issue coin. These were packaged in cardboard holders that did not protect the coins from tarnish. Nicely preserved early sets generally command a 10 to 20 percent premium above listed values. No official mint sets were produced in 1950, 1982 or 1983.

Since 1959 sets have been sealed in a protective plastic envelope. In 1965, 1966 and 1967, Special Mint Sets of higher than normal quality were made as a substitute for proof sets which were not made during that period. Similar specimen sets dated 1964 are reported to exist. The 1966 and 1967 sets were packaged in hard plastic holders.

Privately assembled mint sets, and souvenir sets produced for sale at the Philadelphia or Denver mints, or for special occasions, are valued according to the individual pieces they contain. Only the official government sealed full sets are included in the following list.

Current year sets may be ordered by telephoning 1-800-USA MINT.

Year Minted	Sets Sold	Issue Price	Face Value	Current Value
1947 P-D-S 5,000		$4.87	$4.46	$1,200
1948 P-D-S 6,000		4.92	4.46	600.00
1949 P-D-S 5,000		5.45	4.96	900.00
1951 P-D-S 8,654		6.75	5.46	800.00
1952 P-D-S 11,499		6.14	5.46	750.00
1953 P-D-S 15,538		6.14	5.46	550.00
1954 P-D-S 25,599		6.19	5.46	400.00
1955 P-D-S 49,656		3.57	2.86	190.00
1956 P-D...45,475		3.34	2.64	150.00
1957 P-D...34,324		4.40	3.64	250.00
1958 P-D...50,314		4.43	3.64	200.00
1959 P-D...187,000		2.40	1.82	40.00
1960 P-D...260,485		2.40	1.82	22.00
1961 P-D...223,704		2.40	1.82	40.00

UNCIRCULATED MINT SETS

Year Minted	Sets Sold	Issue Price	Face Value	Current Value
1962 P-D	385,285	$2.40	$1.82	$25.00
1963 P-D	606,612	2.40	1.82	15.00
1964 P-D	1,008,108	2.40	1.82	11.50
1968 P-D-S	2,105,128	2.50	1.33	4.00
1969 P-D-S	1,817,392	2.50	1.33	6.00
1970 P-D-S Lg. date 1¢	2,038,134	2.50	1.33	22.50
1970 P-D-S Sm. date 1¢	Incl. above	2.50	1.33	40.00
1971 P-D-S‡	2,193,396	3.50	1.83	4.25
1972 P-D-S‡	2,750,000	3.50	1.83	4.25
1973 P-D-S	1,767,691	6.00	3.83	25.00
1974 P-D-S	1,975,981	6.00	3.83	8.00
1975 P-D (with 1976 25¢, 50¢, $1)	1,921,488	6.00	3.82	12.00
1776-1976 (3 pieces)	4,908,319	9.00	1.75	16.00
1976 P-D	1,892,513	6.00	3.82	13.00
1977 P-D	2,006,869	7.00	3.82	9.00
1978 P-D	2,162,609	7.00	3.82	9.00
1979 P-D*	2,526,000	8.00	3.82	8.00
1980 P-D-S	2,815,066	9.00	4.82	8.00
1981 P-D-S	2,908,145	11.00	4.82	18.00
1984 P-D	1,832,857	7.00	1.82	8.00
1985 P-D	1,710,571	7.00	1.82	8.00
1986 P-D	1,153,536	7.00	1.82	26.00
1987 P-D	2,890,758	7.00	1.82	8.50
1988 P-D	1,646,204	7.00	1.82	10.00
1989 P-D	1,987,915	7.00	1.82	10.00
1990 P-D	1,809,184	7.00	1.82	9.00
1991 P-D	1,352,101	7.00	1.82	15.00
1992 P-D	1,500,143	7.00	1.82	9.00
1993 P-D	1,297,431	8.00	1.82	10.00
1994 P-D	1,234,813	8.00	1.82	14.00
1995 P-D	1,038,787	8.00	1.82	23.00
1996 P-D plus 1996W dime	1,457,949	8.00	1.92	24.00
1997 P-D	950,473	8.00	1.82	18.00
1998 P-D	1,187,325	8.00	1.82	20.00
1999 P-D (18 pieces)	1,243,867	14.95	3.82	25.00
2000 P-D (20 pieces)	1,416,000	14.95	5.82	20.00
2001 P-D (20 pieces)		14.95	5.82	20.00

‡ Dollar not included.

* S mint dollar not included.

SPECIAL MINT SETS

1965	(2,360,000)	$4.00	$.91	$10.00
1966	(2,261,583)	4.00	.91	9.00
1967	(1,863,344)	4.00	.91	10.00

SOUVENIR SETS

Uncirculated sets were packaged and sold at Philadelphia and Denver gift shops in 1982 and 1983 in place of the "official mint sets" which were not made in those years. A bronze mint medal is packaged with each set. Similar sets were also made in other years.

1982P		$4.00	$.91	$12.00
1982D		4.00	.91	9.00
1983P		4.00	.91	20.00
1983D		4.00	.91	15.00

UNITED STATES REGULAR ISSUES
HALF CENTS — 1793-1857

The half cent is the lowest face value coin struck by the United States. All half cents are scarce, but the series has never enjoyed the popularity of some of the other series, hence the more common dates and varieties are reasonably priced.

There were various intermissions in coinage, and during most of the period 1836 to 1849 the coinage was very small, causing a very noticeable lapse in the series for collectors. While 1796 is the most valuable date, the originals and restrikes of 1831, 1836 and 1840 through 1849, and rare varieties are all difficult to obtain.

The half cent was authorized to be coined April 2, 1792. Originally the weight was to have been 132 grains, but this was changed to 104 grains by the Act of January 14, 1793, before coinage commenced. The weight was again changed to 84 grains January 26, 1796 by presidential proclamation in conformity with the Act of March 3, 1795. Coinage was discontinued by the Act of February 21, 1857. All were coined at the Philadelphia Mint.

+ or – indicates change from previous year	TYPE COIN VALUES									
	G-4	F-12	EF-40	AU-50	MS-60	MS-63	MS-65	PF-60	PF-63	PF-65
Flowing Hair 1793...............	1,500+	3,750+	10,000+	16,000	28,000	48,000	65,000			
Liberty Cap 1794-1797........	210.00	550.00	2,200+	3,500	8,000	13,000	35,000			
Draped Bust 1800-1808	40.00+	55.00+	210.00+	350.00	900.00	2,000	7,000			
Classic Head 1809-1835......	28.00+	45.00	70.00	120.00+	210.00	400.00+	1,900	2,400	4,000	7,500
Coronet Head 1840-1857	28.00	45.00	75.00	120.00+	200.00	375.00	1,600	2,200	3,700	7,000

LIBERTY CAP TYPE 1793-1797

AG-3 ABOUT GOOD—*Clear enough to identify.*
G-4 GOOD—*Outline of bust clear, no details. Date readable. Reverse lettering incomplete.*
VG-8 VERY GOOD—*Some hair details. Reverse lettering complete.*
F-12 FINE—*Most of hair detail shows. Leaves worn but all visible.*
VF-20 VERY FINE—*Hair near ear and forehead worn, other areas distinct. Some details in leaves show.*
EF-40 EXTREMELY FINE—*Light wear on highest parts of head and wreath.*

Values shown for Fine and better copper coins are for those with attractive surfaces and color that are consistent with the amount of normal wear. Coins that are porous, corroded, or similarly defective are worth significantly lower prices.

Head Facing Left 1793

Designer, probably Joseph Wright; weight 6.74 grams; composition: copper; approx. diameter 22 mm; edge: TWO HUNDRED FOR A DOLLAR.

Quan. Minted	AG-3	G-4	VG-8	F-12	VF-20	EF-40
1793 35,334	$800.00	$1,500	$2,300	$3,750	$6,000	$10,000

HALF CENTS
Head Facing Right 1794-1797

1794 — Designer Robert Scot; weight 6.74 grams; composition: copper; approx. diameter 23.5 mm; edge: TWO HUNDRED FOR A DOLLAR.

1795 — Designer John Smith Gardner; weight 6.74 grams; composition: copper; approx. diameter 23.5 mm; edge: TWO HUNDRED FOR A DOLLAR.

1795-1797 (thin planchet) — Weight 5.44 grams; composition: copper; approx. diameter 23.5 mm; edge: plain (some 1797 are either lettered or gripped).

	Quan. Minted	AG-3	G-4	VG-8	F-12	VF-20	EF-40
1794	81,600	$150.00	$300.00	$500.00	$800.00	$1,400	$3,000

Pole to Cap	**Punctuated Date**	**No Pole to Cap**

1795 All kinds............139,690						
1795 Lettered edge, with pole	100.00	250.00	400.00	650.00	1,200	3,000
1795 Lettered edge, punctuated date............	100.00	250.00	400.00	650.00	1,200	3,000
1795 Plain edge, punctuated date............	90.00	210.00	350.00	550.00	1,100	2,200
1795 Plain edge, no pole‡.......	90.00	210.00	350.00	575.00	1,100	2,400
1796 With pole* .... } 1,390	4,000	6,500	10,000	15,000	20,000	35,000
1796 No pole..............	10,000	18,000	27,500	40,000	60,000	—

*The deceptive "Dr. Edwards" struck copy of this coin has a different head and larger letters.

1797, 1 above 1, Plain Edge

1797 All kinds............127,840						
1797 Lettered edge................	300.00	800.00	1,500	2,500	5,000	15,000
1797 Plain edge‡	125.00	250.00	400.00	750.00	1,400	3,500
1797 Gripped edge	3,500	10,000	20,000	—	—	—
1797, 1 above 1, plain edge....	85.00	225.00	350.00	550.00	1,000	2,750

‡Many are struck on cut-down cents and tokens.

HALF CENTS
DRAPED BUST TYPE 1800-1808

A modified reverse design was introduced during 1802, and used through 1808.

Designer Robert Scot: weight 5.44 grams; composition: copper; diameter 23.5 mm; plain edge.

AG-3 ABOUT GOOD—*Clear enough to identify.*
G-4 GOOD—*Bust outline clear, few details, date readable. Reverse lettering worn and incomplete.*
VG-8 VERY GOOD—*Some drapery shows. Date and legends complete.*
F-12 FINE—*Shoulder drapery and hair over brow worn smooth.*
VF-20 VERY FINE—*Only slight wear in above areas. Slight wear on reverse.*
EF-40 EXTREMELY FINE—*Light wear on highest parts of head and wreath.*

1st Reverse
Style of 1800

2nd Reverse

	Quan. Minted	AG-3	G-4	VG-8	F-12	VF-20	EF-40
1800	202,908	$20.00	$40.00	$55.00	$85.00	$165.00	$400.00
1802, 2 over 0, rev. of 1800	} 20,266	4,500	13,500	22,000	32,000		
1802, 2 over 0, 2nd rev...		150.00	450.00	1,000	2,500	7,000	16,000
1803	92,000	18.00	40.00	55.00	100.00	225.00	650.00

Plain 4   **Crosslet 4**   **Stemless Wreath**   **Stems to Wreath**

		AG-3	G-4	VG-8	F-12	VF-20	EF-40
1804 All kinds	1,055,312						
1804 Plain 4, stems		17.00	45.00	80.00	150.00	250.00	650.00
1804 Pl. 4, stemless		15.00	40.00	50.00	60.00	100.00	220.00
1804 Cr. 4, stems		15.00	40.00	50.00	60.00	100.00	220.00
1804 Cr. 4, stemless		15.00	40.00	50.00	60.00	100.00	220.00
1804 "Spiked chin"		20.00	45.00	55.00	90.00	140.00	260.00

1804 "Spiked Chin"   **Small 5**   **Large 5**

		AG-3	G-4	VG-8	F-12	VF-20	EF-40
1805 All kinds	814,464						
1805 Medium 5, stemless		15.00	40.00	55.00	75.00	110.00	225.00
1805 Small 5, stems		200.00	500.00	1,000	2,000	3,500	—
1805 Large 5, stems		15.00	40.00	55.00	75.00	110.00	250.00

HALF CENTS

| Small 0 | Large 6 | 1808, 8 over 7 | Normal Date |

	Quan. Minted	AG-3	G-4	VG-8	F-12	VF-20	EF-40
1806 All kinds	356,000						
1806 Small 6, stems		$40.00	$175.00	$300.00	$450.00	$850.00	$1,800
1806 Small 6, stemless		15.00	40.00	45.00	55.00	90.00	210.00
1806 Large 6, stems		15.00	40.00	45.00	55.00	90.00	210.00
1807	476,000	15.00	40.00	50.00	60.00	115.00	300.00
1808, 8 over 7	} 400,000	50.00	100.00	175.00	400.00	900.00	2,500
1808 Normal date		15.00	40.00	50.00	60.00	115.00	350.00

CLASSIC HEAD TYPE 1809-1836

Designer John Reich. Standards same as previous issue.

G-4 GOOD—*LIBERTY only partly visible on hair band. Lettering, date, stars, worn but visible.*
VG-8 VERY GOOD—*LIBERTY entirely visible on hair band. Lower curls worn.*
F-12 FINE—*Only part wear on LIBERTY and hair at top worn in spots.*
VF-20 VERY FINE—*Lettering clear-cut. Hair only slightly worn.*
EF-40 EXTREMELY FINE—*Light wear on highest points of hair and leaves*
MS-60 UNCIRCULATED—*Typical brown to red surface. No trace of wear.*

| 1809 Normal Date | 1809, 9 over 6 | 1809 Circle Inside 0 |

	Quan. Minted	G-4	VG-8	F-12	VF-20	EF-40	MS-60
1809 All kinds	1,154,572						
1809 Circle inside 0		$30.00	$37.00	$55.00	$90.00	$250.00	$700.00
1809, 9 over 6		30.00	37.00	50.00	75.00	125.00	600.00
1809 Normal date		29.00	35.00	50.00	70.00	100.00	500.00
1810	215,000	32.00	45.00	85.00	130.00	350.00	1,500
1811	63,140	120.00	220.00	500.00	1,200	3,500	6,000
1811 Rev. of 1802. Unofficial restrike. *Ex. Rare*						—	
1825	63,000	30.00	40.00	55.00	75.00	140.00	700.00
1826	234,000	30.00	35.00	50.00	60.00	100.00	400.00

HALF CENTS

13 Stars

12 Stars

	Quan. Minted	G-4	VG-8	F-12	VF-20	EF-40	MS-60
1828, 13 stars	⎫ 606,000	$28.00	$33.00	$45.00	$55.00	$80.00	$245.00
1828, 12 stars	⎬	32.00	35.00	50.00	75.00	175.00	900.00
1829	487,000	28.00	33.00	45.00	55.00	95.00	250.00

**Reverse
1831-1836**

**Reverse
1840-1857**

Beginning in 1831 new coinage equipment and modified dies produced a raised rim on each side of these coins. Proofs and restrikes were made at the mint for sale to collectors. Restrikes are believed to have been struck c. 1858-59.

	Quan. Minted	EF-40	MS-60	Proof-63
1831 Original. (Beware of altered date).....................2,200		$10,000	—	$18,000
1831 Restrike. Lg. berries (Rev. of 1836)			$5,000	8,000
1831 Restrike. Sm. berries (Rev. of 1840-1857)...............				13,000

	Quan. Minted	VG-8	F-12	VF-20	EF-40	MS-60	Proof-63
1832..................51,000*		$34.00	$45.00	$55.00	$70.00	$225.00	$4,500
1833................103,000*		34.00	45.00	55.00	70.00	210.00	4,500
1834................141,000*		34.00	45.00	55.00	70.00	210.00	4,500
1835................398,000*		34.00	45.00	55.00	70.00	210.00	4,500
1836 Original..................							6,500
1836 Restrike. (Rev. of 1840-1857)							8,000

*The figures given here are thought to be correct, although official mint records report these quantities for 1833-36 rather than 1832-35.

No half cents were struck in 1837. Because of the great need for small change, however, a large number of tokens similar in size to current half cents and large cents were issued privately by businessmen who needed them in commerce. One of the most popular pieces is listed and illustrated below.

	G-4	VG-8	F-12	VF-20	EF-40	MS-60
1837 Token (not a coin) ..	$30.00	$40.00	$50.00	$80.00	$140.00	$435.00

HALF CENTS
CORONET TYPE 1840-1857

Brilliant red uncirculated half cents are worth more than prices shown.

Designer Christian Gobrecht; weight 5.44 grams; composition: copper; diameter 23 mm; plain edge.

VG-8 VERY GOOD—*Beads uniformly distinct. Hairlines show in spots.*
F-12 FINE—*Hairlines above ear worn. Beads sharp.*
VF-20 VERY FINE—*Lowest curl shows wear, hair otherwise distinct.*
EF-40 EXTREMELY FINE—*Light wear on highest points of hair and leaves.*
MS-60 UNCIRCULATED—*No trace of wear, light blemishes.*

Both originals and restrikes use reverse of 1840-1857. Originals have large berries, restrikes have small berries in wreath.

	Prof-63		Proof-63
1840 Original	$4,500	1845 Original	$5,500
1840 Restrike	4,200	1845 Restrike	5,000
1841 Original	4,500	1846 Original	5,000
1841 Restrike	4,200	1846 Restrike	4,200
1842 Original	4,600	1847 Original	4,500
1842 Restrike	4,200	1847 Restrike	4,200
1843 Original	4,500	1848 Original	4,500
1843 Restrike	4,200	1848 Restrike	4,200
1844 Original	5,200	1849 Original. Small date	4,800
1844 Restrike	4,200	1849 Restrike. Small date	4,800

Small Date　　　　**Large Date**

Brilliant or red uncirculated half cents are worth more than prices shown

	Quan. Minted	VG-8	F-12	VF-20	EF-40	MS-60	Proof-63
1849 Large date	39,864	$40.00	$50.00	$65.00	$100.00	$310.00	—
1850	39,812	40.00	50.00	65.00	115.00	310.00	$4,500
1851	147,672	35.00	45.00	50.00	75.00	200.00	4,500
1852 Restrike							4,500
1853	129,694	35.00	45.00	50.00	75.00	200.00	
1854	55,358	35.00	45.00	50.00	75.00	200.00	4,500
1855	56,500	35.00	45.00	50.00	75.00	200.00	4,500
1856	40,430	40.00	55.00	60.00	85.00	225.00	4,500
1857	35,180	50.00	70.00	90.00	125.00	300.00	4,500

BIBLIOGRAPHY
Breen, Walter, *Walter Breen's Encyclopedia of United States Half Cents 1793-1857*. South Gate, California, 1983.
Cohen, Roger S., Jr. *American Half Cents—The "Little Half Sisters"*. 2nd Edition, 1982.
Crosby, S. S., *United States Coinage of 1793—Cents and Half Cents*. Boston, 1897.
Frossard, Edward, *United States Cents and Half Cents 1793-1857*. Irvington, New York, 1879.
Gilbert, Ebenezer, *United States Half Cents*. New York, 1916. Hewitt Reprint, Chicago.
Manley, Ronald P., *The Half Cent Die State Book. 1793-1857, United States, 1998.*

LARGE CENTS — 1793-1857

Cents and half cents were the first coins struck under the authority of the United States Government. Coinage began in 1793 with laws specifying that the cent should weigh exactly twice as much as the half cent. Large cents were coined every year from 1793 to 1857 with the exception of 1815, when a lack of copper prevented production. All were coined at the Philadelphia Mint. Mintage records in some cases may be inaccurate, as many of the early pieces were struck later than the dates shown on the coins. Varieties listed are those most significant to collectors. Numerous other die varieties may be found because each of the early dies was individually made. Values of varieties not listed in this guide depend on collector interest, rarity and demand. Proof large cents were first made in 1817; all proofs are rare, as they were not made available to the general public before the mid-1850's.

+ or – indicates change from previous year	**TYPE COIN VALUES**									
	G-4	F-12	EF-40	AU-50	MS-60	MS-63	MS-65	PF-60	PF-63	PF-65
Chain 1793.........................	2,600+	6,000	20,000	40,000	70,000	—				
Wreath 1793 .... 900.00+		2,500+	7,000	10,000	22,000	32,000	60,000			
Liberty Cap 1793-1796 .... 140.00+		425.00+	1,700	2,400	3,600	7,000	20,000			
Draped Bust 1796-1807...... 35.00		110.00	700.00	1,200	2,200	4,500	15,000			
Classic Head 1808-1814..... 37.00+		185.00	900.00	1,800	2,700	8,000	24,000			
Coronet Head 1816-1839.... 13.00+		23.00	90.00	175.00	260.00	425.00	1,200	—		
Braided Hair 1840-1857...... 12.00+		16.00+	50.00	120.00	150.00-	275.00	900.00	2,500	4,500	7,500

FLOWING HAIR, CHAIN TYPE REVERSE 1793

Designer Henry Voigt; weight 13.48 grams; composition: copper; approx. diameter 26-27 mm; edge: bars and slender vine with leaves.

AG-3 ABOUT GOOD—*Date and devices clear enough to identify.*
G-4 GOOD—*Lettering worn but readable. Bust has no detail.*
VG-8 VERY GOOD—*Date and lettering distinct, some details of head visible.*
F-12 FINE—*About half of hair, etc. details show.*
VF-20 VERY FINE—*Ear visible. Most of details can be seen.*
EF-40 EXTREMELY FINE—*Highest points of hair and back of temple show wear.*

Values shown for Fine and better copper coins are for those with attractive surfaces and color that are consistent with the amount of normal wear. Coins that are porous, corroded, or similarly defective are worth significantly lower prices.

Obverse

Ameri. Reverse

America Reverse

	Quan. Minted	AG-3	G-4	VG-8	F-12	VF-20	EF-40
1793 Chain 36,103							
1793 AMERI. in legend....................		$1,400	$3,200	$4,750	$7,000	$13,000	$25,000
1793 AMERICA*		1,200	2,600	3,700	6,000	11,000	20,000

*Varieties with or without periods after date and LIBERTY.

LARGE CENTS

FLOWING HAIR, WREATH TYPE REVERSE 1793

The reverse of this type bears a "single-bow" wreath, as distinguished from the wreath tied with a double bow on the following type. A three-leaf sprig appears above the date on the obverse, and both sides have borders of small beads.

Introduction of this reverse answered criticism of the chain design, but the stronger modeling of the face and hair still failed to gain acceptance as representative of Liberty. After three months' production the design was abandoned in favor of the Liberty Cap type.

Instead of the normal sprig above the date, the rare "strawberry leaf" variety has a spray of trefoil leaves and a small blossom. The trefoils match those found on the normal wreath reverse. It is not clear why this variety was created. All known specimens are badly worn.

Designer Henry Voigt; weight 13.48 grams; composition: copper; approx. diameter 26-28 mm; edge: vine and bars, or lettered ONE HUNDRED FOR A DOLLAR followed by either a single or double leaf.

Wreath Type   **Strawberry Leaf Var.**

	Quan. Minted	AG-3	G-4	VG-8	F-12	VF-20	EF-40
1793 Wreath	63,353						
1793 Vine/bars edge		$400.00	$900.00	$1,300	$2,500	$3,500	$7,000
1793 Lettered edge		550.00	1,000	1,450	2,750	4,000	8,000
1793 Strawberry leaf				4 known			

LIBERTY CAP TYPE 1793-1796

Another major change was made in 1793 to satisfy continuing objections to the obverse portrait. This version appears to have been more successful, as it was continued into 1796. The 1793 pieces had beaded borders, but a border of denticles or "teeth" was adopted in 1794. A famous 1794 variety is the probably whimsical "starred" reverse, with a border of 94 tiny 5-pointed stars under the denticles.

Portrait variations listed below for 1794 are the result of several changes of die engravers. The so-called "Jefferson head" of 1795 is now thought to be a sample for a proposed coinage contract by a private manufacturer, John Harper.

Planchets became too thin for edge lettering after the weight reduction ordered late in 1795. The variety with reeded edge was probably an experimental substitute, rejected in favor of a plain edge.

1793-1795 (thick planchet) — Designer Joseph Wright; weight 13.48 grams; composition: copper; approx. diameter 29 mm; edge: ONE HUNDRED FOR A DOLLAR followed by a single leaf.
1795-1796 (thin planchet) — Designer John Smith Gardner; weight 10.89 grams; composition: copper; approx. diameter 29 mm; plain edge.

1793 Vine and Bars edge   **Lettered edge 1793-1795**
Chain and Wreath type only   ONE HUNDRED FOR A DOLLAR

LARGE CENTS

Beaded Border, 1793 Only

1793-1794

"Head of 1793"
Head is in high
rounded relief

1794 Only

"Head of 1794"
Well defined hair,
hook on lowest curl

1794-1796

"Head of 1795"
Head in low relief,
no hook on lowest curl

1794 Starred Reverse

	Quan. Minted	AG-3	G-4	VG-8	F-12	VF-20	EF-40
1793 Lib. Cap	11,056	$1,000	$2,100	$3,600	$6,500	$15,000	$35,000
1794 All kinds	918,521						
1794 "Head of 1793"		325.00	750.00	1,500	2,500	6,500	14,000
1794 "Head of 1794"		70.00	175.00	275.00	450.00	850.00	2,400
1794 "Head of 1795"		70.00	175.00	275.00	450.00	750.00	2,200
1794 Starred rev.		4,000	8,000	11,000	20,000	40,000	—
1794 No fraction bar		70.00	185.00	325.00	650.00	1,200	3,200
1795 Lettered edge	37,000	80.00	175.00	300.00	600.00	1,000	2,250
1795 Plain edge	501,500	65.00	140.00	225.00	425.00	700.00	1,700
1795 Reeded edge				*4 known*			

1796-1807

Reeded Edge

"Jefferson Head"

This head was modified
slightly in 1798. See
page 82 for details.

1795 Jefferson Head (not a regular mint issue)						
Plain edge	3,000	5,000	9,000	16,000	40,000	
Lettered edge			*3 known*			
1796 Lib. Cap	109,825	90.00	170.00	350.00	600.00	1,400	3,500

LARGE CENTS
DRAPED BUST TYPE 1796-1807

Designer Robert Scot; weight 10.89 grams; composition: copper; approx. diameter 29 mm; plain edge.

AG-3 ABOUT GOOD—*Clear enough to identify.*
G-4 GOOD—*Lettering worn, but clear; date clear. Bust lacks details.*
VG-8 VERY GOOD—*Drapery partly visible. Less wear in date and lettering.*
F-12 FINE—*Hair over brow is smooth, some detail showing in other parts of hair.*
VF-20 VERY FINE—*Hairlines slightly worn. Hair over brow better defined.*
EF-40 EXTREMELY FINE—*Hair above forehead and left of eye outlined and detailed. Only slight wear on olive leaves.*

1794-1796	1795-1798	1796-1807
"Reverse of 1794" Note double leaf at top right; 14-16 leaves left, 16-18 leaves right.	**"Reverse of 1795"** Note single leaf at top right; 17-21 leaves left, 16-20 leaves right.	**"Reverse of 1797"** Note double leaf at top right; 16 leaves left, 19 leaves right.

LIHERTY
error

	Quan. Minted	AG-3	G-4	VG-8	F-12	VF-20	EF-40
1796 Draped Bust	363,375						
1796 Reverse of 1794		$80.00	$150.00	$450.00	$625.00	$1,600	$3,200
1796 Reverse of 1795		70.00	125.00	220.00	475.00	1,100	2,300
1796 Reverse of 1797		60.00	120.00	210.00	450.00	1,000	2,200
1796 LIHERTY error		165.00	300.00	700.00	1,100	3,400	—
1796 Stemless reverse		—					

Gripped Edge

Stems   Stemless

	Quan. Minted	AG-3	G-4	VG-8	F-12	VF-20	EF-40
1797 All kinds	897,510						
1797 Gripped edge, '96 rev.		27.50	75.00	165.00	325.00	600.00	2,000
1797 Plain edge, '96 rev.		35.00	80.00	175.00	325.00	700.00	2,300
1797, '97 rev., stems		25.00	60.00	135.00	185.00	375.00	1,200
1797, '97 rev., stemless		40.00	90.00	200.00	375.00	850.00	3,200

LARGE CENTS

1798, 8 over 7

Style 1 Hair

Style 2 Hair

Style 1 hair appears on all 1796-97, many 1798 varieties and 1800 over 1798. Style 2 hair, used 1798-1807, is most easily recognized by the extra curl near the shoulder.

	Quan. Minted	AG-3	G-4	VG-8	F-12	VF-20	EF-40
1798 All kinds	1,841,745						
1798, 8 over 7		$45.00	$100.00	$200.00	$400.00	$1,500	$3,500
1798, Reverse of 1796		30.00	80.00	175.00	325.00	850.00	3,500
1798, 1st hair style		18.00	40.00	75.00	150.00	325.00	1,200
1798, 2nd hair style		18.00	35.00	70.00	130.00	320.00	1,100

1799, 9 over 8

1800 over 1798

1800, 80 over 79

1799, 9 over 8*	700.00	1,750	3,000	6,750	17,000	—
1799 Nor. date............Incl. above	600.00	1,400	2,500	6,000	15,000	—
1800 All kinds 2,822,175						
1800 over 1798,						
Style 1 hair	18.00	38.00	75.00	175.00	500.00	2,300
1800, 80 over 79,						
Style 2 hair	18.00	36.00	65.00	125.00	350.00	1,400
1800 Normal date	18.00	36.00	65.00	125.00	350.00	1,100

*Mintage for 1799 is included with the 1798 figure.

Fraction 1/000

Corrected Fraction

1801 Reverse, 3 Errors

Error-fraction dies appear on cents of 1801, 1802, and 1803, but all of these dies originated in 1801, possibly all by the same engraver.

LARGE CENTS

	Quan. Minted	AG-3	G-4	VG-8	F-12	VF-20	EF-40
1801 All kinds	1,362,837						
1801 Normal rev.		$16.00	$32.00	$50.00	$130.00	$275.00	$900.00
1801, 3 errors: 1/000, one							
stem & IINITED		40.00	100.00	180.00	500.00	1,100	4,500
1801 Fraction 1/000		15.00	40.00	65.00	160.00	350.00	1,100
1801, 1/100 over 1/000		15.00	45.00	95.00	200.00	500.00	1,300
1802 All kinds	3,435,100						
1802 Normal rev.		15.00	35.00	60.00	110.00	250.00	750.00
1802 Fraction 1/000		15.00	40.00	70.00	150.00	325.00	1,000
1802 Stemless wreath		15.00	35.00	60.00	110.00	250.00	750.00

Values shown for Fine and better copper coins are for those with attractive surfaces and color that are consistent with the amount of normal wear. Coins that are porous, corroded, or similarly defective are worth significantly lower prices.

1803 Small Date Blunt 1	1803 Large Date Pointed 1	Small Fraction	Large Fraction

All small date varieties have a blunt 1 in date. Large dates have pointed 1 and noticeably larger 3.

		AG-3	G-4	VG-8	F-12	VF-20	EF-40
1803 All kinds	3,131,691						
1803 Sm. dt., sm. fract		15.00	35.00	60.00	110.00	250.00	700.00
1803 Sm. dt., lg. fract		15.00	35.00	60.00	110.00	250.00	700.00
1803 Lg. dt., sm. fract		2,000	3,750	7,300	12,500	17,500	
1803 Lg. dt., lg. fract		25.00	50.00	125.00	250.00	600.00	2,000
1803, 1/100 over 1/000		15.00	40.00	80.00	160.00	350.00	1,000
1803 Stemless wreath		15.00	40.00	80.00	160.00	350.00	1,000

1804 With Normal or Broken Dies
(Broken die variety is illustrated)

Broken Dies

All genuine 1804 Cents have a crosslet 4 in the date and a large fraction. The 0 in the date is in line with the O in OF on the reverse of the coin. Values shown are for coins with normal or broken dies.

		AG-3	G-4	VG-8	F-12	VF-20	EF-40
1804	96,500	300.00	600.00	1,200	2,100	3,000	7,000

LARGE CENTS
Restrike of 1804 Cent

1804 Unofficial restrike of 1860 (Uncirculated).. $550.00

A fake 1804 was manufactured from discarded mint dies. An altered 1803 die was used for the obverse and a die of the 1820 cent used for the reverse. They were struck c.1860 to satisfy the demand for this rare date. Known as the "restrike," it was a patchwork job and is easily distinguished from a genuine 1804 cent.

	Quan. Minted	AG-3	G-4	VG-8	F-12	VF-20	EF-40
1805	941,116	$15.00	$35.00	$50.00	$125.00	$300.00	$850.00
1806	348,000	16.00	40.00	70.00	165.00	375.00	1,400

Small 1807, 7 over 6, blunt 1 **Lg. 1807, 7 over 6, pointed 1** **"Comet" Variety**

1807 All kinds	829,221					
1807 Small 7 over 6, Blunt 1	900.00	2,000	3,500	6,750	12,000	25,000
1807 Large 7 over 6	15.00	35.00	50.00	110.00	250.00	675.00
1807 Small fraction	16.00	40.00	55.00	125.00	275.00	725.00
1807 Large fraction	16.00	40.00	55.00	125.00	275.00	725.00
1807 "Comet" variety (die break behind head)	17.00	45.00	60.00	150.00	400.00	1,800

CLASSIC HEAD TYPE 1808-1814

1808 to 1814 — This group does not compare in sharpness and quality to those struck before (1793-1807), nor to those struck after (1816 on). The copper used was "softer," having less metallic impurity. This impaired the wearing quality of the series. For this reason collectors find greater difficulty in obtaining these dates in choice condition.

Designer John Reich. Standards same as previous issue.

LARGE CENTS

AG-3 ABOUT GOOD—*Details clear enough to identify.*
G-4 GOOD—*Legends, stars, date worn, but plain.*
VG-8 VERY GOOD—*LIBERTY all readable. Ear shows. Details worn but plain.*
F-12 FINE—*Hair on forehead and before ear nearly smooth. Ear and hair under ear sharp.*
VF-20 VERY FINE—*All hairlines show some detail. Leaves on reverse show slight wear.*
EF-40 EXTREMELY FINE—*All hairlines sharp. Very slight wear on high points.*

	Quan. Minted	AG-3	G-4	VG-8	F-12	VF-20	EF-40
1808	1,007,000	$15.00	$40.00	$100.00	$200.00	$475.00	$1,000
1809	222,867	36.00	90.00	200.00	375.00	900.00	2,400

1810, 10 over 09	Normal Date	1811, last 1 over 0	Normal Date

1810 All kinds.	1,458,500					
1810, 10 over 09		16.00	40.00	100.00	200.00	500.00	1,100
1810 Normal date		15.00	37.00	70.00	190.00	480.00	950.00
1811 All kinds.	218,025					
1811 Last 1 over 0		25.00	70.00	125.00	400.00	900.00	3,500
1811 Normal date		25.00	70.00	100.00	275.00	700.00	1,350

1812 Small date	1812 Large date	1814 Plain 4	1814 Crosslet 4

1812 Sm. date	} 1,075,500	15.00	37.00	70.00	185.00	450.00	900.00
1812 Lg. date		15.00	37.00	70.00	185.00	450.00	900.00
1813	418,000	20.00	40.00	85.00	200.00	500.00	1,200
1814 Plain 4	} 357,830	15.00	37.00	70.00	185.00	450.00	1,000
1814 Crosslet 4		15.00	37.00	70.00	185.00	450.00	950.00

LARGE CENTS
CORONET TYPE 1816-1857

Designer Robert Scot; weight 10.89 grams; composition: copper; approx. diameter 28-29 mm; plain edge.

G-4 GOOD—*Head details partly visible. Even wear in date and legends.*
VG-8 VERY GOOD—*LIBERTY, date, stars, legends clear. Part of hair cord visible.*
F-12 FINE—*All hairlines show. Hair cords show uniformly.*
VF-20 VERY FINE—*Hair cords only slightly worn. Hairlines only partly worn, all well defined.*
EF-40 EXTREMELY FINE—*Both hair cords stand out sharply. All hairlines sharp.*
MS-60 UNCIRCULATED—*Typical brown to red surface. No trace of wear.*

MATRON HEAD 1816-1835

13 Stars   **15 Stars**

	Quan. Minted	G-4	VG-8	F-12	VF-20	EF-40	MS-60*
1816	2,820,982	$14.00	$17.00	$35.00	$75.00	$150.00	$400.00
1817, 13 stars	} 3,948,400	14.00	17.00	28.00	65.00	125.00	300.00
1817, 15 stars		16.00	25.00	40.00	110.00	400.00	2,000
1818	3,167,000	14.00	17.00	28.00	65.00	125.00	300.00

1819, 9 over 8   **1819 Large Date**   **1819 Small Date**

	Quan. Minted	G-4	VG-8	F-12	VF-20	EF-40	MS-60*
1819 All kinds	2,671,000						
1819, 9 over 8		14.00	18.00	28.00	70.00	210.00	625.00
1819 Large date		13.00	16.00	23.00	60.00	100.00	300.00
1819 Small date		13.00	16.00	23.00	60.00	100.00	300.00

1820, 20 over 19   **1820 Large Date**   **1820 Small Date**
note 1 under 2   **note plain-topped 2**   **note curl-topped 2**

*Values shown are for average condition. Red to bright red uncirculated large cents with attractive surfaces (not cleaned) command higher prices. Beware of slightly worn copper coins that have been cleaned and recolored to simulate uncirculated luster. Cents in VF or better condition with attractive surface and tone may also command higher prices than listed here.

LARGE CENTS

	Quan. Minted	G-4	VG-8	F-12	VF-20	EF-40	MS-60*
1820 All kinds	4,407,550						
1820, 20 over 19		$14.00	$17.00	$35.00	$80.00	$250.00	$700.00
1820 Large date		13.00	16.00	23.00	60.00	100.00	300.00
1820 Small date		13.00	16.00	24.00	65.00	110.00	350.00
1821	389,000	23.00	45.00	100.00	325.00	1,000	5,000
1822	2,072,339	13.00	16.00	27.00	70.00	200.00	750.00

1823, 3 over 2 **1823 Restrike**

1823, 3 over 2 ⎫ Included	50.00	85.00	250.00	525.00	2,000	—
1823 Normal date ⎭ with 1824	50.00	100.00	270.00	600.00	2,400	—
1823 Unofficial restrike, from broken obverse die					325.00	750.00

The 1823 unofficial restrike was made at the same time and by the same people as the 1804 restrike copy (see page 84), using a discarded 1823 obverse and an 1813 reverse die. The dies are heavily rusted (producing lumps on the coin) and most examples have both dies cracked across.

1824, 4 over 2 **1826, 6 over 5**

1824, 4 over 2 ⎫ 1,262,000	15.00	27.00	65.00	225.00	1,000	—
1824 Normal date ⎭	13.00	17.00	35.00	125.00	450.00	2,200
1825 1,461,100	13.00	17.00	25.00	65.00	250.00	1,500
1826, 6 over 5 ⎫ 1,517,425	18.00	34.00	65.00	175.00	700.00	2,200
1826 Normal date ⎭	13.00	16.00	24.00	65.00	175.00	700.00
1827 2,357,732	13.00	16.00	24.00	65.00	140.00	500.00

This date-size appears on cents before 1828

This date-size appears on cents after 1828

1828 Lg. nar. date ⎫ 2,260,624	13.00	16.00	26.00	65.00	160.00	550.00
1828 Sm. wide date ⎭	14.00	20.00	30.00	90.00	225.00	900.00

*See footnote page 86.

LARGE CENTS

This large letter size appears on cents of 1808-1834.

Note individual letter size and proximity.

This medium letter size appears on cents of 1829-1837.

Note isolation of letters, esp. states.

	Quan. Minted	G-4	VG-8	F-12	VF-20	EF-40	MS-60*
1829 Large letters .	1,414,500	$13.00	$15.00	$23.00	$80.00	$135.00	$400.00
1829 Med. letters...		14.00	20.00	50.00	175.00	700.00	—
1830 Large letters .	1,711,500	13.00	15.00	25.00	65.00	140.00	350.00
1830 Med. letters...		20.00	35.00	90.00	325.00	900.00	—
1831 Large letters .	3,359,260	13.00	15.00	23.00	60.00	125.00	300.00
1831 Med. letters...		13.00	15.00	23.00	60.00	150.00	400.00
1832 Large letters .	2,362,000	13.00	15.00	23.00	60.00	125.00	325.00
1832 Med. letters...		13.00	15.00	23.00	60.00	125.00	325.00
1833......................	2,739,000	13.00	15.00	23.00	60.00	125.00	300.00

Large 8 and Stars

Large 8, Small Stars

Small 8, Large Stars

		G-4	VG-8	F-12	VF-20	EF-40	MS-60*
1834 All kinds 1,855,100							
1834 Lg. 8, stars & rev. letters...		13.00	20.00	50.00	110.00	300.00	—
1834 Lg. 8 & stars, med. letters .		100.00	200.00	300.00	600.00	1,750	—
1834 Lg. 8, sm. stars, med. let....		13.00	15.00	23.00	55.00	110.00	325.00
1834 Sm. 8, lg. stars, med. let. ...		13.00	15.00	23.00	55.00	110.00	325.00

Large 8 and Stars, Matron Head

Small 8 and Stars, Matron Head

"Head of 1836" 1835-1837 Slim Bust

		G-4	VG-8	F-12	VF-20	EF-40	MS-60*
1835 All kinds 3,878,400							
1835 Lg. 8 & stars		13.00	15.00	23.00	55.00	175.00	600.00
1835 Sm. 8 & stars		13.00	15.00	23.00	55.00	110.00	300.00
1835 "Head of 1836"		13.00	15.00	23.00	50.00	100.00	285.00
1836............................2,111,000		13.00	15.00	23.00	50.00	100.00	285.00

*See footnote page 86.

LARGE CENTS
YOUNG HEAD 1835-1857

Designer Christian Gobrecht; weight 10.89 grams; composition: copper; diameter 27.5 mm; plain edge.

G-4 GOOD—*Considerably worn. LIBERTY readable.*
VG-8 VERY GOOD—*Hairlines smooth but visible, outline of ear clearly defined.*
F-12 FINE—*Hairlines at top of head and behind ear worn but visible. Braid over brow plain, ear clear.*
VF-20 VERY FINE—*All details more sharp. Hair over brow shows only slight wear.*
EF-40 EXTREMELY FINE—*Hair above ear detailed, but slightly worn.*
MS-60 UNCIRCULATED—*Typical brown to red surface. No trace of wear.*

1829-1837
Medium letters
Note size and
spacing of letters.

"Head of 1838"
Beaded Cords
note slim bust
with beaded cords.

1837-1839
Small letters
note size and
spacing of letters.

	Quan. Minted	G-4	VG-8	F-12	VF-20	EF-40	MS-60*
1837 All kinds	5,558,300						
1837 Pl. crd., med. let		$13.00	$16.00	$23.00	$45.00	$100.00	$275.00
1837 Pl. crd., sm. let		13.00	16.00	24.00	45.00	110.00	325.00
1837 Head of 1838		13.00	16.00	23.00	40.00	90.00	260.00
1838	6,370,200	13.00	16.00	23.00	40.00	90.00	260.00

1839 over 1836
Note closed 9,
plain cords.

Silly Head
Note browlock
at forehead.

Booby Head
Note back tip of
shoulder exposed.

1839 All kinds	3,128,661						
1839, 9 over 6, plain cords		200.00	400.00	1,100	2,200	6,000	—
1839 Head of 1838, beaded cords		13.00	16.00	23.00	45.00	100.00	275.00
1839 Silly Head		14.00	18.00	27.00	60.00	150.00	750.00
1839 Booby Head		13.00	17.00	25.00	50.00	100.00	600.00
1839 Petite head		13.00	16.00	23.00	45.00	100.00	350.00

The last two 1839 heads use a modified reverse that omits the line under CENT (see illustration on page 90).

---

*Values shown are for average condition. Red to bright red uncirculated large cents with attractive surfaces (not cleaned) command higher prices. Beware of slightly worn copper coins that have been cleaned and recolored to simulate uncirculated luster. Cents in VF or better condition with attractive surface and tone may also command higher prices than listed here.

LARGE CENTS

1840 Large Date

1840 Small Date

Small Date over Large 18

	Quan. Minted	G-4	VG-8	F-12	VF-20	EF-40	MS-60*
1840 All kinds	2,462,700						
1840 Large date		$12.00	$14.00	$17.00	$22.00	$70.00	$225.00
1840 Small date		12.00	14.00	17.00	22.00	70.00	225.00
1840 Sm. date, lg. 18		13.00	15.00	20.00	30.00	140.00	450.00
1841 Small date	1,597,367	12.00	14.00	17.00	22.00	100.00	350.00

1842 Small Date

1842 Large Date

Small Letters 1839-1843

		G-4	VG-8	F-12	VF-20	EF-40	MS-60*
1842 Small date	} 2,383,390	12.00	14.00	16.00	22.00	70.00	250.00
1842 Large date		12.00	14.00	16.00	22.00	70.00	225.00

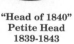

"Head of 1840" Petite Head 1839-1843

"Head of 1844" Mature Head 1843-1857

Large Letters 1843-1857

		G-4	VG-8	F-12	VF-20	EF-40	MS-60*
1843 All kinds	2,425,342						
1843 Petite, sm. let		12.00	14.00	17.00	22.00	70.00	200.00
1843 Petite, lg. let		14.00	19.00	35.00	60.00	150.00	750.00
1843 Mature, lg. let		13.00	15.00	22.00	38.00	100.00	400.00
1844 Normal date	} 2,398,752	12.00	14.00	17.00	25.00	70.00	175.00
1844 over 81 (error)		13.00	18.00	30.00	65.00	200.00	750.00
1845	3,894,804	12.00	14.00	17.00	20.00	65.00	150.00

*See footnote page 89.

LARGE CENTS

1846 Small Date
note squat date
with closed 6

1846 Medium Date
note medium height
with ball-top 6

1846 Tall Date
note vertically-stretched
date with open-mouthed 6

	Quan. Minted	G-4	VG-8	F-12	VF-20	EF-40	MS-60*
1846 All kinds	4,120,800						
1846 Small date.........................		$12.00	$14.00	$16.00	$20.00	$60.00	$150.00
1846 Medium date		12.00	14.00	17.00	22.00	65.00	175.00
1846 Tall date.............................		12.00	15.00	17.00	22.00	70.00	300.00
1847 .... }	6,183,669	12.00	14.00	16.00	20.00	60.00	175.00
1847, 7 over "sm." 7		13.00	16.00	25.00	45.00	125.00	700.00

(1848 Small date is a rare contemporary counterfeit)							
1848.............................	6,415,799	12.00	14.00	16.00	20.00	60.00	200.00
1849.............................	4,178,500	12.00	14.00	16.00	22.00	75.00	250.00
1850.............................	4,426,844	12.00	14.00	16.00	20.00	55.00	150.00

1844, 44 over 81

1851, 51 over 81

1847, 7 over "Small" 7

These are not true overdates, but are some of the more spectacular of several date-punch blunders of the 1844-1854 period. The so-called "overdates" of 1844 and 1851 each have the date punched upside-down, then corrected normally.

1851 Normal date... }	9,889,707	12.00	14.00	16.00	20.00	50.00	150.00
1851 over 81 (error)		13.00	15.00	18.00	37.00	100.00	400.00
1852	5,063,094	12.00	14.00	16.00	20.00	50.00	150.00
1853	6,641,131	12.00	14.00	16.00	20.00	50.00	150.00
1854	4,236,156	12.00	14.00	16.00	20.00	50.00	150.00

*See footnote page 89.

LARGE CENTS

1855 Upright 5's

1855 Slanting 5's

1855 Knob on ear

Original sketches of engraver James B. Longacre's work reveal that slanting 5's were a peculiarity of his work. The figure punch for an upright 5 was probably the work of an apprentice.

	Quan. Minted	G-4	VG-8	F-12	VF-20	EF-40	MS-60*
1855 All kinds 1,574,829							
1855 Upright 5's..........................		$12.00	$14.00	$16.00	$20.00	$50.00	$150.00
1855 Slanting 5's.........................		12.00	14.00	16.00	20.00	50.00	175.00
1855 Slanting 5's, knob on ear ...		12.00	16.00	20.00	35.00	75.00	300.00
1856 Upright 5....... } 2,690,463		12.00	14.00	16.00	20.00	50.00	150.00
1856 Slanting 5......		12.00	14.00	16.00	20.00	50.00	150.00

1857 Large Date

1857 Small Date

		G-4	VG-8	F-12	VF-20	EF-40	MS-60
1857 Large date ..... } 333,456		30.00	40.00	50.00	60.00	85.00	275.00
1857 Small date		35.00	45.00	55.00	65.00	90.00	300.00

*See footnote page 89.

Passing of the Large Cent and Half Cent

By 1857 the cost of making and distributing copper coins had risen. Mint Director Snowden reported that they "barely paid expenses." Both cents and half cents had become unpopular; in fact, they hardly circulated outside of the larger cities. The practice of issuing subsidiary silver coins, which began in 1853, brought about a reform of the copper coinage. The half cent was abandoned and a smaller cent was introduced in 1857.

The law of 1857 brought important benefits to the citizens. By its terms Spanish coins were redeemed and melted at the mint in exchange for new small cents. The decimal system became popular and official thereafter, and the old method of reckoning in reals, medios, shillings, etc., was gradually given up, although the terms, "two bits" and "penny" are still commonly used. The new, convenient small cent won popular favor and soon became a useful instrument of retail trade and a boon to commerce.

For some unexplained reason a few experimental large cent pieces were made dated 1868.

BIBLIOGRAPHY

Grellman, J.R. *Attribution Guide for United States Large Cents 1840-1857*. Bloomington, MN, 1987.
Newcomb, H.R. *United States Copper Cents 1816-1857*. New York, 1944. (Reprinted 1983)
Noyes, William C. *United States Large Cents 1793-1814*. Bloomington, MN, 1991.
Noyes, William C. *United States Large Cents 1816-1839*. Bloomington, MN, 1991.
PENNY-WISE, official publication of Early American Coppers, Inc. (EAC)
Sheldon, Wm. H. *Penny Whimsy (1793-1814)*. New York, 1958. (Reprinted 1965, 1976)
Wright, John D. *The Cent Book 1816-1839*. Bloomington, MN, 1992.

SMALL CENTS — 1856 to Date

The Act of February 21, 1857 provided for the coinage of the new copper-nickel small cent. It also called for Spanish and Mexican coins and old copper cents and half cents in circulation to be called in and exchanged for U.S. silver coins and the new cents. The cent weighed 72 grains with a metallic composition of 88% copper and 12% nickel.

The 1856 Eagle cent, a pattern, was made to show Congress how the new cent would look. Additional proof pieces were struck for sale to collectors. It is believed that between 1,500 and 2,500 pieces were struck in all. These have always been collected as regular issues because of their early widespread popularity. A few 1856 Eagle cents probably went into circulation during the Civil War.

Some 1858-dated cents have been altered into 1856. They are easy to spot because the shape of the 5 is different on the 1858 than it is on the 1856.

There are many varieties known for 1857 and 1858. The 1858 is found with 2 variations. The "Large Letter" design shows the A and M in AMERICA joined, and the "Small Letter" design shows the A and M separated. Minor variations of the reverse designs of corn, wheat, cotton and tobacco appear on 1858 cents. The 1858, 8 over 7 variety can be identified by a small dot, or die defect, in the field above the first 8. During production, this die was ground down to a point where the 7 is no longer visible. These are not as desirable as coins with the 7 showing.

+ or – indicates change from previous year	TYPE COIN VALUES									
	G-4	F-12	EF-40	AU-50	MS-60	MS-63	MS-65	PF-60	PF-63	PF-65
Flying Eagle 1857-1858	16.00+	25.00	100.00	150.00	265.00	575.00+	3,300	1,200	7,000+	20,000+
Indian CN 1859	10.00+	16.00+	85.00	150.00	200.00	425.00+	2,600	550.00	1,200+	4,600
Indian CN 1860-1864..........	6.00+	9.00+	25.00	50.00	75.00	140.00	850.00-	310.00	600.00	2,200
Indian 1864-1909	1.35	1.75	7.00	15.00	25.00	45.00	135.00+	90.00	150.00-	350.00
Lincoln 1909-V.D.B.............	3.25+	3.75+	5.50+	7.00+	12.00+	15.00	50.00+	550.00+	1,500	3,000+

FLYING EAGLE TYPE 1856-1858

Designer James B. Longacre; weight 4.67 grams; composition: .880 copper, .120 nickel; diameter 19 mm; plain edge. All coined at Philadelphia Mint.

G-4 GOOD—*All details worn, but readable.*
VG-8 VERY GOOD—*Feather details and eye of eagle are evident, but worn.*
F-12 FINE—*Eagle head details and feather tips sharp.*
VF-20 VERY FINE—*Feathers in right wing and tail show considerable detail.*
EF-40 EXTREMELY FINE—*Slight wear, all details sharp.*
MS-60 UNCIRCULATED—*No trace of wear. Light blemishes.*

1858, 8 over 7

Large Letters

Small Letters

	Quan. Minted	G-4	VG-8	F-12	VF-20	EF-40	MS-60	Proof-63
1856 ....est.	2,000	$3,700	$4,200	$4,700	$5,200	$5,800	$7,500	$9,000
1857 ....(485)	17,450,000	16.00	17.00	26.00	37.00	110.00	265.00	7,000
1858 Lg. let....(80)	} 24,600,000	16.00	17.00	26.00	37.00	110.00	265.00	7,000
1858 Sm. let.(200)		16.00	17.00	25.00	36.00	100.00	250.00	7,000
1858, 8 over 7 (see picture)			80.00	160.00	310.00	600.00	1,600	

SMALL CENTS
INDIAN HEAD TYPE 1859-1909

The "Indian Head" cent first issued in 1859 is actually a representation of Liberty wearing an Indian headdress, not an actual Indian. The first year featured a Laurel wreath on the reverse. This was changed after one year to the Oak wreath with a small shield. Coins of 1859 and early 1860 show a pointed bust. Those made from late 1860 until 1864 have a more rounded bust. Prior to the issuance of 5 cent nickel pieces in 1866, these coins were commonly referred to as "Nickels" or "Nicks".

COPPER-NICKEL

Designer James B. Longacre; weight 4.67 grams; composition: .880 copper, .120 nickel; diameter 19 mm; plain edge. All coined at Philadelphia Mint.

G-4 GOOD—*No LIBERTY visible.*
VG-8 VERY GOOD—*At least three letters of LIBERTY readable on head band.*
F-12 FINE—*LIBERTY completely visible.*
VF-20 VERY FINE—*Slight but even wear on LIBERTY.*
EF-40 EXTREMELY FINE—*LIBERTY sharp. All other details sharp. Only slight wear on ribbon end.*
MS-60 UNCIRCULATED—*No trace of wear. Light blemishes.*

Without Shield at Top of Wreath	**With Shield on Reverse**
1859 Only	**1860 to 1909**

Variety 1 — Copper-nickel, Laurel Wreath Reverse 1859
Spotted, cleaned or discolored pieces are worth less than values shown.

	Quan. Minted	G-4	VG-8	F-12	VF-20	EF-40	MS-60	Proof-63
1859..........(800)	36,400,000	$10.00	$12.00	$16.00	$35.00	$85.00	$200.00	$1,200

Variety 2 — Copper-nickel, Oak Wreath with Shield 1860-1864

	Quan. Minted	G-4	VG-8	F-12	VF-20	EF-40	MS-60	Proof-63
1860 Pointed bust	20,566,000	9.00	12.00	16.00	22.00	60.00	225.00	
1860.....(1,000)		7.00	9.00	11.00	17.00	45.00	135.00	650.00
1861.....(1,000)	10,100,000	16.00	22.00	27.00	40.00	87.50	185.00	700.00
1862........(550)	28,075,000	6.00	8.00	9.00	15.00	25.00	85.00	600.00
1863........(460)	49,840,000	6.00	8.00	9.00	15.00	25.00	75.00	600.00
1864........(370)	13,740,000	13.00	17.00	24.00	34.00	50.00	130.00	750.00

Variety 3 — Bronze 1864-1909

During the Civil War, all gold, silver and eventually the copper-nickel cent disappeared from circulation. In larger cities, thin copper cent-sized tokens began to be issued by merchants to fill the void left by the missing cents. The Government stepped in and with the act of April 22, 1864, issued its own thin bronze coin and made the issuance of the tokens illegal.

The obverse was redesigned near the end of 1864. A slightly sharper portrait included the designer's initial "L" for Longacre on the lower ribbon behind the neck. This design continued on until 1909 when the design was replaced with the Lincoln cent.

Indian Head Cent with "L"

If the coin is turned slightly (so Indian faces observer) the highlighted details of the "L" will appear to better advantage. The point of the bust is pointed on the variety with "L"; rounded without "L." The "L" is the last initial of the engraver, James B. Longacre.

SMALL CENTS

Designer James B. Longacre; weight 3.11 grams; composition: .950 copper, .050 tin and zinc; diameter 19 mm; plain edge; mints: Philadelphia, San Francisco.

Choice brilliant Unc. and Proof small cents command higher prices. Spotted, cleaned or discolored pieces are worth less.

	Quan. Minted	G-4	VG-8	F-12	VF-20	EF-40	MS-60	Proof-63
1864 All kinds 39,233,714								
1864 No L ....(150)		$5.00	$10.00	$14.00	$27.50	$47.50	$75.00	$700.00
1864 L must show ......(20)		37.50	57.50	90.00	120.00	200.00	350.00	12,500
1865* ...(500+) 35,429,286		6.00	8.00	15.00	20.00	30.00	70.00	400.00
1866 .....(725+) 9,826,500		32.00	37.50	50.00	85.00	150.00	225.00	400.00
1867 .....(625+) 9,821,000		34.00	40.00	55.00	90.00	160.00	235.00	400.00
1868 .....(600+) 10,266,500		32.00	37.50	50.00	85.00	150.00	225.00	400.00
1869 over 9* ...		90.00	125.00	200.00	275.00	300.00	400.00	
1869 .....(600+) 6,420,000		45.00	65.00	175.00	225.00	275.00	400.00	550.00
1870 ..(1,000+) 5,275,000		35.00	60.00	140.00	200.00	275.00	400.00	425.00
1871 .....(960+) 3,929,500		45.00	65.00	200.00	250.00	300.00	425.00	450.00
1872 .....(950+) 4,042,000		57.00	72.00	250.00	290.00	350.00	475.00	500.00

*One variety of 1865 appears to show traces of a 4 under the 5 in the date. On other varieties the tip of the 5 is either plain or curved. The 9 is doubled on some varieties of the 1869; on others it appears to be over an 8, although it is actually a doubled 9. None of these varieties is a true overdate. Varities of 1870, 1871, 1872 and 1873 closed 3, have either a bold or shallow N in CENT.

Closed 3   **Open 3**

	Quan. Minted	G-4	VG-8	F-12	VF-20	EF-40	MS-60	Proof-63
1873 All kinds 11,676,500								
1873 Closed 3 (1,100+)		16.00	25.00	45.00	70.00	150.00	300.00	325.00
1873 Doubled LIBERTY			225.00	550.00	1,000	2,000	5,000	
1873 Open 3		15.00	22.00	40.00	50.00	125.00	165.00	
1874 .....(700+) 14,187,500		13.00	16.00	25.00	40.00	85.00	155.00	300.00
1875 .....(700+) 13,528,000		13.00	20.00	35.00	42.00	85.00	155.00	300.00
1876 ..(1,150+) 7,944,000		23.00	28.00	40.00	55.00	120.00	175.00	325.00
1877 .....(900+) 852,500		425.00	525.00	700.00	850.00	1,250	2,100	2,600
1878 ....(2,350) 5,799,850		23.00	30.00	42.00	70.00	135.00	185.00	275.00
1879 ....(3,200) 16,231,200		5.00	8.00	12.00	25.00	55.00	70.00	180.00
1880 ....(3,955) 38,964,955		2.50	4.00	5.00	7.00	20.00	55.00	180.00
1881 ....(3,575) 39,211,575		2.50	3.00	5.00	7.00	15.00	42.00	180.00
1882 ....(3,100) 38,581,100		2.50	3.00	4.00	8.00	15.00	42.00	180.00
1883 ....(6,609) 45,598,109		2.50	3.00	4.00	7.00	15.00	42.00	180.00
1884 ....(3,942) 23,261,742		3.00	3.50	7.00	10.00	22.00	55.00	220.00
1885 ....(3,790) 11,765,384		5.00	6.00	10.00	20.00	45.00	85.00	180.00
1886 ....(4,290) 17,654,290		2.50	5.00	14.00	38.00	110.00	125.00	175.00

On coins minted in 1859 to mid-1886, the last feather of the headdress points between I and C of AMERICA; on the second variety, from mid-1886 to 1909, it points between C and A.

	Quan. Minted	G-4	VG-8	F-12	VF-20	EF-40	MS-60	Proof-63
1886.....Var. II incl. above		2.75	6.00	15.00	55.00	130.00	250.00	275.00
1887 ....(2,960) 45,226,483		1.50	2.00	3.00	4.50	14.00	45.00	160.00

1888, last 8 over 7
A less prominent variety exists but is valued lower than the clear overdate.

	Quan. Minted	G-4	VG-8	F-12	VF-20	EF-40	MS-60	Proof-63
1888 over 7.. }	37,494,414		650.00	1,000	1,450	2,500	8,000	
1888 .(4,582) }		1.50	2.00	4.00	5.00	16.00	40.00	160.00
1889 .(3,336)	48,869,361	1.50	2.00	2.50	4.00	10.00	35.00	160.00

SMALL CENTS

	Quan. Minted	G-4	VG-8	F-12	VF-20	EF-40	MS-60	Proof-63
1890...(2,740)	57,182,854	$1.50	$1.75	$2.50	$4.00	$10.00	$35.00	$150.00
1891...(2,350)	47,072,350	1.50	1.75	2.50	4.00	10.00	35.00	150.00
1892...(2,745)	37,649,832	1.50	1.75	2.50	4.00	10.00	35.00	150.00
1893...(2,195)	46,642,195	1.50	1.75	2.50	4.00	10.00	35.00	150.00
1894...(2,632) }	16,752,132	2.50	4.00	7.00	10.00	25.00	50.00	150.00
1894 Doubled date ..... }		12.00	20.00	50.00	100.00	175.00	450.00	
1895...(2,062)	38,343,636	1.35	1.75	2.50	3.50	10.00	30.00	150.00
1896...(1,862)	39,057,293	1.35	1.50	2.00	3.00	9.00	30.00	150.00
1897...(1,938)	50,466,330	1.35	1.50	2.00	3.00	9.00	30.00	150.00
1898...(1,795)	49,823,079	1.35	1.50	2.00	3.00	9.00	30.00	150.00
1899...(2,031)	53,600,031	1.35	1.50	2.00	3.00	9.00	30.00	150.00
1900...(2,262)	66,833,764	1.35	1.45	1.75	2.15	7.00	25.00	150.00
1901...(1,985)	79,611,143	1.35	1.45	1.75	2.15	7.00	25.00	150.00
1902...(2,018)	87,376,722	1.35	1.45	1.75	2.15	7.00	25.00	150.00
1903...(1,790)	85,094,493	1.35	1.45	1.75	2.15	7.00	25.00	150.00
1904...(1,817)	61,328,015	1.35	1.45	1.75	2.15	7.00	25.00	150.00
1905...(2,152)	80,719,163	1.35	1.45	1.75	2.15	7.00	25.00	150.00
1906...(1,725)	96,022,255	1.35	1.45	1.75	2.15	7.00	25.00	150.00
1907...(1,475)	108,138,618	1.35	1.45	1.75	2.15	7.00	25.00	150.00

**Location of mint mark S
on reverse of Indian cent
(1908 and 1909 only).**

1908...(1,620)	32,327,987	1.35	1.45	1.75	2.15	8.00	25.00	175.00
1908S.................1,115,000		40.00	45.00	55.00	60.00	90.00	225.00	
1909...(2,175)	14,370,645	2.00	3.00	4.00	5.00	15.00	35.00	200.00
1909S 309,000		235.00	275.00	300.00	350.00	425.00	525.00	

LINCOLN TYPE, WHEAT EARS REVERSE 1909-1958

Victor D. Brenner designed this cent which was issued to commemorate the
hundredth anniversary of Lincoln's birth. The designer's initials VDB appear
on the reverse of a limited quantity of cents of 1909. The initials were
restored, in 1918, to the obverse side on Lincoln's shoulder as illustrated on
page 98. The Lincoln type was the first cent to have the motto IN GOD WE
TRUST.

Matte proof coins were made for collectors from 1909 through 1916, and an
exceptional specimen dated 1917 is also reported to exist.

Designer Victor D. Brenner; weight 3.11 grams; composition: .950 copper, .050 tin and zinc; diameter 19
mm; plain edge; mints: Philadelphia, Denver, San Francisco.

G-4 GOOD—Date worn but apparent. Lines in wheat heads missing. Full rims.
VG-8 VERY GOOD—Half of lines show in upper wheat heads.
F-12 FINE—Wheat lines worn but visible.
VF-20 VERY FINE—Cheek and jaw bones worn but separated. No worn spots on wheat heads.
EF-40 EXTREMELY FINE—Slight wear. All details sharp.
MS-60 UNCIRCULATED—No trace of wear. Light blemishes or discoloration.
MS-63 SELECT UNCIRCULATED—No trace of wear. Slight blemishes. Red-Brown color.
MS-65 CHOICE UNCIRCULATED—No trace of wear. Barely noticeable blemishes. Nearly full red color.

SMALL CENTS

| Location of designer's initials V.D.B. on 1909 reverse only. | No V.D.B. on reverse 1909-1958. | Location of mint mark. |

Variety 1 — Bronze 1909-1942

Choice brilliant uncirculated cents command higher prices. Discolored (brown) or weakly struck pieces are worth less.

	Quan. Minted	G-4	VG-8	F-12	VF-20	EF-40	MS-60	MS-63
1909 V.D.B.	27,995,000	$3.25	$3.50	$3.75	$4.50	$5.50	$12.00	$15.00
1909 V.D.B. Matte prf.(1,194)								1,500
1909S, V.D.B.	484,000	375.00	450.00	500.00	550.00	600.00	800.00	900.00
1909	72,702,618	1.00	1.25	1.75	2.10	2.75	15.00	20.00
1909 Matte proof (2,352)								320.00
1909S	1,825,000	35.00	40.00	55.00	70.00	105.00	140.00	180.00
1909S, S over horiz. S		35.00	40.00	60.00	75.00	110.00	175.00	210.00
1910	146,801,218	.20	.30	.45	.80	2.00	14.00	22.50
1910 Matte proof (4,083)								250.00
1910S	6,045,000	6.00	7.00	8.00	10.00	20.00	65.00	85.00
1911	101,177,787	.20	.35	1.00	1.25	4.00	18.00	30.00
1911 Matte proof (2,411)								275.00
1911D	12,672,000	4.00	5.00	7.00	13.00	35.00	80.00	100.00
1911S	4,026,000	15.00	17.00	19.00	22.50	37.50	135.00	190.00
1912	68,153,060	1.00	1.25	1.75	4.50	8.50	30.00	40.00
1912 Matte proof (2,145)								275.00
1912D	10,411,000	4.50	5.25	6.50	16.00	40.00	125.00	185.00
1912S	4,431,000	10.00	12.00	14.00	18.00	38.00	110.00	160.00
1913	76,532,352	.50	.75	1.25	3.00	10.00	27.50	38.00
1913 Matte proof (2,848)								275.00
1913D	15,804,000	1.75	2.00	4.00	7.00	22.00	80.00	150.00
1913S	6,101,000	6.00	7.00	8.00	12.00	26.00	125.00	175.00
1914	75,238,432	.35	.60	1.50	3.00	10.00	45.00	60.00
1914 Matte proof (1,365)								325.00
1914D*	1,193,000	85.00	115.00	165.00	225.00	450.00	975.00	1,750
1914S	4,137,000	8.00	9.00	11.00	20.00	40.00	225.00	400.00
1915	29,092,120	1.50	1.75	4.00	10.00	35.00	75.00	125.00
1915 Matte proof (1,150)								500.00
1915D	22,050,000	1.25	1.50	2.00	3.75	10.00	60.00	90.00
1915S	4,833,000	6.00	7.00	8.00	12.00	35.00	125.00	225.00
1916	131,833,677	.20	.25	.35	.75	1.50	12.00	25.00
1916 Matte proof (1,050)								700.00
1916D	35,956,000	.25	.40	1.00	2.10	7.25	55.00	100.00
1916S	22,510,000	1.00	1.25	1.75	2.50	8.00	60.00	125.00

Doubled Die Varieties of 1917 and 1936

1917 Doubled die obv.				75.00	200.00	375.00	750.00	1,000
1917	196,429,785	.20	.25	.30	.85	1.50	12.00	25.00
1917 Matte proof								—

*Beware of altered date or mint mark. No V.D.B. on shoulder of genuine 1914D cent.

SMALL CENTS

Designer's initials placed on Lincoln's shoulder next to rim, starting 1918.

Quan. Minted		G-4	VG-8	F-12	VF-20	EF-40	MS-60	MS-63
1917D	55,120,000	$.25	$.35	$.65	$1.50	$7.00	$60.00	$110.00
1917S	32,620,000	.40	.45	.70	1.50	7.00	65.00	125.00
1918	288,104,634	.20	.25	.40	.80	1.50	13.00	25.00
1918D	47,830,000	.25	.35	.65	1.50	5.50	50.00	105.00
1918S	34,680,000	.30	.40	.65	1.50	5.50	60.00	125.00
1919	392,021,000	.15	.25	.40	.60	1.50	11.00	20.00
1919D	57,154,000	.25	.30	.45	1.30	4.00	45.00	80.00
1919S	139,760,000	.15	.25	.40	.80	2.50	35.00	70.00
1920	310,165,000	.15	.25	.35	.40	1.50	10.00	20.00
1920D	49,280,000	.25	.35	.60	1.00	4.00	55.00	100.00
1920S	46,220,000	.25	.35	.60	1.00	4.00	80.00	165.00
1921	39,157,000	.20	.35	.60	1.00	3.00	40.00	70.00
1921S	15,274,000	1.00	1.25	1.75	3.75	15.00	100.00	175.00
1922D		7.00	8.00	10.00	12.00	20.00	75.00	125.00
1922 No D‡	} 7,160,000	250.00	400.00	500.00	600.00	1,500	5,200	14,000
1922 Weak D		25.00	32.00	45.00	65.00	125.00	300.00	500.00
1923	74,723,000	.15	.20	.35	.50	2.00	12.00	22.00
1923S	8,700,000	1.50	2.00	3.00	5.00	18.00	180.00	350.00
1924	75,178,000	.15	.20	.35	.50	3.00	22.00	40.00
1924D	2,520,000	8.00	10.00	12.00	24.00	65.00	240.00	350.00
1924S	11,696,000	.75	1.00	1.50	2.50	12.00	100.00	185.00
1925	139,949,000	.15	.25	.35	.50	1.50	10.00	22.50
1925D	22,580,000	.25	.35	.45	1.00	5.00	50.00	85.00
1925S	26,380,000	.20	.25	.35	.75	5.00	60.00	135.00
1926	157,088,000	.15	.20	.30	.45	1.25	8.00	16.00
1926D	28,020,000	.25	.35	.60	1.30	5.00	50.00	85.00
1926S	4,550,000	2.00	3.00	4.50	5.50	11.00	110.00	200.00
1927	144,440,000	.15	.20	.30	.55	1.25	8.00	16.00
1927D	27,170,000	.25	.35	.50	.85	2.75	30.00	65.00
1927S	14,276,000	.50	.75	1.25	2.25	8.00	65.00	125.00
1928	134,116,000	.15	.20	.30	.55	1.25	8.00	16.00
1928D	31,170,000	.20	.30	.40	.80	2.00	25.00	50.00
1928S*	17,266,000	.35	.40	.70	1.25	3.50	55.00	100.00
1929	185,262,000	.15	.20	.30	.60	1.35	7.50	13.00
1929D	41,730,000	.15	.25	.35	.65	2.00	17.00	32.00
1929S	50,148,000	.15	.25	.35	.60	2.00	10.00	18.00
1930	157,415,000	.10	.15	.25	.40	.90	5.00	10.00
1930D	40,100,000	.15	.20	.30	.45	2.00	12.00	25.00
1930S	24,286,000	.15	.20	.30	.50	1.00	8.00	13.00
1931	19,396,000	.35	.45	.50	.85	1.80	17.00	38.00
1931D	4,480,000	2.50	2.75	3.50	4.25	7.50	50.00	80.00
1931S	866,000	35.00	40.00	42.00	47.00	55.00	70.00	85.00
1932	9,062,000	1.50	1.75	2.00	2.50	3.00	18.00	25.00
1932D	10,500,000	.70	.90	1.20	1.75	2.50	15.00	30.00
1933	14,360,000	.75	.90	1.25	1.50	2.75	16.00	30.00
1933D	6,200,000	1.75	2.00	2.25	3.00	4.00	20.00	25.00
1934	219,080,000	....	.10	.15	.30	.60	4.00	5.00
1934D	28,446,000	.15	.25	.30	.45	1.00	14.00	20.00
1935	245,388,000	....	.10	.15	.20	.40	2.00	3.50
1935D	47,000,000	....	.10	.15	.25	.40	4.00	6.00
1935S	38,702,000	....	.10	.20	.30	.60	10.00	15.00

‡1922 cents with a weak or missing mintmark were made from extremely worn dies that originally struck normal 1922D cents. Three different die pairs were involved; two of them produced "weak D" coins. One die pair (#2, identified by a "strong reverse") is acknowledged as striking "No D" coins. Weak D cents are worth considerably less. Beware of removed mintmark.

*Large and small mint mark varieties, see page 67.

SMALL CENTS

	Quan. Minted	VG-8	F-12	VF-20	EF-40	MS-63	MS-65	Proof-63
1936 ....(5,569)	309,637,569	.....$ .10	$ .15	$ .20	$.30	$1.50	$5.00	$135.00
1936 Doubled die obv.		....		45.00	75.00	200.00	750.00	
1936D.............	40,620,000	10	.20	.30	.45	2.25	8.00	
1936S	29,130,000	10	.25	.40	.55	2.10	8.00	
1937 ....(9,320)	309,179,320	....	.10	.15	.30	1.25	5.00	60.00
1937D.............	50,430,000	10	.15	.25	.35	1.25	6.50	
1937S	34,500,000	10	.20	.30	.40	2.00	9.00	
1938..(14,734)	156,696,734	10	.15	.20	.30	1.50	6.00	40.00
1938D.............	20,010,000	20	.30	.45	.65	2.00	8.00	
1938S	15,180,000	35	.45	.55	.75	3.00	10.00	
1939..(13,520)	316,479,520	....	.10	.15	.25	1.00	3.00	35.00
1939D.............	15,160,000	45	.55	.65	.85	3.50	11.00	
1939S	52,070,000	15	.20	.30	.40	2.00	8.00	
1940..(15,872)	586,825,872	....		.10	.20	1.00	3.00	30.00
1940D.............	81,390,000	....	.10	.15	.25	1.25	4.00	
1940S	112,940,000	....	.10	.15	.25	1.50	5.00	
1941..(21,100)	887,039,100	....		.10	.20	.90	3.00	27.50
1941D.............	128,700,000	....		.10	.25	1.75	7.50	
1941S‡	92,360,000	....	.10	.15	.30	2.10	9.00	
1942..(32,600)	657,828,600	....		.10	.20	.50	2.00	27.50
1942D.............	206,698,000	....		.10	.20	.75	3.00	
1942S	85,590,000	15	.25	.30	.75	5.50	16.00	

‡Large and small mint mark varieties, see page 67.

**1943D,
Boldly
Doubled
Mint Mark**

**1944D,
D over S**

Variety 2 — Zinc-coated Steel 1943, Only

Owing to a shortage of copper during the critical war year 1943, the Treasury Department resorted to the use of zinc-coated steel for our cents. No bronze cents were officially issued in 1943. A few specimens struck on bronze planchets by error are known to exist. Through a similar error, a few of the 1944 cents were struck on steel planchets.

1943 — Weight 2.70 grams; composition: steel, coated with zinc; diameter 19 mm; plain edge.

	Quan. Minted	F-12	VF-20	EF-40	MS-63	MS-65
1943..................................684,628,670		$.20	$.30	$.40	$1.50	$4.00
1943D........................ ⎫		.25	.35	.45	1.50	5.00
1943D Boldly doubled ⎬ 217,660,000						
mint mark................... ⎭		5.00	10.00	15.00	25.00	70.00
1943S................................191,550,000		.35	.50	.60	2.75	10.00

Variety 1 Resumed 1944-1958

Cartridge cases were salvaged for coinage of 1944 through 1946. Although the color was slightly different for uncirculated specimens, the coins proved satisfactory in every respect. The original alloy of 1864-1942 was resumed in 1947.

1944-1946 — Weight 3.11 grams; composition: .950 copper, .050 zinc; diameter 19 mm; plain edge.

	Quan. Minted	VF-20	EF-40	MS-63	MS-65
1944 1,435,400,000		$.10	$.20	$.45	$1.10
1944D............................... ⎫		10	.15	.50	1.50
1944D, D over S .... ⎬ 430,578,000		125.00	175.00	*425.00	1,300
1944S 282,760,000		.10	.20	.50	4.00
1945 1,040,515,000		.10	.15	.40	1.25
1945D 266,268,000		.10	.20	.50	1.50
1945S 181,770,000		.10	.20	.50	4.00

*Value for MS-60 is $200.00. Two varieties exist, but only the one illustrated above is valued at the prices shown here, the other being less obvious and less valuable.

SMALL CENTS

	Quan. minted	VF-20	EF-40	MS-63	MS-65	Proof-65
1946	991,655,000	$.10	$.15	$.50	$1.25	
1946D	315,690,000	.10	.20	.50	2.00	
1946S	} 198,100,000	10	.20	.50	3.00	
1946S, S over D		22.00	70.00	200.00	350.00	
1947	190,555,000	.10	.20	.80	3.00	
1947D	194,750,000	.10	.20	.50	1.25	
1947S	99,000,000	.15	.25	.60	2.25	
1948	317,570,000	.10	.20	.60	1.50	
1948D	172,637,500	.10	.20	.50	1.50	
1948S	81,735,000	.15	.30	.75	2.25	
1949	217,775,000	.10	.20	.50	1.75	
1949D	153,132,500	.10	.20	.50	2.00	
1949S	64,290,000	.20	.30	.80	4.25	
1950 ....(51,386)	272,686,386	.10	.20	.50	1.50	$45.00
1950D	334,950,000	.10	.20	.40	1.00	
1950S	118,505,000	.10	.25	.60	1.25	
1951 ....(57,500)	284,633,500	.10	.25	.55	1.50	35.00
1951D	625,355,000	.10	.15	.30	.60	
1951S	136,010,000	.15	.25	.70	2.00	
1952 ....(81,980)	186,856,980	....	.15	.40	.75	30.00
1952D	746,130,000	....	.15	.40	1.00	
1952S	137,800,004	....	.20	.60	1.25	
1953 ....(128,800)	256,883,800	....	.10	.25	.50	25.00
1953D	700,515,000	....	.10	.25	.70	
1953S	181,835,000	....	.15	.50	1.00	
1954 ....(233,300)	71,873,350	.25	.35	.50	1.25	10.00
1954D	251,552,500	....	.10	.25	.40	
1954S	96,190,000	....	.20	.25	.75	

1955 Doubled Die Error

The popular 1955 doubled die error coins were made from improperly prepared dies that show full-doubled outline of date and legend. Do not confuse these with less valuable pieces showing only minor traces of doubling. Counterfeits exist.

	Quan. minted	VF-20	EF-40	MS-63	MS-65	Proof-65
1955 Doubled die obv. ...... }	330,958,200	$525.00	$600.00	*$1,700	$12,000	
1955 ....(378,200)			.10	.15	.30	$10.00
1955D	563,257,500		.10	.15	.30	
1955S	44,610,000	.30	.40	.50	.70	
1956 ....(669,384)	421,414,384	....		.17	.35	3.00
1956D	1,098,201,100	....		.15	.25	
1957 ....(1,247,952)	283,787,952	....		.15	.25	2.25
1957D	1,051,342,000	....		.15	.20	
1958 ....(875,652)	253,400,652	....		.15	.20	2.50
1958 Doubled die obverse	Rare			—		
1958D	800,953,300	....		.15	.20	

*Value for MS-60 Uncirculated is $1,250.

SMALL CENTS

LINCOLN TYPE, MEMORIAL REVERSE 1959 TO DATE

Frank Gasparro designed the Lincoln Memorial reverse which was introduced in 1959 on the 150th anniversary of Lincoln's birth.

Designer: Obv. V. D. Brenner, Rev. Frank Gasparro.1959-1962; weight 3.11 grams; composition: .950 copper, .050 tin and zinc; diameter 19 mm; plain edge. 1962-1982-composition changed to: .950 copper, .050 zinc. 1982-composition changed to: copper plated zinc. Core is 99.2% zinc, 0.8% copper, with a plating of pure copper. Total content is 97.5% zinc, 2.5% copper. Weight 2.5 grams. Both types issued in 1982. Mints: Philadelphia, Denver, San Francisco.

	Quan. Minted	MS-65	Proof-65
1959 ....(1,149,291)	610,864,291	$.15	$1.50
1959D...	1,279,760,000	.15	

Small Date

Large Date

	Quan. Minted	MS-65	Proof-65
1960 Large date .... } (1,691,602)	588,096,602	.10	1.10
1960 Sm. date.............		3.00	14.00
1960D Large date............................ }	1,580,884,000 ··············	.10	
1960D Small date............................		.20	
1961 ....(3,028,244)	756,373,244..................	.10	1.00
1961D...	1,753,266,700	.10	
1962 ....(3,218,019)	609,263,019..................	.10	1.00
1962D...	1,793,148,400	.10	
1963 ....(3,075,645)	757,185,645..................	.10	1.00
1963D...	1,774,020,400	.10	
1964 ....(3,950,762)	2,652,525,762..................	.10	1.00
1964D...	3,799,071,500	.10	
1965...	1,497,224,900	.20	
1966...	2,188,147,783	.20	
1967...	3,048,667,100	.20	
1968...	1,707,880,970	.25	
1968D...	2,886,269,600	.10	
1968S ....(3,041,506)	261,311,507..................	.10	1.00

In 1969, the dies were modified to strengthen the design, and Lincoln's head was made slightly smaller. In 1973, dies were further modified and engraver's initials FG made larger. The initials were reduced slightly in 1974. During 1982 the dies were again modified and the bust, lettering and date made slightly smaller. One variety of the 1984 cent shows Lincoln's ear doubled. 1,579,324 cents dated 1974 were struck in aluminum as experimental pieces. None was placed in circulation and most were later destroyed. One was preserved for the National Collection in the Smithsonian Institution.

SMALL CENTS

1969S Doubled Die Error	Small Date (High 7)	Large Date (Low 7)	1971S Proof Doubled Die

	Quan. Minted	MS-65	Proof-65
1969	1,136,910,000	$.35	
1969D	4,002,832,200	.15	
1969S (2,934,631)			
	547,309,631	.15	$1.00
1969S Doubled die obv.	—		
1970	1,898,315,000	.25	
1970D	2,891,438,900	.10	
1970S (2,632,810)			
	693,192,814		
1970S Sm. date (high 7)	30.00	60.00	
1970S Lg. date (low 7)..	.15	1.00	
1970S Doubled die obv.	—		
1971	1,919,490,000	.40	
1971D	2,911,045,600	.40	
1971S (3,220,733)			
	528,354,192	.40	1.00

1972 Doubled Die Error

		MS-65	Proof-65
1971S Doubled die obv.			650.00
1972 Doubled die obv.*		450.00	
1972	2,933,255,000	.10	
1972D	2,665,071,400	.15	
1972S (3,260,996)			
	380,200,104	.15	1.00
1973	3,728,245,000	.10	
1973D	3,549,576,588	.10	
1973S (2,760,339)			
	319,937,634	.15	1.00

	Quan. Minted	MS-65	Proof-65
1974	4,232,140,523	$.10	
1974D	4,235,098,000	.10	
1974S (2,612,568)			
	412,039,228	.15	$ 1.00
1975	5,451,476,142	.10	
1975D	4,505,275,300	.10	
1975S Proof (2,845,450)			2.50
1976	4,674,292,426	.10	
1976D	4,221,592,455	.10	
1976S Proof (4,149,730)			2.50
1977	4,469,930,000	.10	
1977D	4,194,062,300	.10	
1977S Proof (3,251,152)			2.50
1978	5,558,605,000	.10	
1978D	4,280,233,400	.10	
1978S Proof (3,127,781)			2.50
1979	6,018,515,000	.10	
1979D	4,139,357,254	.10	
1979S Proof (3,677,175)			
Filled S			3.50
Clear S			4.00
1980	7,414,705,000	.10	
1980D	5,140,098,660	.10	
1980S Proof (3,554,806)			2.00
1981	7,491,750,000	.10	
1981D	5,373,235,677	.10	
1981S Proof (4,063,083)			
Filled S			2.00
Clear S			50.00
1982	10,712,525,000		
Lg. Date		.10	
Sm. Date		.15	
1982D	6,012,979,368		
Lg. date		.10	
1982S Proof (3,857,479)			2.50

*Other slightly doubled varieties exist, but are worth far less.

Copper Plated Zinc

Composition changed to copper plated zinc. Core is 99.2% zinc, 0.8% copper, with a plating of pure copper. Weight is 2.5 grams (approximately 20% lighter than the copper cents)

Large Date	**Small Date**
1982 Lg. date } Incl. above .50	1982D Lg. date } Incl. above .25
1982 Sm. date } .75	1982D Sm. date } .10

SMALL CENTS

1983 Doubled Die Rev.

Doubled Ear Variety

Quan. Minted	MS-65	Proof-65
1983 Doubled die rev.... $200.00		
1983 7,752,355,000	.10	
1983D 6,467,199,428	.10	
1983S Proof.(3,279,126)		$2.50
1984 8,151,079,000	.10	
1984 Doubled ear..........	150.00	
1984D 5,569,238,906	.25	
1984S Proof.(3,065,110)		3.00
1985 5,648,489,887	.10	
1985D 5,287,399,926	.10	
1985S Proof...3,362,821		3.50
1986........4,491,395,493	.25	
1986D 4,442,866,698	.20	
1986S Proof.(3,010,497)		5.00
1987 4,682,466,931	.10	
1987D 4,879,389,514	.10	
1987S Proof.(4,227,728)		3.00
1988 6,092,810,000	.10	
1988D 5,253,740,443	.10	
1988S Proof.(3,262,948)		7.00
1989 7,261,535,000	.10	
1989D 5,345,467,111	.10	
1989S Proof.(3,220,194)		7.00
1990 6,851,765,000	.10	
1990D 4,922,894,533	.10	
1990S Proof.(3,299,559)		3.50
1990 Proof without S....		1,500
1991 5,165,940,000	.10	
1991D 4,158,442,076	.10	
1991S Proof.(2,867,787)		12.00
1992........4,648,905,000	.10	
1992D 4,448,673,300	.10	
1992S Proof.(4,176,560)		4.00

Quan. Minted	MS-65	Proof-65
1993 5,684,705,000	$.10	
1993D 6,426,650,571	.10	
1993S Proof.(3,394,792)		$7.00
1994 6,500,850,000	.10	
1994D 7,131,765,000	.10	
1994S Proof.(3,269,923)		5.00
1995 6,411,440,000	.10	
1995 Double die obv......	35.00	
1995D 7,128,560,000	.10	
1995S Proof(2,797,481)		7.00
1996........6,612,465,000	.10	
1996D 6,510,795,000	.10	
1996S Proof(2,525,265)		3.00
1997 4,622,800,000	.10	
1997D 4,576,555,000	.10	
1997S Proof.(2,796,678)		7.00
1998 5,032,155,000	.10	
1998 Wide AM*............	35.00	
1998D 5,225,353,500	.10	
1998S Proof..................		7.00
1999 5,237,600,000	.10	
1999 Wide AM*............	35.00	
1999D 6,360,065,000	.10	
1999S Proof..................		4.00
2000 5,503,200,000	.10	
2000 Wide AM*.............	35.00	
2000D 8,774,220,000	.10	
2000S Proof..................		3.00
2001 4,959,600,000	.10	
2001D 5,374,990,000	.10	
2001S Proof..................		3.00
2002..............................	.10	
2002D	.10	
2002S Proof..................		3.00

Some of the cents minted since 1994 show the faint trace of a mint mark and are believed to be the result of the letter having been removed from the master die during production of working dies for coinage. So-called "phantom" mint mark pieces were produced in Philadelphia but show traces of either a D or an S. Values for such pieces vary according to date and condition but are not significantly higher than for normal pieces.
*Varieties were made using Proof dies that have a wide space between AM in AMERICA. The letters nearly touch on other Uncirculated cents.

BIBLIOGRAPHY

Fivaz, Bill and Stanton, J.T. *The Cherrypickers' Guide to Rare Die Varieties.* Savannah, 1994.
Lange, David W. *The Complete Guide to Lincoln Cents.* Wolfeboro, N.H. 1996.
Snow, Richard. *Flying Eagle & Indian Cents.* Tucson, AZ, 1992.
Steve, Larry and Flynn, Kevin. *Flying Eagle and Indian Cent Die Varieties.* Jarretteville, MD, 1995.
Taylor, Sol. *The Standard Guide to Lincoln Cent.* Anaheim, CA, 1999.
Wexler, John and Flynn, Kevin. *The Authoritative Reference on Lincoln Cents.* Rancocas, NJ, 1996.

TWO-CENT PIECES — 1864-1873

The Act of April 22, 1864, which changed the weight and composition of the cent, included a provision for the bronze two cent piece. The weight was specified as 96 grains, the alloy being the same as for the cent.

The two cent piece is one of the short-lived issues of United States coinage. The motto "In God We Trust" appeared for the first time on the new coin due largely to the increased religious sentiment during the Civil War crisis.

There are two varieties for the first year of issue, 1864: the small motto, which is scarce, and the large motto. See illustrations below.

1864 Small Motto

1864 Large Motto

On the obverse the D in GOD is narrow on the large motto. The stem to the leaf shows plainly on the small motto variety. There is no stem on the large motto. The first T in TRUST is very close to the ribbon crease at left on the small motto variety; there is a 1mm gap on the large motto variety.

It will be noted that the shield device is very similar to the nickel five cent piece introduced in 1866. Listed Proof mintages are estimates.

+ or − indicates change from previous year	TYPE COIN VALUES									
	G-4	F-12	EF-40	AU-50	MS-60	MS-63	MS-65	PF-60	PF-63	PF-65
1864-1873	11.00+	18.00+	30.00	55.00+	75.00	140.00	400.00	285.00	400.00-	850.00

Designer James B. Longacre; weight 6.22 grams; composition: .950 copper, .050 tin and zinc; diameter 23 mm; plain edge. All coined at Philadelphia Mint.

G-4 GOOD—*At least IN GOD visible.*
VG-8 VERY GOOD—*WE weakly visible.*
F-12 FINE—*Complete motto visible. WE weak.*
EF-40 EXTREMELY FINE—*WE is bold.*
MS-60 UNCIRCULATED—*No trace of wear. Light blemishes.*
MS-63 SELECT UNCIRCULATED—*No trace of wear. Attractive color, very few blemishes.*

Brilliant red choice uncirculated and proof coins command higher prices. Spotted, cleaned or discolored pieces are worth less.

	Quan. Minted	G-4	F-12	VF-20	EF-40	MS-60	Proof-63
1864 Sm. motto	19,847,500	$55.00	$110.00	$175.00	$275.00	$550.00	—
1864 Lg. motto *(100+)*		11.00	18.00	22.00	30.00	75.00	$500.00
1865*...............*(500+)*	13,640,000	11.00	18.00	22.00	30.00	75.00	450.00
1866.................*(725+)*	3,177,000	11.00	19.00	24.00	32.00	75.00	400.00
1867.................*(625+)*	2,938,750	11.00	19.00	24.00	32.00	100.00	400.00
1867 Doubled die		—	—	125.00	175.00	375.00	
1868.................*(600+)*	2,803,750	11.00	19.00	24.00	35.00	120.00	440.00
1869.................*(600+)*	1,546,500	13.00	19.00	24.00	40.00	130.00	440.00
1870.................*(1,000+)*	861,250	13.00	22.00	27.00	60.00	180.00	600.00
1871.................*(960+)*	721,250	15.00	24.00	30.00	75.00	200.00	750.00
1872.................*(950+)*	65,000	90.00	160.00	250.00	400.00	775.00	1,000
1873 Closed 3. Proofs only (Est. 600).			850.00	900.00	1,100		1,500
1873 Open 3. Restrike (Est. 500) (See illustration on page 95)..............................							2,000

*One variety appears to show traces of a 4 under the 5 in the date. Other varieties show the tip of the 5 either plain or curved.

BIBLIOGRAPHY

Flynn, Kevin. *Getting Your Two Cents Worth.* Rancocas, NJ, 1994.
Kliman, Myron M. *The Two Cent Piece and Varieties.* South Laguna, CA, 1977.
Leone, Frank. *Longacre's Two Cent Piece Die Varieties & Errors.* College Point, NY, 1991.

SILVER THREE-CENT PIECES 1851-1873

This smallest of United States silver coins was authorized by Congress March 3, 1851. The first three-cent silver pieces had no lines bordering the six-pointed star. From 1854 through 1858 there were three lines, while issues of the last fifteen years show only two lines. Issues from 1854 through 1873 have an olive sprig over the III and a bundle of three arrows beneath. Nearly the entire production of non-proof coins from 1863 to 1872 was melted in 1873.

+ or – indicates change from previous year		TYPE COIN VALUES							
	G-4	F-12	EF-40	AU-50	MS-60	MS-63	MS-65	PF-60	PF-63	PF-65
Variety 1 1851-1853	18.00+	25.00	52.00	120.00	150.00	250.00	1,000-			
Variety 2 1854-1858	17.00+	25.00+	80.00	170.00-	280.00	625.00	3,800	1,000+	2,400	7,500
Variety 3 1859-1873	17.00+	25.00+	110.00	155.00	275.00	1,100	250.00	450.00	1,400

1851-1853 — Designer James B. Longacre; weight .80 gram; composition: .750 silver, .250 copper; diameter 14 mm; plain edge; mints: Philadelphia, New Orleans.

1854-1873 — Weight .75 gram; composition: .900 silver, .100 copper; diameter 14 mm; plain edge. All coined at Philadelphia Mint.

Mint mark location.

←

G-4 GOOD—*Star worn smooth. Legend and date readable.*
VG-8 VERY GOOD—*Outline of shield defined. Legend and date clear.*
F-12 FINE—*Only star points worn smooth.*
VF-20 VERY FINE—*Only partial wear on star ridges.*
EF-40 EXTREMELY FINE—*Ridges on star points show.*
MS-60 UNCIRCULATED—*No trace of wear. Light blemishes.*

Variety 1 — 1851-1853

	Quan. Minted	G-4	VG-8	F-12	VF-20	EF-40	MS-60	Proof-63
1851 5,447,400		$18.00	$21.00	$25.00	$30.00	$52.00	$150.00	—
1851O 720,000		21.00	24.00	33.00	60.00	125.00	325.00	
1852, 1 over inverted 2......						—		
1852 18,663,500		18.00	21.00	25.00	30.00	52.00	150.00	—
1853 11,400,000		18.00	21.00	25.00	30.00	52.00	150.00	

Variety 2 1854-1858

Well struck specimens command higher prices.

1854 671,000		19.00	22.00	25.00	40.00	85.00	325.00	—
1855 139,000		25.00	33.00	45.00	80.00	165.00	475.00	$2,800
1856 1,458,000		17.00	20.00	25.00	42.00	80.00	280.00	2,700
1857 1,042,000		17.00	20.00	25.00	42.00	85.00	280.00	2,500
1858 ....(300+) 1,604,000		17.00	20.00	25.00	42.00	85.00	280.00	2,400

Variety 3 1859-1873

1862, 2 over 1

1859 ......(800)	365,000	17.00	20.00	25.00	35.00	60.00	155.00	450.00
1860 ...(1,000)	287,000	17.00	20.00	25.00	35.00	60.00	155.00	450.00
1861 ...(1,000)	498,000	17.00	20.00	25.00	35.00	60.00	155.00	450.00
1862, 2 over 1		18.00	22.00	27.00	45.00	75.00	200.00	
1862 ......(550)	343,550	19.00	20.00	25.00	35.00	60.00	155.00	450.00
1863, 3 over 2								1,000
1863 ......(460)	21,460					325.00	550.00	500.00
1864 ......(470)	12,470					325.00	525.00	525.00

[105]

SILVER THREE-CENT PIECES

	Quan. Minted	EF-40	MS-60	Proof-63
1865 ....(500)	8,500	$325.00	$575.00	$575.00
1866 ....(725)	22,725	300.00	575.00	575.00
1867 ....(625)	4,625	350.00	575.00	575.00
1868 ....(600)	4,100	350.00	575.00	575.00
1869, 9 over 8............... }	5,100··········		—	—
1869 ....(600) ʃ	....	375.00	600.00	600.00
1870 ....(1,000)	4,000	350.00	600.00	650.00
1871 ....(960)	4,360	350.00	600.00	650.00
1872 ....(950)	1,950	400.00	625.00	650.00
1873 ....(600)	600 (Closed 3, proof only)			900.00

NICKEL THREE-CENT PIECES 1865-1889

The three-cent pieces struck in nickel composition were designed to replace the silver three-cent coins. Composition is 75% copper and 25% nickel. All were coined at Philadelphia and have plain edges.

+ or – indicates change from previous year	TYPE COIN VALUES								
	G-4	F-12	EF-40	AU-50	MS-60	MS-63	MS-65	PF-60	PF-63	PF-65
1865-1889	11.00+	13.00	20.00+	40.00	85.00	140.00	600.00-	165.00	265.00-	500.00

Designer James B. Longacre; weight 1.94 grams; composition: .750 copper, .250 nickel; diameter 17.9 mm; plain edge. All coined at Philadelphia Mint.

G-4 GOOD—*Date and legends complete though worn. III smooth.*
VG-8 VERY GOOD—*III is half worn. Rims complete.*
VF-20 VERY FINE—*Three-quarters of hair details show.*
EF-40 EXTREMELY FINE—*Slight, even wear.*
MS-60 UNCIRCULATED—*No trace of wear. Light blemishes.*

	Quan. Minted	G-4	VG-8	VF-20	EF-40	MS-60	Proof-63
1865....................(500+)	11,382,000	$11.00	$12.00	$14.00	$20.00	$85.00	$1,000
1866....................(725+)	4,801,000	11.00	12.00	14.00	20.00	85.00	265.00
1867....................(625+)	3,915,000	11.00	12.00	14.00	20.00	85.00	265.00
1868....................(600+)	3,252,000	11.00	12.00	14.00	20.00	85.00	265.00
1869....................(600+)	1,604,000	11.00	12.00	14.00	25.00	100.00	265.00
1870.................(1,000+)	1,335,000	11.00	12.00	16.00	27.00	110.00	265.00
1871....................(960+)	604,000	11.00	12.00	15.00	25.00	120.00	265.00
1872....................(950+)	862,000	11.00	12.00	16.00	25.00	120.00	265.00
1873 Closed 3 .(1,100+)	390,000	11.00	12.00	16.00	25.00	120.00	265.00
1873 Open 3................	783,000	11.00	12.00	16.00	25.00	120.00	
1874....................(700+)	790,000	11.00	12.00	16.00	25.00	120.00	265.00
1875....................(700+)	228,000	13.00	15.00	18.00	30.00	135.00	265.00
1876.................(1,150+)	162,000	13.00	15.00	20.00	35.00	165.00	265.00
1877 (Prfs. only).(510+)	510			900.00	1,100		1,300
1878 (Prfs. only)(2,350)	2,350			450.00	550.00		600.00
1879 ....(3,200)	41,200	45.00	50.00	65.00	90.00	225.00	310.00
1880 ....(3,955)	24,955	65.00	75.00	90.00	120.00	250.00	335.00
1881 ....(3,575)	1,080,575	11.00	12.00	14.00	20.00	90.00	310.00
1882 ....(3,100)	25,300	65.00	70.00	85.00	110.00	260.00	350.00
1883 ....(6,609)	10,609	125.00	150.00	185.00	250.00	350.00	350.00
1884 ....(3,942)	5,642	275.00	300.00	325.00	375.00	525.00	400.00
1885 ....(3,790)	4,790	350.00	400.00	450.00	500.00	700.00	400.00
1886 (Prfs. only)(4,290)	4,290			300.00	350.00		400.00
1887 All kinds } (2,960)	7,961	235.00	275.00	300.00	350.00	500.00	400.00
1887, 7 over 6 ʃ				325.00	375.00		400.00
1888 ....(4,582)	41,083	40.00	45.00	50.00	70.00	250.00	300.00
1889 ....(3,436)	21,561	65.00	75.00	85.00	110.00	235.00	300.00

NICKEL FIVE-CENT PIECES — 1866 to Date

+ or – indicates change from previous year	TYPE COIN VALUES									
	G-4	F-12	EF-40	AU-50	MS-60	MS-63	MS-65	PF-60	PF-63	PF-65
Shield-Rays 1866-1867..........	16.00+	25.00	100.00	150.00	225.00	400.00	2,300	1,200	1,900	3,500
Shield-No Rays 1867-1883	11.00+	15.00+	30.00	50.00	100.00	185.00	625.00	175.00	300.00	600.00
Liberty Head-NC 1883............	4.00+	5.75	9.00	11.00	27.00	45.00	250.00	200.00	235.00	1,000
Liberty Head-WC 1883-1912..	1.25	4.00	20.00	40.00	65.00	110.00	475.00	160.00	180.00	500.00
Buffalo Variety 1 1913...........	5.00	7.00	14.00	20.00	30.00	40.00	125.00	600.00	1,000	2,200
Buffalo Variety 2 1913-1938...	.75	.85	2.00	6.00	13.00	20.00	35.00	550.00	700.00	900.00
Jefferson Wartime 1942-1945.	.50	.60	1.00	2.00	2.25	2.50	6.00	65.00	75.00	90.00

SHIELD TYPE 1866-1883

The shield type nickel was made possible by the Act of May 16, 1866. Its weight was set at 77-16/100 grains (5 grams) with the same composition as the nickel three-cent piece which was authorized in 1865. In 1866 the coin was designed with rays between the stars on the reverse. Some of the pieces minted in 1867 have the same details, but later the rays were eliminated creating two varieties for that year. There was no further change in the type until it was replaced by the Liberty head device in 1883. Only proof pieces were struck in 1877 and 1878.

Designer James B. Longacre; weight 5 grams; composition: .750 copper, .250 nickel; diameter 20.5 mm; plain edge. All coined at Philadelphia Mint.

G-4 GOOD—*All letters in motto readable.*
VG-8 VERY GOOD—*Motto stands out clearly. Rims worn slightly but even. Part of shield lines visible.*
F-12 FINE—*Half of each olive leaf is smooth.*
EF-40 EXTREMELY FINE—*Leaf tips show slight wear. Cross over shield slightly worn.*
MS-60 UNCIRCULATED—*No trace of wear. Light blemishes.*

Variety 1

Rays Between Stars 1866-1867   **1866 Repunched Date**

Sharply struck uncirculated coins are valued higher than the prices shown here

	Quan. Minted	G-4	VG-8	F-12	EF-40	MS-60	Proof-63
1866 Rays...........(200+)	14,742,500	$16.00	$18.00	$25.00	$100.00	$225.00	$1,900
1866 Repunched date...		45.00	65.00	110.00	225.00	500.00	
1867 Rays.............(25+)	2,019,000	16.00	20.00	30.00	120.00	300.00	20,000

Variety 2

Without Rays 1867-1883

**Typical example of 1883, 3 over 2.
Other varieties exist,
as well as pieces with recut 3.**

		Quan. Minted	G-4	VG-8	F-12	EF-40	MS-60	Proof-63
1867 No rays ......(600+)		28,890,500	11.00	13.00	15.00	32.00	100.00	300.00
1868 ....(600+)		28,817,000	11.00	13.00	15.00	32.00	100.00	300.00
1869 ....(600+)		16,395,000	11.00	13.00	15.00	32.00	100.00	300.00
1870 ....(1,000+)		4,806,000	12.00	14.00	17.00	35.00	110.00	300.00
1871 ....(960+)		561,000	30.00	40.00	50.00	110.00	275.00	350.00
1872 ....(950+)		6,036,000	12.00	14.00	17.00	35.00	125.00	300.00
1873 Closed 3 (1,100+)		436,050	13.00	18.00	25.00	80.00	250.00	300.00
1873 Open 3	} 4,113,950		12.00	14.00	17.00	35.00	135.00	—
1873 Lg. over sm. 3							—	—

NICKEL FIVE-CENT PIECES

	Quan. Minted	G-4	VG-8	F-12	EF-40	MS-60	Proof-63
1874 ....(700+)	3,538,000	$12.00	$14.00	$20.00	$45.00	$125.00	$300.00
1875 ....(700+)	2,097,000	14.00	18.00	30.00	55.00	150.00	375.00
1876 ....(1,150+)	2,530,000	13.00	15.00	25.00	45.00	130.00	350.00
1877 (Prfs. only).(510+)	510				1,100		1,500
1878 (Prfs. only)(2,350)	2,350				525.00		700.00
1879 ....(3,200) }	29,100	235.00	300.00	350.00	450.00	600.00	650.00
1879, 9 over 8................							700.00
1880 ....(3,955)	19,955	275.00	350.00	390.00	550.00	650.00	675.00
1881 ....(3,575)	72,375	150.00	175.00	200.00	350.00	500.00	575.00
1882 ....(3,100) } 11,476,000		11.00	13.00	15.00	30.00	100.00	300.00
1883 ....(5,419) }	1,456,919	11.00	13.00	15.00	30.00	100.00	300.00
1883, 3 over 2................		85.00	125.00	200.00	375.00		

LIBERTY HEAD TYPE 1883-1912

In 1883 the type was changed to the familiar "Liberty head." This type first appeared without the word CENTS on the coin, merely a large letter "V." Some of these "centless" coins were gold-plated and passed for five dollars. Later in that year the word CENTS was added to discourage the fradulent practice.

Five 1913 Liberty head nickels were originally owned by Col. E. H. R. Green (son of the famous Hetty Green). These have since been dispersed and are now held in various public and private collections. These were not a regular issue and were never placed in circulation.

Designer Charles E. Barber; weight 5 grams; composition: .750 copper, .250 nickel; diameter 21.2 mm; plain edge; mints: Philadelphia, Denver, San Francisco.

Sharply struck uncirculated coins are valued higher than the prices shown; dull or weakly struck pieces are worth less.

Variety 1 — Without CENTS 1883 Only

G-4 GOOD—No details in head. LIBERTY obliterated.
VG-8 VERY GOOD—At least 3 letters in LIBERTY readable.
F-12 FINE—All letters in LIBERTY show.
VF-20 VERY FINE—LIBERTY bold, including letter I.
EF-40 EXTREMELY FINE—LIBERTY sharp. Corn grains at bottom of wreath show, on reverse.
MS-60 UNCIRCULATED—No trace of wear. Light blemishes.

	Quan. Minted	G-4	VG-8	F-12	VF-20	EF-40	MS-60	Proof-63
1883 without CENTS ....(5,219)	5,479,519	$4.00	$4.50	$5.75	$7.25	$9.00	$27.00	$235.00

Variety 2 — With CENTS 1883-1913

Location of mint mark. →

1883 with CENTS							
(6,783)......16,032,983	9.00	11.00	14.00	23.00	40.00	100.00	180.00
1884 (3,942)......11,273,942	11.00	15.00	20.00	25.00	50.00	125.00	200.00
1885 (3,790)........1,476,490	260.00	285.00	375.00	425.00	625.00	825.00	900.00
1886 (4,290)........3,330,290	85.00	110.00	175.00	225.00	310.00	525.00	550.00
1887 (2,960)......15,263,652	7.00	9.00	18.00	22.00	50.00	100.00	180.00
1888 (4,582)......10,720,483	13.00	17.00	22.00	45.00	60.00	175.00	180.00
1889 (3,336)......15,881,361	4.50	6.00	15.00	18.00	36.00	100.00	180.00
1890 (2,740)......16,259,272	4.25	6.00	15.00	18.00	36.00	100.00	180.00
1891 (2,350)......16,834,350	4.25	6.00	15.00	18.00	36.00	100.00	180.00

NICKEL FIVE-CENT PIECES

	Quan. Minted	G-4	VG-8	F-12	VF-20	EF-40	MS-60	Proof-63
1892 (2,745)	11,699,642	$4.00	$5.00	$15.00	$18.00	$36.00	$100.00	$180.00
1893 (2,195)	13,370,195	4.00	5.00	15.00	18.00	36.00	100.00	180.00
1894 (2,632)	5,413,132	8.00	12.00	50.00	85.00	150.00	200.00	180.00
1895 (2,062)	9,979,884	3.00	4.50	16.00	23.00	42.00	100.00	180.00
1896 (1,862)	8,842,920	4.50	7.00	18.00	23.00	42.00	100.00	180.00
1897 (1,938)	20,428,735	2.00	3.00	7.00	10.00	23.00	90.00	180.00
1898 (1,795)	12,532,087	2.00	3.00	7.00	10.00	23.00	90.00	180.00
1899 (2,031)	26,029,031	1.75	2.00	6.00	9.00	23.00	90.00	180.00
1900 (2,262)	27,255,995	1.25	1.50	4.00	7.00	21.00	65.00	180.00
1901 (1,985)	26,480,213	1.25	1.50	4.00	7.00	21.00	65.00	180.00
1902 (2,018)	31,489,579	1.25	1.50	4.00	7.00	21.00	65.00	180.00
1903 (1,790)	28,006,725	1.25	1.50	4.00	7.00	21.00	65.00	180.00
1904 (1,817)	21,404,984	1.25	1.50	4.00	7.00	21.00	65.00	180.00
1905 (2,152)	29,827,276	1.25	1.50	4.00	7.00	21.00	65.00	180.00
1906 (1,725)	38,613,725	1.25	1.50	4.00	7.00	21.00	65.00	180.00
1907 (1,475)	39,214,800	1.25	1.50	4.00	7.00	21.00	65.00	180.00
1908 (1,620)	22,686,177	1.25	1.50	4.00	7.00	21.00	80.00	180.00
1909 (4,763)	11,590,526	1.50	2.00	4.25	8.00	23.00	90.00	180.00
1910 (2,405)	30,169,353	1.25	1.50	4.00	7.00	20.00	65.00	180.00
1911 (1,733)	39,559,372	1.25	1.50	4.00	7.00	20.00	65.00	180.00
1912 (2,145)	26,236,714	1.25	1.50	4.00	7.00	20.00	65.00	180.00
1912D	8,474,000	1.40	1.75	6.00	15.00	47.50	210.00	
1912S	238,000	50.00	65.00	100.00	250.00	500.00	800.00	

1913 Liberty head *(5 known)* ....2001 auction............$1,840,000

INDIAN HEAD or BUFFALO TYPE 1913-1938

These pieces are known as Buffalo, Bison or Indian Head nickels. In the first year of issue, 1913, there were two distinct varieties, the first showing the bison on a mound, and the second with the base redesigned to a thinner, straight line.

James E. Fraser designed this nickel employing three different Indians as models. His initial F is beneath the date. The bison was modeled after "Black Diamond" in the New York Zoological Gardens.

Matte proof coins were made for collectors from 1913 to 1917.

Designer James Earle Fraser; weight 5 grams; composition: .750 copper, .250 nickel; diameter 21.2 mm; plain edge; mints: Philadelphia, Denver, San Francisco.

G-4 GOOD — *Legends and date readable. Horn worn off.*
VG-8 VERY GOOD — *Half horn shows.*
F-12 FINE — *Three-quarters of horn shows. Obv. rim intact.*
VF-20 VERY FINE — *Full horn shows. Indian's cheekbone worn.*
EF-40 EXTREMELY FINE — *Full horn. Slight wear on Indian's hair ribbon.*
MS-63 SELECT UNCIRCULATED — *No trace of wear. Light blemishes. Attractive mint luster.*

Variety 1 — FIVE CENTS on Raised Ground

	Quan. Minted	G-4	VG-8	F-12	VF-20	EF-40	MS-63	Matte Proof-63
1913 Var. 1 (1,520)	30,993,520	$5.00	$6.00	$7.00	$8.00	$14.00	$45.00	$1,000
1913D Var. 1	5,337,000	9.00	10.00	11.00	15.00	25.00	72.00	
1913S Var. 1	2,105,000	15.00	19.00	23.00	30.00	48.00	115.00	

NICKEL FIVE-CENT PIECES
Variety 2 — FIVE CENTS in Recess

Mint mark below
FIVE CENTS.

1916 Doubled Die Obverse

1918D, 8 over 7

	Quan. Minted	G-4	VG-8	F-12	VF-20	EF-40	MS-63	Matte Proof-63
1913 Var. 2 (1,514).........29,858,700		$6.00	$7.00	$8.00	$10.00	$14.00	$55.00	$800.00
1913D Var. 2 4,156,000		50.00	55.00	70.00	80.00	90.00	260.00	
1913S Var. 2............1,209,000		110.00	150.00	200.00	220.00	275.00	600.00	
1914, 4 over 3				350.00	500.00	850.00		
1914 (1,275).........20,665,738		11.00	13.00	15.00	18.00	22.00	75.00	700.00
1914D.....................3,912,000		45.00	52.00	70.00	80.00	150.00	375.00	
1914S 3,470,000		13.00	15.00	20.00	28.00	42.00	375.00	
1915 (1,050).........20,987,270		4.00	5.00	6.25	8.00	17.00	65.00	850.00
1915D.....................7,569,000		12.00	16.00	25.00	40.00	65.00	310.00	
1915S 1,505,000		16.00	22.00	50.00	75.00	150.00	750.00	
1916 (600).........63,498,066		2.25	2.75	3.00	4.00	8.00	60.00	1,400
1916 Doubled die obv.............		1,800	3,200	5,000	7,000	10,000	40,000	
1916D...................13,333,000		8.00	10.00	14.00	25.00	52.00	230.00	
1916S 11,860,000		4.00	7.00	10.00	20.00	43.00	300.00	
1917 51,424,019		1.25	1.75	2.50	6.00	10.00	75.00	—
1917D.....................9,910,000		7.00	9.00	20.00	45.00	85.00	600.00	
1917S 4,193,000		8.00	12.00	30.00	60.00	120.00	700.00	
1918 32,086,314		1.75	2.00	3.00	7.00	20.00	175.00	
1918D, 8 over 7 ⎫ ⎬ 8,362,000		350.00	650.00	1,000	2,200	5,000	37,500	
1918D .... ⎭		7.00	12.00	22.00	80.00	160.00	800.00	
1918S 4,882,000		6.50	13.00	25.00	70.00	150.00	2,300	
1919 60,868,000		1.00	1.25	1.50	3.00	7.50	80.00	
1919D‡.....................8,006,000		8.00	12.00	30.00	80.00	175.00	1,200	
1919S‡ 7,521,000		5.00	11.00	25.00	65.00	175.00	1,200	
1920 63,093,000		1.00	1.25	1.50	3.00	9.00	85.00	
1920D‡.....................9,418,000		5.50	9.00	18.00	75.00	220.00	1,300	
1920S 9,689,000		2.50	5.00	14.00	70.00	150.00	1,200	
1921 10,663,000		1.50	2.00	3.25	10.00	30.00	200.00	
1921S‡ 1,557,000		30.00	40.00	85.00	350.00	675.00	1,900	
1923 35,715,000		1.00	1.25	1.50	3.00	9.00	100.00	
1923S‡ 6,142,000		2.50	4.00	9.00	85.00	225.00	650.00	
1924 21,620,000		1.00	1.25	1.50	4.00	10.00	100.00	
1924D.....................5,258,000		3.50	5.00	12.00	58.00	160.00	775.00	
1924S 1,437,000		7.00	13.00	55.00	400.00	1,000	3,000	
1925 35,565,100		1.50	2.00	2.50	3.50	10.00	75.00	
1925D‡.....................4,450,000		5.25	11.00	27.00	65.00	145.00	600.00	
1925S 6,256,000		3.00	6.00	12.00	50.00	140.00	1,800	
1926 44,693,000		.75	.85	1.00	2.00	6.50	55.00	
1926D‡.....................5,638,000		3.75	6.50	16.00	65.00	120.00	450.00	
1926S 970,000		8.00	14.00	40.00	310.00	650.00	5,500	
1927 37,981,000		.75	.85	1.00	1.75	7.00	55.00	
1927D.....................5,730,000		1.50	3.00	5.00	15.00	60.00	250.00	
1927S 3,430,000		1.00	1.75	3.00	20.00	70.00	1,800	
1928 23,411,000		.75	.85	1.00	2.00	6.00	50.00	
1928D.....................6,436,000		1.00	2.00	4.00	9.00	27.00	82.00	
1928S 6,936,000		1.00	1.25	2.00	6.00	17.00	550.00	

‡Uncirculated pieces with full sharp details are worth considerably more.

NICKEL FIVE-CENT PIECES

	Quan. Minted	G-4	VG-8	F-12	VF-20	EF-40	MS-63	Proof-65
1929	36,446,000	$.75	$.85	$1.00	$1.75	$4.50	$50.00	
1929D	8,370,000	.85	1.00	1.50	4.50	20.00	85.00	
1929S	7,754,000	.75	.85	1.00	2.00	10.00	75.00	
1930	22,849,000	.75	.85	1.00	1.75	4.00	40.00	
1930S	5,435,000	.75	.85	1.00	1.75	7.00	80.00	
1931S	1,200,000	5.00	6.00	7.00	9.00	15.00	70.00	
1934	20,213,003	.75	.85	1.00	1.50	4.00	40.00	
1934D*	7,480,000	.75	.85	1.10	2.00	10.00	75.00	
1935	58,264,000	.75	.85	1.00	1.25	2.25	24.00	
1935 Doubled die reverse				75.00	125.00	350.00	1,600	
1935D	12,092,000	.75	.85	1.25	3.00	9.50	50.00	
1935S	10,300,000	.75	.85	1.00	1.25	2.50	40.00	
1936 (4,420)	119,001,420	.75	.85	1.00	1.25	2.25	25.00	$1,000
1936D	24,814,000	.75	.85	1.00	1.25	2.50	25.00	
1936D 3 1/2 legs				350.00	850.00			
1936S	14,930,000	.75	.85	1.00	1.25	2.25	25.00	
1937 (5,769)	79,485,769	.75	.85	1.00	1.25	2.00	20.00	900.00

*Large and small mint mark varieties exist, see page 67.
Uncirculated pieces with full sharp details are worth considerably more.

1937D "3-Legged" Variety
A similar variety exists for 1936-D

1938 D over S

1937D All kinds ...	17,826,000	.75	.85	1.00	1.25	2.00	25.00
1937D 3-Legged...		150.00	230.00	300.00	365.00	450.00	3,200
1937S	5,635,000	.75	.85	1.00	1.25	2.00	20.00
1938D	} 7,020,000	1.00	1.25	1.50	2.00	3.00	20.00
1938D, D over S‡ .				10.00	15.00	23.00	60.00

‡Varieties exist.

JEFFERSON TYPE 1938 to Date

This nickel was designed by Felix Schlag. He won an award of $1,000 in a competition with some 390 artists. His design established the definite public approval of portrait and pictorial themes rather than symbolic devices on our coinage.

Designer Felix Schlag; weight 5 grams; composition: 1938-1942, 1946- , .750 copper, .250 nickel; 1942-1945, .560 copper, .350 silver, .090 manganese; diameter 21.2 mm; plain edge; mints: Philadelphia, Denver, San Francisco. Net weight 1942-1945: .05626 oz. pure silver.

VG-8 VERY GOOD—*Second porch pillar from right nearly gone, other three still visible but weak.*
F-12 FINE—*Cheekbone worn flat. Hairlines and eyebrow faint. Second pillar weak, especially at bottom.*
VF-20 VERY FINE—*Second pillar plain and complete on both sides.*
EF-40 EXTREMELY FINE—*Cheekbone, hairlines, eyebrow slightly worn but well defined. Base of triangle above pillars visible but weak.*
MS-65 CHOICE UNCIRCULATED—*No trace of wear. Barely noticeable blemishes.*

1939 Doubled Monticello and Five Cents

Uncirculated pieces with fully struck steps are valued higher.

NICKEL FIVE-CENT PIECES

	Quan. Minted	F-12	VF-20	EF-40	MS-63	MS-65	Proof-63
1938 ....(19,365)	19,515,365	$ .25	$ .40	$ .55	$3.00	$6.00	$45.00
1938D	5,376,000	1.45	1.65	2.25	5.00	7.00	
1938S	4,105,000	2.25	3.00	3.50	5.00	8.00	
1939 ....(12,535)	120,627,535	.25	.35	.50	1.25	2.00	45.00
1939 Doubled MONTICELLO and FIVE CENTS		35.00	50.00	60.00	300.00	600.00	
1939D	3,514,000	4.50	5.50	9.00	50.00	70.00	
1939S	6,630,000	.90	1.25	2.30	20.00	28.00	
1940 ....(14,158)	176,499,158		.20	.35	1.00	1.75	37.50
1940D	43,540,000		.25	.40	2.00	3.75	
1940S	39,690,000		.30	.60	2.00	3.50	
1941 ....(18,720)	203,283,720		.15	.30	1.00	1.50	27.50
1941D	53,432,000		.20	.35	2.00	4.00	
1941S‡	43,445,000		.25	.45	2.25	5.75	
1942 ....(29,600)	49,818,600		.25	.40	2.00	4.00	27.50
1942D	} 13,938,000	.75	1.00	2.00	25.00	40.00	
1942D over horiz. D.		30.00	50.00	75.00	275.00	700.00	

‡Large and small mint mark varieties, see page 67.

Wartime Alloy Variety 1942-1945

On October 8, 1942, the wartime five-cent piece composed of copper (56%), silver (35%) and manganese (9%) was introduced to eliminate nickel, a critical war material. A larger mint mark was placed above the dome. Letter P (Philadelphia) was used for the first time, indicating the change of alloy.

Location of mint mark

1943 3 over 2

1943 Doubled Eye

	Quan. Minted	F-12	VF-20	EF-40	MS-63	MS-65	Proof-63
1942P ....(27,600)	57,900,600	.60	.75	2.00	7.00	12.00	75.00
1942S	32,900,000	.60	.75	1.50	6.00	13.00	
1943P, 3 over 2		45.00	65.00	90.00	225.00	450.00	
1943P......................	} 271,165,000	.60	.75	1.00	3.50	6.00	
1943P Doubled eye		20.00	30.00	45.00	125.00	300.00	
1943D	15,294,000	.60	.75	1.00	3.50	7.00	
1943S	104,060,000	.60	.75	1.10	3.25	6.00	
1944P*	119,150,000	.60	.75	1.00	3.25	6.00	
1944D	32,309,000	.60	.75	1.25	7.00	9.00	
1944S......................	21,640,000	.60	.75	1.25	5.00	9.00	
1945P......................	119,408,100	.60	.75	1.00	3.50	7.00	
1945P Doubled die rev..................		10.00	20.00	40.00	100.00	200.00	
1945D	37,158,000	.60	.75	1.15	3.50	7.00	
1945S......................	58,939,000	.60	.75	.75	2.50	6.00	

*1944 nickels without mint marks are counterfeits. Genuine pieces of other dates struck in nickel by error are known to exist.

Prewar composition and mint mark style resumed 1946-1967

	Quan. Minted	VF-20	EF-40	MS-63	Proof-65
1946................................161,116,000			$.20	$.85	
1946D.............................45,292,200		$.20	.30	.90	
1946S 13,560,000		.25	.35	1.00	
1947.................................95,000,000			.20	.50	
1947D.............................37,822,000			.25	1.00	
1947S 24,720,000		.25	.35	.80	

NICKEL FIVE-CENT PIECES

	Quan. Minted	VF-20	EF-40	MS-63	Proof-65
1948	89,348,000		$.20	$.70	
1948D	44,734,000	$.25	.40	1.25	
1948S	11,300,000	.35	.40	1.25	
1949	60,652,000	.15	.25	1.50	
1949D }	36,498,000		.30	1.25	
1949D, D over S }		35.00	75.00	200.00	
1949S	9,716,000	.40	.75	2.25	
1950 ....(51,386)	9,847,386	.40	.70	2.00	$37.50
1950D	2,630,030	5.00	6.00	8.00	
1951 ....(57,500)	28,609,500	.20	.30	1.25	35.00
1951D	20,460,000	.20	.30	1.50	
1951S	7,776,000	.50	.90	3.00	
1952 ....(81,980)	64,069,980		.20	.80	27.50
1952D	30,638,000	.30	.65	2.00	
1952S	20,572,000	.20	.30	.75	
1953 ....(128,800)	46,772,800		.20	.30	27.50
1953D	59,878,600		.20	.30	
1953S	19,210,900	.20	.30	.50	

1954S, S over D

1955D, D over S*

	Quan. Minted	VF-20	EF-40	MS-63	Proof-65
1954 ....(233,300)	47,917,350		.15	.40	15.00
1954D	117,183,060		.15	.30	
1954S }	29,384,000	.15	.20	.30	
1954S, S over D }		6.00	14.00	40.00	
1955 ....(378,200)	8,266,200	.50	.60	1.00	10.00
1955D }	74,464,100		.15	.25	
1955D, D over S* }		7.00	15.00	55.00	
1956 ....(669,384)	35,885,384		.15	.25	3.00
1956D	67,222,940		.15	.25	
1957 ....(1,247,952)	39,655,952		.15	.25	2.00
1957D	136,828,900		.15	.20	
1958 ....(875,652)	17,963,652		.20	.35	2.50
1958D	168,249,120		.15	.20	
1959 ....(1,149,291)	28,397,291		.15	.30	1.25
1959D	160,738,240			.15	
1960 ....(1,691,602)	57,107,602			.15	.75
1960D	192,582,180			.15	
1961 ....(3,028,144)	76,668,244			.15	.75
1961D	229,342,760			.15	
1962 ....(3,218,019)	100,602,019			.15	.75
1962D	280,195,720			.15	
1963 ....(3,075,645)	178,851,645			.15	.75
1963D	276,829,460			.15	
1964 ....(3,950,762)	1,028,622,762			.15	.75
1964D	1,787,297,160			.15	
1965	136,131,380			.15	
1966	156,208,283			.15	—‡
1967	107,325,800			.15	

*Varieties exist. Value is for that illustrated.
‡Two presentation pieces were given to the designer.

NICKEL FIVE-CENT PIECES

The designer's initials FS were added below the bust starting in 1966, and dies were further remodeled to strengthen the design in 1971, 1972, 1977 and 1982. Mint mark position was moved to the obverse starting in 1968.

	Quan.Minted	MS-63	Proof-65
1968D..........91,227,880		$.15	
1968S (3,041,506)			
..................103,437,510		.15	$.75
1969D.........202,807,500		.15	
1969S (2,934,631)			
..................123,099,631		.15	.75
1970D.........515,485,380		.15	
1970S (2,632,810)			
..................241,464,814		.15	.75
1971 106,884,000		.65	
1971D.........316,144,800		.25	
1971 Proof without S*...			600.00
1971S Proof.(3,220,733)			1.00
1972 202,036,000		.15	
1972D.........351,694,600		.15	
1972S Proof (3,260,996)			1.00
1973 384,396,000		.15	
1973D.........261,405,000		.15	
1973S Proof (2,760,339)			1.00
1974 601,752,000		.15	
1974D.........277,373,000		.25	
1974S Proof.(2,612,568)			1.00
1975 181,772,000		.50	
1975D.........401,875,300		.15	
1975S Proof.(2,845,450)			1.00
1976 367,124,000		.30	
1976D.........563,964,147		.30	
1976S Proof.(4,149,730)			1.00
1977 585,376,000		.15	
1977D.........297,313,422		.35	
1977S Proof.(3,251,152)			1.00
1978 391,308,000		.15	
1978D.........313,092,780		.15	
1978S Proof.(3,127,781)			1.00
1979 463,188,000		.15	
1979D.........325,867,672		.15	
1979S Proof.(3,677,175)			
Filled S			1.00
Clear S			1.50
1980P.........593,004,000		.15	
1980D.........502,323,448		.15	
1980S Proof.(3,554,806)			.75
1981P.........657,504,000		.15	
1981D.........364,801,843		.15	
1981S Proof.(4,063,083)			1.25
1982P.........292,355,000		1.00	
1982D.........373,726,544		1.50	
1982S Proof.(3,857,479)			1.50
1983P.........561,615,000		1.50	
1983D.........536,726,276		1.00	
1983S Proof.(3,279,126)			2.25
1984P.........746,769,000		$1.25	
1984D.........517,675,146		.30	
1984S Proof.(3,065,110)			$3.00
1985P.........647,114,962		.20	
1985D.........459,747,446		.20	
1985S Proof.(3,362,821)			2.25
1986P.........536,883,483		.25	
1986D.........361,819,140		.80	
1986S Proof.(3,010,497)			5.00
1987P.........371,499,481		.15	
1987D.........410,590,604		.15	
1987S Proof.(4,227,728)			2.25
1988P.........771,360,000		.15	
1988D.........663,771,652		.15	
1988S Proof.(3,262,948)			3.00
1989P.........898,812,000		.15	
1989D.........570,842,474		.15	
1989S Proof.(3,220,194)			3.00
1990P.........661,636,000		.15	
1990D.........663,938,503		.15	
1990S Proof.(3,299,559)			3.00
1991P.........614,104,000		.20	
1991D.........436,496,678		.20	
1991S Proof.(2,867,787)			3.50
1992P.........399,552,000		.25	
1992D.........450,565,113		.15	
1992S Proof.(4,176,560)			3.00
1993P.........412,076,000		.15	
1993D.........406,084,135		.15	
1993S Proof.(3,394,792)			3.00
1994P.........722,160,000		.10	
1994P Special Unc.**			
..........................167,703		60.00	
1994D.........715,762,110		.10	
1994S Proof.(3,269,923)			3.00
1995P.........774,156,000		.10	
1995D.........888,112,000		.25	
1995S Proof.(2,797,481)			4.00
1996P.........829,332,000		.10	
1996D.........817,736,000		.10	
1996S Proof.(2,525,265)			2.00
1997P.........470,972,000		.10	
1997P Special Unc.**			
..........................25,000		170.00	
1997D.........466,640,000		.15	
1997S Proof.(2,796,678)			2.00
1998P 688,272,000		.10	
1998D 635,360,000		.10	
1998S Proof			2.00
1999P......1,212,000,000		.10	
1999D......1,066,720,000		.10	
1999S Proof			3.00

*1971 proof nickels without mint mark were made in error. See pages 67 and 69.
**Special "frosted" uncirculated pieces were included in the 1993 Thomas Jefferson commemorative dollar packaging (sold in 1994) and the 1997 Botanic Gardens Sets. They resemble proof coins.

NICKEL FIVE-CENT PIECES

	Quan.Minted	MS-63	Proof-65
2000P	846,240,000	$.10	
2000D	1,509,520,000	.10	
2000S Proof			$2.00
2001P	675,704,000	.10	
2001D	627,680,000	.10	
2001S Proof			2.00
2002P		.10	
2002D		.10	
2002S Proof			3.00

BIBLIOGRAPHY

Fletcher, Edward L., Jr. *The Shield Five Cent Series*. Ormond Beach, FL, 1994.

Lange, David W. *The Complete Guide to Buffalo Nickels*. Virginia Beach, VA, 2000.

Nagengast, Bernard. *The Jefferson Nickel Analyst*. Sidney, Ohio, 1979.

Peters, Gloria and Mahon, Cynthia. *The Complete Guide to Shield and Liberty Head Nickels*. Virginia Beach, VA, 1995.

Wescott, Michael. *The United States Nickel Five-Cent Piece*. Wolfeboro, NH, 1991.

HALF DIMES 1794-1873

The half-dime types present the same general characteristics as larger United States silver coins. Authorized by the Act of April 2, 1792, they were not coined until February, 1795, although some were dated 1794. At first the weight was 20.8 grains, and fineness 892.4. By the Act of January 18, 1837, the weight was slightly reduced to 20 5/8 grains and the fineness changed to .900. Finally the weight was reduced to 19.2 grains by the Act of February 21, 1853. Both half dimes and dimes offer many varieties in the early dates.

+ or – indicates change from previous year	TYPE COIN VALUES									
	G-4	F-12	EF-40	AU-50	MS-60	MS-63	MS-65	PF-60	PF-63	PF-65
Flowing Hair 1794-1795..........	550.00	950.00	2,200	3,200	4,500	7,500	*23,000*			
Drpd Bust, SE 1796-1797	650.00	1,100	3,200	4,500	6,200	13,000	*80,000*			
Drpd Bust, HE 1800-1805.......	475.00	750.00	2,200	3,500	5,000	9,000	*28,000*			
Cap Bust 1829-1837	18.00+	32.00+	110.00	225.00	300.00	600.00	2,800			
Lib Seated-NS 1837-1838.......	25.00	46.00	185.00	325.00	600.00	900.00	3,200			
Lib Seated-Stars 1838-1859 ...	8.00	11.00	40.00	90.00	160.00	275.00	1,300	500.00	1,200	4,500
Lib. Seat-Arr. 1853-1855	8.00	11.00	40.00	100.00	185.00	400.00	2,000	4,000+	7,000	16,000
Lib. Seat-Leg. 1860-1873	8.00	11.00	30.00	65.00	135.00	210.00	1,200	260.00	500.00	1,900

FLOWING HAIR TYPE 1794-1795

Designer Robert Scot; weight 1.35 grams; composition: .8924 silver, .1076 copper; approx. diameter 16.5 mm; reeded edge. All coined at Philadelphia Mint.

AG-3 ABOUT GOOD—*Details clear enough to identify.*
G-4 GOOD—*Eagle, wreath, bust outlined but lack details.*
VG-8 VERY GOOD—*Some details remain on face. All lettering readable.*
F-12 FINE—*Hair ends show. Hair at top smooth.*
VF-20 VERY FINE—*Hairlines at top show. Hair about ear defined.*
EF-40 EXTREMELY FINE—*Hair above forehead and at neck well defined but shows some wear.*
MS-60 UNCIRCULATED—*No trace of wear. Light blemishes.*

	Quan. Minted	AG-3	G-4	VG-8	F-12	VF-20	EF-40	MS-60
1794	} 86,416	$350.00	$725.00	$850.00	$1,200	$1,900	$3,200	$6,500
1795		275.00	550.00	650.00	950.00	1,400	2,200	4,500

DRAPED BUST TYPE, SMALL EAGLE REVERSE 1796-1797

Designer Robert Scot; weight 1.35 grams; composition: .8924 silver, .1076 copper; approx. diameter 16.5 mm; reeded edge. All coined at Philadelphia Mint.

AG-3 ABOUT GOOD—*Details clear enough to identify.*
G-4 GOOD—*Date, stars, LIBERTY readable. Bust outlined but no details.*
VG-8 VERY GOOD—*Some details show.*
F-12 FINE—*Hair and drapery lines worn, but visible.*
VF-20 VERY FINE—*Only left of drapery indistinct.*
EF-40 EXTREMELY FINE—*All hairlines show details.*
MS-60 UNCIRCULATED—*No trace of wear. Light blemishes.*

	Quan. Minted	AG-3	G-4	VG-8	F-12	VF-20	EF-40	MS-60
1796, 6 over 5....	} 10,230	$425.00	$725.00	$900.00	$1,400	$2,500	$4,200	$16,000
1796 Nor. date ..		375.00	650.00	800.00	1,200	2,000	3,400	9,000
1796 LIKERTY		375.00	675.00	825.00	1,300	2,100	3,500	11,000
1797, 15 stars....	} 44,527	350.00	700.00	825.00	1,100	1,900	3,200	6,200
1797, 16 stars....		350.00	700.00	825.00	1,100	1,900	3,200	6,500
1797, 13 stars....		350.00	700.00	825.00	1,100	2,200	3,750	10,000

HALF DIMES
DRAPED BUST TYPE, HERALDIC EAGLE REVERSE 1800-1805

1800 LIBEKTY

	Quan. Minted	AG-3	G-4	VG-8	F-12	VF-20	EF-40	MS-60
1800	24,000	$200.00	$475.00	$575.00	$750.00	$1,100	$2,200	$5,000
1800 LIBEKTY	16,000	200.00	475.00	575.00	750.00	1,100	2,200	5,000
1801	27,760	200.00	525.00	625.00	850.00	1,450	2,400	5,750
1802	3,060	5,000	9,000	13,500	22,500	35,000	60,000	—
1803 Large 8 ... ⎫	37,850	200.00	500.00	600.00	800.00	1,200	2,400	5,500
1803 Small 8 ... ⎭		200.00	500.00	600.00	800.00	1,200	2,500	5,500
1805	15,600	275.00	650.00	800.00	1,000	1,600	3,300	—

CAPPED BUST TYPE 1829-1837

Designer William Kneass; weight 1.35 grams; composition: .8924 silver, .1076 copper; approx. diameter 15.5 mm; reeded edge. All coined at Philadelphia Mint.

G-4 GOOD—*Bust outlined, no detail. Date and legend readable.*
VG-8 VERY GOOD—*Complete legend and date plain. At least 3 letters of LIBERTY show clearly.*
F-12 FINE—*All letters in LIBERTY show.*
VF-20 VERY FINE—*Full rims. Ear and shoulder clasp show plainly.*
EF-40 EXTREMELY FINE—*Ear very distinct, eyebrow and hair well defined.*
MS-60 UNCIRCULATED—*No trace of wear. Light blemishes.*

	Quan. Minted	G-4	VG-8	F-12	VF-20	EF-40	MS-60
1829	1,230,000	$19.00	$26.00	$33.00	$55.00	$110.00	$300.00
1830	1,240,000	19.00	26.00	33.00	55.00	110.00	300.00
1831	1,242,700	18.00	25.00	32.00	55.00	110.00	300.00
1832	965,000	20.00	30.00	35.00	57.50	125.00	325.00
1833	1,370,000	18.00	25.00	32.00	55.00	110.00	325.00
1834 ⎫	1,480,000	18.00	25.00	32.00	55.00	110.00	300.00
1834, 3 over inverted 3 ⎭		23.00	30.00	32.00	100.00	200.00	500.00
1835 All kinds	2,760,000						
1835 Lg. date and 5c		18.00	25.00	32.00	55.00	110.00	300.00
1835 Lg. date, sm. 5c		18.00	25.00	32.00	55.00	110.00	300.00
1835 Sm. date, lg. 5c		18.00	25.00	32.00	55.00	110.00	300.00
1835 Sm. date and 5c		18.00	25.00	32.00	55.00	110.00	300.00
1836 Small 5c ⎫	1,900,000	18.00	25.00	32.00	55.00	110.00	300.00
1836 Large 5c ⎬		18.00	25.00	32.00	55.00	110.00	300.00
1836, 3 over inverted 3 ⎭		23.00	30.00	50.00	100.00	200.00	500.00
1837 Small 5c ⎫	871,000	23.00	30.00	45.00	85.00	160.00	1,000
1837 Large 5c ⎭		18.00	25.00	30.00	55.00	110.00	300.00

LIBERTY SEATED TYPE 1837-1873
Variety 1 — No Stars on Obverse 1837-1838

Designer Christian Gobrecht; weight 1.34 grams; composition: .900 silver, .100 copper; diameter 15.5 mm; reeded edge; mints: Philadelphia, New Orleans.

G-4 GOOD—*LIBERTY on shield smooth. Date and letters readable.*
VG-8 VERY GOOD—*At least 3 letters in LIBERTY are visible.*
F-12 FINE—*Entire LIBERTY visible, weak spots.*
VF-20 VERY FINE—*Entire LIBERTY strong and even.*
EF-40 EXTREMELY FINE—*LIBERTY and scroll edges distinct.*
MS-60 UNCIRCULATED—*No trace of wear. Light blemishes.*

HALF DIMES

	Quan. Minted	G-4	VG-8	F-12	VF-20	EF-40	MS-60
1837 Sm. date		$25.00	$35.00	$46.00	$90.00	$185.00	$650.00
1837 Lg. date	1,405,000	25.00	35.00	46.00	90.00	185.00	600.00
1838O No stars	70,000	65.00	100.00	190.00	350.00	500.00	1,650

No Drapery from Elbow 1837-1840

Drapery from Elbow Starting 1840

From 1838 through 1859 mint mark is located above bow on reverse. Large, medium or small mint mark varieties occur for several dates.

Variety 2 — Stars on Obverse 1838-1853

1838 No Drapery		9.00	10.00	12.00	25.00	50.00	300.00
1838 Small stars.....	2,225,000	16.00	25.00	50.00	75.00	150.00	650.00
1839 No Drapery...........1,069,150		9.00	10.00	14.00	27.50	55.00	300.00
1839O No Drapery.........1,034,039		11.00	14.00	19.00	30.00	60.00	400.00
1840 No Drapery...........1,034,000		9.00	11.00	13.00	27.50	55.00	300.00
1840O No Drapery...........695,000		10.00	12.00	18.00	40.00	80.00	475.00
1840 Drapery 310,085		14.00	22.00	45.00	75.00	150.00	550.00
1840O Drapery.................240,000		25.00	40.00	80.00	150.00	325.00	2,200
1841 1,150,000		9.00	10.00	12.00	20.00	45.00	185.00
1841O 815,000		11.00	15.00	23.00	40.00	80.00	600.00
1842 815,000		8.00	9.00	11.00	20.00	45.00	185.00
1842O 350,000		20.00	30.00	50.00	175.00	400.00	—
1843 1,165,000		8.00	9.00	11.00	20.00	45.00	185.00
1844 430,000		8.00	9.00	11.00	22.00	47.50	185.00
1844O 220,000		60.00	100.00	175.00	350.00	900.00	—
1845 1,564,000		8.00	9.00	11.00	20.00	45.00	185.00
1846 27,000		160.00	250.00	375.00	600.00	1,350	—
1847 1,274,000		8.00	9.00	11.00	20.00	45.00	185.00
1848 Med. date		8.00	9.00	11.00	20.00	45.00	185.00
1848 Lg. date	668,000	10.00	15.00	25.00	40.00	100.00	400.00
1848O 600,000		10.00	15.00	30.00	50.00	95.00	400.00
1849, 9 over 6..........		10.00	15.00	25.00	35.00	75.00	350.00
1849, 9 over 8..........	1,309,000	10.00	15.00	30.00	45.00	100.00	400.00
1849 Nor. date		8.00	9.00	11.00	20.00	45.00	185.00
1849O 140,000		25.00	35.00	70.00	200.00	450.00	—
1850 955,000		8.00	9.00	11.00	20.00	45.00	185.00
1850O 690,000		11.00	15.00	25.00	50.00	100.00	550.00
1851 781,000		8.00	9.00	11.00	20.00	45.00	185.00
1851O 860,000		11.00	14.00	22.00	35.00	75.00	500.00
1852 1,000,500		8.00	9.00	11.00	20.00	45.00	185.00
1852O 260,000		20.00	30.00	55.00	110.00	250.00	—
1853 No arrows.................135,000		24.00	32.50	60.00	100.00	200.00	600.00
1853O No arrows 160,000		135.00	200.00	300.00	500.00	1,000	—

HALF DIMES
Variety 3 — Arrows at Date 1853-1855

As on the dimes, quarters and halves, arrows were placed at the sides of the date for a short period starting in 1853. They were placed there to denote the reduction of weight under the terms of the Act of February 21, 1853.

Weight 1.24 grams; composition: .900 silver, .100 copper; diameter 15.5 mm; reeded edge, mints: Philadelphia, New Orleans, San Francisco

	Quan. Minted	G-4	VG-8	F-12	VF-20	EF-40	MS-60	Proof-63
1853	13,210,020	$8.00	$9.00	$11.00	$17.00	$40.00	$185.00	
1853O	2,200,000	9.00	12.00	16.00	25.00	60.00	275.00	
1854	5,740,000	8.00	9.00	11.00	17.00	40.00	200.00	
1854O	1,560,000	9.00	12.00	15.00	24.00	60.00	350.00	
1855	1,750,000	8.00	9.00	12.00	18.00	45.00	200.00	$7,000
1855O	600,000	15.00	20.00	30.00	45.00	100.00	500.00	

Variety 2 Resumed 1856-1859

1858 Over Inverted Date

1856	4,880,000	8.00	9.00	11.00	18.00	40.00	160.00	2,500
1856O	1,100,000	10.00	14.00	20.00	32.00	70.00	550.00	
1857	7,280,000	8.00	9.00	11.00	18.00	40.00	160.00	2,100
1857O	1,380,000	9.00	12.00	16.00	30.00	65.00	450.00	
1858	3,500,000	8.00	9.00	11.00	18.00	40.00	160.00	1,400
1858 Repunched high date		20.00	35.00	75.00	125.00	225.00	600.00	
1858 over inverted date....		25.00	30.00	55.00	110.00	200.00	550.00	
1858O	1,660,000	8.00	9.00	16.00	30.00	60.00	300.00	
1859O	560,000	10.00	17.50	25.00	40.00	85.00	300.00	
1859	340,000	10.00	17.50	25.00	40.00	85.00	200.00	1,400

A new die was utilized in 1859 at the Philadelphia Mint, in which the stars are hollow in the center and the arms of Liberty are slimmer.

During the years 1859 and 1860 interesting half dime patterns were made which do not bear our nation's identity. These are transitional pieces, not made for circulation, but struck at the time the inscription UNITED STATES OF AMERICA was being transferred from the reverse to the obverse.

1859 Obv. of 59, rev. of 60	....	20	10,000
1860 Obv. of 59, rev. of 60 (with stars)	....	100	2,500

Variety 4 — Legend on Obverse 1860-1873

HALF DIMES

Mint mark below bow 1860-1869, 1872-1873.

Mint mark above bow 1870-1872.

so-called 1861, 1 over 0

	Quan. Minted	G-4	VG-8	F-12	VF-20	EF-40	MS-60	Proof-63
1860 Legend								
(1,000)	799,000	$8.00	$9.00	$11.00	$15.00	$32.00	$150.00	$700.00
1860O	1,060,000	8.00	9.00	12.00	20.00	40.00	200.00	
1861 ..(1,000)	3,361,000	8.00	9.00	11.00	14.00	30.00	150.00	600.00
1861, "1 over 0"		20.00	30.00	50.00	110.00	225.00	550.00	
1862 ....(550)	1,492,550	8.00	9.00	11.00	15.00	32.00	150.00	600.00
1863.... (460)	18,460	120.00	160.00	200.00	275.00	375.00	600.00	800.00
1863S	100,000	16.00	25.00	35.00	50.00	120.00	650.00	
1864 .....(470)	48,470	250.00	350.00	400.00	500.00	650.00	900.00	1,000
1864S	90,000	30.00	40.00	65.00	100.00	200.00	700.00	
1865 .....(500)	13,500	225.00	275.00	325.00	400.00	550.00	800.00	1,000
1865S	120,000	15.00	25.00	30.00	55.00	100.00	800.00	
1866 .....(725)	10,725	200.00	250.00	325.00	400.00	500.00	800.00	800.00
1866S	120,000	13.00	20.00	27.00	55.00	110.00	600.00	
1867 .....(625)	8,625	275.00	350.00	500.00	600.00	650.00	800.00	800.00
1867S	120,000	15.00	20.00	27.50	60.00	110.00	400.00	
1868 .....(600)	89,200	35.00	50.00	85.00	120.00	240.00	500.00	600.00
1868S	280,000	10.00	13.00	15.00	25.00	50.00	300.00	
1869 .....(600)	208,600	8.00	10.00	15.00	20.00	40.00	225.00	500.00
1869S	230,000	10.00	13.00	15.00	25.00	50.00	300.00	
1870 ..(1,000)	536,000	8.00	9.00	11.00	14.00	30.00	150.00	500.00
1870S	Unique		Bowers Auction Sale 1986				253,000	
1871 .....(960)	1,873,960	8.00	9.00	11.00	14.00	30.00	150.00	500.00
1871S	161,000	11.00	16.00	30.00	50.00	90.00	275.00	
1872 .....(950)	2,947,950	8.00	9.00	11.00	14.00	30.00	135.00	500.00
1872S All kinds ..837,000								
1872S mm. above bow		8.00	9.00	11.00	14.00	30.00	135.00	
1872S mm. below bow		8.00	9.00	11.00	14.00	30.00	135.00	
1873 (Closed 3 only)								
.......(600)	712,600	8.00	9.00	11.00	14.00	30.00	135.00	500.00
1873S (Closed 3 only)								
	324,000	8.00	9.00	11.00	14.00	30.00	135.00	

BIBLIOGRAPHY

Blythe, Al. *The Complete Guide to Liberty Seated Half Dimes*. Virginia Beach, VA, 1992.
Breen, Walter. *United States Half Dimes: A Supplement*. New York, 1958.
Logan, Russell, and McClosky. *Federal Half Dimes 1792 – 1837*. Manchester, MI, 1998.
Newlin, H. P. *The Early Half-Dimes of the United States*. Philadelphia, 1883 (reprinted 1933).
Valentine, D. W. *The United States Half Dimes*. New York, 1931 (reprinted 1975).

DIMES — 1796 to Date

The designs of the dimes, first coined in 1796, follow closely those of the half dimes up through the Liberty seated type. The dimes in each instance weigh twice as much as the half dimes.

+ or – indicates change from previous year			TYPE COIN VALUES							
	G-4	F-12	EF-40	AU-50	MS-60	MS-63	MS-65	PF-60	PF-63	PF-65
Drpd Bust, SE 1796-1797 ...	900.00	1,900	4,750	6,000	8,500–	13,000	*50,000*			
Drpd Bust, HE 1798-1807 ...	350.00	600.00	1,500	2,400	3,500	7,000	*28,000*			
Cap Bust lg. 1809-1828	18.00+	35.00	275.00	600.00	850.00	1,900	8,500			
Cap Bust sm. 1828-1837	17.00+	25.00+	175.00	375.00–	600.00	1,300	5,800			
Lib Seated-NS 1837-1838...	25.00	65.00	475.00	750.00	1,000	1,800	6,500			
Lib. Seated-Stars 1838-1860..	8.00	11.00	35.00	90.00	275.00	500.00	3,200	500.00	1,200	4,000
Lib. Seat-Arr. 1853-1855	8.00	11.00	40.00	100.00	300.00	680.00	3,000	2,500	9,000+	*35,000*
Lib. Seat-Leg. 1860-1891 ...	8.00	10.00	20.00	60.00	140.00–	200.00	1,100	285.00	500.00–	1,400–
Lib. Seat-Arr. 1873-1874	10.00	16.00	125.00	275.00	550.00	900.00	4,500	600.00	1,000	4,500
Barber 1892-1916...............	1.25	4.00	20.00	50.00	90.00	140.00	700.00	250.00	400.00	1,600
Mercury 1916-1945	.60	.75	1.25	2.50	5.75	8.00	17.00	100.00	130.00	175.00
Roosevelt 1946-1964..........	.60	.60	.60	.60	.65	.75	1.00	1.00	1.00	1.25

DRAPED BUST TYPE, SMALL EAGLE REVERSE 1796-1797

Designer Robert Scot; weight 2.70 grams; composition: .8924 silver, .1076 copper; approx. diameter 19 mm; reeded edge. All coined at Philadelphia Mint.

AG-3 ABOUT GOOD—*Details clear enough to identify.*
G-4 GOOD—*Date readable. Bust outlined, but no detail.*
VG-8 VERY GOOD—*All but deepest drapery folds worn smooth. Hairlines nearly gone and curls lack detail.*
F-12 FINE—*All drapery lines visible. Hair partly worn.*
VF-20 VERY FINE—*Only left side of drapery is indistinct.*
EF-40 EXTREMELY FINE—*Hair well outlined and shows details.*
MS-60 UNCIRCULATED—*No trace of wear. Light blemishes.*

1796   **1797, 16 Stars**

	Quan. Minted	AG-3	G-4	VG-8	F-12	VF-20	EF-40	MS-60
1796......................	22,135	$400.00	$900.00	$1,500	$1,850	$2,750	$4,500	$8,500
1797, 16 stars...	25,261	400.00	900.00	1,500	1,900	2,800	4,750	8,500
1797, 13 stars...		400.00	900.00	1,500	1,900	2,800	4,750	8,500

DRAPED BUST TYPE, HERALDIC EAGLE REVERSE 1798-1807

1798 All kinds 27,550							
1798 over 97, 16 stars on rev.	235.00	500.00	600.00	800.00	1,100	2,150	5,250
1798 over 97, 13 stars	650.00	1,700	2,250	3,500	6,000	—	
1798.................................	225.00	475.00	575.00	700.00	1,000	1,800	4,000
1798 Small 8	325.00	650.00	800.00	1,200	1,900	3,000	9,000
1800........................21,760	250.00	475.00	575.00	750.00	1,100	2,000	5,000

DIMES

	Quan. Minted	AG-3	G-4	VG-8	F-12	VF-20	EF-40	MS-60
1801	34,640	$250.00	$475.00	$600.00	$850.00	$1,600	$3,500	$7,500
1802	10,975	250.00	600.00	1,000	1,500	2,500	5,000	15,000
1803	33,040	250.00	475.00	575.00	800.00	1,200	2,500	6,500
1804 All kinds	8,265							
1804, 13 stars on rev.		450.00	900.00	1,500	2,200	4,000	7,500	—
1804, 14 stars on rev.		475.00	1,000	1,750	2,500	4,500	8,500	12,000
1805, 4 ber.	} 120,780	150.00	350.00	500.00	600.00	800.00	1,500	4,000
1805, 5 ber.		150.00	350.00	500.00	600.00	800.00	2,000	6,000
1807	165,000	150.00	350.00	500.00	600.00	800.00	1,500	3,500

CAPPED BUST TYPE 1809-1837

Designer John Reich; weight 2.70 grams; composition: .8924 silver, .1076 copper; approx. diameter 18.8 mm; reeded edge. All coined at Philadelphia Mint. Diameter c. 18.5 mm from 1828 to 1837.

AG-3 ABOUT GOOD—*Details clear enough to identify.*
G-4 GOOD—*Date, letters and stars discernible. Bust outlined, no details.*
VG-8 VERY GOOD—*Legends and date plain. Minimum of 3 letters in LIBERTY.*
F-12 FINE—*Full LIBERTY. Ear and shoulder clasp visible. Part of rim shows both sides.*
VF-20 VERY FINE—*LIBERTY distinct. Full rim. Ear and clasp plain and distinct.*
EF-40 EXTREMELY FINE—*LIBERTY sharp. Ear distinct. Hair above eye well defined.*
MS-60 UNCIRCULATED—*No trace of wear. Light blemishes.*

Variety 1 — Wide Border 1809-1828

	Quan. Minted	G-4	VG-8	F-12	VF-20	EF-40	MS-60
1809	51,065	$85.00	$140.00	$275.00	$475.00	$900.00	$3,750
1811 over 9	65,180	60.00	90.00	175.00	400.00	800.00	3,000

1814 Small Date   **1814 Large Date**

	Quan. Minted	G-4	VG-8	F-12	VF-20	EF-40	MS-60
1814 Sm. date	} 421,500	$50.00	$75.00	$100.00	$200.00	$400.00	$1,800
1814 Lg. date		22.00	27.00	47.00	135.00	350.00	1,000
1814 STATESOFAMERICA		50.00	75.00	100.00	200.00	400.00	1,800
1820 STATESOFAMERICA		20.00	25.00	50.00	140.00	350.00	1,600

DIMES

1820 Large 0

1821 Small Date

1821 Large Date

	Quan. Minted	G-4	VG-8	F-12	VF-20	EF-40	MS-60
1820 Lg. 0	} 942,587	$18.00	$23.00	$35.00	$100.00	$325.00	$900.00
1820 Sm. 0		18.00	23.00	35.00	100.00	325.00	950.00
1821 Sm. date	} 1,186,512	19.00	23.00	40.00	110.00	325.00	1,000
1821 Lg. date		18.00	23.00	35.00	95.00	300.00	900.00
1822	100,000	325.00	450.00	800.00	1,200	2,300	7,500

1823, 3 over 2

Small E's

Large E's

	G-4	VG-8	F-12	VF-20	EF-40	MS-60
1823, 3 over 2, All kinds 440,000						
1823, 3 over 2, small E's	18.00	23.00	35.00	95.00	300.00	1,200
1823, 3 over 2, large E's	18.00	23.00	35.00	95.00	300.00	1,200

1824, 4 over 2

Large Date

Small Date

		G-4	VG-8	F-12	VF-20	EF-40	MS-60
1824, 4 over 2	} 510,000	20.00	25.00	50.00	225.00	500.00	1,750
1825		18.00	23.00	35.00	90.00	275.00	850.00
1827	1,215,000	18.00	23.00	35.00	90.00	275.00	850.00
1827, 7 over 5	Rare						
1828 Both vars	125,000						
1828 Lg. date, curl base 2		40.00	50.00	70.00	150.00	425.00	2,000

Variety 2 — Modified Design 1828-1837

New mint equipment was used to make the small date 1828 dimes and subsequent issues. Unlike earlier coinage, these have beaded borders and a uniform diameter. Large date has curl base knob 2; small date has square base knob 2.

1829 Small 10c

Large 10c

1829 Curl base 2

1830, 30 over 29

	Quan. Minted	G-4	F-12	VF-20	EF-40	MS-60
1828 Small date, sq. base 2		$25.00	$70.00	$150.00	$325.00	$1,200

DIMES

	Quan. Minted	G-4	F-12	VF-20	EF-40	MS-60
1829 All kinds..............	770,000					
1829 Curl base 2		$3,000	$5,000	$10,000		
1829 Small 10c		18.00	30.00	65.00	$200.00	$750.00
1829 Medium 10c		18.00	30.00	65.00	200.00	750.00
1829 Large 10c		20.00	35.00	70.00	225.00	900.00
1830 All kinds..............	510,000					
1830, 30 over 29		35.00	80.00	150.00	350.00	1,500
1830 Large 10c		17.00	25.00	55.00	175.00	600.00
1830 Small 10c		17.00	25.00	55.00	175.00	600.00
1831..............................	771,350	17.00	25.00	55.00	175.00	600.00
1832.................................	522,500	17.00	25.00	55.00	175.00	600.00
1833..............................	} 485,000	17.00	25.00	55.00	175.00	600.00
1833 Last 3 high..........		17.00	25.00	55.00	175.00	650.00
1834 Small 4		17.00	25.00	55.00	175.00	700.00
1834 Large 4	} 635,000	17.00	25.00	55.00	175.00	650.00
1835 1,410,000		17.00	25.00	55.00	175.00	600.00
1836 1,190,000		17.00	25.00	55.00	175.00	600.00
1837 359,500		17.00	25.00	55.00	175.00	600.00

LIBERTY SEATED TYPE 1837-1891

Variety 1 — No Stars on Obverse 1837-1838

Designer Christian Gobrecht; weight 2.67 grams; composition: .900 silver, .100 copper; diameter 17.9 mm; reeded edge; mints: Philadelphia, New Orleans.

G-4 GOOD —*LIBERTY on shield smooth. Date and letters readable.*
F-12 FINE —*Entire LIBERTY visible, weak spots.*
VF-20 VERY FINE —*Entire LIBERTY strong and even.*
EF-40 EXTREMELY FINE —*LIBERTY and scroll edges distinct.*
MS-60 UNCIRCULATED —*No trace of wear. Light blemishes.*

**No Drapery From Elbow
No Stars on Obverse**

Mint marks on Liberty seated dimes are placed on the reverse within, or below, the wreath. Size of mint mark varies on many dates.

1837 Large date...........	} 682,500	25.00	65.00	250.00	475.00	1,000
1837 Small date...........		25.00	65.00	250.00	475.00	1,000
1838O..................................406,034		32.00	90.00	300.00	625.00	2,500

Variety 2 — Stars on Obverse 1838-1853

**No Drapery from Elbow
Tilted Shield**

1838 Small Stars

1838 Large Stars

1838 Small stars	} 1,992,500	16.00	45.00	70.00	150.00	700.00
1838 Large stars		10.00	12.50	20.00	50.00	350.00
1838 Partial drapery .		18.00	45.00	75.00	160.00	800.00
1839 1,053,115		8.50	13.00	24.00	60.00	275.00
1839O..............................1,323,000		10.00	16.00	35.00	75.00	450.00
1840 981,500		8.00	12.00	22.00	50.00	275.00
1840O..............................1,175,000		9.50	18.00	37.50	80.00	900.00
1841 Proof, see page 125.						

DIMES

**Drapery from Elbow
Upright Shield**

	Quan. Minted	G-4	F-12	VF-20	EF-40	MS-60	Proof-63
1840	377,500	$25.00	$75.00	$135.00	$300.00	—	
1841	1,622,500	8.00	12.00	20.00	45.00	$300.00	—*
1841O	2,007,500	9.00	15.00	35.00	65.00	850.00	
1842	1,887,500	8.00	12.00	18.00	40.00	300.00	
1842O	2,020,000	9.00	13.00	40.00	125.00	—	
1843	1,370,000	8.00	12.00	18.00	40.00	300.00	
1843O	150,000	35.00	100.00	225.00	500.00	—	
1844	72,500	160.00	370.00	575.00	950.00	2,000	
1845	1,755,000	8.00	12.00	18.00	40.00	300.00	
1845O	230,000	15.00	50.00	180.00	450.00	—	
1846	31,300	75.00	150.00	300.00	625.00	—	
1847	245,000	12.00	30.00	55.00	115.00	750.00	
1848	451,500	10.00	20.00	40.00	80.00	400.00	
1849	839,000	8.00	12.00	20.00	45.00	300.00	
1849O	300,000	12.00	30.00	100.00	225.00	—	
1850	1,931,500	8.00	12.00	18.00	45.00	300.00	
1850O	510,000	10.00	20.00	60.00	100.00	900.00	
1851	1,026,500	8.00	12.00	18.00	40.00	300.00	
1851O	400,000	12.00	25.00	70.00	150.00	1,600	
1852	1,535,500	8.00	12.00	18.00	40.00	275.00	
1852O	430,000	14.00	35.00	100.00	200.00	1,500	
1853 No arrows	95,000	40.00	90.00	160.00	275.00	750.00	

*1841 Small stars, no drapery, upright shield. One proof and one VF known. 1973 M.A.N.A. sale $52,000.

Variety 3 — Arrows at Date 1853-1855

Weight 2.49 grams; composition: .900 silver, .100 copper; diameter 17.9 mm, reeded edge; mints: Philadelphia, New Orleans, San Francisco, Carson City.

1853-1855	**1856-1860**	
Arrows at Date	**Small Date, Arrows Removed**	

1853 with arrows	12,078,010	8.00	11.00	16.00	40.00	300.00	
1853O	1,100,000	9.00	12.00	25.00	85.00	700.00	
1854	4,470,000	8.00	11.00	16.00	40.00	300.00	$10,000
1854O	1,770,000	9.00	12.00	22.50	60.00	500.00	
1855	2,075,000	8.00	10.00	16.00	40.00	350.00	9,000

Variety 2 Resumed 1856-1860

1856 Lg. date	⎱ 5,780,000	8.00	10.00	15.00	40.00	300.00	
1856 Sm. date	⎰	8.00	10.00	15.00	35.00	275.00	2,750
1856O	1,180,000	8.00	10.00	18.00	50.00	425.00	
1856S	70,000	80.00	225.00	425.00	700.00	—	

DIMES

	Quan. Minted	G-4	F-12	VF-20	EF-40	MS-60	Proof-63
1857	5,580,000	$8.00	$10.00	$15.00	$35.00	$275.00	$2,750
1857O	1,540,000	8.00	11.00	20.00	45.00	350.00	
1858 ....(300+)	1,540,000	8.00	11.00	15.00	35.00	275.00	2,000
1858O	290,000	12.00	35.00	75.00	135.00	550.00	
1858S	60,000	75.00	150.00	275.00	575.00	—	
1859 ....(800)	430,000	8.00	11.00	20.00	50.00	275.00	1,500
1859O	480,000	9.00	12.00	40.00	80.00	375.00	
1859S	60,000	75.00	175.00	350.00	800.00	3,000	
1860S	140,000	20.00	45.00	100.00	250.00	—	

In 1859 an interesting dime pattern was made which does not bear our nation's identity. It is a "transitional" piece, not made for circulation, but struck at the time the inscription UNITED STATES OF AMERICA was being transferred from the reverse to the obverse.

1859 15,000

Variety 4 — Legend on Obverse 1860-1873

		G-4	F-12	VF-20	EF-40	MS-60	Proof-63
1860 ....(1,000)	607,000	8.00	11.00	18.00	30.00	200.00	800.00
1860O	40,000	275.00	700.00	1,000	2,400	—	
1861* ....(1,000)	1,884,000	8.00	11.00	18.00	30.00	175.00	800.00
1861S	172,500	32.00	80.00	175.00	325.00	1,500	
1862 ....(550)	847,550	8.00	11.00	18.00	30.00	185.00	700.00
1862S	180,750	25.00	50.00	140.00	200.00	1,300	
1863 ....(460)	14,460	250.00	450.00	575.00	725.00	1,100	800.00
1863S	157,500	24.00	45.00	80.00	175.00	1,000	
1864 ....(470)	11,470	200.00	350.00	450.00	575.00	900.00	800.00
1864S	230,000	18.00	40.00	60.00	120.00	900.00	
1865 ....(500)	10,500	215.00	375.00	550.00	675.00	1,000	850.00
1865S	175,000	20.00	45.00	80.00	200.00	2,000	
1866 ....(725)	8,725	225.00	475.00	575.00	750.00	1,200	800.00
1866S	135,000	20.00	40.00	80.00	175.00	1,400	
1867 ....(625)	6,625	300.00	600.00	700.00	900.00	1,500	950.00
1867S	140,000	22.00	50.00	100.00	200.00	1,750	
1868 ....(600)	464,600	8.00	15.00	35.00	70.00	350.00	600.00
1868S	260,000	12.00	25.00	60.00	125.00	350.00	
1869 ....(600)	256,600	10.00	18.00	40.00	80.00	400.00	600.00
1869S	450,000	10.00	17.00	35.00	80.00	350.00	
1870 ....(1,000)	471,500	8.00	10.00	17.50	35.00	200.00	600.00
1870S	50,000	200.00	250.00	350.00	475.00	1,500	
1871 ....(960)	907,710	8.00	10.00	18.00	30.00	300.00	600.00
1871CC	20,100	750.00	1,400	2,500	4,000	—	
1871S	320,000	15.00	30.00	50.00	120.00	600.00	
1872 ....(950)	2,396,450	8.00	10.00	18.00	30.00	150.00	600.00
1872CC	35,480	300.00	800.00	1,500	3,250	—	
1872S	190,000	20.00	60.00	100.00	225.00	1,200	
1873 Closed 3 (1,100)	1,508,000	8.00	10.00	18.00	30.00	200.00	600.00
1873 Open 3	60,000	20.00	45.00	85.00	150.00	450.00	
1873CC (Unique)	12,400		CSNS auction 1999			650,000	

*Dies modified slightly during 1861. First variety with only five vertical lines in top of shield is scarcer than the later variety.

DIMES

Variety 5 — Arrows at Date 1873-1874

In 1873 the dime was increased in weight to 2.50 grams. Arrows at date in 1873 and 1874 indicate this change.

Weight 2.50 grams; composition: .900 silver, .100 copper; diameter 17.9 mm; reeded edge; mints: Philadelphia, New Orleans, San Francisco, Carson City.

	Quan. Minted	G-4	F-12	VF-20	EF-40	MS-60	Proof-63
1873 ....(800)	2,378,500	$10.00	$20.00	$45.00	$125.00	$550.00	$1,200
1873 Doubled die obverse		30.00	100.00	350.00	1,000		
1873CC.............................18,791		650.00	1,800	3,200	4,750	—	
1873S...............................455,000		15.00	30.00	60.00	140.00	900.00	
1874 ....(700)	2,940,000	10.00	20.00	45.00	125.00	550.00	1,200
1874CC...............................10,817		2,000	4,200	7,000	12,000	—	
1874S................................240,000		20.00	50.00	85.00	175.00	900.00	

Variety 4 Resumed 1875-1891

	Quan. Minted	G-4	F-12	VF-20	EF-40	MS-60	Proof-63
1875 ....(700)	10,350,700	8.00	10.00	12.00	20.00	140.00	500.00
1875CC Below bow							
All kinds 4,645,000		10.00	12.00	20.00	45.00	300.00	
1875CC Above bow		9.00	11.00	15.00	30.00	200.00	
1875S Below bow							
All kinds 9,070,000		8.00	10.00	12.00	20.00	140.00	
1875S Above bow		8.00	10.00	12.00	30.00	200.00	
1876 ....(1,150)	11,461,150	8.00	10.00	12.00	20.00	140.00	500.00
1876CC...........................8,270,000		8.00	10.00	12.00	25.00	200.00	
1876S...........................10,420,000		8.00	10.00	12.00	24.00	140.00	
1877 ....(510)	7,310,510	8.00	10.00	12.00	20.00	140.00	550.00
1877CC...........................7,700,000		8.00	10.00	12.00	24.00	200.00	
1877S...........................2,340,000		9.00	11.00	14.00	25.00	175.00	
1878 ....(800)	1,678,000	8.00	10.00	12.00	22.00	140.00	500.00
1878CC................................200,000		35.00	80.00	125.00	250.00	700.00	
1879 ....(1,100)	15,100	150.00	250.00	300.00	400.00	600.00	550.00
1880 ....(1,355)	37,355	100.00	180.00	250.00	350.00	600.00	550.00
1881 ....(975)	24,975	100.00	180.00	250.00	350.00	550.00	550.00
1882 ....(1,100)	3,911,100	8.00	10.00	12.00	20.00	140.00	500.00
1883 ....(1,039)	7,675,712	8.00	10.00	12.00	20.00	140.00	500.00
1884 ....(875)	3,366,380	8.00	10.00	12.00	20.00	140.00	500.00
1884S................................564,969		13.00	24.00	45.00	75.00	700.00	
1885 ....(930)	2,533,427	8.00	10.00	12.00	20.00	140.00	500.00
1885S.................................43,690		300.00	700.00	1,200	2,000	5,500	
1886 ....(886)	6,377,570	8.00	10.00	12.00	20.00	140.00	500.00
1886S................................206,524		20.00	40.00	60.00	100.00	550.00	
1887 ....(710)	11,283,939	8.00	10.00	12.00	20.00	140.00	500.00
1887S...........................4,454,450		8.00	10.00	12.00	20.00	140.00	
1888 ....(832)	5,496,487	8.00	10.00	12.00	20.00	140.00	500.00
1888S...........................1,720,000		8.00	10.00	12.00	25.00	200.00	
1889 ....(711)	7,380,711	8.00	10.00	12.00	20.00	140.00	500.00
1889S................................972,678		10.00	20.00	40.00	75.00	425.00	
1890 ....(590)	9,911,541	8.00	10.00	12.00	20.00	140.00	500.00
1890S, large S..............1,423,076		10.00	18.00	37.50	65.00	275.00	
1890S, small S ....rare				—	—		

DIMES

	Quan. Minted	G-4	F-12	VF-20	EF-40	MS-60	Proof-63
1891 ....(600)	15,310,600	$8.00	$10.00	$12.00	$20.00	$140.00	$600.00
1891O..........................	4,540,000	8.00	10.00	20.00	35.00	200.00	
1891O, O over O		50.00	110.00	150.00	225.00	—	
1891S	3,196,116	8.00	10.00	15.00	28.00	225.00	

BARBER or LIBERTY HEAD TYPE 1892-1916

Designed by Charles E. Barber, Chief Engraver of the Mint, who also designed the 25- and 50-cent pieces. His initial B is at the truncation of the neck.

Designer Charles E. Barber; weight 2.50 grams; composition: .900 silver, .100 copper; diameter 17.9 mm; reeded edge; mints: Philadelphia, Denver, New Orleans, San Francisco. Net weight: .07234 oz. pure silver.

G-4 GOOD—Date and letters plain. LIBERTY is obliterated.
VG-8 VERY GOOD—At least 3 letters visible in LIBERTY.
F-12 FINE—All letters in LIBERTY visible, though some are weak.
VF-20 VERY FINE—All letters of LIBERTY evenly plain.
EF-40 EXTREMELY FINE—All letters in LIBERTY are sharp, distinct. Headband edges are distinct.
MS-60 UNCIRCULATED—No trace of wear. Light blemishes.

Mint mark location is on the reverse below the wreath.

	Quan. Minted	G-4	VG-8	F-12	VF-20	EF-40	MS-60	Proof-63
1892...(1,245)	12,121,245	$3.00	$5.00	$13.00	$18.00	$25.00	$100.00	$400.00
1892O................3,841,700		6.50	10.00	20.00	30.00	40.00	150.00	
1892S 990,710		37.00	65.00	135.00	175.00	200.00	360.00	
1893, 3 over 2 } 3,340,792					—	180.00	450.00	800.00
1893......(792) }		6.00	9.00	15.00	22.00	35.00	150.00	400.00
1893O................1,760,000		16.00	30.00	90.00	110.00	135.00	275.00	
1893S 2,491,401		7.50	17.00	23.00	37.00	50.00	225.00	
1894......(972)	1,330,972	8.50	20.00	80.00	100.00	125.00	250.00	400.00
1894O...................720,000		37.00	65.00	160.00	210.00	300.00	1,000	
1894S 24			Bowers-Eliasberg Sale 1996					465,000
1895......(880)	690,880	60.00	95.00	275.00	375.00	425.00	600.00	400.00
1895O...................440,000		210.00	300.00	675.00	1,000	1,600	3,200	
1895S 1,120,000		20.00	35.00	85.00	125.00	175.00	425.00	
1896......(762)	2,000,762	6.00	15.00	30.00	50.00	60.00	160.00	400.00
1896O 610,000		45.00	75.00	200.00	250.00	350.00	700.00	
1896S....................575,056		50.00	80.00	190.00	240.00	300.00	650.00	
1897......(731)	10,869,264	1.30	1.50	4.00	8.00	20.00	115.00	400.00
1897O 666,000		40.00	70.00	240.00	300.00	375.00	725.00	
1897S................1,342,844		8.00	18.00	65.00	80.00	110.00	375.00	
1898......(735)	16,320,735	1.30	1.50	4.00	8.00	20.00	110.00	400.00
1898O 2,130,000		5.00	13.00	70.00	95.00	135.00	425.00	
1898S................1,702,507		4.00	8.00	18.00	30.00	45.00	275.00	
1899......(846)	19,580,846	1.30	1.50	4.00	8.00	20.00	110.00	400.00
1899O 2,650,000		4.00	8.00	60.00	80.00	125.00	350.00	
1899S................1,867,493		4.00	8.00	12.00	20.00	35.00	250.00	
1900......(912)	17,600,912	1.30	1.50	4.00	8.00	20.00	110.00	400.00
1900O 2,010,000		8.00	15.00	80.00	100.00	200.00	550.00	
1900S................5,168,270		3.00	4.00	8.00	12.00	25.00	160.00	
1901......(813)	18,860,478	1.30	1.50	4.00	7.00	20.00	90.00	400.00
1901O	5,620,000	2.50	4.00	11.00	18.00	45.00	325.00	

DIMES

	Quan. Minted	G-4	VG-8	F-12	VF-20	EF-40	MS-60	Proof-63
1901S	593,022	$45.00	$75.00	$285.00	$350.00	$425.00	$850.00	
1902......(777)	21,380,777	1.25	1.50	4.00	7.00	20.00	90.00	$400.00
1902O	4,500,000	2.75	4.00	12.00	22.00	40.00	350.00	
1902S	2,070,000	3.50	8.00	40.00	50.00	75.00	325.00	
1903......(755)	19,500,755	1.25	2.00	4.00	7.00	20.00	90.00	400.00
1903O	8,180,000	2.50	3.00	8.00	12.00	30.00	250.00	
1903S	613,300	40.00	70.00	300.00	400.00	675.00	1,000	
1904......(670)	14,601,027	1.25	1.50	4.00	7.00	20.00	90.00	400.00
1904S	800,000	25.00	45.00	125.00	190.00	235.00	600.00	
1905......(727)	14,552,350	1.25	1.50	4.00	7.00	20.00	90.00	400.00
1905O	} 3,400,000	2.50	6.00	25.00	36.00	55.00	225.00	
1905O Micro O*		10.00	20.00	75.00	110.00	175.00	600.00	
1905S	6,855,199	2.00	4.00	7.00	13.00	30.00	200.00	
1906......(675)	19,958,406	1.25	1.50	4.00	7.00	20.00	90.00	400.00
1906D	4,060,000	2.50	3.25	7.00	12.00	25.00	135.00	
1906O	2,610,000	3.00	8.00	40.00	50.00	70.00	200.00	
1906S	3,136,640	2.00	4.00	11.00	20.00	35.00	225.00	
1907......(575)	22,220,575	1.25	1.50	4.00	7.00	20.00	90.00	400.00
1907D	4,080,000	1.75	2.75	8.00	13.00	32.00	250.00	
1907O	5,058,000	1.75	4.00	30.00	40.00	55.00	185.00	
1907S	3,178,470	2.00	4.00	9.00	15.00	40.00	300.00	
1908......(545)	10,600,545	1.25	1.50	4.00	7.00	20.00	90.00	400.00
1908D	7,490,000	1.50	2.00	7.00	10.00	25.00	110.00	
1908O	1,789,000	2.75	9.00	40.00	55.00	75.00	275.00	
1908S	3,220,000	2.00	3.00	8.00	15.00	32.00	250.00	
1909......(650)	10,240,650	1.25	1.50	4.00	7.00	20.00	90.00	400.00
1909D	954,000	3.00	10.00	60.00	80.00	120.00	400.00	
1909O	2,287,000	2.00	4.00	10.00	20.00	30.00	175.00	
1909S	1,000,000	4.00	12.00	65.00	100.00	150.00	525.00	
1910......(551)	11,520,551	1.25	1.50	4.00	7.00	20.00	90.00	400.00
1910D	3,490,000	1.50	3.00	8.00	15.00	35.00	180.00	
1910S	1,240,000	2.00	6.00	45.00	70.00	90.00	325.00	
1911......(543)	18,870,543	1.25	1.50	4.00	7.00	20.00	90.00	400.00
1911D	11,209,000	1.25	1.50	4.00	7.00	20.00	100.00	
1911S	3,520,000	1.50	3.00	8.00	13.00	30.00	140.00	
1912......(700)	19,350,000	1.25	1.50	3.00	7.00	20.00	90.00	400.00
1912D	11,760,000	1.25	1.50	4.00	7.00	20.00	90.00	
1912S	3,420,000	2.00	3.00	6.00	10.00	25.00	160.00	
1913......(622)	19,760,622	1.25	1.50	4.00	7.00	20.00	90.00	400.00
1913S	510,000	7.50	15.00	65.00	100.00	175.00	400.00	
1914......(425)	17,360,655	1.25	1.50	4.00	7.00	20.00	90.00	450.00
1914D	11,908,000	1.25	1.50	4.00	7.00	20.00	90.00	
1914S	2,100,000	2.00	3.00	6.00	14.00	30.00	150.00	
1915......(450)	5,620,450	1.25	1.50	4.00	7.00	20.00	90.00	500.00
1915S	960,000	2.00	5.00	30.00	35.00	55.00	250.00	
1916	18,490,000	1.25	1.50	4.00	7.00	20.00	90.00	
1916S	5,820,000	1.25	1.50	4.00	7.00	20.00	90.00	

*Normal and "microscopic" mint mark varieties, see page 67.

WINGED LIBERTY HEAD or "MERCURY" TYPE 1916-1945

Although this coin is commonly called the "Mercury Dime," the main device is in fact a representation of Liberty. The wings crowning her cap are intended to symbolize liberty of thought. The designer's monogram AW is right of neck.

Designer Adolph A. Weinman; weight 2.50 grams; composition: .900 silver, .100 copper; diameter 17.9 mm; reeded edge; mints: Philadelphia, Denver, San Francisco. Net weight: .07234 oz. pure silver.

DIMES

G-4 GOOD—*Letters and date clear. Lines and bands in fasces are obliterated.*
VG-8 VERY GOOD—*One-half of sticks discernible in fasces.*
F-12 FINE—*All sticks in fasces are defined. Diagonal bands worn nearly flat.*
VF-20 VERY FINE—*The two crossing diagonal bands must show.*
EF-40 EXTREMELY FINE—*Diagonal bands show only slight wear. Braids and hair before ear show clearly.*
AU-50 ABOUT UNCIRCULATED—*Slight trace of wear. Most mint luster is present.*
MS-63 SELECT UNCIRCULATED—*No trace of wear. Light blemishes. Attractive mint luster.*
MS-65 CHOICE UNCIRCULATED—*No trace of wear. Barely noticeable blemishes.*

**Mint mark location
is on reverse,
left of fasces.**

*Uncirculated values shown are for average pieces with minimum blemishes,
those with sharp strikes and split bands on reverse are worth much more.*

	Quan. Minted	G-4	VG-8	F-12	VF-20	EF-40	AU-50	MS-63
1916	22,180,080	$2.50	$3.50	$5.00	$6.00	$9.00	$17.00	$45.00
1916D	264,000	500.00	700.00	1,250	1,600	2,400	3,200	5,500
1916S	10,450,000	3.00	4.00	6.00	10.00	15.00	22.00	60.00
1917	55,230,000	1.25	1.75	2.00	5.00	6.00	11.00	55.00
1917D	9,402,000	3.50	5.00	9.00	17.00	40.00	75.00	325.00
1917S	27,330,000	1.50	2.50	4.00	6.00	10.00	25.00	160.00
1918	26,680,000	2.00	3.00	5.00	10.00	22.00	35.00	125.00
1918D	22,674,800	2.00	3.00	4.50	9.50	20.00	40.00	225.00
1918S	19,300,000	2.00	2.50	4.00	7.00	15.00	35.00	225.00
1919	35,740,000	2.00	2.50	3.25	5.00	7.50	20.00	100.00
1919D	9,939,000	3.00	4.50	7.00	16.00	32.00	60.00	425.00
1919S	8,850,000	3.00	3.50	6.00	12.00	30.00	60.00	450.00
1920	59,030,000	1.50	1.75	3.00	5.00	7.00	12.00	70.00
1920D	19,171,000	2.00	2.50	4.50	7.00	20.00	40.00	325.00
1920S	13,820,000	2.00	3.00	4.00	7.00	17.00	37.00	275.00
1921	1,230,000	25.00	40.00	85.00	200.00	425.00	600.00	1,400
1921D	1,080,000	40.00	65.00	120.00	250.00	500.00	675.00	1,600
1923*	50,130,000	1.50	2.00	3.00	4.00	6.00	12.00	45.00
1923S	6,440,000	2.00	3.00	6.00	11.00	50.00	85.00	375.00
1924	24,010,000	1.50	2.00	3.00	5.00	9.00	19.00	90.00
1924D	6,810,000	1.50	3.00	4.50	10.00	40.00	85.00	300.00
1924S	7,120,000	2.00	3.00	4.00	8.00	35.00	80.00	500.00
1925	25,610,000	1.50	2.00	2.50	4.00	7.00	14.00	70.00
1925D	5,117,000	3.50	4.50	11.00	30.00	90.00	175.00	650.00
1925S	5,850,000	2.00	3.00	6.00	11.00	55.00	90.00	450.00
1926	32,160,000	1.25	1.50	2.25	3.00	6.00	12.00	55.00
1926D	6,828,000	2.00	3.00	4.00	7.00	18.00	50.00	225.00
1926S	1,520,000	5.50	7.00	15.00	37.00	190.00	385.00	1,400
1927	28,080,000	1.25	1.50	2.25	3.00	6.00	11.00	50.00
1927D	4,812,000	3.00	4.00	5.00	17.00	40.00	80.00	350.00
1927S	4,770,000	2.00	2.50	3.50	6.00	17.00	45.00	450.00
1928	19,480,000	1.25	1.50	2.00	4.00	6.00	14.00	45.00
1928D	4,161,000	3.00	4.00	7.00	15.00	40.00	75.00	300.00
1928S‡	7,400,000	1.50	2.00	3.00	4.50	13.00	45.00	200.00
1929	25,970,000	1.25	1.50	2.00	3.50	5.00	9.00	30.00
1929D	5,034,000	2.50	3.00	5.00	8.00	12.00	16.00	38.00

* Coins dated 1923D are counterfeit.

‡ Large and small mint marks. See page 67.

DIMES

Quan. Minted	G-4	VG-8	F-12	VF-20	EF-40	AU-50	MS-63
1929S 4,730,000	$1.50	$2.00	$3.00	$4.00	$7.00	$18.00	$40.00
1930*...............6,770,000	1.50	1.75	2.50	4.00	6.00	12.00	45.00
1930S 1,843,000	2.75	3.00	4.50	6.00	13.00	40.00	100.00
1931 3,150,000	1.25	2.00	3.50	5.00	10.00	19.00	50.00
1931D...............1,260,000	5.00	6.00	9.00	18.00	30.00	45.00	100.00
1931S 1,800,000	3.00	3.50	5.00	8.50	13.00	30.00	80.00

*Dimes dated 1930D are counterfeit.

Quan. Minted	F-12	VF-20	EF-40	MS-63	MS-65	Proof-65
1934 24,080,000	$1.00	$1.25	$3.00	$15.00	$30.00	
1934D‡............................6,772,000	1.50	2.00	5.50	42.00	85.00	
1935 58,830,000	1.00	1.25	2.00	12.00	33.00	
1935D...................10,477,000	1.50	2.00	6.00	40.00	70.00	
1935S 15,840,000	1.00	1.25	4.00	20.00	35.00	
1936 ....(4,130) 87,504,130	1.00	2.00	2.50	15.00	30.00	$1,200
1936D...................16,132,000	1.50	2.75	5.00	25.00	40.00	
1936S 9,210,000	1.00	2.00	3.00	16.00	28.00	
1937 ....(5,756) 56,865,756	1.00	1.25	2.25	12.00	22.00	500.00
1937D...........................14,146,000	1.00	2.00	3.00	24.00	40.00	
1937S 9,740,000	1.00	2.00	3.00	22.00	35.00	
1938 ....(8,728) 22,198,728	1.00	2.00	2.75	15.00	22.00	325.00
1938D........................5,537,000	1.75	2.50	4.00	17.00	30.00	
1938S 8,090,000	1.00	2.00	3.00	15.00	25.00	
1939 ....(9,321) 67,749,321	1.00	1.25	2.50	11.00	20.00	300.00
1939D..........................24,394,000	1.00	1.25	2.50	12.00	20.00	
1939S 10,540,000	1.25	1.75	3.00	20.00	40.00	
1940.........(11,827) 65,361,827	.70	.85	1.25	8.00	17.00	275.00
1940D...........................21,198,000	.70	.85	1.25	13.00	20.00	
1940S 21,560,000	.70	.85	1.25	11.00	20.00	
1941 ....(16,557) 175,106,557	.70	.85	1.25	8.00	17.00	175.00
1941D.............................45,634,000	.70	.85	1.25	10.00	17.00	
1941S‡ 43,090,000	.70	.85	1.25	11.00	20.00	

1942, 2 over 1   **1942D, 2 over 1**

		F-12	VF-20	EF-40	MS-63	MS-65	Proof-65
1942, 2 over 1.........	} 205,432,329	250.00	290.00	450.00	2,900	6,500	
1942 ....(22,329)		.60	.80	1.25	8.00	17.00	175.00
1942D, 2 over 1......	} 60,740,000	325.00	325.00	500.00	2,500	5,000	
1942D.....................		.60	.80	1.25	10.00	20.00	
1942S 49,300,000		.60	.80	1.25	12.00	22.00	
1943 191,710,000		.60	.80	1.25	8.00	17.00	
1943D.............................71,949,000		.60	.80	1.25	10.00	20.00	
1943S 60,400,000		.60	.80	1.25	10.00	20.00	
1944 231,410,000		.60	.80	1.25	8.00	17.00	
1944D.............................62,224,000		.60	.80	1.25	8.00	22.00	
1944S 49,490,000		.60	.80	1.25	10.00	20.00	
1945 159,130,000		.60	.80	1.25	8.00	17.00	
1945D.............................40,245,000		.60	.80	1.25	8.00	20.00	
1945S Normal	} 41,920,000	.60	.80	1.25	8.00	22.00	
1945S Micro S‡......		1.25	2.00	4.00	25.00	65.00	

‡Large and small mint mark varieties, see page 67.

DIMES
ROOSEVELT TYPE 1946 to Date

John R. Sinnock (whose initials JS are at the truncation of the neck) designed this dime showing a portrait of Franklin D. Roosevelt. The design has heavier lettering and a more modernistic character than preceding types.

Mint mark on reverse 1946-1964.　**Mint mark on obverse starting 1968.**

Silver Coinage — 1946-1964

Designer John R. Sinnock; weight 2.50 grams; composition: .900 silver, .100 copper; diameter 17.9 mm; reeded edge; mints: Philadelphia, Denver, San Francisco, West Point. Net weight: .07234 oz. pure silver.

VF-20 VERY FINE—*Hair above ear slightly worn. All vertical lines on torch plain.*
EF-40 EXTREMELY FINE—*All lines of torch, flame and hair very plain.*
MS-60 UNCIRCULATED—*No trace of wear. Light blemishes.*
MS-63 SELECT UNCIRCULATED—*No trace of wear. Very light blemishes. Attractive mint luster.*
MS-65 CHOICE UNCIRCULATED—*No trace of wear. Barely noticeable blemishes.*

	Quan. Minted	EF-40	MS-63	MS-65	Proof-65
1946	255,250,000	$.60	$1.00	$2.00	
1946D	61,043,500	.60	1.25	3.00	
1946S	27,900,000	.60	2.50	4.00	
1947	121,520,000	.60	2.00	3.00	
1947D	46,835,000	.60	4.00	6.00	
1947S	34,840,000	.60	3.00	5.00	
1948	74,950,000	.60	5.00	10.00	
1948D	52,841,000	.60	4.00	9.00	
1948S	35,520,000	.60	4.00	9.00	
1949	30,940,000	1.25	15.00	25.00	
1949D	26,034,000	1.00	5.00	12.00	
1949S	13,510,000	2.50	22.00	40.00	
1950 ....(51,386)	50,181,500	.60	3.00	6.00	$30.00
1950D	46,803,000	.60	3.00	6.00	
1950S .... } 1950S, S over D .... }	20,440,000	.60	14.00	22.00	
		75.00	350.00		
1951 ....(57,500)	103,937,602	.60	1.25	3.00	25.00
1951D	56,529,000	.60	1.50	3.00	
1951S	31,630,000	.60	8.00	16.00	
1952 ....(81,980)	99,122,073	.60	1.75	3.00	24.00
1952D	122,100,000	.60	1.75	4.00	
1952S	44,419,500	.60	4.00	10.00	
1953 ....(128,800)	53,618,920	.60	1.75	4.00	23.00
1953D	136,433,000	.60	2.00	3.00	
1953S	39,180,000	.60	2.00	2.75	
1954 ....(233,300)	114,243,503	.60	1.50	2.75	10.00
1954D	106,397,000	.60	1.50	3.00	
1954S	22,860,000	.60	1.50	3.00	
1955 ....(378,200)	12,828,381	.60	1.50	4.00	9.00
1955D	13,959,000	.60	1.50	3.00	
1955S	18,510,000	.60	.85	2.50	
1956 ....(669,384)	109,309,384	.60	.85	1.00	3.00
1956D	108,015,100	.60	.85	1.00	

DIMES

1960 Proof Doubled Die Obverse

1964D Doubled Die Reverse

	Quan. Minted	EF-40	MS-63	MS-65	Proof-65
1957 ....(1,247,952)	161,407,952	*$.60*	*$.75*	*$1.00*	$2.50
1957D 113,354,330		*.60*	*.75*	*1.00*	
1958 ....(875,652)	32,785,652	*.60*	*.75*	*1.00*	3.00
1958D 136,564,600		*.60*	*.75*	*1.00*	
1959 ....(1,149,291)	86,929,291	*.60*	*.75*	*1.00*	1.50
1959D 164,919,790		*.60*	*.75*	*1.00*	
1960 ....(1,691,602)	72,081,602	*.60*	*.75*	*1.00*	1.50
1960 Doubled die obverse					300.00
1960D 200,160,400		*.60*	*.75*	*1.00*	
1961 ....(3,028,244)	96,758,244	*.60*	*.75*	*1.00*	1.25
1961D 209,146,550		*.60*	*.75*	*1.00*	
1962 ....(3,218,019)	75,668,019	*.60*	*.75*	*1.00*	1.25
1962D 334,948,380		*.60*	*.75*	*1.00*	
1963 ....(3,075,645)	126,725,645	*.60*	*.75*	*1.00*	1.25
1963 Proof doubled die reverse					400.00
1963D 421,476,530		*.60*	*.75*	*1.00*	
1964* ....(3,950,762)	933,310,762	*.60*	*.75*	*1.00*	1.25
1964D* 1,357,517,180		*.60*	*.75*	*1.00*	
1964D Doubled die reverse		50.00	250.00	300.00	

*Variations of 9 in date have either pointed or straight tail.
Note: Prices in italic are based on silver bullion value.

Clad Coinage — 1965 to date

Weight 2.27 grams; composition: outer layers of copper-nickel (.750 copper, .250 nickel) bonded to inner core of pure copper; diameter 17.9 mm; reeded edge. Silver Proofs: pre-1965 standards.

Quan. Minted	MS-65	Proof-65		Quan. Minted	MS-65	Proof-65
1965 1,652,140,570	$.35		1975S Proof*.(2,845,450)			$1.25
1966 1,382,734,540	.35		1976 568,760,000	$.40	
1967 2,244,007,320	.30		1976D 695,222,774	.40	
1968 424,470,400	.25		1976S Proof...(4,149,730)		.85
1968D 480,748,280	.25		1977 796,930,000	.25	
1968S Proof*.(3,041,506)		$.85	1977D 376,607,228	.25	
1969 145,790,000	.75		1977S Proof...(3,251,152)		.85
1969D 563,323,870	.25		1978 663,980,000	.25	
1969S Proof...(2,934,631)		.85	1978D 282,847,540	.25	
1970 345,570,000	.25		1978S Proof...(3,127,781)		.85
1970D 754,942,100	.25		1979 315,440,000	.25	
1970S Proof*.(2,632,810)		.85	1979D 390,921,184	.25	
1971 162,690,000	.40		1979S Proof...(3,677,175)		
1971D 377,914,240	.40		Filled S		.75
1971S Proof...(3,220,733)		.85	Clear S		1.50
1972 431,540,000	.25		1980P...........735,170,000	.20	
1972D 330,290,000	.25		1980D 719,354,321	.20	
1972S Proof...(3,260,996)		.85	1980S Proof...(3,554,806)		.75
1973 315,670,000	.25		1981P...........676,650,000	.20	
1973D 455,032,426	.25		1981D 712,284,143	.20	
1973S Proof...(2,760,339)		.85	1981S Proof...(4,063,083)		.75
1974 470,248,000	.25		1982 (no mint mark)* 200.00		
1974D 571,083,000	.25		1982P...........519,475,000	2.50	
1974S Proof...(2,612,568)		1.00	1982D 542,713,584	1.00	
1975 585,673,900	.30		1982S Proof...(3,857,479)		1.00
1975D 313,705,300	.25				

*1968, 1970, and 1975 proof dimes without S mint mark were made in error. Some of the 1982 business strike dimes were also made without a mint mark. See page 69.

DIMES

Quan. Minted	MS-65	Proof-65		Quan. Minted	MS-65	Proof-65
1983P 647,025,000	$2.00		1995P 1,125,500,000	$.20	
1983D 730,129,224	1.00		1995D 1,274,890,000	.30	
1983S Proof*(3,279,126)		$1.00	1995S Proof..(2,117,496)		$15.00
1984P 856,669,000	.30		1995S Silver		
1984D 704,803,976	.50		Proof ....(679,985)		16.00
1984S Proof .(3,065,110)		1.50	1996P 1,421,163,000	.20	
1985P 705,200,962	.50		1996D 1,400,300,000	.20	
1985D 587,979,970	.40		1996W‡ 1,457,000	6.50	
1985S Proof .(3,362,821)		1.00	1996S Proof .(1,750,244)		2.00
1986P 682,649,693	.75		1996S Silver		
1986D 473,326,970	.60		Proof .... (775,021)		6.00
1986S Proof .(3,010,497)		1.50	1997P 991,640,000	.20	
1987P 762,709,481	.20		1997D 979,810,000	.20	
1987D 653,203,402	.20		1997S Proof .(2,055,000)		3.00
1987S Proof .(4,227,728)		1.50	1997S Silver		
1988P 1,030,550,000	.20		Proof ....(741,678)		15.00
1988D 962,385,489	.20		1998P 1,163,000,000	.20	
1988S Proof .(3,262,948)		2.00	1998D 1,172,250,000	.20	
1989P 1,298,400,000	.20		1998S Proof....................		2.00
1989D 896,535,597	.20		1998S Silver		
1989S Proof .(3,220,194)		2.00	Proof ....(878,792)		6.00
1990P 1,034,340,000	.20		1999P 2,164,000,000	.20	
1990D 839,995,824	.20		1999D 1,397,750,000	.20	
1990S Proof .(3,299,559)		1.75	1999S Proof....................		2.00
1991P 927,220,000	.20		1999S Silver		
1991D 601,241,114	.20		Proof ....(800,000)		4.00
1991S Proof .(2,867,787)		2.50	2000P 1,842,500,000	.20	
1992P 593,500,000	.20		2000D 1,818,700,000	.20	
1992D 616,273,932	.20		2000S Proof .(2,968,900)		1.50
1992S Proof .(2,858,981)		5.00	2000S Silver		
1992S Silver			Proof ....(856,400)		3.00
Proof ......(1,317,579)		6.00	2001P 1,369,590,000	.20	
1993P 766,180,000	.20		2001D 1,412,800,000	.20	
1993D 750,110,166	.20		2001S Proof....................		1.50
1993S Proof .(2,633,439)		4.00	2001S Silver Proof.........		3.00
1993S Silver			2002P		.20
Proof ....(761,353)		5.00	2002D		.20
1994P 1,189,000,000	.20		2002S Proof....................		1.50
1994D 1,303,268,110	.20		2002S Silver Proof.........		3.00
1994S Proof .(2,484,594)		4.00			
1994S Silver					
Proof ....(785,329)		6.75			

*1983S proof dimes without S mint mark were made in error. See page 69.
‡Issued in mint sets only.

BIBLIOGRAPHY

Ahwash, Kamal M. *Encyclopedia of United States Liberty Seated Dimes 1837-1891.* Kamal Press, 1977.
Davis, David; Logan, Russell; Lovejoy, Allen; McCloskey, John; Subjack, William. *Early United States Dimes 1796-1837.* Ypsilanti, Michigan, 1984.
Greer, Brian, *The Complete Guide to Liberty Seated Dimes.* Virginia Beach, VA, 1992.
Kosoff, A. *United States Dimes from 1796.* New York, 1945.
Lange, David W. *The Complete Guide to Mercury Dimes.* Virginia Beach, VA 1993.
Lawrence, David, *The Complete Guide to Barber Dimes.* Virginia Beach, VA 1991.

TWENTY-CENT PIECES — 1875-1878

This short-lived coin was authorized by the Act of March 3, 1875. Soon after the appearance of the first twenty-cent pieces, people complained about the similarity in design and size to the quarter dollar. The eagle is very similar to that used on the Trade Dollar, but the edge of this coin is plain. Mint mark is positioned on the reverse below the eagle. Most of the 1876CC coins were melted at the mint and never released.

↑ or indicates change from previous year	TYPE COIN VALUES									
	G-4	F-12	EF-40	AU-50	MS-60	MS-63	MS-65	PF-60	PF-63	PF-65
1875-1878	50.00	70.00	160.00	300.00	475.00	1,000	5,300	850.00	1,800	8,000+

Designer William Barber; weight 5 grams; composition: .900 silver, .100 copper; diameter 22 mm; plain edge; mints: Philadelphia, Carson City, San Francisco.

G-4 GOOD—*LIBERTY on shield obliterated. Letters and date legible.*
VG-8 VERY GOOD—*One or two letters in LIBERTY may show. Other details will be bold.*
F-12 FINE—*At least 3 letters of LIBERTY show.*
VF-20 VERY FINE—*LIBERTY completely readable, but partly weak.*
EF-40 EXTREMELY FINE—*LIBERTY sharp. Only slight wear on high points of the coin*
MS-60 UNCIRCULATED—*No trace of wear. Light blemishes.*

	Quan. Minted	G-4	VG-8	F-12	VF-20	EF-40	MS-60	Proof-63
1875	(2,790) 39,700	$55.00	$67.00	$80.00	$100.00	$200.00	$600.00	$1,800
1875CC	133,290	60.00	65.00	80.00	135.00	225.00	750.00	
1875S	1,155,000	50.00	55.00	70.00	100.00	160.00	475.00	—
1876	(1,260) 15,900	85.00	110.00	150.00	210.00	325.00	800.00	2,000
1876CC	10,000						60,000	
1877	(350) 350				1,500	1,600		2,800
1878	(600) 600				1,300	1,400		2,500

QUARTER DOLLARS — 1796 to Date

Authorized in 1792, this denomination was not issued until four years later. The first coinage, dated 1796, follows the pattern of the early half-dimes and dimes by the absence of a mark of value. In 1804 the value "25c" was added to the reverse. Figures were used until 1838 when the term "QUAR. DOL." appeared. It was not until 1892 that the value was spelled out entirely.

The first type weighed 104 grains which remained standard until modified to 103⅛ grains by the Act of January 18, 1837. As with the dime and half dime, the weight was reduced and arrows placed at the date in 1853. Rays were placed in the field of the reverse during that year only.

The law of 1873 also affected the quarter, for the weight was slightly increased and arrows again placed at the date.

Proofs of some dates prior to 1856 are known to exist, and all are rare.

+ or – indicates change from previous year	TYPE COIN VALUES									
	G-4	F-12	EF-40	AU-50	MS-60	MS-63	MS-65	PF-60	PF-63	PF-65
Drpd Bust-SE 1796	4,000	8,250	15,000	17,500	25,000	32,000	95,000			
Drpd Bust-HE 1804-1807	200.00	400.00	1,700	2,500	4,500	8,500+	45,000			
Lg. Bust 1815-1828	50.00	100.00	625.00	1,100	2,000	3,800	16,000			
Sm. Bust 1831-1838	40.00+	55.00	225.00	600.00	800.00	2,200	13,500			
Lib. Seated-NM 1838-1865	13.00	20.00	50.00	125.00	325.00	575.00	4,000	450.00	1,100	5,000
Lib. Seat-A&R 1853	13.00+	20.00	150.00	375.00	950.00	2,400	16,500			
Lib. Seat-Arr. 1854-1855	12.00	20.00	75.00	225.00	500.00	1,200	7,800			
Lib. Seat-WM 1866-1891	12.00	20.00	45.00	120.00	250.00	475.00	1,700	350.00	600.00	2,000
Lib. Seat-Arr. 1873-1874	13.00	25.00	200.00	400.00	750.00	1,600	4,000	750.00	1,400	6,500
Barber 1892-1916	3.25+	17.00	60.00	100.00	150.00	275.00	1,200-	350.00	600.00	1,700
Stand Lib. 1 1916-1917	13.00	27.00	60.00	100.00	180.00	275.00	750.00			
Stand Lib. 2 1917-1930	2.50	6.00	25.00	55.00	115.00	175.00	460.00			
Washington 1932-1964	1.25	1.50	1.75	1.85	2.00	2.50	6.00+	2.75	3.00	3.50

QUARTER DOLLARS
DRAPED BUST TYPE, SMALL EAGLE REVERSE 1796

Designer Robert Scot; weight 6.74 grams; composition: .8924 silver, .1076 copper; approx. diameter 27.5 mm; reeded edge. All coined at Philadelphia.

AG-3 ABOUT GOOD—*Details clear enough to identify.*
G-4 GOOD—*Date readable. Bust outlined, but no detail.*
VG-8 VERY GOOD—*All but deepest drapery folds worn smooth. Hairlines nearly gone and curls lack detail.*
F-12 FINE—*All drapery lines visible. Hair partly worn.*
VF-20 VERY FINE—*Only left side of drapery is indistinct.*
EF-40 EXTREMELY FINE—*Hair well outlined and detailed.*
MS-60 UNCIRCULATED—*No trace of wear. Light blemishes.*

	Quan. Minted	AG-3	G-4	VG-8	F-12	VF-20	EF-40	MS-60
1796	6,146	$1,800	$4,000	$5,500	$8,250	$12,000	$15,000	$25,000

DRAPED BUST TYPE, HERALDIC EAGLE REVERSE 1804-1807

1804	6,738	500.00	1,000	2,000	2,750	3,600	7,750	—
1805	121,394	100.00	200.00	275.00	400.00	800.00	1,700	4,500
1806, 6 over 5	} 206,124	100.00	200.00	275.00	400.00	850.00	2,000	5,000
1806		100.00	200.00	275.00	400.00	800.00	1,700	4,500
1807	220,643	100.00	200.00	275.00	400.00	800.00	1,700	4,500

CAPPED BUST TYPE 1815-1838
Variety 1 — Large Size 1815-1828

Designer John Reich; weight 6.74 grams; composition: .8924 silver, .1076 copper; approx. diameter 27 mm; reeded edge. All coined at Philadelphia.

AG-3 ABOUT GOOD—*Details clear enough to identify.*
G-4 GOOD—*Date, letters and stars readable. Hair under headband smooth. Cap lines worn smooth.*
VG-8 VERY GOOD—*Rim well defined. Main details visible. Full LIBERTY on cap. Hair above eye nearly smooth.*
F-12 FINE—*All hairlines show but drapery has only part details. Shoulder clasp distinct.*
VF-20 VERY FINE—*All details show, but some wear. Clasp and ear sharp.*
EF-40 EXTREMELY FINE—*All details show distinctly. Hair well outlined.*
MS-60 UNCIRCULATED—*No trace of wear. Light blemishes.*

QUARTER DOLLARS

	Quan. Minted	AG-3	G-4	VG-8	F-12	VF-20	EF-40	MS-60
1815	89,235	$25.00	$50.00	$70.00	$100.00	$300.00	$750.00	$2,300
1818, 8 over 5	} 361,174	25.00	50.00	70.00	125.00	350.00	750.00	2,500
1818 Normal date		25.00	50.00	70.00	100.00	300.00	650.00	2,000
1819 Small 9	} 144,000	25.00	50.00	70.00	100.00	300.00	650.00	2,000
1819 Large 9		25.00	50.00	70.00	100.00	300.00	650.00	2,000

1820 Small 0	**1820 Large 0**	**1822, 25 over 50c**

	Quan. Minted	AG-3	G-4	VG-8	F-12	VF-20	EF-40	MS-60
1820 Small 0	} 127,444	25.00	50.00	70.00	100.00	250.00	650.00	2,000
1820 Large 0		25.00	50.00	70.00	100.00	250.00	650.00	2,000
1821	216,851	25.00	50.00	70.00	100.00	250.00	650.00	2,000
1822 All kinds	64,080	25.00	50.00	85.00	125.00	350.00	800.00	2,750
1822, 25 over 50c		500.00	1,600	2,200	3,500	5,000	8,200	12,000
1823, 3 over 2	17,800	4,000	9,000	14,000	20,000	25,000	38,000	—

1825, 5 over 2 (wide date)	**1825, 5 over 3 or 4 (close date)**

	Quan. Minted	AG-3	G-4	VG-8	F-12	VF-20	EF-40	MS-60
1824, 4 over 2	} 168,000	35.00	80.00	110.00	190.00	500.00	1,300	5,000
1825, 5 over 2		25.00	75.00	100.00	175.00	400.00	1,000	3,000
1825, 5 over 4		25.00	50.00	60.00	100.00	250.00	625.00	2,000
1827 Original (Curled base 2 in 25c) 4,000 Minted								60,000
1827 Restrike (Square base 2 in 25c)								25,000
1828 All kds	102,000	25.00	50.00	60.00	100.00	225.00	625.00	2,000
1828, 25 over 50c		50.00	100.00	200.00	350.00	800.00	1,500	6,000

Variety 2 — Reduced Size, No Motto on Reverse 1831-1838

Designer William Kneass; weight 6.74 grams; composition: .8924 silver, .1076 copper; diameter 24.3 mm; reeded edge. All coined at Philadelphia.

G-4 GOOD—*Bust well defined. Hair under headband smooth. Date, letters, stars readable. Scant rims.*
VG-8 VERY GOOD—*Details apparent but worn on high spots. Rims strong. Full LIBERTY.*
F-12 FINE—*All hairlines visible. Drapery partly worn. Shoulder clasp distinct.*
VF-20 VERY FINE—*Only top spots worn. Clasp sharp. Ear distinct.*
EF-40 EXTREMELY FINE—*Hair details and clasp are bold and clear.*
MS-60 UNCIRCULATED—*No trace of wear. Light blemishes.*

QUARTER DOLLARS

Small Letters (1831)　　　　　　　　**Large Letters**

	Quan. Minted	G-4	VG-8	F-12	VF-20	EF-40	MS-60
1831 Small letters........ }	398,000	$40.00	$47.00	$55.00	$90.00	$225.00	$800.00
1831 Large letters........		40.00	47.00	55.00	90.00	225.00	800.00
1832 320,000		40.00	47.00	55.00	90.00	225.00	800.00
1833 156,000		45.00	55.00	65.00	125.00	275.00	1,400
1834 286,000		40.00	47.00	55.00	90.00	225.00	800.00
1835 1,952,000		40.00	47.00	55.00	90.00	225.00	800.00
1836 472,000		40.00	47.00	55.00	90.00	225.00	800.00
1837 252,400		40.00	47.00	55.00	90.00	225.00	800.00
1838 366,000		40.00	47.00	55.00	90.00	225.00	800.00

LIBERTY SEATED TYPE 1838-1891
Variety 1 — No Motto Above Eagle 1838-1853

Designer Christian Gobrecht; weight 6.68 grams; composition: .900 silver, .100 copper; diameter 24.3 mm; reeded edge; mints: Philadelphia, New Orleans.

G-4 GOOD—*Scant rim. LIBERTY on shield worn off. Date and letters readable.*
VG-8 VERY GOOD—*Rim fairly defined, at least 3 letters in LIBERTY evident.*
F-12 FINE—*LIBERTY complete, but partly weak.*
VF-20 VERY FINE—*LIBERTY strong.*
EF-40 EXTREMELY FINE—*Complete LIBERTY and edges of scroll. Clasp shows plainly.*
MS-60 UNCIRCULATED—*No trace of wear. Light blemishes.*

No Drapery from Elbow　　　　　　**Drapery from Elbow**

Mint mark location is on the reverse below the eagle.

		G-4	VG-8	F-12	VF-20	EF-40	MS-60
1838 No drapery.................466,000		13.00	17.00	27.00	60.00	275.00	1,100
1839 No drapery.................491,146		13.00	17.00	27.00	60.00	275.00	900.00
1840O No drapery..............382,200		13.00	17.00	27.00	60.00	275.00	1,000
1840 Drapery.....................188,127		18.00	25.00	45.00	80.00	175.00	1,100
1840O Drapery....................43,000		20.00	30.00	55.00	100.00	250.00	1,500
1841 120,000		40.00	50.00	100.00	160.00	225.00	800.00
1841O...................................452,000		15.00	22.00	40.00	70.00	165.00	800.00

Small Date　　　　　　**Large Date**

		G-4	VG-8	F-12	VF-20	EF-40	MS-60
1842 Small date. Proofs only..........							25,000
1842 Large date 88,000		75.00	100.00	150.00	250.00	400.00	2,400

QUARTER DOLLARS

	Quan. Minted	G-4	VG-8	F-12	VF-20	EF-40	MS-60
1842O Small date ..... }	769,000	$375.00	$500.00	$900.00	$1,500	$3,000	—
1842O Large date ...... }		16.00	20.00	30.00	70.00	175.00	$2,000
1843............................	645,600	13.00	16.00	20.00	40.00	85.00	550.00
1843O	968,000	17.00	27.00	42.50	80.00	225.00	1,500
1844............................	421,200	13.00	16.00	25.00	45.00	90.00	550.00
1844O	740,000	15.00	20.00	45.00	90.00	200.00	1,100
1845............................	922,000	13.00	16.00	20.00	40.00	80.00	550.00
1846............................	510,000	13.00	16.00	25.00	45.00	90.00	550.00
1847............................	734,000	13.00	16.00	20.00	40.00	80.00	550.00
1847O	368,000	20.00	30.00	60.00	120.00	225.00	1,750
1848............................	146,000	25.00	35.00	65.00	125.00	175.00	1,100
1849............................	340,000	16.00	22.00	40.00	70.00	150.00	800.00
1849O	‡incl. below	350.00	475.00	800.00	1,650	3,000	—
1850............................	190,800	20.00	35.00	50.00	75.00	150.00	800.00
1850O	412,000	25.00	35.00	50.00	70.00	135.00	1,300
1851............................	160,000	25.00	40.00	60.00	125.00	170.00	850.00
1851O	88,000	150.00	225.00	400.00	600.00	1,200	3,500
1852............................	177,060	30.00	40.00	60.00	135.00	200.00	750.00
1852O	96,000	175.00	250.00	400.00	600.00	1,300	6,000
1853* Recut date, no arrows or rays	44,200	175.00	250.00	350.00	500.00	650.00	2,800

‡Coinage for 1849O included with 1850O.
*Beware of altered 1858.

Variety 2 — Arrows at Date, Rays Around Eagle 1853 Only

The reduction in weight is indicated by the arrows at the date. Rays were added on the reverse side in the field around the eagle. The arrows were retained through 1855, but the rays were omitted after 1853.

Weight 6.22 grams; composition: .900 silver, .100 copper; diameter 24.3 mm; reeded edge; mints: Philadelphia, New Orleans, San Francisco, Carson City.

1853, 3 over 4   1854O, Huge O

	Quan. Minted	G-4	VG-8	F-12	VF-20	EF-40	MS-60
1853.............................. }	15,210,020	13.00	15.00	20.00	40.00	150.00	950.00
1853, 3 over 4.............. }		35.00	70.00	100.00	150.00	350.00	1,800
1853O	1,332,000	15.00	20.00	30.00	60.00	200.00	2,500

Variety 3 — Arrows at Date, No Rays 1854-1855

	Quan. Minted	G-4	VG-8	F-12	VF-20	EF-40	MS-60
1854............................	12,380,000	12.00	14.00	20.00	30.00	80.00	500.00
1854O .... }	1,484,000	13.00	16.00	22.00	45.00	100.00	800.00
1854O Huge O .... }		75.00	135.00	200.00	300.00	650.00	—
1855............................	2,857,000	12.00	14.00	20.00	30.00	80.00	550.00
1855O	176,000	35.00	50.00	100.00	250.00	350.00	2,750
1855S..........................	396,400	35.00	50.00	75.00	140.00	300.00	1,800

Variety 1 Resumed 1856-1865

	Quan. Minted	G-4	VG-8	F-12	VF-20	EF-40	MS-60	Proof-63
1856.................7,264,000		$13.00	$15.00	$20.00	$25.00	$50.00	$375.00	$4,250
1856O 968,000		13.00	16.00	25.00	40.00	100.00	1,100	

QUARTER DOLLARS

	Quan. Minted	G-4	VG-8	F-12	VF-20	EF-40	MS-60	Proof-63
1856S	} 286,000	$30.00	$42.00	$70.00	$200.00	$350.00	$2,100	
1856S, S over S		35.00	60.00	125.00	275.00	500.00	—	
1857	9,644,000	13.00	15.00	20.00	25.00	50.00	325.00	$2,750
1857O	1,180,000	13.00	15.00	22.00	30.00	75.00	1,000	
1857S	82,000	50.00	90.00	170.00	350.00	575.00	2,500	
1858 (300+)	7,368,000	13.00	15.00	20.00	25.00	50.00	325.00	2,250
1858O	520,000	15.00	19.00	30.00	45.00	125.00	1,300	
1858S	121,000	40.00	60.00	100.00	225.00	500.00		
1859 (800)	1,344,000	14.00	16.00	20.00	25.00	60.00	375.00	1,250
1859O	260,000	16.00	25.00	40.00	65.00	95.00	1,200	
1859S	80,000	75.00	115.00	185.00	300.00	700.00	—	
1860 (1,000)	805,400	14.00	16.00	20.00	25.00	50.00	400.00	1,100
1860O	388,000	14.00	19.00	30.00	45.00	75.00	1,000	
1860S	56,000	100.00	175.00	325.00	750.00	3,000	—	
1861 (1,000)	4,854,600	13.00	15.00	20.00	25.00	50.00	300.00	1,100
1861S	96,000	50.00	85.00	200.00	300.00	700.00	4,000	
1862 (550)	932,550	14.00	16.00	22.00	30.00	60.00	325.00	1,100
1862S	67,000	40.00	60.00	100.00	225.00	475.00	2,200	
1863 (460)	192,060	23.00	32.00	45.00	65.00	120.00	600.00	1,100
1864 (470)	94,070	45.00	60.00	90.00	125.00	225.00	800.00	1,100
1864S	20,000	200.00	300.00	550.00	900.00	1,750	—	
1865 (500)	59,300	40.00	60.00	90.00	130.00	250.00	700.00	1,100
1865S	41,000	65.00	85.00	130.00	300.00	500.00	2,350	
1866	Unique							—

The 1866 proof quarter, half and dollar without motto are not mentioned in the Director's Report, and were not issued for circulation.

Variety 4 — Motto Above Eagle 1866-1873

The motto IN GOD WE TRUST was added to the reverse side in 1866. As on the half dollar and silver dollar, the motto has been retained since that time.

1866 (725)	17,525	225.00	300.00	450.00	550.00	750.00	1,800	900.00
1866S	28,000	140.00	200.00	300.00	600.00	900.00	3,000	
1867 (625)	20,625	110.00	150.00	200.00	300.00	475.00	1,000	900.00
1867S	48,000	125.00	175.00	275.00	400.00	650.00	3,800	
1868 (600)	30,000	90.00	115.00	175.00	250.00	300.00	800.00	900.00
1868S	96,000	55.00	75.00	120.00	200.00	475.00	2,500	
1869 (600)	16,600	175.00	225.00	325.00	450.00	700.00	1,500	900.00
1869S	76,000	60.00	90.00	150.00	225.00	475.00	2,400	
1870 (1,000)	87,400	40.00	55.00	85.00	150.00	250.00	800.00	900.00
1870CC	8,340	1,600	2,700	5,200	9,000	15,000	—	
1871 (960)	119,160	25.00	35.00	50.00	100.00	150.00	650.00	800.00
1871CC	10,890	1,100	2,100	3,200	6,500	12,000	—	
1871S	30,900	225.00	325.00	400.00	550.00	850.00	2,750	
1872 (950)	182,950	20.00	30.00	50.00	80.00	140.00	775.00	800.00

QUARTER DOLLARS

	Quan. Minted	G-4	VG-8	F-12	VF-20	EF 40	MS-60	Proof-63
1872CC	22,850	$325.00	$500.00	$1,000	$2,000	$3,500	$11,000	
1872S	83,000	350.00	550.00	1,000	1,400	1,800	7,500	
1873 Cl. 3 (600)	40,600	75.00	150.00	225.00	350.00	500.00	1,800	$800.00
1873 Open 3	172,000	20.00	30.00	50.00	75.00	175.00	500.00	
1873CC	4,000	*5 known*				—	150,000	

Variety 5 — Arrows at Date 1873-1874

Arrows were placed at the date in the years 1873 and 1874 to denote the change of weight from 6.22 to 6.25 grams.

Weight 6.25 grams; composition: .900 silver, .100 copper; diameter 24.3 mm; reeded edge; mints: Philadelphia, San Francisco, Carson City, New Orleans.

	Quan. Minted	G-4	VG-8	F-12	VF-20	EF 40	MS-60	Proof-63
1873 .....(540)	1,271,700	13.00	16.00	25.00	60.00	200.00	750.00	1,400
1873CC	12,462	1,300	2,200	4,500	6,750	11,000	30,000	
1873S	156,000	18.00	25.00	50.00	75.00	250.00	1,100	
1874 .....(700)	471,900	13.00	18.00	30.00	65.00	200.00	750.00	1,400
1874S	392,000	18.00	25.00	50.00	75.00	250.00	850.00	

Variety 4 Resumed 1875-1891

1877S, S over horizontal S

	Quan. Minted	G-4	VG-8	F-12	VF-20	EF 40	MS-60	Proof-63
1875 .....(700)	4,293,500	12.00	14.00	20.00	25.00	45.00	250.00	600.00
1875CC	140,000	50.00	75.00	125.00	225.00	450.00	1,500	
1875S	680,000	22.00	35.00	55.00	100.00	175.00	600.00	
1876 ..(1,150)	17,817,150	12.00	14.00	20.00	25.00	45.00	250.00	600.00
1876CC*	4,944,000	12.00	15.00	24.00	35.00	60.00	425.00	
1876S	8,596,000	12.00	14.00	20.00	25.00	45.00	250.00	
1877 .....(510)	10,911,710	12.00	14.00	20.00	25.00	45.00	250.00	600.00
1877CC	4,192,000	12.00	15.00	22.00	35.00	65.00	425.00	
1877S	8,996,000	12.00	14.00	20.00	25.00	45.00	250.00	
1877S over horizontal S		—	—	60.00	135.00	225.00	700.00	
1878 .....(800)	2,260,800	12.00	14.00	20.00	25.00	45.00	250.00	600.00
1878CC	996,000	15.00	25.00	40.00	65.00	100.00	500.00	
1878S	140,000	75.00	125.00	185.00	250.00	400.00	1,300	
1879 ..(1,100)	14,700	110.00	125.00	185.00	215.00	290.00	550.00	600.00
1880 ..(1,355)	14,955	110.00	125.00	185.00	215.00	290.00	550.00	600.00
1881 .....(975)	12,975	140.00	165.00	230.00	265.00	310.00	550.00	600.00

*Variety with fine edge reeding is scarcer than that with normally spaced reeding.

QUARTER DOLLARS

	Quan. Minted	G-4	VG-8	F-12	VF-20	EF-40	MS-60	Proof-63
1882 ....(1,100)	16,300	$120.00	$140.00	$200.00	$265.00	$310.00	$575.00	$600.00
1883 ....(1,039)	15,439	115.00	135.00	210.00	265.00	310.00	550.00	600.00
1884 ....(875)	8,875	210.00	250.00	275.00	325.00	350.00	675.00	700.00
1885 ....(930)	14,530	115.00	135.00	200.00	265.00	310.00	600.00	600.00
1886 ....(886)	5,886	240.00	300.00	400.00	450.00	600.00	825.00	700.00
1887 ....(710)	10,710	150.00	200.00	300.00	350.00	400.00	650.00	600.00
1888 ....(832)	10,833	150.00	200.00	300.00	350.00	400.00	650.00	600.00
1888S..............	1,216,000	12.00	14.00	20.00	25.00	45.00	250.00	
1889 ....(711)	12,711	120.00	140.00	200.00	265.00	310.00	600.00	800.00
1890 ....(590)	80,590	50.00	55.00	95.00	115.00	175.00	500.00	650.00
1891 ....(600)	3,920,600	12.00	14.00	20.00	25.00	45.00	250.00	600.00
1891O.............	68,000	120.00	160.00	275.00	425.00	750.00	2,750	
1891S..............	2,216,000	12.00	14.00	22.00	32.00	55.00	300.00	

BARBER or LIBERTY HEAD TYPE 1892-1916

Like other silver coins of this type, the quarter dollars minted from 1892 to 1916
were designed by Charles E. Barber. His initial B is found at the truncation of
the neck of Liberty. There are two varieties of the 1892 reverse: 1) Eagle's wing
covers only half of E in UNITED. 2) Eagle's wing covers most of E. Coins of the
first variety reverse are somewhat scarcer than those of the second variety.

Designer Charles E. Barber; weight 6.25 grams; composition: .900 silver, .100 copper; diameter 24.3
mm; reeded edge; mints: Philadelphia, Denver, New Orleans, San Francisco. Net weight: .18084 oz.
pure silver.

GOOD—Date and legends readable. LIBERTY worn off headband.
VG-8 VERY GOOD—Minimum of 3 letters in LIBERTY readable.
F-12 FINE—LIBERTY completely readable but not sharp.
VF-20 VERY FINE—All letters in LIBERTY evenly plain.
EF-40 EXTREMELY FINE—LIBERTY bold, and its ribbon distinct.
MS-60 UNCIRCULATED—No trace of wear. Light blemishes.

Mint mark location is on the reverse below the eagle.

	Quan. Minted	G-4	VG-8	F-12	VF-20	EF-40	MS-60	Proof-63
1892 .....(1,245)	8,237,245	$4.00	$6.00	$18.00	$26.00	$65.00	$175.00	$600.00
1892O	2,640,000	5.00	8.00	20.00	30.00	70.00	250.00	
1892S	964,079	14.00	25.00	40.00	55.00	125.00	400.00	
1893 ....(792)	5,444,815	4.00	6.00	17.00	26.00	65.00	200.00	600.00
1893O	3,396,000	4.50	7.00	25.00	35.00	75.00	250.00	
1893S	1,454,535	5.00	10.00	32.00	55.00	100.00	400.00	
1894 ....(972)	3,432,972	4.00	6.00	22.00	32.00	65.00	200.00	600.00
1894O	2,852,000	4.50	7.00	27.00	40.00	80.00	300.00	
1894S	2,648,821	4.50	7.00	27.00	40.00	80.00	300.00	
1895 ....(880)	4,440,880	4.00	6.00	22.00	30.00	70.00	200.00	600.00
1895O	2,816,000	4.50	7.00	30.00	40.00	85.00	325.00	
1895S	1,764,681	6.00	11.00	35.00	50.00	100.00	325.00	
1896 ....(762)	3,874,762	4.00	6.00	22.00	30.00	70.00	210.00	600.00
1896O	1,484,000	5.00	10.00	50.00	185.00	300.00	750.00	
1896S	188,039	275.00	450.00	650.00	950.00	1,700	4,000	
1897 ....(731)	8,140,731	4.00	6.00	17.00	26.00	65.00	160.00	600.00
1897O	1,414,800	7.00	12.00	65.00	165.00	340.00	750.00	

QUARTER DOLLARS

	Quan. Minted	G-4	VG-8	F-12	VF-20	EF-40	MS-60	Proof-63
1897S	542,229	$15.00	$30.00	$125.00	$175.00	$300.00	$900.00	
1898....(735)	11,100,735	3.75	5.00	17.00	28.00	65.00	160.00	$600.00
1898O	1,868,000	5.00	9.00	45.00	80.00	175.00	550.00	
1898S	1,020,592	4.50	9.00	30.00	40.00	80.00	400.00	
1899....(846)	12,624,846	3.75	5.00	20.00	30.00	70.00	160.00	600.00
1899O	2,644,000	6.00	11.00	25.00	40.00	85.00	375.00	
1899S	708,000	7.50	15.00	27.00	50.00	85.00	400.00	
1900....(912)	10,016,912	3.25	5.00	18.00	27.00	70.00	160.00	600.00
1900O	3,416,000	6.00	12.00	45.00	70.00	120.00	500.00	
1900S	1,858,585	4.50	8.00	20.00	32.00	70.00	350.00	
1901....(813)	8,892,813	3.25	5.00	17.00	25.00	65.00	160.00	600.00
1901O	1,612,000	20.00	40.00	75.00	160.00	350.00	750.00	
1901S	72,664	1,750	3,000	4,500	5,750	7,500	14,500	
1902....(777)	12,197,744	3.25	5.00	17.00	28.00	65.00	160.00	600.00
1902O	4,748,000	4.50	6.00	22.00	40.00	85.00	400.00	
1902S	1,524,612	8.00	10.00	25.00	45.00	85.00	450.00	
1903....(755)	9,670,064	3.25	5.00	17.00	26.00	65.00	160.00	600.00
1903O	3,500,000	4.00	7.00	25.00	40.00	85.00	375.00	
1903S	1,036,000	8.00	12.00	35.00	55.00	100.00	425.00	
1904....(670)	9,588,813	3.25	5.00	17.00	26.00	60.00	160.00	600.00
1904O	2,456,000	4.50	8.00	35.00	60.00	175.00	700.00	
1905....(727)	4,968,250	3.25	6.00	17.00	26.00	60.00	160.00	600.00
1905O	1,230,000	8.00	13.00	55.00	90.00	175.00	425.00	
1905S	1,884,000	6.00	9.00	25.00	40.00	85.00	300.00	
1906....(675)	3,656,435	3.25	5.00	17.00	28.00	65.00	160.00	600.00
1906D	3,280,000	3.25	6.00	20.00	32.00	70.00	220.00	
1906O	2,056,000	3.75	6.00	24.00	35.00	80.00	250.00	
1907....(575)	7,192,575	3.25	5.00	17.00	27.00	65.00	160.00	600.00
1907D	2,484,000	3.25	5.00	20.00	32.00	75.00	250.00	
1907O	4,560,000	3.25	5.00	20.00	30.00	65.00	220.00	
1907S	1,360,000	4.00	6.00	30.00	40.00	100.00	400.00	
1908....(545)	4,232,545	3.25	5.00	20.00	30.00	60.00	160.00	600.00
1908D	5,788,000	3.25	5.00	20.00	30.00	65.00	200.00	
1908O	6,244,000	3.25	5.00	17.00	29.00	60.00	200.00	
1908S	784,000	8.00	15.00	55.00	100.00	220.00	650.00	
1909....(650)	9,268,650	3.25	5.00	20.00	28.00	60.00	160.00	600.00
1909D	5,114,000	3.25	5.00	17.00	28.00	70.00	200.00	
1909O	712,000	10.00	16.00	55.00	120.00	210.00	700.00	
1909S	1,348,000	3.75	6.00	22.00	35.00	75.00	300.00	
1910....(551)	2,244,551	3.25	5.00	20.00	30.00	65.00	160.00	600.00
1910D	1,500,000	3.25	6.00	22.00	35.00	85.00	350.00	
1911....(543)	3,720,543	3.25	5.00	17.00	25.00	60.00	160.00	600.00
1911D	933,600	3.25	8.00	75.00	175.00	275.00	650.00	
1911S	988,000	3.25	5.00	28.00	40.00	110.00	350.00	
1912....(700)	4,400,700	3.25	5.00	17.00	25.00	65.00	160.00	600.00
1912S	708,000	3.25	5.00	27.00	40.00	90.00	350.00	
1913....(613)	484,613	10.00	14.00	55.00	140.00	400.00	950.00	750.00
1913D	1,450,800	3.25	5.00	17.00	30.00	80.00	230.00	
1913S	40,000	435.00	700.00	1,800	2,900	3,400	4,750	
1914....(380)	6,244,610	3.25	5.00	17.00	30.00	65.00	160.00	750.00
1914D	3,046,000	3.25	5.00	17.00	30.00	65.00	170.00	
1914S	264,000	50.00	80.00	125.00	175.00	375.00	800.00	
1915....(450)	3,480,450	3.25	5.00	17.00	30.00	65.00	160.00	750.00
1915D	3,694,000	3.25	5.00	17.00	30.00	65.00	160.00	
1915S	704,000	3.75	6.00	17.00	35.00	75.00	250.00	
1916	1,788,000	3.25	5.00	17.00	30.00	65.00	150.00	
1916D	6,540,800	3.25	5.00	17.00	30.00	65.00	150.00	

QUARTER DOLLARS
STANDING LIBERTY TYPE 1916-1930

This type quarter was designed by Hermon A. MacNeil. The left arm of Liberty is upraised uncovering a shield in the attitude of protection. Her right hand bears the olive branch of peace. MacNeil's initial M is located above and to the right of the date.

There was a modification in 1917 because of public resentment to Liberty's exposed breast. The reverse has a new arrangement of the stars and the eagle is higher.

In 1925 a depression was made in the pedestal on which Liberty stands and which bears the date. On the earlier issues the dates wore off easily because they were too high and were not protected by other features of the coin. The new "recessed" dates proved more durable as a result of this change.

No proof coins of this type were officially issued, but specimen strikings of the first variety, dated 1917, are known to exist.

Designer Hermon A. MacNeil. Standards same as previous issue; mints: Philadelphia, Denver, San Francisco.

G-4 GOOD—*Date and lettering readable. Top of date worn. Liberty's right leg and toes worn off. Left leg and drapery lines show much wear.*
VG-8 VERY GOOD—*Distinct date. Toes show faintly. Drapery lines visible above her left leg.*
F-12 FINE—*High curve of right leg flat from thigh to ankle. Left leg shows only slight wear. Drapery lines over right thigh seen only at sides of leg.*
VF-20 VERY FINE—*Garment line across right leg will be worn but show at sides.*
EF-40 EXTREMELY FINE—*Flattened only at high spots. Her toes are sharp. Drapery lines across right leg are evident.*
MS-63 SELECT UNCIRCULATED—*No trace of wear. Light blemishes. Attractive mint luster.*

(Some modifications must be made for grading variety 2.)

Uncirculated pieces with fully struck head of Liberty are worth more than double the prices listed below.

Mint mark location is on obverse at left of date.

Variety 1

No Stars Below Eagle

	Quan. Minted	G-4	VG-8	F-12	VF-20	EF-40	MS-63
1916	52,000	$1,400	$1,900	$2,600	$3,400	$3,750	$7,500
1917 Variety 1	8,740,000	13.00	16.00	27.00	35.00	60.00	275.00
1917D Variety 1	1,509,200	16.00	18.00	30.00	50.00	85.00	350.00
1917S Variety 1	1,952,000	16.00	20.00	32.00	55.00	130.00	400.00

Variety 2

1918S, 8 over 7

Stars Below Eagle

1917 Variety 2	13,880,000	13.00	16.00	20.00	27.50	45.00	200.00
1917D Variety 2	6,224,400	25.00	30.00	47.00	65.00	90.00	275.00
1917S Variety 2	5,552,000	21.00	25.00	40.00	52.00	75.00	260.00
1918	14,240,000	14.00	17.00	25.00	32.00	45.00	180.00

QUARTER DOLLARS

	Quan. Minted	G-4	VG-8	F-12	VF-20	EF-40	MS-63
1918D	7,380,000	$20.00	$28.00	$40.00	$55.00	$80.00	$375.00
1918S Norm. date	} 11,072,000	16.00	18.00	25.00	28.00	45.00	300.00
1918S, 8 over 7		1,100	1,500	2,000	2,500	4,500	22,000
1919	11,324,000	25.00	35.00	45.00	50.00	65.00	200.00
1919D	1,944,000	60.00	80.00	120.00	200.00	300.00	1,250
1919S	1,836,000	60.00	80.00	120.00	225.00	375.00	1,600
1920	27,860,000	13.00	15.00	20.00	25.00	35.00	195.00
1920D	3,586,400	30.00	40.00	65.00	90.00	115.00	600.00
1920S	6,380,000	20.00	23.00	28.00	35.00	50.00	700.00
1921	1,916,000	70.00	100.00	150.00	200.00	285.00	800.00
1923	9,716,000	13.00	16.00	23.00	30.00	40.00	200.00
1923S	1,360,000	160.00	210.00	300.00	375.00	475.00	900.00
1924	10,920,000	15.00	17.00	23.00	27.00	35.00	175.00
1924D	3,112,000	40.00	55.00	65.00	80.00	100.00	225.00
1924S	2,860,000	20.00	25.00	30.00	38.00	90.00	850.00

Recessed Date Style 1925-1930

1925	12,280,000	2.50	3.50	6.00	18.00	29.00	175.00
1926	11,316,000	2.50	3.50	6.00	18.00	29.00	175.00
1926D	1,716,000	6.00	9.00	15.00	22.00	50.00	185.00
1926S	2,700,000	3.00	5.00	11.00	21.00	90.00	650.00
1927	11,912,000	2.50	3.50	6.00	14.00	25.00	175.00
1927D	976,000	5.00	8.00	14.00	35.00	80.00	220.00
1927S	396,000	9.00	15.00	50.00	150.00	1,000	5,500
1928	6,336,000	2.50	3.50	6.00	14.00	25.00	185.00
1928D	1,627,600	4.00	7.00	10.00	18.00	35.00	185.00
1928S*	2,644,000	4.00	5.00	8.00	17.00	31.00	185.00
1929	11,140,000	2.50	3.50	6.00	14.00	25.00	175.00
1929D	1,358,000	5.00	8.00	10.00	17.00	35.00	185.00
1929S	1,764,000	2.50	5.00	6.00	14.00	30.00	185.00
1930	5,632,000	2.50	3.50	6.00	14.00	25.00	175.00
1930S	1,556,000	2.50	3.50	6.00	14.00	25.00	200.00

*Large and small mint mark varieties, see page 67.

WASHINGTON TYPE 1932 to Date

This type was intended to be a commemorative issue marking the two-hundredth anniversary of Washington's birth. John Flanagan, a New York sculptor, was the designer; his initials, JF, can be found at the base of Washington's neck. The mint mark is on the reverse below wreath, 1932 to 1964.

Weight 6.25 grams; composition: .900 silver, .100 copper; diameter 24.3 mm; reeded edge. Net weight: .18084 oz. pure silver; mints: Philadelphia, Denver, San Francisco.

VG-8 VERY GOOD—Wing tips outlined. Rims are fine and even. Tops of letters at rim are flattened.
F-12 FINE—Hairlines about ear are visible. Tiny feathers on eagle's breast are faintly visible.
VF-20 VERY FINE—Most hair details show. Wing feathers are clear.
EF-40 EXTREMELY FINE—Hairlines sharp. Wear spots confined to top of eagle's legs and center of breast.
MS-63 SELECT UNCIRCULATED—No trace of wear. Light blemishes. Attractive mint luster.
MS-65 CHOICE UNCIRCULATED—No trace of wear. Barely noticeable blemishes.

1934 Doubled Die

[145]

QUARTER DOLLARS
Silver Coinage — 1932-1964

	Quan. Minted	VG-8	F-12	VF-20	EF-40	MS-63	MS-65
1932	5,404,000	$3.00	$4.00	$6.00	$8.00	$35.00	$250.00
1932D	436,800	60.00	70.00	100.00	175.00	1,500	8,500
1932S	408,000	60.00	65.00	80.00	90.00	600.00	3,500
1934 Light motto	} 31,912,052	*1.75*	2.50	3.50	6.00	34.00	130.00
1934 Hvy. motto		*1.75*	2.50	3.50	6.00	30.00	100.00
1934 Doubled die			60.00	95.00	140.00	600.00	2,100
1934D	3,527,200	3.00	4.00	8.00	11.00	260.00	1,100
1935	32,484,000	*1.75*	2.00	3.00	5.00	30.00	75.00
1935D	5,780,000	3.00	4.00	8.00	15.00	250.00	500.00
1935S	5,660,000	2.25	3.00	5.00	10.00	90.00	200.00

1937 Doubled Die Obverse	**1942D Doubled Die Obverse**	**1943 Doubled Die Obverse**

	Quan. Minted	VF-20	EF-40	MS-63	MS-65	Proof-65
1936	(3,837) 41,303,837	$2.25	$4.00	$25.00	$60.00	$900.00
1936D	5,374,000	15.00	40.00	400.00	750.00	
1936S	3,828,000	6.00	10.00	75.00	150.00	
1937	(5,542) 19,701,542	2.25	4.00	25.00	75.00	400.00
1937 Doubled die obverse		125.00	250.00	475.00	1,800	
1937D	7,189,600	6.00	8.00	50.00	120.00	
1937S	1,652,000	11.00	18.00	130.00	225.00	
1938	(8,045) 9,480,045	10.00	14.00	70.00	140.00	250.00
1938S	2,832,000	8.00	12.00	65.00	130.00	
1939	(8,795) 33,548,795	2.25	3.00	22.00	55.00	175.00
1939D	7,092,000	5.00	8.00	40.00	90.00	
1939S	2,628,000	6.00	10.00	80.00	140.00	
1940	(11,246) 35,715,246	2.00	3.00	16.00	40.00	165.00
1940D	2,797,600	6.00	13.00	70.00	140.00	
1940S	8,244,000	2.00	3.50	20.00	45.00	
1941	(15,287) 79,047,287	*1.50*	2.00	10.00	40.00	125.00
1941D	16,714,800	*1.50*	3.00	30.00	50.00	
1941S*	16,080,000	*1.50*	3.00	30.00	75.00	
1942	(21,123) 102,117,123	*1.50*	2.00	6.00	35.00	125.00
1942D	17,487,200	*1.50*	3.00	20.00	45.00	
1942D Doubled die obverse		275.00	375.00	1,500	—	
1942S	19,384,000	2.00	6.00	65.00	120.00	
1943	99,700,000	*1.50*	2.00	7.00	30.00	
1943 Doubled die obverse		150.00	225.00	800.00	—	
1943D	16,095,600	*1.50*	3.00	20.00	35.00	
1943S	21,700,000	*1.50*	3.00	30.00	50.00	
1943S Doubled die obverse		100.00	150.00	600.00	1,500	
1944	104,956,000	*1.50*	*1.75*	6.00	30.00	
1944D	14,600,800	*1.50*	2.00	13.00	32.00	
1944S	12,560,000	*1.50*	2.00	13.00	35.00	
1945	74,372,000	*1.50*	*1.75*	5.00	25.00	
1945D	12,341,600	*1.50*	*1.75*	14.00	40.00	
1945S	17,004,001	*1.50*	*1.75*	8.00	30.00	
1946	53,436,000	*1.50*	*1.75*	6.00	30.00	
1946D	9,072,800	*1.50*	*1.75*	6.00	25.00	
1946S	4,204,000	*1.50*	*1.75*	6.00	35.00	
1947	22,556,000	*1.50*	*1.75*	8.00	25.00	
1947D	15,338,400	*1.50*	*1.75*	7.00	25.00	
1947S	5,532,000	*1.50*	*1.75*	8.00	35.00	
1948	35,196,000	*1.50*	*1.75*	5.00	22.00	

*Large and small mint mark varieties, see page 67.

QUARTER DOLLARS

	Quan. Minted	VF-20	EF-40	MS-63	MS-65	Proof-65
1948D	16,766,800	$1.50	$1.75	$6.00	$25.00	
1948S	15,960,000	1.50	1.75	6.00	35.00	
1949	9,312,000	1.50	2.00	25.00	40.00	
1949D	10,068,400	1.50	1.75	15.00	35.00	
1950 ....(51,386)	24,971,512	1.50	1.75	6.00	10.00	$55.00
1950D	} 21,075,600	1.50	1.75	5.00	12.00	
1950D, D over S		70.00	125.00	300.00	525.00	
1950S	} 10,284,004	1.50	1.75	10.00	20.00	
1950S, S over D		90.00	150.00	400.00	700.00	
1951........(57,500)	43,505,602	1.50	1.75	6.00	11.00	40.00
1951D	35,354,800	1.50	1.75	5.00	10.00	
1951S	9,048,000	1.50	1.75	18.00	32.00	
1952........(81,980)	38,862,073	1.50	1.75	4.00	12.00	30.00
1952D	49,795,200	1.50	1.75	4.00	12.00	
1952S	13,707,800	1.50	1.75	12.00	25.00	
1953....(128,800)	18,664,920	1.50	1.75	5.00	12.00	23.00
1953D	56,112,400	1.50	1.75	5.00	12.00	
1953S	14,016,000	1.50	1.75	5.00	13.00	
1954........(233,300)	54,645,503	1.50	1.75	4.00	10.00	17.00
1954D	42,305,500	1.50	1.75	4.00	10.00	
1954S	11,834,722	1.50	1.75	4.00	10.00	
1955........(378,200)	18,558,381	1.50	1.75	4.00	10.00	13.00
1955D	3,182,400	1.50	1.75	2.50	7.00	
1956........(669,384)	44,813,384	1.50	1.75	3.00	6.00	6.00
1956D	32,334,500	1.50	1.75	4.00	7.00	
1957......(1,247,952)	47,779,952	1.50	1.75	4.00	7.00	4.50
1957D	77,924,160	1.50	1.75	3.00	6.00	
1958........(875,652)	7,235,652	1.50	1.75	2.50	6.00	5.00
1958D	78,124,900	1.50	1.75	2.50	6.00	
1959......(1,149,291)	25,533,291	1.50	1.75	3.00	7.00	3.50
1959D	62,054,232	1.50	1.75	2.50	6.00	
1960......(1,691,602)	30,855,602	1.50	1.75	2.50	6.00	3.50
1960D	63,000,324	1.50	1.75	2.50	6.00	
1961......(3,028,244)	40,064,244	1.50	1.75	2.50	6.00	3.50
1961D	83,656,928	1.50	1.75	2.50	6.00	
1962......(3,218,019)	39,374,019	1.50	1.75	2.50	6.00	3.50
1962D	127,554,756	1.50	1.75	2.50	6.00	
1963......(3,075,645)	77,391,645	1.50	1.75	2.50	6.00	3.50
1963D	135,288,184	1.50	1.75	2.50	6.00	
1964......(3,950,762)	564,341,347	1.50	1.75	2.50	6.00	3.50
1964D	704,135,528	1.50	1.75	2.50	6.00	

Clad Coinage — 1965 to Date

Proof coins from 1937 through 1972 were made from special dies with high relief and minor detail differences. Some of the circulation coins of 1956-1964 and 1969D-1972D were also made from reverse dies with these same features. A variety of the 1964D quarter occurs with the modified reverse normally found only on the clad coins.

Weight 5.67 grams; composition: outer layers of copper-nickel (.750 copper, .250 nickel) bonded to inner core of pure copper; diameter 24.3 mm; reeded edge.

Starting in 1968 mint mark is on obverse at right of ribbon.

QUARTER DOLLARS

	Quan. Minted	MS-65	Proof-65
1965	1,819,717,540	$1.00	
1966	821,101,500	1.00	
1967	1,524,031,848	1.00	
1968	220,731,500	1.00	
1968D	101,534,000	1.00	
1968S Proof	(3,041,506)		$1.50
1969	176,212,000	2.00	
1969D	114,372,000	1.50	
1969S Proof	(2,934,631)		1.50
1970	136,420,000	1.00	
1970D	417,341,364	1.00	
1970S Proof	(2,632,810)		1.50
1971	109,284,000	$1.00	
1971D	258,634,428	1.00	
1971S Proof	(3,220,733)		$1.50
1972	215,048,000	1.00	
1972D	311,067,732	1.00	
1972S Proof	(3,260,996)		1.50
1973	346,924,000	1.00	
1973D	232,977,400	1.00	
1973S Proof	(2,760,339)		1.50
1974	801,456,000	1.00	
1974D	353,160,300	1.00	
1974S Proof	(2,612,568)		1.50

Lightweight, thin quarters of 1970D were struck on metal intended for dimes.

BICENTENNIAL COINAGE DATED 1776-1976

In October of 1973, the Treasury announced an open contest for the selection of suitable designs for the Bicentennial reverses of the quarter, half dollar and dollar, with $5,000 to be awarded to each winner. Twelve semifinalists were chosen, and from these the symbolic entry of Jack L. Ahr was selected for the quarter reverse. It features a Colonial drummer facing left, with a victory torch encircled by thirteen stars at the upper left. Except for the dual dating, 1776-1976, the obverse remained unchanged. Only pieces with this dual dating were coined during 1975 and 1976. They were struck for general circulation and included in all the mint's offerings of proof and uncirculated sets.

Designers John Flanagan and Jack L. Ahr. Silver issue: weight 5.75 grams; composition: outer layers of .800 silver, .200 copper bonded to inner core of .209 silver, .791 copper. Copper-nickel issue: weight 5.67 grams; composition: outer layers of .750 copper, .250 nickel bonded to inner core of pure copper. Diameter 24.3 mm; reeded edge. Net weight of silver issues: .0739 oz. pure silver.

	Quan. Minted	MS-65	Proof-65
1776-1976 Copper-nickel clad	809,784,016	$1.00	
1776-1976D Copper-nickel clad	860,118,839	1.00	
1776-1976S Copper-nickel clad	(7,059,099)		$1.25
1776-1976S Silver clad	*11,000,000	2.25	
1776-1976S Silver clad	(*4,000,000)		3.00

*Approximate mintage.

Eagle Reverse Resumed (Dies slightly modified to lower relief)

	Quan. Minted	MS-65	Proof-65
1977	468,556,000	$1.00	
1977D	256,524,978	1.00	
1977S Proof	(3,251,152)		$1.25
1978	521,452,000	1.00	
1978D	287,373,152	1.00	
1978S Proof	(3,127,781)		1.25
1979	515,708,000	1.00	
1979D	489,789,780	1.00	
1979S Proof	(3,677,175)		
Filled S			$1.25
Clear S			1.75
1980P	635,832,000	$1.00	
1980D	518,327,487	1.00	
1980S Proof	(3,554,806)		1.25
1981P	601,716,000	1.00	
1981D	575,722,833	1.00	

QUARTER DOLLARS

	Quan. Minted	MS-65	Proof-65
1981S Proof..(4,063,083)			$2.00
1982P..........500,931,000		$4.00	
1982D 480,042,788		3.00	
1982S Proof..(3,857,479)			2.00
1983P..........673,535,000		15.00	
1983D 617,806,446		9.00	
1983S Proof..(3,279,126)			2.00
1984P..........676,545,000		1.50	
1984D 546,483,064		2.00	
1984S Proof..(3,065,110)			2.50
1985P..........775,818,962		2.50	
1985D 519,962,888		2.25	
1985S Proof..(3,362,821)			2.00
1986P..........551,199,333		3.50	
1986D 504,298,660		4.00	
1986S Proof..(3,010,497)			3.00
1987P..........582,499,481		1.00	
1987D 655,594,696		1.00	
1987S Proof..(4,227,728)			2.00
1988P..........562,052,000		1.25	
1988D 596,810,688		1.00	
1988S Proof..(3,262,948)			2.25
1989P..........512,868,000		1.00	
1989D 896,535,597		1.00	
1989S Proof..(3,220,194)			2.25
1990P..........613,792,000		1.00	
1990D 927,638,181		1.00	
1990S Proof..(3,299,559)			3.00
1991P..........570,968,000		1.00	
1991D 630,966,693		1.00	
1991S Proof..(2,867,787)			3.00

	Quan. Minted	MS-65	Proof-65
1992P..........384,764,000		$1.00	
1992D 389,777,107		1.50	
1992S Proof..(2,858,981)			$3.00
1992S Silver Proof........(1,317,579)			5.00
1993P..........639,276,000		1.00	
1993D 645,476,128		1.00	
1993S Proof..(2,633,439)			7.00
1993S Silver Proof...........(761,353)			7.00
1994P..........825,600,000		1.00	
1994D 880,034,110		1.00	
1994S Proof..(2,484,594)			3.00
1994S Silver Proof...........(785,329)			5.00
1995P.......1,004,336,000		1.00	
1995D 1,103,216,000		1.00	
1995S Proof..(2,117,496)			15.00
1995S Silver Proof...........(679,985)			13.00
1996P..........925,040,000		1.00	
1996D 906,868,000		1.00	
1996S Proof..(1,750,244)			3.00
1996S Silver Proof...........(775,021)			8.00
1997P..........595,740,000		1.00	
1997D 599,680,000		1.00	
1997S Proof..(2,055,000)			7.00
1997S Silver Proof...........(741,678)			15.00
1998P 896,268,000		1.00	
1998D 821,000,000		1.00	
1998S Proof....................			8.00
1998S Silver Proof...........(878,792)			9.00

STATEHOOD QUARTER DOLLARS — 1999-

The United States Mint 50 State Quarters Program begun in 1999 will produce a series of 50 quarter dollar coins with special designs honoring each state. Five different designs will be issued each year during the period 1999-2008. States are being commemorated in the order of their entrance into statehood.

These are all legal tender coins of standard weight and composition. The obverse side depicting President George Washington has been modified slightly to include some of the wording previously used on the reverse. The modification was authorized by special legislation, and carried out by Mint Sculptor-Engraver William Cousins, whose initials have been added to the truncation of Washington's neck adjacent to those of the original designer, John Flanagan.

Each state theme is being proposed, and approved, by the governor of the state. Final designs will be created by mint personnel.

Circulation coins are made at the Philadelphia and Denver mints. Proof coins are made in San Francisco.

Weight 5.67 grams; composition: outer layers of copper-nickel (.750 copper, .250 nickel) bonded to inner core of pure copper; diameter 24.3 mm reeded edge. Silver Proof: pre-1965 standards.

QUARTER DOLLARS
Statehood Quarters

	Quan. Minted	AU-50	MS-63	MS-65	Proof-65
1999P Delaware 373,400,000		$.50	$1.25	$3.00	
1999D Delaware 401,424,000		.50	1.25	3.00	
1999S Delaware Proof					$5.00
1999S Delaware Silver Proof	(800,000)				10.00
1999P Pennsylvania 349,000,000		.50	1.50	4.00	
1999D Pennsylvania 358,332,000		.50	1.25	3.00	
1999S Pennsylvania Proof........					5.00
1999S Pennsylvania Silver Proof ..	(800,000)				10.00

1999P New Jersey 363,200,000		.40	.75	1.50	
1999D New Jersey 299,028,000		.45	1.00	3.00	
1999S New Jersey Proof					5.00
1999S New Jersey Silver Proof....	(800,000)				10.00
1999P Georgia 451,188,000		.40	.75	1.25	
1999D Georgia 488,744,000		.40	.75	1.25	
1999S Georgia Proof					5.00
1999S Georgia Silver Proof	(800,000)				10.00
1999P Connecticut 688,744,000		.35	.60	1.00	
1999D Connecticut 657,880,000		.35	.60	1.00	
1999S Connecticut Proof					5.00
1999S Connecticut Silver Proof ...	(800,000)				10.00
2000P Massachusetts 628,600,000		.35	.60	1.00	
2000D Massachusetts 535,184,000		.35	.60	1.00	
2000S Massachusetts Proof	(937,600)				5.00
2000S Massachusetts Silver Proof .	(856,400)				8.00
2000P Maryland 678,200,000		.35	.60	1.00	
2000D Maryland 556,532,000		.35	.60	1.00	
2000S Maryland Proof	(937,600)				5.00
2000S Maryland Silver Proof	(856,400)				8.00
2000P South Carolina 742,576,000		.35	.60	1.00	
2000D South Carolina 566,208,000		.35	.60	1.00	
2000S South Carolina Proof	(937,600)				5.00
2000S South Carolina Silver Proof .	(856,400)				8.00

QUARTER DOLLARS

	Quan. Minted	AU-50	MS-63	MS-65	Proof-65
2000P New Hampshire 673,040,000		$.35	$.50	$1.00	
2000D New Hampshire 495,976,000		.35	.50	1.00	
2000S New Hampshire Proof ..... (937,600)					$5.00
2000S New Hampshire Silver Proof (856,400)					8.00
2000P Virginia 943,000,000		.35	.50	1.00	
2000D Virginia 651,616,000		.35	.50	1.00	
2000S Virginia Proof .... (937,600)					5.00
2000S Virginia Silver Proof .... (856,400)					8.00
2001P New York 655,400,000		.35	.50	1.00	
2001D New York 619,640,000		.35	.50	1.00	
2001S New York Proof...........					5.00
2001S New York Silver Proof					8.00
2001P North Carolina 627,600,000		.35	.50	1.00	
2001D North Carolina 427,876,000		.35	.50	1.00	
2001S North Carolina Proof					5.00
2001S North Carolina Silver Proof .					8.00
2001P Rhode Island 423,000,000		.35	.50	1.00	
2001D Rhode Island 447,100,000		.35	.50	1.00	
2001S Rhode Island Proof					5.00
2001S Rhode Island Silver Proof ..					8.00
2001P Vermont 423,400,000		.35	.50	1.00	
2001D Vermont 459,404,000		.35	.50	1.00	
2001S Vermont Proof...........					5.00
2001S Vermont Silver Proof					8.00
2001P Kentucky 353,000,000		.35	.50	1.00	
2001D Kentucky 370,564,000		.35	.50	1.00	
2001S Kentucky Proof					5.00
2001S Kentucky Silver Proof					8.00
2002P Tennessee		.35	.50	1.00	
2002D Tennessee		.35	.50	1.00	
2002S Tennessee Proof					5.00
2002S Tennessee Silver Proof					8.00
2002P Ohio		.35	.50	1.00	
2002D Ohio		.35	.50	1.00	
2002S Ohio Proof					5.00
2002S Ohio Silver Proof					8.00
2002P Louisiana		.35	.50	1.00	
2002D Louisiana		.35	.50	1.00	
2002S Louisiana Proof...........					5.00
2002S Louisiana Silver Proof					8.00
2002P Indiana		.35	.50	1.00	
2002D Indiana		.35	.50	1.00	
2002S Indiana Proof					5.00
2002S Indiana Silver Proof					8.00
2002P Mississippi		.35	.50	1.00	
2002D Mississippi		.35	.50	1.00	
2002S Mississippi Proof					5.00
2002S Mississippi Silver Proof					8.00

QUARTER DOLLARS

2003 Illinois
2003 Alabama
2003 Maine
2003 Missouri
2003 Arkansas

2004 Michigan
2004 Florida
2004 Texas
2004 Iowa
2004 Wisconsin

2005 California
2005 Minnesota
2005 Oregon
2005 Kansas
2005 West Virginia

2006 Nevada
2006 Nebraska
2006 Colorado
2006 North Dakota
2006 South Dakota

2007 Montana
2007 Washington
2007 Idaho
2007 Wyoming   .
2007 Utah

2008 Oklahoma
2008 New Mexico
2008 Arizona
2008 Alaska
2008 Hawaii

Some Statehood quarters were accidentally made with disoriented dies and are valued higher than ordinary pieces. Normal United States coins have dies oriented in "coin alignment," where the reverse appears upside down when the coin is rotated from right to left. Values for the rotated die quarters vary according to the amount of shifting. The most valuable are those that are shifted 180 degrees so that both sides appear upright when the coin is turned over (medal alignment).

QUARTER DOLLARS

BIBLIOGRAPHY

Briggs, Larry. *The Comprehensive Encyclopedia of United States Seated Quarters*. Lima, Ohio, 1991.
Browning, A. W. *The Early Quarter Dollars of the United States 1796-1838*. New York, 1925.
    (Reprinted 1992)
Cline, J. H. *Standing Liberty Quarters*. 3rd edition, 1996.
Duphorne, R. *The Early Quarter Dollars of The United States*. 1975.
Fivaz, Bill and Stanton, J.T. *The Cherrypickers' Guide to Rare Die Varieties*. Savannah, 1991.
Haseltine, J. W. *Type Table of United States Dollars, Half Dollars and Quarter Dollars*. Philadelphia,
    1881 (reprinted 1927, 1968).
Kelman, Keith N. *Standing Liberty Quarters*. N.H., 1976.
Lawrence, David. *The Complete Guide to Barber Quarters*. Virginia Beach, VA, 1989.

HALF DOLLARS — 1794 to Date

The half dollar, authorized by the Act of April 2, 1792, was not minted until December, 1794. The early types of this series have been extensively collected by die varieties, of which many exist for most dates. Valuations given below are in each case for the most common variety; scarcer ones as listed by Overton (see bibliography) generally command higher prices.

The weight of the half dollar was 208 grains and its fineness .8924 when first issued. This standard was not changed until 1837 when the law of January 18, 1837 specified 206¼ grains, .900 fine. This fineness continued in use until 1965.

Arrows at the date in 1853 indicate the reduction of weight to 192 grains, in conformity with the Act of February 21, 1853. During that year only, rays were added to the field on the reverse side to identify the lighter coins. Arrows remained in 1854 and 1855.

The 1866 proof quarter, half and dollar without motto are not mentioned in the Director's Report, and were not issued for circulation.

In 1873 the weight was raised by law to 192.9 grains and arrows were again placed at the date, to be removed in 1875.

+ or – indicates change from previous year	TYPE COIN VALUES									
	G-4	F-12	EF-40	AU-50	MS-60	MS-63	MS-65	PF-60	PF-63	PF-65
Flowing Hair 1794-1795	450.00	900.00	4,500	8,500	17,000	37,500	130,000			
Drpd. Bust, SE 1796-1797 ..	10,000	17,000	40,000-	58,000	95,000					
Drpd. Bust, HE 1801-1807 ..	130.00	225.00	625.00	2,000	4,750	11,000	45,000			
Cap Bust Type 1807-1836 ...	32.00	42.00	80.00	200.00	525.00	1,300	7,500			
Cap Bust, RE 1836-1839	32.00	42.00	125.00	375.00	800.00	2,000	13,000			
Lib. Seated-NM 1839-1866 .	16.00	33.00	75.00	150.00	400.00	900.00	5,500	475.00	900.00	5,500
Lib. Seated-A&R 1853	16.00	38.00	225.00	450.00	1,300	3,500	21,000			
Lib .Seat-Arr. 1854-1855	16.00	35.00	90.00	250.00	650.00	1,500	8,000			
Lib. Seat-WM 1866-1891	15.00	30.00	60.00	150.00	375.00	650.00-	3,250-	500.00	800.00	3,000
Lib. Seat-Arr. 1873-1874.....	21.00	38.00	225.00	450.00	850.00	2,000	17,500	900.00	2,000	10,000
Barber 1892-1915	6.00	25.00	125.00	275.00	385.00	750.00	3,000	475.00	700.00	3,000
Lib. Walking 1916-1947	3.00	3.50	6.00	12.00	25.00	40.00+	110.00	325.00	375.00	435.00
Franklin 1948-1963	2.00	2.00	3.50	3.75	5.00+	7.00+	40.00	8.00	9.00	18.00
Kennedy 1964 Silver		2.00	3.25	3.50	3.75	4.00	6.00			8.00

FLOWING HAIR TYPE 1794-1795

Designer Robert Scot; weight 13.48 grams; composition: .8924 silver, .1076 copper; approx. diameter 32.5 mm; edge: FIFTY CENTS OR HALF A DOLLAR with decorations between words.

AG-3 ABOUT GOOD—*Clear enough to identify.*
G-4 GOOD—*Date and letters sufficient to be readable. Main devices outlined, but lack details.*
VG-8 VERY GOOD—*Major details discernible. Letters well formed but worn.*
F-12 FINE—*Hair ends distinguishable. Top hairlines show, but otherwise worn smooth.*
VF-20 VERY FINE—*Hair in center shows some detail. Other details more bold.*
EF-40 EXTREMELY FINE—*Hair above head and down neck detailed, with slight wear.*

2 Leaves under Wings

	Quan. Minted	AG-3	G-4	VG-8	F-12	VF-20	EF-40
1794 23,464		$750.00	$1,100	$2,400	$3,200	$5,750	$12,500

HALF DOLLARS

	Quan. Minted	AG-3	G-4	VG-8	F-12	VF-20	EF-40
1795 All kinds	299,680	$225.00	$450.00	$600.00	$900.00	$1,800	$4,500
1795 Recut date		225.00	450.00	600.00	900.00	1,850	4,800
1795 3 leaves under each wing.		450.00	950.00	1,700	3,000	6,000	11,000

Varieties of 1795 are known with final S in STATES over D, with A in STATES over E, and with Y in LIBERTY over a star. All are scarce. Some 1795 half dollars were weight-adjusted by inserting a silver plug in the center of the blank planchet before striking the coin.

DRAPED BUST TYPE, SMALL EAGLE REVERSE 1796-1797

Designer Robert Scot; weight 13.48 grams; composition: .8924 silver, .1076 copper; approx. diameter 32.5 mm; edge: FIFTY CENTS OR HALF A DOLLAR with decorations between words.

AG-3 ABOUT GOOD—*Clear enough to identify.*
G-4 GOOD—*Date and letters sufficient to be readable. Main devices outlined, but lack details.*
VG-8 VERY GOOD—*Major details discernible. Letters well formed but worn.*
F-15 FINE—*Hair ends distinguishable. Top hairlines show, but otherwise worn smooth.*
VF-20 VERY FINE—*Right side of drapery slightly worn. Left side to curls is smooth.*
EF-40 EXTREMELY FINE—*All lines in drapery on bust will show distinctly around to hair curls.*

1796, 15 Stars		**1796, 16 Stars**

	Quan. Minted	AG-3	G-4	VG-8	F-12	VF-20	EF-40
1796, 15 stars		$7,500	$10,000	$12,000	$17,000	$24,000	$40,000
1796, 16 stars	} 3,918	8,000	11,000	13,000	19,000	27,000	46,000
1797, 15 stars		7,500	10,000	12,000	17,000	24,000	40,000

DRAPED BUST TYPE, HERALDIC EAGLE REVERSE
1801-1807

	Quan. Minted	G-4	VG-8	F-12	VF-20	EF-40	MS-60
1801	30,289	$200.00	$290.00	$550.00	$1,100	$2,300	$10,000
1802	29,890	175.00	250.00	450.00	850.00	2,100	10,000
1803 Small 3	} 188,234	150.00	200.00	325.00	550.00	1,300	7,250
1803 Large 3		130.00	160.00	250.00	475.00	900.00	6,000

HALF DOLLARS

| 1805, 5 over 4 | | 1806, 6 over 5 |

	Quan. Minted	G-4	VG-8	F-12	VF-20	EF-40	MS-60
1805, 5 over 4	} 211,722	$160.00	$300.00	$450.00	$700.00	$2,100	$14,000
1805 Normal date ..		130.00	160.00	225.00	400.00	800.00	6,500

Knobbed Top 6, Small Stars   **Branch Stem through Claw**

Pointed Top 6   **Branch Stem Not Through Claw**

		G-4	VG-8	F-12	VF-20	EF-40	MS-60
1806 All kinds	839,576						
1806, 6 over 5		130.00	160.00	225.00	400.00	800.00	5,200
1806, 6 over inverted 6		160.00	225.00	550.00	875.00	1,600	8,500
1806 Knobbed 6, large stars (traces of overdate)		130.00	160.00	225.00	350.00	625.00	4,750
1806 Knobbed 6, small stars ...		130.00	160.00	225.00	350.00	625.00	4,750
1806 Knobbed 6, stem not through claw			Rare				
1806 Pointed 6, stem through claw*		130.00	160.00	225.00	350.00	625.00	4,750
1806 Pointed 6, stem not through claw		130.00	160.00	225.00	350.00	625.00	4,750
1807	301,076	130.00	160.00	225.00	350.00	625.00	4,750

*One variety shows E in STATES over A.

CAPPED BUST TYPE, Lettered Edge 1807-1836

John Reich designed this capped head concept of Liberty. The head of Liberty facing left was used on all U.S. silver coin denominations for the next thirty years. Reich was the first artist to consistently include the denomination on our gold and silver coins. A German immigrant, John Reich became an engraver for the mint after having been freed from a bond of servitude by a mint official.

Designer John Reich; weight 13.48 grams; composition: .8924 silver, .1076 copper; approx. diameter 32.5 mm; edge varieties, 1807-1814: FIFTY CENTS OR HALF A DOLLAR; 1814-1831: star added between DOLLAR and FIFTY; 1832-1836: vertical lines added between words.

G-4 GOOD—*Date and letters readable. Bust worn smooth with outline distinct.*
VG-8 VERY GOOD—*LIBERTY visible but faint. Legends distinguishable. Clasp at shoulder visible. Curl above it nearly smooth.*
F-12 FINE—*Clasp and adjacent curl clearly outlined with slight details.*
VF-20 VERY FINE—*Clasp at shoulder clear. Curl has wear on highest point. Hair over brow distinguishable.*
EF-40 EXTREMELY FINE—*Clasp and adjacent curl fairly sharp. Brow and hair above distinct. Curls well defined.*
AU-50 ABOUT UNCIRCULATED—*Trace of wear on hair over eye, and over ear.*
MS-60 UNCIRCULATED—*No trace of wear. Light blemishes. May have slide marks from storage handling.*

HALF DOLLARS
First style (Variety 1) 1807-1808

1807 Small Stars   **1807 Large Stars**   **1807, 50 over 20**

	Quan. Minted	G-4	F-12	VF-20	EF-40	AU-50	MS-60
1807 All kinds..............	750,500						
1807 Small stars......................		$55.00	$185.00	$350.00	$700.00	$2,100	$3,500
1807 Large stars......................		50.00	160.00	300.00	600.00	2,000	4,000
1807 Same, 50 over 20		45.00	125.00	250.00	450.00	1,900	3,500
1807 "Bearded" Liberty............		375.00	725.00	1,200	2,600	7,700	—
1808, 8 over 7........	1,368,600	45.00	85.00	150.00	350.00	900.00	1,800
1808		40.00	55.00	90.00	250.00	500.00	1,200

Remodeled Portrait and Eagle 1809-1836

1809 Experimental edge, xxxx between words.

1809 Experimental edge, IIIII between words.

HALF DOLLARS

	Quan. Minted	G-4	F-12	VF-20	EF-40	AU-50	MS-60
1809 All Kinds	1,405,810						
1809 Normal edge		$38.00	$55.00	$90.00	$225.00	$550.00	$1,200
1809 xxxx edge		40.00	60.00	100.00	250.00	750.00	1,600
1809 ıııııı edge		40.00	60.00	100.00	250.00	600.00	1,500
1810	1,276,276	38.00	55.00	90.00	200.00	500.00	1,200

"Punctuated" Date 18.11

1811 Small 8

1811 Large 8

1812, 2 over 1, Small 8

1812, 2 over 1, Large 8

1811 All kinds	1,203,644						
1811 (18.11) 11 over 10		38.00	75.00	125.00	325.00	550.00	1,300
1811 Small 8		35.00	52.00	80.00	160.00	400.00	1,000
1811 Large 8		35.00	52.00	80.00	160.00	400.00	1,000
1812 All kinds	1,628,059						
1812, 2 over 1, small 8		40.00	75.00	165.00	275.00	675.00	2,200
1812, 2 over 1, large 8		1,300	3,500	6,000	10,000	—	—
1812 Normal		35.00	47.00	80.00	150.00	350.00	850.00
1812 Single leaf below wing		675.00	1,000	2,000	3,500	6,000	—

1813, 50 C. over UNI

Single leaf below wing

1814, 4 over 3

1814 E over A in STATES

1813 ⎫	1,241,903	35.00	47.00	70.00	135.00	350.00	900.00
1813, 50C over UNI ⎭		38.00	75.00	125.00	250.00	600.00	1,500
1814 All kinds	1,039,075						
1814, 4 over 3		45.00	75.00	125.00	300.00	625.00	1,200
1814 E over A in STATES		38.00	52.00	85.00	225.00	550.00	1,000
1814 Normal		35.00	47.00	75.00	200.00	425.00	950.00
1814 Single leaf below wing		45.00	80.00	130.00	425.00	1,100	2,000

[158]

HALF DOLLARS

1817, 7 over 3   **1817, 7 over 4**   **1817 Punctuated Date**

	Quan. Minted	G-4	F-12	VF-20	EF-40	AU-50	MS-60
1815, 5 over 2	47,150	$650.00	$1,300	$1,800	$2,700	$4,500	$8,500
1817, All kinds	1,215,567						
1817, 7 over 3		75.00	200.00	350.00	700.00	1,300	3,000
1817, 7 over 4		V. Rare	70,000	110,000	—		
1817 Dated 181.7		35.00	52.00	75.00	175.00	350.00	900.00
1817 Normal		35.00	52.00	60.00	135.00	300.00	850.00
1817 Single leaf below wing		40.00	70.00	100.00	300.00	800.00	1,750

1818, 1st 8 Small, 2nd 8 over 7   **1818, 1st 8 Large, 2nd 8 over 7**

1819 Small 9 over 8   **1819 Large 9 over 8**

1818 All kinds	1,960,322						
1818, 8 over 7, small 8		38.00	52.00	70.00	150.00	500.00	1,100
1818, 8 over 7, large 8		38.00	52.00	70.00	150.00	500.00	1,100
1818 Normal		35.00	42.00	60.00	135.00	300.00	800.00
1819 All kinds	2,208,000						
1819 Small 9 over 8		35.00	47.00	70.00	150.00	325.00	900.00
1819 Large 9 over 8		35.00	47.00	70.00	150.00	325.00	900.00
1819 Normal		32.00	42.00	60.00	120.00	300.00	800.00

1820, 20 over 19   **1820, 20 over 19**   **Curl Base, No Knob 2,**
Square Base 2   **Curl Base 2**   **Small Date**

1820 All kinds	751,122						
1820, 20 over 19, square 2		38.00	60.00	125.00	250.00	600.00	1,200
1820, 20 over 19, curl 2		38.00	60.00	125.00	250.00	600.00	1,200
1820 Curl base 2, small date		32.00	47.00	75.00	175.00	450.00	1,000

HALF DOLLARS

**Square Base, Knob 2,
Large Date**

**Square Base, No Knob 2,
Large Date**

	Quan. Minted	G-4	F-12	VF-20	EF-40	AU-50	MS-60
1820 Sq. base knob 2, lg. date		$32.00	$47.00	$75.00	$175.00	$400.00	$1,000
1820 Sq. base no knob 2, lg. date		32.00	47.00	75.00	175.00	400.00	1,000
1820 No serifs on E's		200.00	300.00	400.00	600.00	2,000	—
1821 1,305,797		32.00	47.00	70.00	125.00	350.00	900.00
1822 1,559,573		38.00	60.00	85.00	150.00	250.00	600.00
1822, 2 over 1		45.00	100.00	125.00	225.00	500.00	1,400

1823 Broken 3   **1823 Patched 3**   **1823 Ugly 3**

		G-4	F-12	VF-20	EF-40	AU-50	MS-60
1823 All kinds 1,694,200							
1823 Broken 3		42.00	80.00	100.00	225.00	400.00	1,000
1823 Patched 3		40.00	70.00	90.00	200.00	400.00	1,000
1823 Ugly 3		32.00	42.00	55.00	110.00	250.00	575.00
1823 Normal		32.00	42.00	55.00	110.00	250.00	575.00

**"Various Dates"
(probably 4 over
2 over 0)**   **1824, 4 over 1**   **1824, 4 over 4**   **1824, 4 over 4**

**4 over 4 varieties are easily mistaken for the
scarcer 4 over 1 variety. Notice the distance
between the 2's and 4's in the illustrations.**

		G-4	F-12	VF-20	EF-40	AU-50	MS-60
1824 All kinds 3,504,954							
1824 over various dates		32.00	42.00	55.00	110.00	225.00	575.00
1824, 4 over 1		32.00	42.00	55.00	100.00	225.00	575.00
1824, 4 over 4 (2 var.)		32.00	42.00	55.00	110.00	250.00	700.00
1824 Normal		32.00	42.00	55.00	100.00	225.00	575.00
1825 2,943,166		32.00	42.00	55.00	100.00	200.00	525.00
1826 4,004,180		32.00	42.00	55.00	100.00	200.00	525.00
1827 All kinds 5,493,400							
1827, 7 over 6		32.00	42.00	60.00	125.00	300.00	800.00
1827 Sq. base 2		32.00	42.00	55.00	100.00	200.00	525.00
1827 Curl base 2		32.00	42.00	55.00	100.00	200.00	525.00

HALF DOLLARS

1828 Curl Base, Knob 2

1828 Square Base 2, Large 8's

1828 Square Base 2, Small 8's

1828 Large Letters

1828 Small Letters

	Quan. Minted	G-4	F-12	VF-20	EF-40	AU-50	MS-60
1828 All kinds	3,075,200						
1828 Curl base, no knob 2		$32.00	$40.00	$55.00	$80.00	$200.00	$525.00
1828 Curl base, knob 2		38.00	60.00	85.00	125.00	275.00	700.00
1828 Sq. base 2, lg. 8's		32.00	42.00	55.00	80.00	200.00	525.00
1828 Sq. base 2, sm. 8's, lg. let		32.00	42.00	55.00	80.00	200.00	525.00
1828 Sq. base 2, sm. 8's & let		32.00	47.00	75.00	125.00	275.00	800.00
1829, 9 over 7	} 3,712,156	32.00	42.00	55.00	120.00	300.00	750.00
1829		32.00	42.00	55.00	80.00	200.00	525.00
1829 Large letters		38.00	47.00	60.00	100.00	300.00	900.00

1830 Small 0

1832 Large Letters Reverse

Raised segment lines to right, 1830.

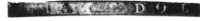

Raised segment lines to left, 1830-1831.

Adopted edge 1830-1836.

1830 Small 0	} 4,764,800	32.00	42.00	55.00	80.00	200.00	525.00
1830 Large 0		32.00	42.00	55.00	80.00	200.00	525.00
1830 Large letters		1,000	2,000	3,000	4,500	9,000	—
1831	5,873,660	32.00	42.00	55.00	80.00	200.00	525.00
1832 Normal	} 4,797,000	32.00	42.00	55.00	80.00	200.00	525.00
1832 Large letters		32.00	42.00	55.00	80.00	200.00	525.00
1833	5,206,000	32.00	42.00	55.00	80.00	200.00	525.00

HALF DOLLARS

1834 Large Date   1834 Small Date

1834 Lg. Letters Reverse   1834 Sm. Letters Reverse   1836, 50 over 00

Proofs of 1833, 1834 and 1835 with crushed edge lettering use the same reverse die as the 1836 with beaded border reverse. All are very rare.

Portrait Modified Slightly 1834-1836

	Quan. Minted	G-4	F-12	VF-20	EF-40	AU-50	MS-60
1834 All kinds	6,412,004						
1834 Lg. date & let		$32.00	$42.00	$55.00	$80.00	$200.00	$525.00
1834 Large date, small letters		32.00	42.00	55.00	80.00	200.00	525.00
1834 Small date, stars, letters		32.00	42.00	55.00	80.00	200.00	525.00
1835	5,352,006	32.00	42.00	55.00	80.00	200.00	525.00
1836		32.00	42.00	55.00	80.00	200.00	525.00
1836 over 1336 }	6,545,000	38.00	47.00	75.00	125.00	250.00	625.00
1836, 50 over 00 }		40.00	65.00	100.00	175.00	500.00	1,250
1836 Beaded border on reverse		35.00	50.00	85.00	190.00	420.00	900.00

Variety 2 — Reeded Edge, Reverse "50 CENTS" 1836-1837

Designer Christian Gobrecht; weight 13.36 grams; composition: .900 silver, .100 copper; diameter 30 mm; reeded edge; mints: Philadelphia.

G-4 GOOD—*LIBERTY discernible on headband.*
VG-8 VERY GOOD—*Minimum of 3 letters in LIBERTY must be clear.*
F-12 FINE—*LIBERTY complete.*
VF-20 VERY FINE—*LIBERTY is sharp. Shoulder clasp is clear.*
EF-40 EXTREMELY FINE—*LIBERTY sharp and strong. Hair details show.*
MS-60 UNCIRCULATED—*No trace of wear. Light blemishes.*

	Quan. Minted	G-4	VG-8	F-12	VF-20	EF-40	MS-60
1836	1,200	$625.00	$775.00	$1,000	$1,200	$1,800	$7,000
1837	3,629,820	32.00	38.00	42.00	70.00	125.00	800.00

HALF DOLLARS

Variety 3 — Reeded Edge, Reverse "HALF DOL." 1838-1839

The 1838O was the first branch mint half dollar, though not mentioned in the Director's report. The New Orleans chief coiner stated that only 20 were struck. In 1838-39 the mint mark appears on the obverse; thereafter, through 1915, all mint marks are placed on the reverse.

	Quan. Minted	G-4	VG-8	F-12	VF-20	EF-40	MS-60
1838	3,546,000	$32.00	$40.00	$50.00	$85.00	$185.00	$800.00
1838O	(20)						75,000
1839	1,392,976	32.00	40.00	50.00	85.00	185.00	900.00
1839 Small letters reverse					—	—	
1839O	178,976	120.00	160.00	225.00	375.00	650.00	3,000

LIBERTY SEATED TYPE 1839-1891

Variety 1 — No Motto Above Eagle 1839-1853

Designer Christian Gobrecht; weight 13.36 grams; composition: .900 silver, .100 copper; diameter 30.6 mm; reeded edge; mints: Philadelphia, New Orleans.

G-4 GOOD—*Scant rim. LIBERTY on shield worn off. Date and letters readable.*
VG-8 VERY GOOD—*Rim fairly defined. At least 3 letters in LIBERTY are evident.*
F-12 FINE—*LIBERTY complete, but weak.*
VF-20 VERY FINE—*LIBERTY mostly sharp.*
EF-40 EXTREMELY FINE—*LIBERTY entirely sharp. Scroll edges and clasp distinct.*
MS-60 UNCIRCULATED—*No trace of wear. Light blemishes.*

1839 No drapery from elbow	35.00	50.00	115.00	275.00	650.00	4,500

HALF DOLLARS
Modified obverse, drapery from elbow. Small letters in legend 1839-1841.

Drapery from Elbow Starting 1839	Small Letters in Legend 1839-41	1840 (only) with Medium Letters and Large Eagle

	Quan. Minted	G-4	VG-8	F-12	VF-20	EF-40	MS-60
1839	1,972,400	$22.50	$30.00	$45.00	$70.00	$125.00	$550.00
1840 Sm. letters	1,435,008	20.00	35.00	50.00	80.00	135.00	550.00
1840 Med. letters*	} 855,100	100.00	160.00	225.00	300.00	575.00	2,500
1840O		20.00	30.00	45.00	60.00	110.00	550.00
1841	310,000	30.00	42.00	85.00	140.00	250.00	1,200
1841O	401,000	17.00	26.00	40.00	60.00	125.00	750.00
1842 Sm. date, sm. letters					—		
1842O Sm. date, sm. letters	203,000	525.00	825.00	1,300	2,100	3,900	—

*Struck at the New Orleans Mint from a reverse die of the previous style without mint mark.

Modified reverse with large letters in legend 1842-1853.

Small Date

Medium Date

Large Letter Reverse

1844O Double Date

1842 Sm. date	} 2,012,764	25.00	40.00	55.00	80.00	150.00	950.00
1842 Med. date		17.00	30.00	45.00	60.00	110.00	600.00
1842O Med. date	754,000	18.00	26.00	36.00	55.00	110.00	625.00
1843	3,844,000	17.00	24.00	33.00	42.00	80.00	450.00
1843O	2,268,000	17.00	24.00	33.00	42.00	80.00	450.00
1844	1,766,000	17.00	24.00	33.00	42.00	80.00	450.00
1844O	} 2,005,000	17.00	24.00	33.00	42.00	80.00	450.00
1844O Double date		225.00	425.00	725.00	1,100	2,200	4,500
1845	589,000	20.00	26.00	45.00	55.00	125.00	600.00
1845O	} 2,094,000	17.00	24.00	33.00	42.00	80.00	550.00
1845O No drapery‡		30.00	45.00	60.00	90.00	200.00	700.00

‡Drapery missing because of excessive die polishing.

HALF DOLLARS

In 1846 the date size was again enlarged. The 1846 medium date is approximately the size of the 1842 medium date shown. Tall date is similar to 1853. See illustrations of cents on page 91.

	Quan. Minted	G-4	VG-8	F-12	VF-20	EF-40	MS-60
1846 Med. date. All kinds	2,210,000	$17.00	$24.00	$35.00	$45.00	$90.00	$525.00
1846 Tall date		19.00	24.00	35.00	45.00	90.00	600.00
1846 over horizontal 6 (error)		100.00	150.00	250.00	350.00	500.00	2,750
1846O Med. date	} 2,304,000	19.00	25.00	35.00	45.00	110.00	600.00
1846O Tall date		125.00	225.00	325.00	500.00	900.00	3,000
1847, 7 over 6	} 1,156,000	1,600	2,500	3,000	4,000	5,500	—
1847 Normal date		17.00	24.00	35.00	45.00	90.00	500.00
1847O	2,584,000	17.00	24.00	35.00	45.00	110.00	600.00
1848	580,000	30.00	40.00	60.00	100.00	175.00	1,000
1848O	3,180,000	19.00	24.00	35.00	45.00	90.00	600.00
1849	1,252,000	19.00	24.00	35.00	45.00	110.00	700.00
1849O	2,310,000	19.00	24.00	35.00	45.00	90.00	600.00
1850	227,000	150.00	200.00	250.00	300.00	550.00	1,400
1850O	2,456,000	19.00	24.00	35.00	45.00	90.00	600.00
1851	200,750	200.00	300.00	400.00	500.00	700.00	1,500
1851O	402,000	19.00	24.00	35.00	45.00	90.00	600.00
1852	77,130	275.00	400.00	550.00	700.00	900.00	1,600
1852O	144,000	45.00	75.00	125.00	175.00	375.00	1,300
1853O			110,000	160,000	225,000		

Variety 2 — Arrows at Date, Rays Around Eagle 1853 Only

Weight 12.44 grams; composition: .900 silver, .100 copper; diameter 30.6 mm; reeded edge; mints: Philadelphia, New Orleans, San Francisco, Carson City.

1853	3,532,708	16.00	21.00	38.00	85.00	225.00	1,300
1853O All kinds	1,328,000	17.00	23.00	42.00	100.00	250.00	2,300

Variety 3 — Arrows at Date, No Rays 1854-1855

1854	2,982,000	16.00	20.00	35.00	45.00	90.00	650.00
1854O	5,240,000	16.00	20.00	35.00	45.00	90.00	650.00
1855 over 1854	} 759,500	50.00	100.00	200.00	375.00		1,600
1855 Normal date		16.00	20.00	35.00	45.00	90.00	650.00
1855O	3,688,000	16.00	20.00	35.00	45.00	90.00	700.00
1855S	129,950	300.00	400.00	650.00	1,400	2,750	—

Variety 1 Design Resumed 1856-1866

1856	938,000	16.00	20.00	33.00	40.00	75.00	400.00
1856O	2,658,000	16.00	20.00	33.00	40.00	75.00	400.00
1856S	211,000	30.00	45.00	60.00	125.00	300.00	3,000
1857	1,988,000	16.00	20.00	33.00	40.00	75.00	400.00
1857O	818,000	18.00	23.00	35.00	45.00	80.00	700.00
1857S	158,000	35.00	50.00	90.00	175.00	350.00	2,750

HALF DOLLARS

	Quan. Minted	G-4	VG-8	F-12	VF-20	EF-40	MS-60	Proof-63
1858......(300+)	4,226,000	$16.00	$20.00	$33.00	$40.00	$75.00	$400.00	$2,500
1858O	7,294,000	16.00	20.00	33.00	40.00	75.00	400.00	
1858S	476,000	21.00	25.00	35.00	65.00	140.00	800.00	
1859......(800)	748,000	16.00	20.00	33.00	40.00	75.00	450.00	1,300
1859O	2,834,000	16.00	20.00	33.00	40.00	75.00	400.00	
1859S	566,000	21.00	25.00	35.00	60.00	135.00	800.00	
1860.....(1,000)	303,700	21.00	25.00	34.00	45.00	90.00	700.00	1,000
1860O	1,290,000	16.00	20.00	33.00	40.00	75.00	400.00	
1860S	472,000	21.00	24.00	35.00	50.00	80.00	600.00	
1861.....(1,000)	2,888,400	16.00	20.00	33.00	40.00	75.00	400.00	900.00
1861O	2,532,633	16.00	20.00	33.00	40.00	85.00	400.00	
1861O Cracked obv.		50.00	75.00	125.00	175.00	250.00	900.00	

The 1861O quantity includes 330,000 struck under the United States government, 1,240,000 for the State of Louisiana after it seceded from the Union, and 962,633 after Louisiana joined the Confederate States of America. As all these 1861O coins were struck from U.S. dies, it is impossible to distinguish one from another. They should not be confused with the very rare Confederate half dollar of 1861 (see pgs. 308-309) which has a distinctive reverse.

	Quan. Minted	G-4	VG-8	F-12	VF-20	EF-40	MS-60	Proof-63
1861S	939,500	16.00	19.00	33.00	40.00	75.00	500.00	
1862......(550)	253,550	22.50	30.00	38.00	90.00	125.00	625.00	1,000
1862S	1,352,000	16.00	19.00	33.00	40.00	75.00	450.00	
1863......(460)	503,660	21.00	24.00	35.00	45.00	90.00	500.00	1,000
1863S	916,000	16.00	19.00	33.00	40.00	75.00	400.00	
1864......(470)	379,570	25.00	35.00	50.00	75.00	100.00	550.00	1,000
1864S	658,000	16.00	19.00	33.00	40.00	80.00	400.00	
1865......(500)	511,900	21.00	24.00	35.00	45.00	85.00	600.00	1,000
1865S	675,000	16.00	19.00	33.00	40.00	80.00	500.00	
1866S No motto	60,000	60.00	85.00	150.00	300.00	550.00	4,500	
1866		*Unique*—(see similar quarter and dollar)						—

**Variety 4 —
"In God We Trust"
Above Eagle
1866-1873
1875-1891**

	Quan. Minted	G-4	VG-8	F-12	VF-20	EF-40	MS-60	Proof-63
1866......(725)	745,625	15.00	19.00	30.00	40.00	70.00	375.00	800.00
1866S	994,000	15.00	19.00	30.00	40.00	75.00	400.00	
1867......(625)	449,925	20.00	30.00	50.00	65.00	125.00	475.00	800.00
1867S	1,196,000	15.00	19.00	30.00	40.00	75.00	400.00	
1868......(600)	418,200	25.00	35.00	55.00	90.00	175.00	500.00	800.00
1868S	1,160,000	15.00	19.00	30.00	40.00	85.00	475.00	
1869......(600)	795,900	16.00	21.00	35.00	50.00	100.00	500.00	800.00
1869S	656,000	16.00	21.00	35.00	50.00	100.00	500.00	
1870.....(1,000)	634,900	15.00	19.00	30.00	40.00	90.00	375.00	800.00
1870CC	54,617	450.00	750.00	1,500	2,600	6,500	—	
1870S	1,004,000	15.00	19.00	30.00	40.00	75.00	450.00	
1871......(960)	1,204,560	15.00	19.00	30.00	40.00	65.00	425.00	800.00
1871CC	153,950	100.00	160.00	250.00	400.00	1,000	5,750	
1871S	2,178,000	16.00	22.00	40.00	50.00	75.00	500.00	

HALF DOLLARS

	Quan. Minted	G-4	VG-8	F-12	VF-20	EF-40	MS-60	Proof-63
1872........(950)	881,550	$16.00	$23.00	$40.00	$50.00	$70.00	$450.00	$800.00
1872CC 257,000		50.00	80.00	150.00	275.00	550.00	3,000	
1872S 580,000		20.00	30.00	50.00	75.00	125.00	1,000	
1873 Closed 3 ....(600)	587,600	19.00	29.00	45.00	70.00	110.00	475.00	800.00
1873 Open 3...........214,200					3,200	5,200	12,500	
1873CC 122,500		95.00	175.00	275.00	450.00	1,000	6,500	
1873S No arrows 5,000				Unknown in any collection.				

Variety 5 — Arrows at Date 1873-1874

Arrows were placed at the date to denote a change in weight from 12.44 to 12.50 grams.

Weight 12.50 grams; composition: .900 silver, .100 copper; diameter 30.6 mm; reeded edge; mints: Philadelphia, Carson City, San Francisco.

1873........(550)	1,815,700	21.00	26.00	38.00	80.00	225.00	850.00	2,000
1873CC 214,560		75.00	125.00	225.00	400.00	1,200	5,000	
1873S 228,000		35.00	50.00	90.00	150.00	300.00	1,750	
1874........(700)	2,360,300	21.00	25.00	38.00	80.00	225.00	850.00	2,000
1874CC 59,000		175.00	300.00	500.00	850.00	1,400	7,500	
1874S 394,000		30.00	35.00	60.00	125.00	275.00	1,400	

Variety 4 Resumed 1875-1891

1875........(700)	6,027,500	15.00	19.00	30.00	40.00	60.00	375.00	700.00
1875CC 1,008,000		19.00	30.00	50.00	65.00	125.00	600.00	
1875S 3,200,000		15.00	20.00	40.00	50.00	75.00	350.00	
1876.....(1,150)	8,419,150	15.00	19.00	30.00	40.00	60.00	325.00	700.00
1876CC 1,956,000		18.00	20.00	35.00	50.00	80.00	600.00	
1876S 4,528,000		15.00	19.00	30.00	40.00	60.00	375.00	
1877........(510)	8,304,510	15.00	19.00	30.00	40.00	60.00	325.00	700.00
1877, 7 over 6......................				300.00	600.00	900.00		
1877CC 1,420,000		18.00	25.00	45.00	60.00	90.00	625.00	
1877S 5,356,000		15.00	19.00	30.00	40.00	60.00	375.00	
1878........(800)	1,378,400	15.00	19.00	30.00	40.00	60.00	375.00	700.00
1878CC 62,000		200.00	300.00	450.00	750.00	1,350	4,500	
1878S 12,000		6,000	8,000	10,000	14,000	18,000	30,000	
1879.....(1,100)	5,900	150.00	175.00	225.00	300.00	400.00	775.00	700.00
1880.....(1,355)	9,755	150.00	175.00	225.00	300.00	350.00	725.00	700.00
1881........(975)	10,975	150.00	175.00	225.00	300.00	350.00	725.00	700.00
1882.....(1,100)	5,500	160.00	200.00	250.00	320.00	400.00	825.00	700.00
1883.....(1,039)	9,039	150.00	175.00	225.00	300.00	350.00	725.00	700.00
1884........(875)	5,275	160.00	200.00	275.00	320.00	400.00	875.00	700.00
1885........(930)	6,130	150.00	175.00	225.00	300.00	350.00	825.00	700.00
1886........(886)	5,886	150.00	175.00	275.00	325.00	375.00	825.00	700.00
1887........(710)	5,710	150.00	175.00	275.00	375.00	425.00	925.00	700.00
1888........(832)	12,833	140.00	170.00	225.00	300.00	325.00	725.00	700.00
1889........(711)	12,711	140.00	170.00	225.00	300.00	325.00	725.00	700.00
1890........(590)	12,590	140.00	170.00	225.00	300.00	325.00	725.00	700.00
1891........(600)	200,600	30.00	40.00	50.00	75.00	120.00	550.00	700.00

HALF DOLLARS
BARBER or LIBERTY HEAD TYPE 1892-1915

Like the dime and quarter dollar, this type was designed by Charles E. Barber, whose initial B is at the truncation of the neck.

Designer Charles E. Barber; weight 12.50 grams; composition: .900 silver, .100 copper; diameter 30.6 mm; reeded edge; mints: Philadelphia, Denver, New Orleans, San Francisco.

G-4 GOOD—*Date and legends readable. LIBERTY worn off headband.*
VG-8 VERY GOOD—*Minimum of 3 letters readable in LIBERTY.*
F-12 FINE—*LIBERTY completely readable, but not sharp.*
VF-20 VERY FINE—*All letters in LIBERTY evenly plain.*
EF-40 EXTREMELY FINE—*LIBERTY bold, and its ribbon distinct.*
MS-60 UNCIRCULATED—*No trace of wear. Light blemishes.*

Mint mark location on reverse below eagle.

	Quan. Minted	G-4	VG-8	F-12	VF-20	EF-40	MS-60	Proof-63
1892.....(1,245)	935,245	$18.00	$25.00	$40.00	$85.00	$175.00	$450.00	$800.00
1892O	390,000	120.00	175.00	250.00	300.00	425.00	850.00	
1892O Micro O*		500.00	900.00	1,500	2,000	3,750	9,000	
1892S	1,029,028	110.00	130.00	185.00	260.00	375.00	850.00	
1893........(792)	1,826,792	13.00	18.00	40.00	75.00	160.00	500.00	700.00
1893O	1,389,000	18.00	26.00	55.00	120.00	250.00	500.00	
1893S	740,000	80.00	100.00	150.00	275.00	380.00	1,000	
1894........(972)	1,148,972	13.00	25.00	55.00	85.00	175.00	500.00	700.00
1894O	2,138,000	10.00	16.00	50.00	100.00	250.00	500.00	
1894S	4,048,690	9.00	12.00	40.00	75.00	195.00	450.00	
1895........(880)	1,835,218	9.00	12.00	40.00	75.00	165.00	475.00	700.00
1895O	1,766,000	12.00	16.00	45.00	90.00	220.00	525.00	
1895S	1,108,086	16.00	22.50	55.00	100.00	250.00	525.00	
1896........(762)	950,762	12.00	17.00	40.00	85.00	185.00	500.00	700.00
1896O	924,000	18.00	21.00	70.00	140.00	325.00	1,200	
1896S	1,140,948	55.00	75.00	100.00	190.00	350.00	1,150	
1897........(731)	2,480,731	8.00	9.00	23.00	65.00	130.00	400.00	700.00
1897O	632,000	55.00	80.00	285.00	550.00	800.00	1,500	
1897S	933,900	95.00	120.00	250.00	375.00	700.00	1,250	
1898........(735)	2,956,735	7.00	9.00	25.00	75.00	135.00	400.00	700.00
1898O	874,000	14.00	24.00	80.00	175.00	350.00	800.00	
1898S	2,358,550	10.00	15.00	35.00	85.00	200.00	700.00	
1899........(846)	5,538,846	7.00	9.00	25.00	75.00	150.00	400.00	700.00
1899O	1,724,000	9.00	12.00	40.00	90.00	200.00	600.00	
1899S	1,686,411	9.00	12.00	40.00	85.00	200.00	525.00	
1900........(912)	4,762,912	6.50	8.00	25.00	75.00	130.00	400.00	700.00
1900O	2,744,000	7.00	10.00	37.00	85.00	250.00	650.00	
1900S	2,560,322	7.00	10.00	32.00	80.00	185.00	550.00	
1901........(813)	4,268,813	6.50	8.00	25.00	70.00	125.00	400.00	700.00
1901O	1,124,000	8.00	13.00	40.00	100.00	290.00	1,200	
1901S	847,044	15.00	25.00	90.00	200.00	500.00	1,400	
1902........(777)	4,922,777	6.50	8.00	25.00	70.00	120.00	400.00	700.00
1902O	2,526,000	8.00	11.00	35.00	75.00	170.00	600.00	

*Normal and "microscopic" mint mark varieties, see page 67.

HALF DOLLARS

	Quan. Minted	G-4	VG-8	F-12	VF-20	EF-40	MS-60	Proof-63
1902S	1,460,670	$7.00	$11.00	$40.00	$85.00	$200.00	$525.00	
1903 .....(755)	2,278,755	6.00	8.00	25.00	75.00	130.00	400.00	$700.00
1903O	2,100,000	6.50	10.00	40.00	80.00	180.00	525.00	
1903S	1,920,772	6.50	11.00	40.00	85.00	200.00	525.00	
1904 .....(670)	2,992,670	6.00	8.00	25.00	65.00	130.00	400.00	700.00
1904O	1,117,600	10.00	13.00	50.00	100.00	285.00	1,000	
1904S	553,038	14.00	25.00	120.00	285.00	550.00	2,000	
1905 .....(727)	662,727	9.00	11.00	40.00	80.00	225.00	500.00	700.00
1905O	505,000	10.00	18.00	65.00	135.00	235.00	625.00	
1905S	2,494,000	6.00	8.00	35.00	75.00	180.00	525.00	
1906 .....(675)	2,638,675	6.00	8.00	25.00	65.00	125.00	385.00	700.00
1906D	4,028,000	6.00	8.00	25.00	70.00	140.00	385.00	
1906O	2,446,000	6.00	8.00	35.00	75.00	165.00	600.00	
1906S	1,740,154	6.00	8.00	35.00	75.00	200.00	500.00	
1907 .....(575)	2,598,575	6.00	8.00	25.00	65.00	125.00	400.00	700.00
1907D	3,856,000	6.00	8.00	25.00	65.00	140.00	385.00	
1907O	3,946,600	6.00	8.00	25.00	65.00	140.00	400.00	
1907S	1,250,000	6.50	10.00	55.00	100.00	300.00	800.00	
1908 .....(545)	1,354,545	6.00	8.00	25.00	65.00	125.00	400.00	700.00
1908D	3,280,000	6.00	8.00	25.00	65.00	125.00	400.00	
1908O	5,360,000	6.00	8.00	25.00	65.00	125.00	400.00	
1908S	1,644,828	6.00	9.00	40.00	80.00	185.00	650.00	
1909 .....(650)	2,368,650	6.00	8.00	25.00	65.00	125.00	385.00	700.00
1909O	925,400	8.00	10.00	40.00	90.00	225.00	650.00	
1909S	1,764,000	6.00	8.00	25.00	70.00	175.00	500.00	
1910 .....(551)	418,551	8.00	13.00	50.00	100.00	260.00	600.00	700.00
1910S	1,948,000	6.00	8.00	25.00	75.00	160.00	500.00	
1911 .....(543)	1,406,543	6.00	8.00	25.00	65.00	125.00	385.00	700.00
1911D	695,080	6.00	10.00	30.00	80.00	165.00	440.00	
1911S	1,272,000	6.50	9.00	28.00	75.00	150.00	500.00	
1912 .....(700)	1,550,700	6.00	8.00	25.00	65.00	125.00	400.00	700.00
1912D	2,300,800	6.00	8.00	25.00	65.00	125.00	400.00	
1912S	1,370,000	6.00	8.00	25.00	75.00	165.00	420.00	
1913 .....(627)	188,627	19.00	27.00	110.00	190.00	325.00	900.00	950.00
1913D	534,000	6.00	9.00	30.00	75.00	180.00	425.00	
1913S	604,000	6.00	9.00	40.00	80.00	185.00	550.00	
1914 .....(380)	124,610	30.00	45.00	160.00	325.00	500.00	900.00	1,200
1914S	992,000	6.00	9.00	30.00	75.00	175.00	470.00	
1915 .....(450)	138,450	21.00	28.00	80.00	190.00	350.00	850.00	1,100
1915D	1,170,400	6.00	8.00	25.00	70.00	125.00	385.00	
1915S	1,604,000	6.00	8.00	25.00	70.00	125.00	400.00	

LIBERTY WALKING TYPE 1916-1947

This type was designed by A. A. Weinman whose monogram AAW appears under the tip of the wing feathers. On the 1916 coins and some of the 1917 coins the mint mark is located on the obverse below the motto.

Designer Adolph A. Weinman; weight 12.50 grams; composition: .900 silver, .100 copper; diameter 30.6 mm; reeded edge; mints: Philadelphia, Denver, San Francisco. Net weight: .36169 oz. pure silver.

G-4 GOOD—*Rims are defined. Motto IN GOD WE TRUST readable.*
VG-8 VERY GOOD—*Motto is distinct. About half of skirt lines at left are clear.*
F-12 FINE—*All skirt lines evident, but worn in spots. Details in sandal below motto are clear.*
VF-20 VERY FINE—*Skirt lines sharp including leg area. Little wear on breast and right arm.*
EF-40 EXTREMELY FINE—*All skirt lines bold.*
MS-60 UNCIRCULATED—*No trace of wear. Light blemishes.*
MS-65 CHOICE UNCIRCULATED—*No trace of wear. Barely noticeable blemishes.*

HALF DOLLARS

Locations of mint mark.

Choice uncirculated, well struck specimens are worth more than values listed.

See pg. 6 for information on higher grade coins.

	Quan. Minted	G-4	VG-8	F-12	VF-20	EF-40	MS-60	Proof-65
1916	608,000	$24.00	$32.00	$55.00	$120.00	$150.00	$260.00	
1916D (Obv.)	1,014,400	20.00	25.00	35.00	80.00	135.00	250.00	
1916S (Obv.)	508,000	75.00	85.00	130.00	300.00	500.00	900.00	
1917	12,292,000	4.00	6.00	9.00	18.00	32.00	120.00	
1917D (Obv.)	765,400	13.00	17.00	35.00	85.00	135.00	450.00	
1917D (Rev.)	1,940,000	10.00	15.00	25.00	75.00	175.00	700.00	
1917S (Obv.)	952,000	16.00	26.00	50.00	240.00	650.00	1,800	
1917S (Rev.)	5,554,000	5.00	7.00	14.00	25.00	45.00	275.00	
1918	6,634,000	6.00	9.00	16.00	40.00	130.00	450.00	
1918D	3,853,040	6.00	9.00	20.00	50.00	150.00	800.00	
1918S	10,282,000	5.00	7.00	14.00	25.00	50.00	400.00	
1919	962,000	16.00	19.00	35.00	125.00	400.00	950.00	
1919D	1,165,000	12.00	16.00	42.00	140.00	500.00	2,500	
1919S	1,552,000	12.00	16.00	30.00	120.00	600.00	2,000	
1920	6,372,000	5.00	6.00	11.00	20.00	50.00	250.00	
1920D	1,551,000	8.00	10.00	25.00	120.00	325.00	1,100	
1920S	4,624,000	5.00	7.00	15.00	40.00	150.00	625.00	
1921	246,000	100.00	135.00	200.00	550.00	1,400	3,000	
1921D	208,000	140.00	180.00	250.00	720.00	2,000	2,700	
1921S	548,000	20.00	27.00	100.00	525.00	4,250	8,000	
1923S	2,178,000	8.00	10.00	18.00	45.00	200.00	1,100	
1927S	2,392,000	5.00	6.00	11.00	25.00	85.00	600.00	
1928S‡	1,940,000	6.00	7.00	12.00	30.00	100.00	600.00	
1929D	1,001,200	6.00	7.00	10.00	18.00	70.00	250.00	
1929S	1,902,000	6.00	7.00	10.00	18.00	70.00	250.00	
1933S	1,786,000	6.00	7.00	9.00	12.00	45.00	475.00	
1934	6,964,000	*3.00*	*3.50*	*4.00*	5.00	11.00	50.00	
1934D‡	2,361,400	*3.00*	*3.50*	*4.50*	7.00	25.00	100.00	
1934S	3,652,000	*3.00*	*3.50*	*4.50*	6.00	25.00	225.00	
1935	9,162,000	*3.00*	*3.50*	*4.50*	6.00	8.00	40.00	
1935D	3,003,800	*3.00*	*3.50*	*4.50*	6.00	25.00	110.00	
1935S	3,854,000	*3.00*	*3.50*	*4.50*	6.00	23.00	135.00	
1936..(3,901)	12,617,901	*3.00*	*3.50*	*4.50*	6.00	8.00	40.00	$2,800
1936D	4,252,400	*3.00*	*3.50*	*4.50*	6.00	16.00	75.00	
1936S	3,884,000	*3.00*	*3.50*	*4.50*	6.00	16.00	110.00	
1937..(5,728)	9,527,728	*3.00*	*3.50*	*4.50*	6.00	8.00	37.00	800.00
1937D	1,676,000	5.00	6.00	8.00	10.00	28.00	150.00	
1937S	2,090,000	4.00	5.00	6.00	9.00	18.00	115.00	
1938..(8,152)	4,118,152	*3.00*	*3.50*	*4.50*	6.00	10.00	60.00	575.00
1938D	491,600	22.00	25.00	30.00	45.00	100.00	400.00	

‡Large and small mint mark varieties, see page 67. Pieces dated 1928D are counterfeit.

HALF DOLLARS

	Quan. Minted	F-12	VF-20	EF-40	MS-60	MS-63	Proof-65
1939.............(8,808)	6,820,808	$3.50	$4.00	$6.00	$40.00	$55.00	$575.00
1939D............................4,267,800		3.50	6.00	10.00	40.00	55.00	
1939S 2,552,000		5.00	8.00	12.00	100.00	120.00	
1940...........(11,279)	9,167,279	3.50	4.00	6.00	30.00	40.00	500.00
1940S............................4,550,000		3.50	4.00	6.00	30.00	40.00	
1941*.........(15,412)	24,207,412	3.50	4.00	6.00	30.00	40.00	*450.00
1941D.........................11,248,400		3.50	4.00	6.00	35.00	45.00	
1941S 8,098,000		3.50	4.00	6.00	75.00	120.00	
1942...........(21,120)	47,839,120	3.50	4.00	6.00	30.00	40.00	435.00
1942D.........................10,973,800		3.50	4.00	6.00	30.00	60.00	
1942S‡ 12,708,000		3.50	4.00	6.00	38.00	60.00	
1943.........................53,190,000		3.50	4.00	6.00	30.00	40.00	
1943D.........................11,346,000		3.50	4.00	6.00	50.00	65.00	
1943S 13,450,000		3.50	4.00	6.00	40.00	50.00	
1944.........................28,206,000		3.50	4.00	6.00	30.00	40.00	
1944D...........................9,769,000		3.50	4.00	6.00	35.00	42.00	
1944S 8,904,000		3.50	4.00	6.00	35.00	45.00	
1945.........................31,502,000		3.50	4.00	6.00	30.00	40.00	
1945D...........................9,966,800		3.50	4.00	6.00	32.00	40.00	
1945S 10,156,000		3.50	4.00	6.00	32.00	40.00	
1946.........................12,118,000		3.50	4.00	6.00	30.00	40.00	
1946 Doubled die reverse.............		10.00	30.00	50.00	200.00	325.00	
1946D...........................2,151,000		5.00	8.00	9.00	35.00	40.00	
1946S 3,724,000		3.50	4.00	6.00	38.00	40.00	
1947............................4,094,000		3.50	4.00	6.00	35.00	40.00	
1947D...........................3,900,600		3.50	4.00	6.00	35.00	40.00	

*Proofs struck with or without designer's initials.

‡Large and small mint mark varieties exist, see page 67.

FRANKLIN-LIBERTY BELL TYPE 1948-1963

The Benjamin Franklin half dollar and the Roosevelt dime were both designed by John R. Sinnock whose initials appear below the shoulder. The Liberty Bell is similar to that used by Sinnock on the 1926 Sesquicentennial commemorative half dollar modeled from a sketch by John Frederick Lewis.

Designer John R. Sinnock; weight 12.50 grams; composition: .900 silver, .100 copper; diameter 30.6 mm; reeded edge; mints: Philadelphia, Denver, San Francisco. Net weight: .36169 oz. pure silver.

VF-20 VERY FINE—At least half of the lower and upper incused lines on the rim of the bell must show.
EF-40 EXTREMELY FINE—Wear spots appear at top of end curls and hair back of ears. On reverse, Liberty Bell will show wear at top and on lettering.
MS-63 SELECT UNCIRCULATED—No trace of wear. Light blemishes. Attractive mint luster.
MS-65 CHOICE UNCIRCULATED—No trace of wear. Barely noticeable blemishes.

Mint mark location.

Choice, well struck uncirculated halves command higher prices.

HALF DOLLARS

	Quan. Minted	VF-20	EF-40	MS-60	MS-63	Proof-65
1948	3,006,814	$4.00	$5.00	$15.00	$20.00	
1948D	4,028,600	3.00	4.50	9.00	15.00	
1949	5,614,000	3.00	4.50	30.00	45.00	
1949D	4,120,600	3.00	4.50	32.00	45.00	
1949S	3,744,000	4.50	10.00	50.00	70.00	
1950.........(51,386)	7,793,509	3.50	4.50	22.00	30.00	$325.00
1950D	8,031,600	3.00	3.50	20.00	30.00	
1951............(57,500)	16,859,602	3.00	3.50	10.00	15.00	230.00
1951D	9,475,200	3.00	3.50	22.00	30.00	
1951S	13,696,000	3.00	3.50	22.00	35.00	
1952...........(81,980)	21,274,073	3.00	3.50	7.50	16.00	135.00
1952D	25,395,600	3.00	3.50	7.00	12.00	
1952S	5,526,000	3.00	3.50	35.00	40.00	
1953...........(128,800)	2,796,920	3.50	6.00	14.00	20.00	90.00
1953D	20,900,400	3.00	3.50	7.00	11.00	
1953S	4,148,000	3.00	4.00	15.00	20.00	
1954...........(233,300)	13,421,503	3.00	3.50	6.00	11.00	55.00
1954D	25,445,580	3.00	3.50	6.00	10.00	
1954S	4,993,400	3.00	3.50	7.00	12.00	
1955...........(378,200)	2,876,381	6.00	6.50	7.00	10.00	50.00
1956...........(669,384)	4,701,384	3.00	4.00	6.00	10.00	22.00
1957........(1,247,952)	6,361,952	3.00	4.00	6.50	11.00	22.00
1957D	19,966,850	3.00	3.50	6.25	10.00	
1958...........(875,652)	4,917,652	3.00	4.00	6.00	10.00	25.00
1958D	23,962,412	3.00	3.50	6.00	8.00	
1959........(1,149,291)	7,349,291	3.00	4.00	6.00	9.00	23.00
1959D	13,053,750	3.00	3.50	6.00	9.00	
1960........(1,691,602)	7,715,602	3.00	4.00	6.00	8.00	23.00
1960D	18,215,812	3.00	3.50	6.00	8.00	

**1961 Proof
Doubled Die**

1961........(3,028,244)	11,318,244	3.00	4.00	6.00	8.00	18.00
1961 Double die proof						1,200
1961D	20,276,442	3.00	3.50	5.00	8.00	
1962........(3,218,019)	12,932,019	3.00	3.50	5.00	7.00	18.00
1962D	35,473,281	3.00	3.50	5.00	7.00	
1963........(3,075,645)	25,239,645	3.00	3.50	5.00	7.00	18.00
1963D	67,069,292	3.00	3.50	5.00	7.00	

KENNEDY TYPE 1964 to Date

Gilroy Roberts, former Chief Engraver of the Mint, designed the obverse of this coin. His stylized initials are on the truncation of the forceful bust of President John F. Kennedy. The reverse, which uses the presidential coat of arms for the motif, is the work of Chief Engraver Frank Gasparro. A few of the pieces dated 1971D and 1977D were struck in silver clad by error.

HALF DOLLARS

Designers Gilroy Roberts and Frank Gasparro. 1964–: Standards same as previous issue; 1965-1970: weight 11.50 grams; composition: outer layers of .800 silver, .200 copper bonded to inner core of .209 silver, .791 copper; 1971: weight 11.34 grams; composition: outer layers of copper-nickel (.750 copper, .250 nickel) bonded to inner core of pure copper; diameter 30.6 mm; reeded edge. Net weight: 1964 .36169 oz. pure silver. 1965-1970 .1479 oz. pure silver, mints: Philadelphia, Denver, San Francisco.

1964 Mint mark location

1968 Mint mark location

Silver Coinage 1964

	Quan. Minted	MS-63	Proof-65
1964	277,254,766	$4.00	
1964	(3,950,762)		$8.00

	Quan. Minted	MS-63	Proof-65
1964 Heavily accented hair	incl. above		$20.00
1964D	156,205,446	$4.00	

Silver Clad Coinage 1965-1970

	Quan. Minted	MS-63	Proof-65
1965	65,879,366	1.75	
1966	108,984,932	1.75	
1967	295,046,978	1.75	
1968D	246,951,930	1.75	
1968S Proof..	(3,041,506)		3.00

	Quan. Minted	MS-63	Proof-65
1969D	129,881,800	1.75	
1969S Proof..	(2,934,631)		3.00
1970D	*2,150,000	15.00	
1970S Proof..	(2,632,810)		9.00

*Issued only in mint sets

Copper-Nickel Clad Coinage

Design was slightly modified several times between 1971 and 1995.

1974D Doubled Die Obverse

(Note prominent doubling of RUS.)

	Quan. Minted	MS-63	Proof-65
1971	155,164,000	$1.25	
1971D	302,097,424	1.25	
1971S Proof..	(3,220,733)		$3.00
1972	153,180,000	1.50	
1972D	141,890,000	1.50	
1972S Proof..	(3,260,996)		3.00
1973	64,964,000	1.50	

	Quan. Minted	MS-63	Proof-65
1973D	83,171,400	$1.25	
1973S Proof..	(2,760,339)		$2.50
1974	201,596,000	1.25	
1974D	79,066,300	1.25	
1974D Double die obv.		150.00	
1974S Proof..	(2,612,568)		2.50

HALF DOLLARS
BICENTENNIAL COINAGE DATED 1776-1976

In an open contest for the selection of suitable designs for the special Bicentennial reverses of the quarter, half dollar and dollar, Seth G. Huntington's winning entry was featured on the half dollar. It shows Independence Hall in Philadelphia as the center device. The obverse was unchanged except for the dual dating 1776-1976. They were the only coins struck during 1975 and 1976 and were used for general circulation as well as being included in proof and uncirculated sets.

Designers Gilroy Roberts and Seth Huntington. Silver clad: weight 11.50 grams; composition: outer layers of .800 silver, .200 copper bonded to inner core of .209 silver, .791 copper; copper-nickel clad: weight 11.34 grams; composition: outer layers of copper-nickel (.750 copper, .250 nickel) bonded to inner core of pure copper; diameter 30.6 mm; reeded edge. Net weight: silver clad coinage .14792 oz. pure silver. Silver Proofs: pre-1965 standards.

	Quan. Minted	MS-63	Proof-65
1776-1976 Copper-nickel clad	234,308,000	$1.25	
1776-1976D Copper-nickel clad	287,565,248	1.25	
1776-1976S Copper-nickel clad	(7,059,099)		$1.75
1776-1976S Silver clad	*11,000,000	4.00	
1776-1976S Silver clad	*(4,000,000)		5.00

*Approximate mintage.

Eagle Reverse Resumed

	Quan. Minted	MS-63	Proof-65		Quan. Minted	MS-63	Proof-65
1977	43,598,000	$1.50		1983S Proof..	(3,279,126)		$3.50
1977D	31,449,106	1.50		1984P	26,029,000	$2.00	
1977S Proof..	(3,251,152)		$2.50	1984D	26,262,158	2.00	
1978	14,350,000	1.75		1984S Proof..	(3,065,110)		4.00
1978D	13,765,799	2.50		1985P	18,706,962	2.00	
1978S Proof..	(3,127,781)		2.50	1985D	19,814,034	2.25	
1979	68,312,000	1.50		1985S Proof..	(3,362,821)		4.00
1979D	15,815,422	1.50		1986P	13,107,633	6.00	
1979S Proof..	(3,677,175)			1986D	15,336,145	4.00	
Filled S			2.50	1986S Proof..	(3,010,497)		10.00
Clear S			15.00	1987P	*2,890,758	4.00	
1980P	44,134,000	1.25		1987D	*2,890,758	4.00	
1980D	33,456,449	1.25		1987S Proof..	(4,227,728)		4.00
1980S Proof..	(3,554,806)		2.50	1988P	13,626,000	3.25	
1981P	29,544,000	1.50		1988D	12,000,096	3.00	
1981D	27,839,533	1.25		1988S Proof..	(3,262,948)		6.00
1981S Proof..	(4,063,083)		2.50	1989P	24,542,000	2.00	
1982P	10,819,000	2.50		1989D	23,000,216	1.75	
1982D	13,140,102	2.50		1989S Proof..	(3,220,194)		5.00
1982S Proof..	(3,857,479)		2.50	1990P	22,278,000	2.00	
1983P	34,139,000	3.50		1990D	20,096,242	3.00	
1983D	32,472,244	3.50		1990S Proof..	(3,299,559)		5.00

*Not issued for circulation; included with uncirculated and souvenir sets.

HALF DOLLARS

	Quan. Minted	MS-63	Proof-65
1991P	14,874,000	$2.00	
1991D	15,054,678	3.50	
1991S Proof	(2,867,787)		$12.00
1992P	17,628,000	1.50	
1992D	17,000,106	2.50	
1992S Proof	(2,858,981)		10.00
1992S Silver			
Proof	(1,317,579)		13.00
1993P	15,510,000	1.50	
1993D	15,000,006	1.50	
1993S Proof	(2,633,439)		14.00
1993S Silver			
Proof	(761,353)		25.00
1994P	23,718,000	1.00	
1994D	23,828,110	1.25	
1994S Proof	(2,484,594)		8.00
1994S Silver			
Proof	(785,329)		30.00
1995P	26,496,000	1.00	
1995D	26,288,000	1.00	
1995S Proof	(2,117,496)		30.00
1995S Silver			
Proof	(679,985)		80.00
1996P	24,442,000	1.00	
1996D	24,744,000	1.00	
1996S Proof	(1,750,244)		8.00
1996S Silver			
Proof	(775,021)		40.00
1997P	20,882,000	1.00	
1997D	19,876,000	1.50	
1997S Proof	(2,055,000)		20.00
1997S Silver			
Proof	(741,678)		75.00

	Quan. Minted	MS-63	Proof-65
1998P	15,646,000	$1.25	
1998D	15,064,000	1.25	
1998S Proof			$12.50
1998S Silver			
Proof	(878,792)		25.00
1998S Silver			
Matte Finish			250.00
1999P	8,900,000	1.00	
1999D	10,682,000	1.00	
1999S Proof			10.00
1999S Silver			
Proof	(800,000)		15.00
2000P	22,600,000	1.25	
2000D	19,466,000	1.25	
2000S Proof	(2,968,900)		6.00
2000S Silver			
Proof	(856,400)		10.00
2001P	21,200,000	1.25	
2001D	19,504,000	1.00	
2001S Proof			7.00
2001S Silver Proof			12.00
2002P		1.00	
2002D		1.00	
2002S Proof			7.00
2002S Silver Proof			12.00

BIBLIOGRAPHY

Beistle, M. L. *Register of United States Half Dollar Die Varieties and Sub-Varieties.* Shippensburg, PA, 1929. (Reprinted 1964)

Fox, Bruce. *The Complete Guide to Walking Liberty Half Dollars.* Virginia Beach, VA, 1993.

Haseltine, J. W. *Type Table of United States Dollars, Half Dollars and Quarter Dollars.* Philadelphia, 1881 (reprinted 1927, 1968).

Lawrence, David. *The Complete Guide to Barber Halves.* Virginia Beach, VA, 1991.

Overton, Al C. *Early Half Dollar Die Varieties 1794-1836.* Colorado Springs, 1967. Third Edition, 1990, edited by Donald Parsley.

Peterson, Glenn R. *The Ultimate Guide to Attributing Bust Half Dollars.* Rocky River, OH, 2000.

Wiley, Randy and Bugert, Bill. *The Complete Guide to Liberty Seated Half Dollars.* Virginia Beach, VA, 1993.

SILVER DOLLARS — 1794 to Date

The silver dollar was authorized by Congress April 2, 1792. Weight and fineness were specified at 416 grains and 892.4 fine. The first issues appeared in 1794 and until 1804 all silver dollars had the value stamped on the edge: HUNDRED CENTS, ONE DOLLAR OR UNIT. After a lapse in coinage of the silver dollar during the period 1804 to 1835, coins were made with either plain or reeded edges and the value was placed on the reverse side.

The weight was changed by the law of January 18, 1837 to 412$\frac{1}{2}$ grains, fineness .900. The coinage was discontinued by the Act of February 12, 1873 and reauthorized by the Act of February 28, 1878. The dollar was again discontinued after 1935, and since then only the copper-nickel pieces first authorized in 1971 have been coined for circulation. See bullion coins on page 333.

ORIGIN OF THE DOLLAR

The word *Dollar* evolves from German *Thaler*, the name given to the first large-sized European silver coin. Designed as a substitute for the gold *Florin*, the coin originated in the Tyrol in 1484. So popular did these large silver coins become during the 16th century that many other countries struck similar pieces, giving them names derived from "thaler". In the Netherlands the coin was called *Rijksdaalder*, in Denmark *Rigsdaler*, in Italy *Tallero*, in Poland *Talar*, in France *Jocandale*, in Russia *Jefimok*. All these names are abbreviations of "Joachimsthaler." Until the discovery of the great silver deposits in Mexican and South American mines, the mint with the greatest output of large silver coins was that of Joachimsthal in the Bohemian Erzgebirge.

The Spanish Dollar, or piece-of-eight, was widely used and familiar to everyone in the English-American colonies. It was only natural therefore that the word "dollar" was adopted officially as the standard monetary unit of the United States by Congress on July 6, 1785. The Continental Dollar of 1776 is described on page 33.

+ or − indicates change from previous year	TYPE COIN VALUES									
	G-4	F-12	EF-40	AU-50	MS-60	MS-63	MS-65	PF-60	PF-63	PF-65
Flowing Hair 1794-1795......	850.00+	1,900+	5,000+	8,000+	*30,000+*	42,000+	250,000+			
Drpd Bust, SE 1795-1798...	775.00+	1,700+	5,500+	8,000+	29,000+	*45,000+*	*175,000+*			
Drpd Bust, HE 1798-1804...	500.00+	1,000+	2,000+	4,500+	12,500+	*25,000+*	125,000	80,000		
Lib Seat-NM 1840-1866......	100.00	175.00	275.00	550.00	850.00	2,800	18,000	1,500	3,250	*12,000*
Lib. Seat-WM 1866-1873....	100.00	175.00	300.00	575.00	1,100	3,000	23,000	1,500	3,000	*10,000*
U.S. Trade Dol 1873-1883 ..	45.00	90.00	140.00	250.00	450.00	1,350	8,500	1,000	2,300	7,200
Morgan Dol 1878-1921.......	*8.00*	*9.00*	11.00+	12.00+	17.00	25.00	90.00	850.00	1,500	5,200
Peace Dol 1921-1935..........	*8.00*	*9.00*	10.00	11.00	14.00	25.00	100.00-			

FLOWING HAIR TYPE 1794-1795

Varieties listed are those most significant to collectors, but numerous minor variations may be found because each of the early dies was individually made. Blanks were weighed before the dollars were struck and overweight pieces were filed to remove excess silver. Coins showing old "adjustment marks" may be worth less than values shown here. Some Flowing Hair type dollars of 1795 were weight-adjusted by inserting a small (8mm) silver plug in the center of the blank planchet before striking the coin. Values of variations not listed in this guide depend on collector interest and demand. Values shown here for uncirculated pieces are for well struck, attractive coins with a minimum of surface marks.

Designer Robert Scot; weight 26.96 grams; composition: .8924 silver, .1076 copper; approx. diameter 39-40 mm; edge: HUNDRED CENTS ONE DOLLAR OR UNIT with decorations between words.

AG-3 ABOUT GOOD —*Clear enough to identify.*
G-4 GOOD —*Date and letters readable. Main devices outlined, but lack details.*
VG-8 VERY GOOD —*Major details discernible. Letters well formed but worn.*
F-12 FINE —*Hair ends distinguishable. Top hairlines show, but otherwise worn smooth.*
VF-20 VERY FINE —*Hair in center shows some detail. Other details more bold.*
EF-40 EXTREMELY FINE —*Hair well defined but will show some wear.*
MS-60 UNCIRCULATED —*No trace of wear. Light blemishes.*

SILVER DOLLARS

	Quan. Minted	AG-3	G-4	VG-8	F-12	VF-20	EF-40	MS-60
1794	1,758	$7,000	$10,000	$16,000	$25,000	$50,000	$95,000	$240,000

Two Leaves Beneath Each Wing   **Three Leaves Beneath Each Wing**   **Silver Plug 1795**

	Quan. Minted	AG-3	G-4	VG-8	F-12	VF-20	EF-40	MS-60
1795 Two leaves		$600.00	$850.00	$1,100	$2,000	$2,400	$7,000	$37,000
1795 Three leaves	160,295	600.00	850.00	1,000	1,900	3,200	6,500	30,000
1795 Silver plug		650.00	1,000	1,450	2,500	4,650	8,500	55,000

DRAPED BUST TYPE, SMALL EAGLE REVERSE 1795-1798

AG-3 ABOUT GOOD—*Clear enough to identify.*
G-4 GOOD—*Bust outlined, no detail. Date readable, some leaves evident.*
VG-8 VERY GOOD—*Drapery worn except deepest folds. Hairlines smooth.*
F-12 FINE—*All drapery lines distinguishable. Hairlines near cheek and neck show some detail.*
VF-20 VERY FINE—*Left side of drapery worn smooth.*
EF-40 EXTREMELY FINE—*Drapery shows distinctly. Hair well outlined and detailed.*
MS-60 UNCIRCULATED—*No trace of wear. Light blemishes.*

1795 Off-center bust	42,738	600.00	850.00	975.00	1,750	2,650	5,350	25,000
1795 Centered bust		600.00	850.00	975.00	1,750	2,650	5,350	25,000

SILVER DOLLARS

Small Date

Large Date

Small Letters

Large Letters

	Quan. Minted	AG-3	G-4	VG-8	F-12	VF-20	EF-40	MS-60
1796 All kinds	72,920							
1796 Sm. dt. sm. let.		$600.00	$850.00	$1,000	$1,850	$2,750	$5,500	$35,000
1796 Sm. date, lg. let		575.00	800.00	950.00	1,750	2,600	5,350	29,000
1796 Lg. date, sm. let.		575.00	800.00	950.00	1,750	2,600	5,350	32,000
1797 All kinds	7,776							
1797, 10 stars left, 6 right		550.00	775.00	1,000	1,750	2,750	5,500	29,000
1797, 9 stars l., 7 r., lg. let.		550.00	775.00	950.00	1,700	2,600	5,500	29,000
1797, 9 stars l., 7 r., sm. let		975.00	1,275	2,000	2,950	4,650	9,750	55,000
1798 All kinds	327,536							
1798, 15 stars on obverse		900.00	1,250	1,700	2,500	3,200	6,800	35,000
1798, 13 stars on obverse		750.00	975.00	1,200	1,900	3,000	5,900	10,000

HERALDIC EAGLE REVERSE 1798-1804

G-4 GOOD—*Letters and date readable. E PLURIBUS UNUM illegible.*
VG-8 VERY GOOD—*Motto partially readable. Only deepest drapery details visible. All other lines smooth.*
F-12 FINE—*All drapery lines distinguishable. Hairlines near cheek and neck show some detail.*
VF-20 VERY FINE—*Left side of drapery worn smooth.*
EF-40 EXTREMELY FINE—*Drapery is distinct. Hair well detailed.*
MS-60 UNCIRCULATED—*No trace of wear. Light blemishes.*

The two earliest reverse dies of 1798 have five vertical lines in the stripes in the shield. All dollar dies thereafter have four vertical lines.

4 vertical lines in shield

	Quan. Minted	G-4	VG-8	F-12	VF-20	EF-40	MS-60
1798 Knob 9, 5 vertical lines		$525.00	$625.00	$1,000	$1,650	$2,100	$13,500
1798 Knob 9, 4 vertical lines		500.00	600.00	1,000	1,800	2,300	—
1798 Knob 9, 10 arrows		550.00	700.00	1,400	2,000	2,500	—
1798 Pointed 9, Close date		500.00	600.00	1,000	1,600	2,000	13,500
1798 Pointed 9, Wide date		500.00	600.00	1,000	1,600	2,000	13,500

SILVER DOLLARS

1799 over 98, Stars 7 and 6   **Stars 8 and 5**

	Quan. Minted	G-4	VG-8	F-12	VF-20	EF-40	MS-60
1798 Pointed 9, 5 vertical lines		$550.00	$650.00	$1,250	$1,850	$2,500	—
1798 Pointed 9, 10 arrows		500.00	600.00	1,000	1,600	2,000	$12,500
1798 Pointed 9, 4 berries		500.00	600.00	1,100	1,700	2,200	—
1799 All kinds...................	423,515						
1799 9 over 8 rev. with 15 stars		500.00	600.00	1,000	1,650	2,200	13,500
1799 9 over 8 rev. with 13 stars		500.00	600.00	1,000	1,600	2,100	13,000
1799 Irregular date, 15-star rev....		525.00	650.00	1,100	1,750	2,200	—
1799 Irregular date, 13-star rev....		600.00	700.00	1,250	2,000	2,500	—
1799 Normal date...........................		500.00	600.00	1,000	1,600	2,000	12,500
1799 Stars - 8 left, 5 right..............		550.00	675.00	1,100	1,800	2,250	14,500
1800 All kinds...................	220,920						
1800 Very wide date, low 8............		500.00	600.00	1,000	1,600	2,100	14,500
1800 "Dotted date" from die breaks		500.00	600.00	1,000	1,600	2,100	—
1800 Only 12 arrows		500.00	600.00	1,000	1,600	2,000	13,000
1800 Normal dies		500.00	600.00	1,000	1,600	2,000	13,000
1800 AMERICAI		500.00	600.00	1,000	1,600	2,000	12,500
1801 54,454		500.00	600.00	1,100	1,700	2,650	19,500
1801 Proof restrike (rev. struck from first die of 1804 dollar).						(Proof)	100,000

1802 over 1   **Small 3**   **Large 3**

	Quan. Minted	G-4	VG-8	F-12	VF-20	EF-40	MS-60
1802 All kinds......................	41,650						
1802 2 over 1, narrow date		525.00	625.00	1,000	1,750	2,650	13,500
1802 2 over 1, wide date		500.00	600.00	950.00	1,700	2,600	13,500
1802 Narrow normal date..............		500.00	600.00	900.00	1,600	2,200	13,000
1802 Wide normal date.................		550.00	650.00	1,100	1,750	2,350	—
1802 Proof restrike.........................						(Proof)	80,000
1803 Small 3................. }	85,634	500.00	600.00	1,000	1,600	2,600	15,500
1803 Large 3		500.00	600.00	1,000	1,600	2,600	15,500
1803 Proof restrike.........................						(Proof)	90,000

SILVER DOLLARS
THE 1804 DOLLAR

FIRST REVERSE

SECOND REVERSE

Note position of words
STATES OF
with relation to clouds.

Compare
with first
reverse.

1804 First reverse, Original (Childs specimen sold for $4,140,000 in 1999.)
1804 Second reverse, Restrike (Adams specimen sold for $874,000 in 2001.)
1804 Second reverse, Restrike with plain edge. Unique in Smithsonian.

The 1804 dollar is one of the most publicized rarities in the entire series of United States coins. There are specimens known as originals (first reverse), of which eight are known, and restrikes (second reverse), of which seven are known, one of which has a plain edge.

Numismatists have found that the 1804 "original" dollars were struck at the mint in the 1834-35 period, for use in presentation proof sets. The first known specimen, a proof, was obtained from a mint officer by Mr. Stickney on May 9, 1843, in exchange for an "Immune Columbia" piece in gold. Later, in 1859, the pieces known as restrikes and electrotypes were made at the mint to supply the needs of collectors who wanted specimens of these dollars.

Evidence that these pieces were struck during the later period is based on the fact that the 1804 dollars differ from issues of 1803 or earlier and conform more closely to those struck after 1836, their edges or borders having beaded segments and raised rim, not elongated denticles such as are found on the earlier dates.

Although the mint records state that 19,570 dollars were coined in 1804, in no place does it mention that they were dated 1804. It was the practice in those days to use old dies as long as they were serviceable with no regard in the annual reports for the dating of the coins. It is probable that the 1804 total for dollars actually covered coins that were dated 1803.

BIBLIOGRAPHY

Bolender, M. H. *The United States Early Silver Dollars from 1794 to 1803*. 3rd edition. Iola, WI, 1982. (Reprinted 1987)

Bowers, Q. David. *The Rare Silver Dollars Dated 1804*. Wolfeboro, NH, 1999.

Bowers, Q. David. *Silver Dollars and Trade Dollars of the United States: A Complete Encyclopedia*. Wolfeboro, NH, 1993.

Haseltine, J. W. *Type Table of United States Dollars, Half Dollars and Quarter Dollars*. Philadelphia, 1881 (reprinted 1927, 1968).

Newman, Eric P. and Bressett, Kenneth E. *The Fantastic 1804 Dollar*. Racine, WI, 1962.

SILVER DOLLARS
GOBRECHT DOLLARS — 1836-1839

Suspension of silver dollar coinage was lifted in 1831; however, not until 1835 were steps taken to resume coinage. Late in that year Director R.M. Patterson ordered Engraver Christian Gobrecht to prepare a pair of dies from designs by Thomas Sully and Titian Peale. The first obverse die bore the seated figure of Liberty on the obverse with the inscription C. GOBRECHT F. (F. is an abbreviation for the Latin word *Fecit* or "made it") below the base of Liberty. On the reverse was a large eagle flying left surrounded by twenty-six stars and the legend UNITED STATES OF AMERICA ONE DOLLAR. Criticism may have forced Gobrecht's name to be moved to the base of Liberty and, with this new die, pieces were struck in late 1836 on the 1792 standard of 416 grains.

In early 1837 the weight was lowered to 412$\frac{1}{2}$ grains and pieces were struck in March, 1837, using the dies of 1836. To distinguish the 1837 coinage from that of 1836, the reverse die was oriented in "medal" fashion.

Between 1855 and 1870 the Mint produced restrikes to satisfy collector demand. Mules (mismatched combinations of dies) were also struck in the 1850's and are rare. Restrikes and mules are seldom seen in worn condition.

Dollars issued for circu-

Original 1836 die alignment
using either "coin" ↑↓ turn
or "medal" ↑ ↑ turn.

Die alignment of original
issues dated 1838 and 1839
and all restrikes.

lation in 1836, 1837, and 1839 are found with different die alignments. The "original" issue of December 1836 has the normal "coin" alignment (reverse upright when coin is flipped around a <u>horizontal</u> axis) with the eagle flying upward. These coins were usually made on 416 grain planchets. The "second original" issue of March, 1837 (made from dies dated 1836) differs from the 1836 issue in that the dies are oriented in a "medal" alignment: reverse upright when the coin is rotated around a <u>vertical</u> axis. The first ones struck, perhaps 125-150 coins, had the eagle flying upward as in 1836. The reverse die then rotated for 50-75 coins until it settled into a position with the eagle flying level, remaining there for the remaining 400 or so of the total 600 struck. These coins were made from heavy planchets prepared by the mint in 1836 before the standard changed in 1837.

Restrikes use the same die combination as originals but with the eagle flying level when rotated (see illustrations). Mules with wrong edge or die combinations also exist and are extremely rare.

SILVER DOLLARS
CIRCULATION ISSUES AND PATTERNS

	VF-20	EF-40	Proof-60
1836 C. GOBRECHT F. below base. Rev. Eagle flying upward amid stars. Plain edge ↑↓ . Pattern			—
1836 C. GOBRECHT F. on base. Rev. as above. Plain edge ↑↓ . Circulation issue. 1,000 struck..............	$4,000	$5,500	$8,500
1836 As above. Plain edge medal turn. Eagle flying upward or level. Circulation issue struck in 1837 on new standard. 600 struck....................................	4,500	5,750	9,000

	VF-20	EF-40	Proof-60
1838 Similar obv., designer's name omitted, stars added around border. Rev. Eagle flying in plain field. Reeded edge. Medal turn. (Pattern)			—
1839 As above. Reeded edge. Medal turn, eagle level. Circulation issue. 300 struck	5,000	7,000	11,000

RESTRIKES

Restrikes were produced between 1857 and 1870 and are not official coins. All have the eagle flying level.

1836 Name below base. Eagle in starry field. Plain edge............................	25,000
1836 Name on base. Plain or reeded edge (reeded edge is rare)	10,000
1838 Designer's name omitted. Plain or reeded edge. (plain edge is rare)	17,500
1839 Same as above. Plain or reeded edge. (plain edge is rare)................	12,500

[182]

SILVER DOLLARS

LIBERTY SEATED TYPE — HERALDIC EAGLE 1840-1873

Starting in 1840 silver dollars were issued for general circulation, but by spring 1853 the silver content of such pieces was worth more than the face value, and later issues were not seen in circulation but were used mainly in export trade. This situation continued through the late 1860s. The seated figure of Liberty device was adopted for the obverse, but the flying eagle design was rejected in favor of the more familiar form with olive branch and arrows used for the other silver denominations.

The 1866 proof quarter, half and dollar without motto are not mentioned in the Director's Report, and were not issued for circulation.

Mint mark location is on the reverse below eagle.

Designer Christian Gobrecht; weight 26.73 grams; composition: .900 silver, .100 copper; diameter 38.1 mm; reeded edge; mints: Philadelphia, New Orleans, Carson City, San Francisco. Net weight: .77344 oz. pure silver.

VG-8 VERY GOOD—*Any 3 letters of LIBERTY at least two-thirds complete.*
F-12 FINE—*All 7 letters of LIBERTY visible though weak.*
VF-20 VERY FINE—*LIBERTY is strong but its ribbon shows slight wear.*
EF-40 EXTREMELY FINE—*Horizontal lines of shield complete. Eagle's eye plain.*
MS-60 UNCIRCULATED—*No trace of wear. Light marks or blemishes.*

	Quan. Minted	VG-8	F-12	VF-20	EF-40	MS-60	Proof-60
1840	61,005	$160.00	$200.00	$250.00	$400.00	$1,800	$7,500
1841	173,000	135.00	185.00	235.00	350.00	1,200	8,500
1842	184,618	135.00	175.00	225.00	325.00	1,000	7,500
1843	165,100	135.00	175.00	225.00	325.00	1,400	7,500
1844	20,000	200.00	250.00	315.00	525.00	2,750	7,500
1845	24,500	200.00	250.00	315.00	525.00	3,500	8,000
1846	110,600	135.00	175.00	235.00	325.00	1,200	7,500
1846O	59,000	200.00	250.00	300.00	500.00	3,750	
1847	140,750	135.00	185.00	235.00	375.00	1,200	7,500
1848	15,000	325.00	425.00	600.00	775.00	3,000	7,500
1849	62,600	150.00	210.00	275.00	425.00	1,500	7,500
1850	7,500	400.00	550.00	800.00	1,200	4,700	7,500
1850O	40,000	240.00	325.00	600.00	1,200	6,000	
1851 Original, high date	1,300	4,000	8,500	10,000	12,000	20,000	20,000
1851 Restrike, date centered							16,000
1852 Original	1,100	3,000	7,500	8,000	10,000	17,000	
1852 Restrike							12,000
1853	46,110	210.00	275.00	365.00	500.00	2,100	12,000
1854	33,140	950.00	1,200	1,800	3,000	5,500	10,000
1855	26,000	800.00	1,100	1,500	2,500	5,500	10,000
1856	63,500	250.00	325.00	435.00	900.00	3,000	5,000
1857	94,000	250.00	325.00	435.00	900.00	2,250	4,500
1858	Estimated *(300+)*	2,500	3,200	4,800	5,500		6,000

SILVER DOLLARS

	Quan. Minted	VG-8	F-12	VF-20	EF-40	MS-60	Proof-63
1859..............(800)	256,500	$225.00	$325.00	$425.00	$550.00	$2,000	$3,500
1859O 360,000		125.00	170.00	200.00	275.00	850.00	
1859S..............................20,000		300.00	375.00	600.00	1,200	7,000	
1860...........(1,330)	218,930	250.00	300.00	400.00	500.00	1,200	3,500
1860O 515,000		125.00	175.00	200.00	275.00	850.00	
1861...........(1,000)	78,500	425.00	550.00	800.00	1,000	2,800	3,500
1862..............(550)	12,090	375.00	475.00	700.00	950.00	3,000	3,500
1863..............(460)	27,660	275.00	300.00	400.00	600.00	2,300	3,250
1864..............(470)	31,170	180.00	250.00	350.00	550.00	2,200	3,250
1865..............(500)	47,000	180.00	250.00	350.00	500.00	2,200	3,250
1866 *(2 known)*..............							—

Motto "In God We Trust" Added to Reverse 1866-1873

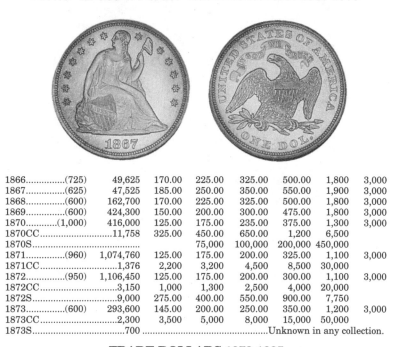

	Quan. Minted	VG-8	F-12	VF-20	EF-40	MS-60	Proof-63
1866..............(725)	49,625	170.00	225.00	325.00	500.00	1,800	3,000
1867..............(625)	47,525	185.00	250.00	350.00	550.00	1,900	3,000
1868..............(600)	162,700	170.00	225.00	325.00	500.00	1,800	3,000
1869..............(600)	424,300	150.00	200.00	300.00	475.00	1,800	3,000
1870...........(1,000)	416,000	125.00	175.00	235.00	375.00	1,300	3,000
1870CC...........................11,758		325.00	450.00	650.00	1,200	6,500	
1870S....................................		75,000	100,000	200,000	450,000		
1871..............(960)	1,074,760	125.00	175.00	200.00	325.00	1,100	3,000
1871CC..............................1,376		2,200	3,200	4,500	8,500	30,000	
1872..............(950)	1,106,450	125.00	175.00	200.00	300.00	1,100	3,000
1872CC..............................3,150		1,000	1,300	2,500	4,000	20,000	
1872S..............................9,000		275.00	400.00	550.00	900.00	7,750	
1873..............(600)	293,600	145.00	200.00	250.00	350.00	1,200	3,000
1873CC..............................2,300		3,500	5,000	8,000	15,000	50,000	
1873S....................................700					Unknown in any collection.		

TRADE DOLLARS 1873-1885

This coin was issued for circulation in the Orient to compete with dollar-size coins of other countries. It weighed 420 grains compared to 412½ grains, the weight of the regular silver dollar.

Many of the pieces that circulated in the Orient were counterstamped with Oriental characters, known as "chop marks". These are generally valued lower than normal pieces.

When first coined they were legal tender in the United States to the extent of $5.00, but with the decline in price of silver bullion Congress repealed the legal tender provision in 1876 and authorized the Treasury to limit coinage to export demand. In 1887 a law was passed authorizing the Treasury to redeem, for six months, all Trade dollars that were not mutilated.

The Trade dollars of 1884 and 1885 were unknown to collectors generally

TRADE DOLLARS 1873 - 1885

until 1908. None is listed in the Director's Report and numismatists believe that they are not a part of the regular mint issue. After 1878, strikings were specimen proofs only.

The law authorizing Trade dollars was repealed in February, 1887.

Designer William Barber; weight 27.22 grams; composition: .900 silver, .100 copper; diameter 38.1 mm; reeded edge; mints: Philadelphia, Carson City, San Francisco. Net weight: .7874 oz. pure silver.

VG-8 VERY GOOD—About half of mottoes IN GOD WE TRUST and E PLURIBUS UNUM will show. Rim on both sides well defined.
F-12 FINE—Mottoes and LIBERTY readable but worn.
EF-40 EXTREMELY FINE—Mottoes and LIBERTY are sharp. Only slight wear on rims.
MS-60 UNCIRCULATED—No trace of wear. Light blemishes.

**1875S
S over CC**

Mint mark location on reverse above letter "D" in dollar.

	Quan. Minted	VG-8	F-12	EF-40	MS-60	Proof-63
1873 ....(865)	397,500	$85.00	$100.00	$200.00	$550.00	$2,300
1873CC 124,500		130.00	175.00	475.00	1,500	
1873S 703,000		85.00	100.00	225.00	900.00	
1874 ....(700)	987,800	85.00	100.00	200.00	450.00	2,300
1874CC 1,373,200		90.00	115.00	200.00	900.00	
1874S 2,549,000		75.00	95.00	175.00	450.00	
1875 ....(700)	218,900	150.00	300.00	550.00	1,300	2,400
1875CC 1,573,700		85.00	100.00	250.00	750.00	
1875S 4,487,000		75.00	95.00	140.00	450.00	
1875S, S over CC........................		200.00	275.00	700.00	2,200	
1876 ....(1,150)	456,150	75.00	95.00	145.00	450.00	2,400
1876CC 509,000		85.00	100.00	300.00	1,300	
1876S 5,227,000		75.00	90.00	145.00	450.00	
1877 ....(510)	3,039,710	75.00	90.00	145.00	500.00	2,400
1877CC 534,000		125.00	185.00	325.00	1,100	
1877S 9,519,000		75.00	90.00	145.00	450.00	
1878 ....(900)		....		1,000		2,400
1878CC *97,000		400.00	575.00	1,600	6,000	
1878S 4,162,000		75.00	90.00	145.00	450.00	
1879 ....(1,541)		....		900.00		2,300
1880 ....(1,987)		....		900.00		2,300
1881 ....(960)		....		1,000		2,300
1882 ....(1,097)		....		900.00		2,300
1883 ....(979)		....		1,000		2,400
1884 ....(10)		....				100,000
1885 ....(5)		....				250,000

*44,148 Trade dollars were melted on July 19, 1878. Many of these may have been 1878CC.

BIBLIOGRAPHY
Willem, John M. *The United States Trade Dollar.* Second edition, Racine, Wis., 1965.

SILVER DOLLARS
LIBERTY HEAD OR MORGAN TYPE 1878-1921

The coinage law of 1873 made no provision for the standard silver dollar. During the lapse in coinage of this denomination the gold dollar became the unit coin, and the trade dollar was used for our commercial transactions with the Orient.

Resumption of coinage of the silver dollar was authorized by the Act of February 28, 1878, known as the Bland-Allison Act. The weight ($412\frac{1}{2}$ grains) and fineness (.900) were to conform with the Act of January 18, 1837.

George T. Morgan, formerly a pupil of Wyon in the Royal Mint in London, designed the new dollar. His initial M is found at the truncation of the neck, at the last tress. It also appears on the reverse on the left-hand loop of the ribbon.

Coinage of the silver dollar was suspended after 1904 when the bullion supply became exhausted. Under provisions of the Pittman Act of 1918, 270,232,722 silver dollars were melted and later, in 1921, coinage of the silver dollar was resumed. The Morgan design, with some slight refinements, was employed until the new Peace design was adopted later in that year.

Varieties listed are those most significant to collectors. Numerous other variations exist. Values are shown for the most common pieces. Prices of variations not listed in this guide depend on collector interest and demand.

Sharply struck, "proof-like" coins have a highly reflective surface and are very scarce, usually commanding substantial premiums.

BIBLIOGRAPHY
Bowers, Q. David. *Silver Dollars and Trade Dollars of the United States; a Complete Encyclopedia.* Wolfeboro, NH, 1993.

Fay, Michael S., and Jeff Oxman. *The Top 100 Morgan Dollar Varieties.* Morris Planes, NJ, 1997.

Highfill, John W. *The Comprehensive U.S. Silver Dollar Encyclopedia.* Broken Arrow, OK, 1992.

Van Allen, Leroy C. and Mallis, A. George. *Comprehensive Catalogue and Encyclopedia of U.S. Morgan and Peace Silver Dollars.* New York. 1997.

Designer George T. Morgan; weight 26.73 grams; composition: .900 silver, .100 copper; diameter 38.1 mm; reeded edge; mints: Philadelphia, New Orleans, Carson City, Denver, San Francisco. Net weight: .77344 oz. pure silver.

Mint mark location is on reverse below wreath.

First Reverse 1878 Only

8 Tail Feathers, 1878 Philadelphia Only

Second Reverse	Third Reverse	

Parallel top arrow feather, concave breast.

Slanted top arrow feather, convex breast.

1878 doubled tail feathers

SILVER DOLLARS

VF-20 VERY FINE — *Two-thirds of hairlines from top of forehead to ear must show. Ear well defined. Feathers on eagle's breast worn.*

EF-40 EXTREMELY FINE — *All hairlines strong and ear bold. Eagle's feathers all plain but slight wear on breast and wing tips.*

AU-50 ABOUT UNCIRCULATED — *Slight trace of wear. Most of mint luster is present although marred by bag marks.*

MS-60 UNCIRCULATED — *No trace of wear. Has full mint luster but may be noticeably marred by scuff marks or bag abrasions.*

MS-63 SELECT UNCIRCULATED — *No trace of wear, full mint luster, few noticeable surface marks.*

MS-65 UNCIRCULATED — *Many Morgan dollars in this grade are very rare and command much higher prices. The most common dates sell for approximately $90.00.*

See page 6 for information on investment grade coins.

	Quan. Minted	VF-20	EF-40	AU-50	MS-60	MS-63	Proof-63
1878, 8 tail feathers.(500)	750,000	$18.00	$22.00	$33.00	$90.00	$125.00	$2,300
1878, 7 tail feathers.(250)	9,759,550						
1878 Clear doubled tail feathers		20.00	25.00	45.00	95.00	145.00	
1878, 7 feathers, 2nd reverse		13.00	16.00	23.00	40.00	65.00	
1878, 7 feathers, 3rd reverse		15.00	18.00	25.00	40.00	135.00	6,000
1878CC	2,212,000	45.00	50.00	75.00	130.00	150.00	
1878S	9,774,000	13.00	15.00	21.00	35.00	45.00	
1879 (1,100)	14,807,100	12.00	14.00	16.00	25.00	45.00	1,900
1879CC CC over CC	756,000	115.00	300.00	600.00	1,400	3,000	
1879CC Clear CC		125.00	350.00	750.00	1,600	3,200	
1879O	2,887,000	12.00	14.00	18.00	65.00	130.00	
1879S Second reverse	9,110,000	15.00	20.00	35.00	90.00	325.00	
1879S Third reverse		12.00	14.00	16.00	25.00	35.00	
1880, 8 over 7*	12,601,355	16.00	20.00	30.00	70.00	250.00	
1880 (1,355)		12.00	13.00	15.00	21.00	45.00	2,400

1880CC, 80 over 79‡

1880CC, 8 over high 7*

1880CC, 8 over low 7

	Quan. Minted	VF-20	EF-40	AU-50	MS-60	MS-63	Proof-63
1880CC All kinds	591,000						
1880CC, 80 over 79, 2nd rev. ‡		85.00	110.00	160.00	210.00	320.00	
1880CC, 8 over 7, 2nd rev.		85.00	110.00	160.00	185.00	275.00	
1880CC, 8 over high 7, 3rd rev.*		70.00	100.00	130.00	165.00	250.00	
1880CC, 8 over low 7, 3rd. rev.		70.00	100.00	130.00	165.00	250.00	
1880CC Third reverse		70.00	100.00	130.00	165.00	225.00	
1880O, 8 over 7*	5,305,000	14.00	20.00	30.00	70.00	375.00	
1880O		12.00	14.00	18.00	50.00	275.00	
1880S, 8 over 7*	8,900,000	13.00	17.00	20.00	30.00	40.00	
1880S, 0 over 9		13.00	17.00	20.00	30.00	40.00	
1880S		12.00	14.00	16.00	20.00	30.00	
1881 (984)	9,163,984	12.00	13.00	17.00	24.00	40.00	1,700
1881CC	296,000	130.00	140.00	160.00	230.00	275.00	
1881O	5,708,000	12.00	13.00	15.00	21.00	38.00	
1881S	12,760,000	12.00	13.00	15.00	20.00	30.00	
1882 (1,100)	11,101,100	12.00	13.00	15.00	21.00	35.00	1,600
1882CC	1,133,000	45.00	55.00	65.00	90.00	120.00	
1882O	6,090,000	12.00	13.00	15.00	20.00	35.00	
1882O, O over S*		17.00	20.00	45.00	135.00	850.00	

*Several die varieties. Values shown are for the most common.

‡7 and 9 show within the 80, no tip below second 8.

Proof Morgan Dollars where indicated in mintage record (quantity shown in parenthesis) are valued approximately as follows:

    Proof-60 $850.00   **Proof-65 $5,200**

SILVER DOLLARS

	Quan. Minted	VF-20	EF-40	AU-50	MS-60	MS-63	Proof-63
1882S 9,250,000		$12.00	$13.00	$15.00	$22.00	$35.00	
1883 ....(1,039)	12,291,039	12.00	13.00	15.00	20.00	33.00	$1,500
1883CC 1,204,000		45.00	50.00	60.00	90.00	100.00	
1883O................................8,725,000		12.00	13.00	15.00	20.00	30.00	
1883S 6,250,000		14.00	25.00	125.00	400.00	1,400	
1884 ....(875)	14,070,875	12.00	13.00	15.00	20.00	33.00	1,500
1884CC 1,136,000		50.00	60.00	65.00	90.00	100.00	
1884O................................9,730,000		12.00	13.00	15.00	20.00	30.00	
1884S 3,200,000		16.00	32.00	225.00	3,500	23,000	
1885 ....(930)	17,787,930	12.00	13.00	15.00	20.00	30.00	1,500
1885CC 228,000		210.00	235.00	250.00	275.00	290.00	
1885O................................9,185,000		12.00	13.00	15.00	20.00	30.00	
1885S 1,497,000		15.00	20.00	50.00	120.00	180.00	
1886 ....(886)	19,963,886	12.00	13.00	15.00	20.00	30.00	1,500
1886O................................10,710,000		14.00	18.00	70.00	300.00	2,500	
1886S 750,000		32.00	47.00	70.00	160.00	250.00	
1887, 7 over 6 } (710)	20,290,710	22.00	35.00	85.00	200.00	650.00	
1887...............		12.00	13.00	15.00	20.00	30.00	1,500
1887O, 7 over 6........ }	11,550,000	25.00	40.00	100.00	325.00	2,300	
1887O.........................		13.00	15.00	21.00	40.00	110.00	
1887S 1,771,000		15.00	18.00	35.00	75.00	160.00	

**1888O
Doubled Die
Obverse
"Hot Lips"
variety**

**1901 Doubled Die Reverse
Note Tail Feathers**

		VF-20	EF-40	AU-50	MS-60	MS-63	Proof-63
1888 ....(832)	19,183,832	12.00	13.00	15.00	20.00	30.00	1,500
1888O..............................12,150,000		12.00	14.00	15.00	23.00	35.00	
1888O Doubled die obv		50.00	125.00	320.00	1,300	—	
1888S 657,000		35.00	45.00	80.00	165.00	250.00	
1889 ....(811)	21,726,811	12.00	13.00	15.00	20.00	30.00	1,500
1889CC 350,000		500.00	1,000	2,800	6,750	16,500	
1889O..............................11,875,000		14.00	17.00	30.00	100.00	225.00	
1889S 700,000		23.00	33.00	55.00	130.00	200.00	
1890 ....(590)	16,802,590	12.00	13.00	15.00	21.00	35.00	1,600
1890CC 2,309,041		45.00	50.00	100.00	275.00	400.00	
1890O..............................10,701,000		13.00	16.00	25.00	35.00	75.00	
1890S 8,230,373		13.00	16.00	25.00	35.00	75.00	
1891 ....(650)	8,694,206	13.00	16.00	25.00	40.00	135.00	1,600
1891CC 1,618,000		45.00	55.00	100.00	260.00	300.00	
1891O................................7,954,529		14.00	18.00	30.00	90.00	225.00	
1891S 5,296,000		13.00	15.00	22.00	40.00	85.00	
1892 ....(1,245)	1,037,245	15.00	24.00	50.00	120.00	275.00	1,600
1892CC 1,352,000		65.00	120.00	210.00	425.00	775.00	
1892O................................2,744,000		15.00	18.00	55.00	100.00	225.00	
1892S 1,200,000		40.00	150.00	1,500	14,500	45,000	

For Proof-60 and Proof-65 Morgan dollar prices see page 187.

SILVER DOLLARS

	Quan. Minted	VF-20	EF-40	AU-50	MS-60	MS-63	Proof-63
1893 ....(792)	378,792	$90.00	$150.00	$200.00	$350.00	$750.00	$2,000
1893CC 677,000		250.00	550.00	825.00	1,450	3,600	
1893O 300,000		135.00	225.00	550.00	1,400	5,500	
1893S*...............................100,000		2,000	4,250	13,500	40,000	80,000	
1894 ....(972)	110,972	350.00	450.00	600.00	950.00	3,500	3,000
1894O 1,723,000		35.00	50.00	150.00	600.00	3,000	
1894S 1,260,000		55.00	100.00	210.00	400.00	700.00	
1895‡ ....(880)	12,880		‡14,000	‡15,500	‡18,000		24,000
1895O.............................450,000		150.00	250.00	800.00	10,000	31,000	
1895S 400,000		200.00	400.00	725.00	1,500	3,500	
1896 ....(762)	9,976,762	12.00	13.00	15.00	22.00	30.00	1,500
1896O.............................4,900,000		14.00	17.00	110.00	750.00	6,500	
1896S 5,000,000		45.00	140.00	375.00	725.00	1,500	
1897 ....(731)	2,822,731	12.00	13.00	15.00	22.00	30.00	1,500
1897O.............................4,004,000		13.00	17.00	100.00	550.00	4,200	
1897S 5,825,000		12.00	14.00	20.00	37.00	60.00	
1898 ....(735)	5,884,735	12.00	13.00	15.00	22.00	30.00	1,500
1898O.............................4,440,000		13.00	14.00	16.00	22.00	30.00	
1898S 4,102,000		16.00	24.00	60.00	160.00	250.00	
1899 ....(846)	330,846	35.00	45.00	65.00	85.00	120.00	1,500
1899O.............................12,290,000		13.00	15.00	16.00	24.00	36.00	
1899S 2,562,000		20.00	35.00	85.00	200.00	270.00	
1900 ....(912)	8,830,912	12.00	13.00	15.00	22.00	30.00	1,500
1900O....................⎫		12.00	13.00	15.00	25.00	35.00	
1900O, O over CC+ ...⎬ 12,590,000		30.00	45.00	100.00	185.00	325.00	
1900S 3,540,000		21.00	33.00	70.00	180.00	220.00	
1901* ....(813)	6,962,813	28.00	55.00	275.00	1,600	15,000	2,500
1901 Double die reverse................		175.00	450.00	1,600	—	—	
1901O.............................13,320,000		12.00	14.00	16.00	25.00	32.00	
1901S 2,284,000		25.00	45.00	160.00	180.00	475.00	
1902 ....(777)	7,994,777	12.00	14.00	22.00	35.00	75.00	1,500
1902O.............................8,636,000		12.00	14.00	16.00	22.00	30.00	
1902S 1,530,000		75.00	90.00	125.00	210.00	300.00	
1903 ....(755)	4,652,755	18.00	25.00	28.00	35.00	55.00	1,500
1903O.............................4,450,000		140.00	150.00	200.00	250.00	300.00	
1903S 1,241,000		75.00	250.00	1,000	2,600	4,200	
1904 ....(650)	2,788,650	14.00	17.00	30.00	60.00	275.00	1,600
1904O.............................3,720,000		12.00	13.00	15.00	22.00	30.00	
1904S 2,304,000		45.00	170.00	500.00	900.00	1,800	
1921.............................44,690,000		9.50	10.00	11.00	17.00	25.00	—
1921D 20,345,000		10.00	11.00	12.00	25.00	40.00	
1921S 21,695,000		10.00	11.00	12.00	25.00	45.00	

*Authentication is recommended. Beware of altered mint mark.

‡Beware of removed mint mark. Values are for Proofs; business strikes are not known to exist.

+Several die varieties.

For Proof-60 and Proof-65 Morgan dollar prices see page 187.

PEACE TYPE 1921-1935

The dollar issued from 1921 to 1935 was a commemorative peace coin, which might easily have been a half dollar. The Peace Dollar, in fact, was issued without congressional sanction, under the terms of the Pittman Act, which referred to the bullion and in no way affected the design.

Anthony De Francisci, a medalist, designed this dollar. His monogram is located in the field of the coin under the neck of Liberty.

The new Peace Dollar was placed in circulation January 3, 1922. 1,006,473 pieces were struck in December, 1921.

The high relief of the 1921 design was found impractical for coinage and was slightly modified in 1922 after 35,401 coins were made and most of them melted at the mint. The rare matte and satin finish proof specimens of 1922 are of both the high relief style of 1921, as well as of the normal relief.

SILVER DOLLARS

Legislation dated August 3, 1964 authorized the coinage of 45 million silver dollars, and 316,076 dollars of the Peace design dated 1964 were struck at the Denver mint in 1965. Plans for completing this coinage were subsequently abandoned and all of these coins were melted. None were preserved or released for circulation.

Designer Anthony De Francisci; weight 26.73 grams; composition: .900 silver, .100 copper; diameter 38.1 mm; reeded edge; mints: Philadelphia, Denver, San Francisco. Net weight: .77344 oz. pure silver.

Mint mark location is on reverse below ONE.

VF-20 VERY FINE—*Hair over eye well worn. Some strands over ear well defined. Some eagle feathers on top and outside edge of right wing will show.*

EF-40 EXTREMELY FINE—*Hairlines over brow and ear are strong though slightly worn. Outside wing feathers at right and those at top are visible but faint.*

AU-50 ABOUT UNCIRCULATED—*Slight trace of wear. Most of mint luster is present although marred by contact marks.*

MS-60 UNCIRCULATED—*No trace of wear. Has full mint luster but may be noticeably marred by stains, surface marks or bag abrasions.*

MS-63 SELECT UNCIRCULATED—*No trace of wear, full mint luster, few noticeable surface marks.*

MS-65 CHOICE UNCIRCULATED—*No trace of wear, full mint luster, and only minute surface marks.*

	Quan. Minted	VF-20	EF-40	AU-50	MS-60	MS-63	Matte Proof-65
1921 high relief	1,006,473	$42.00	$50.00	$85.00	$145.00	$225.00	$30,000
1922 high relief	35,401			—			30,000
1922 normal relief	51,737,000	9.00	10.00	11.00	14.00	25.00	30,000
1922D	15,063,000	9.00	10.00	11.00	20.00	35.00	
1922S	17,475,000	9.00	10.00	12.00	20.00	50.00	
1923	30,800,000	9.00	10.00	11.00	14.00	25.00	
1923D	6,811,000	9.00	10.00	13.00	45.00	90.00	
1923S	19,020,000	9.00	10.00	13.00	20.00	60.00	
1924	11,811,000	10.00	10.00	13.00	15.00	27.00	
1924S	1,728,000	14.00	20.00	50.00	170.00	350.00	
1925	10,198,000	10.00	11.00	13.00	14.00	27.00	
1925S	1,610,000	11.00	14.00	25.00	55.00	125.00	
1926	1,939,000	10.00	12.00	16.00	25.00	45.00	
1926D	2,348,700	10.00	13.00	27.00	50.00	115.00	
1926S	6,980,000	10.00	12.00	16.00	30.00	60.00	
1927	848,000	18.00	24.00	38.00	55.00	100.00	
1927D	1,268,900	15.00	22.00	65.00	120.00	225.00	
1927S	866,000	15.00	20.00	55.00	110.00	225.00	
1928	360,649	150.00	170.00	180.00	220.00	300.00	
1928S	1,632,000	15.00	20.00	40.00	125.00	275.00	
1934	954,057	16.00	20.00	35.00	65.00	115.00	
1934D*	1,569,500	15.00	20.00	35.00	75.00	180.00	
1934S	1,011,000	50.00	140.00	425.00	1,100	2,400	
1935	1,576,000	13.00	17.00	25.00	50.00	70.00	
1935S‡	1,964,000	13.00	18.00	65.00	135.00	260.00	

*Large and small mint mark varieties, see page 67.
‡Varieties exist with either 3 or 4 rays below ONE, and are of equal value.

EISENHOWER DOLLARS 1971-1978

Honoring both President Dwight D. Eisenhower and the first landing of man on the moon, this design is the work of Chief Engraver Frank Gasparro, whose initials are on the truncation and below the eagle. The reverse is an adaptation of the official Apollo 11 insignia. Collectors' coins were struck in 40% silver composition, and the circulation issue is copper-nickel.

Since 1971, the dies for the Eisenhower dollar have been modified several times by changing the relief, strengthening the design and making the world above the eagle more clearly defined.

Low relief (variety I) dies, with flattened world and three islands off Florida, were used for all copper-nickel issue of 1971, uncirculated silver of 1971, and most copper-nickel coins of 1972.

High relief (varity II) dies, with round world and weak or indistinct islands, were used for all proofs of 1971, all silver issues of 1972, and the reverse of some exceptional and scarce Philadelphia copper-nickel coins of 1972.

Improved high relief reverse dies (variety III), were used for late 1972 Philadelphia copper-nickel coins and for all subsequent issues. Modified high relief dies were also used on all issues begining in 1973.

A few 1974D and 1977D dollars in silver clad composition were made in error.

Designer Frank Gasparro. Silver issue: weight 24.59 grams; composition: outer layers of .800 silver, .200 copper bonded to inner core of .209 silver, .791 copper. Copper-nickel issue: weight 22.68 grams; composition: outer layers of .750 copper, .250 nickel bonded to inner core of pure copper. Diameter 38.1 mm; reeded edge; mints: Philadelphia, Denver, San Francisco. Net weight of silver issues: .3161 oz. pure silver.

Mint mark location is above the date.

	Proof	Quan. Minted Regular	EF-40	MS-63	Proof-65
1971 Copper-nickel clad		47,799,000	$1.50	$3.50	
1971D Copper-nickel clad		68,587,424	1.50	2.50	
1971S Silver clad	(4,265,234)	6,868,530		6.50	$7.00
1972 Copper-nickel clad, variety I		⎫	2.00	5.00	
1972 Copper-nickel clad, variety II		⎬ 75,890,000	5.00	50.00	
1972 Copper-nickel clad, variety III		⎭	2.00	5.00	
1972D Copper-nickel clad		92,548,511	1.50	2.50	
1972S Silver clad	(1,811,631)	2,193,056		6.50	7.00
1973 Copper-nickel clad		*2,000,056		9.00	
1973D Copper-nickel clad		*2,000,000		9.00	
1973S Copper-nickel clad	(2,760,339)				7.50
1973S Silver clad	(1,013,646)	1,883,140		7.00	27.50
1974 Copper-nickel clad		27,366,000	1.50	3.00	
1974D Copper-nickel clad		45,517,000	1.50	3.00	
1974S Copper-nickel clad	(2,612,568)				7.00
1974S Silver clad	(1,306,579)	1,900,156		6.00	7.00

*1,769,258 of each sold only in sets and not released for circulation. Unissued coins destroyed at mint.

EISENHOWER DOLLARS

BICENTENNIAL COINAGE DATED 1776-1976

The national significance of the Bicentennial of the United States was high-lighted with the adoption of new reverse designs for the quarter, half dollar and dollar. Nearly a thousand entries were submitted after the Treasury announced in October of 1973 that an open contest was to be held for the selection of the new designs. After the field was narrowed down to twelve semifinalists, the judges chose the rendition of the Liberty Bell superimposed on the moon to appear on the dollar coins. This design is the work of Dennis R. Williams.

The obverse remained unchanged except for the dual date 1776-1976, which appeared on all dollars made during 1975 and 1976. These dual-dated coins were included in the various offerings of proof and uncirculated coins made by the mint. They were also struck for general circulation. The lettering was modified early in 1975 to produce a more attractive design.

Designers Frank Gasparro and Dennis R. Williams. Silver issue: weight 24.59 grams; composition: outer layers of .800 silver, .200 copper bonded to inner core of .209 silver, .791 copper. Copper-nickel issue: weight 22.68 grams; composition: outer layers of .750 copper, .250 nickel bonded to inner core of pure copper. Diameter 38.1 mm; reeded edge; mints: Philadelphia, Denver, San Francisco. Net weight of silver issues: .3161 oz. pure silver.

Reverse Var. 2

Variety 1: Design in low relief, bold lettering on reverse. Variety 2: Sharp design, delicate lettering on reverse.

	Quan. Minted	EF-40	MS-63	Proof-65
1776-1976 Copper-nickel clad, variety 1	4,019,000	$1.50	$5.00	
1776-1976 Copper-nickel clad, variety 2	113,318,000	1.50	3.00	
1776-1976 Silver clad, variety 2				—
1776-1976D Copper-nickel clad, variety 1	21,048,710	1.50	3.00	
1776-1976D Copper-nickel clad, variety 2	82,179,564	1.50	3.00	
1776-1976S Copper-nickel clad, variety 1	(2,845,450)			$7.00
1776-1976S Copper-nickel clad, variety 2	(4,149,730)			7.00
1776-1976S Silver clad, variety 1	* 11,000,000		12.00	
1776-1976S Silver clad, variety 1	*(4,000,000)			11.00

*Approximate mintage.

EAGLE REVERSE RESUMED

1977 Copper-nickel clad	12,596,000	1.50	3.50	
1977D Copper-nickel clad	32,983,006	1.50	3.00	
1977S Copper-nickel clad	(3,251,152)			6.00
1978 Copper-nickel clad	25,702,000	1.50	2.50	
1978D Copper-nickel clad	33,012,890	1.50	3.00	
1978S Copper-nickel clad	(3,127,781)			7.00

BIBLIOGRAPHY

Wexler, Crawford, and Flynn. *The Authoritative Reference on Eisenhower Dollars.* Rancocas, NJ, 1998.

ANTHONY DOLLARS 1979-1999

Intended to honor this pioneer in women's rights, legislation dated October 10, 1978, provided for the issuance of the Susan B. Anthony dollar coin. Both obverse and reverse designs were the work of Chief Engraver of the U.S. Mint, Frank Gasparro, whose initials FG are located below the portrait and the eagle.

Placement of Susan B. Anthony's likeness on the dollar represented the first time that a woman, other than a mythical figure, has appeared on a circulating U.S. coin. The reverse design is the same as that used on the Eisenhower dollar. Mint marks P, D or S appear on the obverse, slightly above Anthony's right shoulder.

The size of this coin caused it to be confused with the quarter and half dollar, and it failed to gain widespread public acceptance. No coins were made for circulation from 1981 to 1998. In 1999 additional pieces were made to meet the needs of vending machines.

Designer Frank Gasparro; weight 8.1 grams; composition: outer layers of copper-nickel (.750 copper, .250 nickel) bonded to inner core of pure copper; diameter 26.5 mm; reeded edge; mints: Philadelphia, Denver, San Francisco.

1979S Filled S (Type I)

1979S Clear S (Type II)
1981S First S (Type I, filled)

1981S Clear S
(Type II, clear)

1979 Narrow Rim
(Far Date)

1979 Wide Rim
(Near Date)

	Quan. Minted	MS-63	Proof-65
1979P*	360,222,000		
Narrow rim		$1.50	
Wide rim		9.00	
1979D	288,015,744	1.75	
1979S	109,576,000	2.00	
1979S Proof	(3,677,175)		
Filled S			$10.00
Clear S			100.00
1980P	27,610,000	1.75	
1980D	41,628,708	1.75	

	Quan. Minted	MS-63	Proof-65
1980S	20,422,000	$2.00	
1980S Proof	(3,554,806)		$10.00
1981P‡	3,000,000	6.00	
1981D‡	3,250,000	6.00	
1981S‡	3,492,000	6.00	
1981S Proof	(4,063,083)		8.50
1981S Proof clear S			180.00
1999P	29,592,000	2.00	
1999P Proof			10.00
1999D	11,776,000	2.50	

*The obverse design was modified in 1979 to widen the border rim. Late issues of 1979P and subsequent issues have the wide rim. Dies for the 1999 coins were further modified to strengthen details on the reverse.

‡Issued only in Mint sets.

SACAGAWEA DOLLARS 2000-

The design of this coin was selected in national competition from among 120 submissions that were considered by a panel appointed by Treasury Secretary Robert Rubin. The adopted motif depicts Sacagawea, a young Native American Shoshone as conceived by artist Glenna Goodacre. On her back she carries Jean Baptiste, her infant son. The reverse shows an eagle in flight designed by mint engraver Thomas D. Rogers, Sr.

The composition exemplifies the spirit of Liberty, Peace, and Freedom shown by Sacagawea in her conduct as interpreter and guide to explorers Meriwether Louis and William Clark during their famed journey westward from the Great Northern Plains to the Pacific.

These coins have a distinctive golden color and a plain edge to distinguish them from other denominations or coins of a similar size. The change in composition and appearance was mandated under the United States Dollar Coin Act of 1997.

Several distinctive finishes can be identified on the Sacagawea dollars as a result of the mint attempting to adjust the dies, blanks, strikes or finishing to produce coins with minimum spotting and a better surface color. One group of 5,000 pieces, dated 2000, with a special finish were presented to sculptor Glenna Goodacre in payment for the obverse design. Unexplained error coins made from mismatched dies (a 50-state quarter obverse combined with a Sacagawea dollar reverse) are extremely rare.

Designers: Obv. Glenna Goodacre; Rev. Thomas D. Rogers, Sr.; weight 8.1 grams; composition: pure copper core with outer layers of manganese brass. The alloy contains .770 copper, .120 zinc, .070 manganese, and .040 nickel; diameter 26.5 mm; plain edge; mints: Philadelphia, Denver, San Francisco; 22-karat gold numismatic specimens dated 2000W were struck at West Point in 1999.

	Quan. Minted	MS-63	Proof-65
2000P	767,140,000	$2.00	
2000D	518,916,000	2.00	
2000S Proof			$8.00
2001P	62,468,000	1.50	
2001D	70,939,500	1.50	
2001S Proof			8.00

SACAGAWEA DOLLARS 2000-
SPECIAL MILLENNIUM SET

	Unc.
2000D Sacagawea dollar, 2000(W) silver eagle dollar, Series 1999 $1 Federal Reserve note	$110.00

GOLD

Gold has served as money or established the monetary value of currencies longer than any other material. The use of gold coins was widespread in Europe by the fourth century B.C.

The earliest coins circulated in the United States were foreign coins, mostly gold, brought from Europe. The Coinage Act in 1792 established an independent monetary system with the dollar as the basic United States monetary unit containing 24$\frac{3}{4}$ grains of fine gold, based on the world price of $19.39 a troy ounce (480 grains). Congress changed the gold specification in 1834 and again in 1837, when it set the dollar price of gold at $20.67 an ounce.

In 1934, United States citizens were prohibited from holding monetary gold in this country; this was extended in 1961 to gold held abroad as well. The dollar price was then set at $35 per ounce. Use of gcld in international trade was further restricted as the price rose. The government revalued it at $38 per ounce in 1972, then $42.22 in 1973. It has fluctuated widely over the past few years. All restrictions on holding gold were removed in 1975.

GOLD DOLLARS 1849-1889

Coinage of the gold dollar was authorized by the Act of March 3, 1849. The weight was 25.8 grains, fineness .900. The first type, struck until 1854, is known as the Liberty Head or small-sized type.

In 1854 the piece was made larger in diameter and thinner. The design was changed to a feather headdress on a female, generally referred to as the Indian Head or large-sized type. In 1856 the type was changed slightly by enlarging the size of the head.

+ or − indicates change from previous year	TYPE COIN VALUES									
	F-12	VF-20	EF-40	AU-50	MS-60	MS-63	MS-65	PF-60	PF-63	PF-65
Liberty Hd Type 1 1849-1854	100.00	125.00+	145.00+	160.00	275.00-	800.00	4,500-			
Indian Hd Type 2 1854-1856	160.00	275.00	350.00	550.00	2,500	16,000-	50,000-			
Indian Hd Type 3 1856-1889	100.00	125.00	145.00+	160.00	275.00-	800.00	1,800-	2,400	4,250	9,000

> Values of common gold coins have been based on the current bullion price of gold, $280 per oz., and may vary with the prevailing spot price. The weight and content is stated in the introduction to each series, and may be used to recalculate bullion value.

LIBERTY HEAD TYPE 1849-1854

Designer James B. Longacre; weight 1.672 grams; composition: .900 gold, .100 copper; diameter 13 mm; reeded edge; mints: Philadelphia, Charlotte, Dahlonega, New Orleans, San Francisco. Net weight: .04837 oz. pure gold.

VF-20 VERY FINE —*LIBERTY on headband complete and readable. Knobs on coronet are defined.*
EF-40 EXTREMELY FINE —*Slight wear on Liberty's hair. Knobs on coronet sharp.*
AU-50 ABOUT UNCIRCULATED —*Trace of wear on head band. Nearly full luster.*
MS-60 UNCIRCULATED —*No trace of wear. Light marks and blemishes.*

Type 1
With closed or open wreath.

Mint mark is below wreath.

	Quan. Minted	VF-20	EF-40	AU-50	MS-60
1849 Open wreath—All kinds*	688,567	$135.00	$165.00	$215.00	$400.00
1849 Closed wreath (ends closer to numeral)		135.00	160.00	210.00	400.00
1849C Closed wreath	} 11,634	550.00	1,000	2,300	7,500
1849C Open wreath (Ex. Rare)		200,000	325,000	—	—
1849D Open wreath	21,588	550.00	1,000	1,500	4,500
1849O Open wreath	215,000	140.00	220.00	350.00	850.00
1850	481,953	125.00	160.00	200.00	375.00
1850C	6,966	600.00	1,450	3,000	8,000
1850D	8,382	600.00	1,200	2,500	8,000
1850O	14,000	250.00	350.00	750.00	3,250

*The variety with smaller head and no L on truncation is valued higher.

GOLD DOLLARS

	Quan. Minted	VF-20	EF-40	AU-50	MS-60	Proof-63
1851	3,317,671	$125.00	$145.00	$160.00	$275.00	
1851C	41,267	475.00	700.00	1,200	2,500	
1851D	9,882	500.00	850.00	1,750	4,750	
1851O	290,000	150.00	190.00	250.00	700.00	
1852	2,045,351	125.00	145.00	160.00	275.00	
1852C	9,434	500.00	1,000	1,700	4,600	
1852D	6,360	700.00	1,250	2,100	8,500	
1852O	140,000	130.00	190.00	375.00	1,500	
1853	4,076,051	125.00	145.00	160.00	275.00	
1853C	11,515	600.00	1,100	1,900	6,000	
1853D	6,583	675.00	1,250	2,500	8,500	
1853O	290,000	150.00	175.00	250.00	650.00	
1854	855,502	125.00	145.00	160.00	275.00	—
1854D	2,935	800.00	2,000	5,000	13,000	
1854S	14,632	300.00	450.00	850.00	2,200	

INDIAN HEAD TYPE, Small Head 1854-1856

Standards same as previous issue. Diameter changed to 15 mm.

Type 2

VF-20 VERY FINE —*Feather curl tips outlined but details worn.*
EF-40 EXTREMELY FINE —*Slight wear on tips of feather curls on head dress.*
AU-50 ABOUT UNCIRCULATED —*Trace of wear on feathers, nearly full luster.*
MS-60 UNCIRCULATED —*No trace of wear. Light marks and blemishes.*

	Quan. Minted	VF-20	EF-40	AU-50	MS-60	Proof-63
1854	783,943	$275.00	$350.00	$550.00	$2,500	—
1855	758,269	275.00	350.00	550.00	2,500	—
1855C	9,803	1,100	2,400	6,000	18,000	
1855D	1,811	2,500	5,500	10,000	28,000	
1855O	55,000	425.00	700.00	1,500	6,000	
1856S	24,600	625.00	1,100	1,850	6,500	

INDIAN HEAD TYPE, Large Head 1856-1889

Type 3

VF-20 VERY FINE —*Curled feathers have slight detail. Details worn smooth at eyebrow, hair below headdress and behind ear and bottom curl.*
EF-40 EXTREMELY FINE —*Slight wear above and to right of eye and on top of curled feathers.*
AU-50 ABOUT UNCIRCULATED —*Trace of wear on feathers, nearly full luster.*
MS-60 UNCIRCULATED —*No trace of wear. Light marks and blemishes.*

	Quan. Minted	VF-20	EF-40	AU-50	MS-60	Proof-63
1856 Upright 5	1,762,936	$125.00	$160.00	$200.00	$500.00	
1856 Slant 5		125.00	145.00	165.00	300.00	$10,000
1856D	1,460	3,600	5,250	7,500	26,000	
1857	774,789	125.00	145.00	165.00	285.00	10,000
1857C	13,280	550.00	1,300	3,100	12,500	
1857D	3,533	700.00	1,750	3,250	11,000	
1857S	10,000	475.00	650.00	1,300	5,800	
1858	117,995	125.00	145.00	165.00	285.00	6,000
1858D	3,477	750.00	1,450	2,400	9,000	
1858S	10,000	300.00	500.00	1,300	5,750	
1859	(80) 168,324	125.00	145.00	165.00	285.00	5,000
1859C	5,235	575.00	1,400	3,400	12,000	
1859D	4,952	725.00	1,300	2,300	9,000	
1859S	15,000	250.00	600.00	1,600	5,500	
1860	(154) 36,668	135.00	150.00	170.00	400.00	4,200
1860D	1,566	2,750	4,000	7,000	23,000	

GOLD DOLLARS

	Quan. Minted	VF-20	EF-40	AU-50	MS-60	Proof-63
1860S	13,000	$275.00	$400.00	$750.00	$2,500	
1861 ....(349)	527,499	125.00	145.00	165.00	275.00	$5,000
1861D		6,250	9,500	16,500	34,000	
1862 ....(35)	1,361,390	125.00	145.00	165.00	275.00	5,500
1863 ....(50)	6,250	400.00	800.00	1,750	4,000	6,000
1864 ....(50)	5,950	300.00	450.00	650.00	1,100	6,500
1865 ....(25)	3,725	350.00	550.00	750.00	1,450	6,500
1866 ....(30)	7,130	325.00	450.00	550.00	900.00	5,000
1867 ....(50)	5,250	350.00	500.00	700.00	1,100	5,500
1868 ....(25)	10,525	200.00	325.00	550.00	900.00	6,200
1869 ....(25)	5,925	300.00	450.00	650.00	900.00	6,500
1870 ....(35)	6,335	210.00	325.00	450.00	800.00	5,000
1870S	3,000	400.00	650.00	1,250	2,500	
1871 ....(30)	3,930	225.00	325.00	385.00	700.00	5,000
1872 ....(30)	3,530	225.00	325.00	450.00	850.00	6,500
1873 Closed 3 ....(25)	1,825	250.00	550.00	900.00	1,800	10,000
1873 Open 3	123,300	125.00	145.00	165.00	275.00	
1874 ....(20)	198,820	125.00	145.00	165.00	275.00	7,500
1875 ....(20)	420	1,900	3,250	4,500	6,500	15,000
1876 ....(45)	3,245	200.00	300.00	450.00	750.00	5,000
1877 ....(20)	3,920	200.00	300.00	450.00	675.00	6,500
1878 ....(20)	3,020	200.00	275.00	425.00	700.00	5,000
1879 ....(30)	3,030	145.00	175.00	325.00	600.00	5,000
1880 ....(36)	1,636	150.00	175.00	225.00	425.00	5,000
1881 ....(87)	7,707	145.00	165.00	225.00	400.00	5,000
1882 ....(125)	5,125	145.00	165.00	225.00	400.00	4,250
1883 ....(207)	11,007	140.00	160.00	225.00	400.00	4,250
1884 ....(1,006)	6,236	140.00	160.00	225.00	400.00	4,250
1885 ....(1,105)	12,261	140.00	160.00	225.00	400.00	4,250
1886 ....(1,016)	6,016	140.00	160.00	225.00	400.00	4,250
1887 ....(1,043)	8,543	140.00	160.00	225.00	400.00	4,250
1888 ....(1,079)	16,580	140.00	160.00	225.00	400.00	4,250
1889 ....(1,779)	30,729	140.00	160.00	225.00	400.00	4,250

BIBLIOGRAPHY

Akers, David W., *Gold Dollars* (and other gold denominations). Englewood, Ohio, 1975.
Bowers, Q. David, *United States Gold Coins. An Illustrated History.* Wolfeboro, NH, 1982.
Breen, Walter, *Major Varieties of U.S. Gold Dollars* (and other gold denominations). Chicago, 1964.

QUARTER EAGLES ($2.50 GOLD PIECES)—1796-1929

Authorized by the Act of April 2, 1792, they weighed 67.5 grains, 916 2/3 fine until the weight was changed to 64.5 grains, fineness 899.225, by the Act of June 28, 1834. The Act of January 18, 1837 established fineness at .900. Most dates before 1834 are rare. The first issue was struck in 1796, most of which had no stars on the obverse.

Proofs of some dates prior to 1855 are known to exist, and all are rare.

TYPE COIN VALUES

+ or – indicates change from previous year

	F-12	VF-20	EF-40	AU-50	MS-60	MS-63	MS-65	PF-60	PF-63	PF-65
Cap Bust Right-NS 1796	12,000	22,500	40,000	60,000	145,000	220,000				
Cap Bust Right 1796-1807......	3,000	4,000	5,500	8,000	18,000	40,000	110,000			
Cap Bust Left-Lg. 1808	9,000	14,500	21,000	35,000+	55,000+	120,000				
Cap Bust Left-Sm. 1821-1827	3,000	3,650	5,000	6,000	15,000	27,500	75,000			
Cap Bust Left-Sm. 1829-1834	3,000	3,750	4,500	6,500+	10,000	18,000	38,000			
Classic Head 1834-1839	210.00+	275.00+	450.00	700.00	1,800	6,000	27,500			
Lib Coronet 1840-1907............	110.00	130.00	155.00	170.00	285.00	800.00	1,500-	2,250	5,000	13,000
Indian Head 1908-1929	110.00	150.00+	165.00+	180.00+	235.00	650.00	2,800	2,600	6,000	14,000

QUARTER EAGLES ($2.50 GOLD PIECES)
CAPPED BUST TO RIGHT 1796-1807

Designer Robert Scot; weight 4.37 grams; composition: .9167 gold, .0833 silver and copper; approx. diameter 20 mm; reeded edge.

F-12 FINE—*Hair worn smooth on high spots. E PLURIBUS UNUM weak but readable.*
VF-20 VERY FINE—*Some wear on high spots.*
EF-40 EXTREMELY FINE—*Only slight wear on hair and cheek.*
AU-50 ABOUT UNCIRCULATED—*Trace of wear on cap, hair, cheek and drapery.*
MS-60 UNCIRCULATED—*No trace of wear. Light blemishes.*

No Stars on Obverse 1796 Only   **Stars on Obverse 1796-1807**

	Quan. Minted	F-12	VF-20	EF-40	AU-50	MS-60
1796 No stars on obverse	963	$12,000	$22,500	$40,000	$65,000	$140,000
1796 Stars on obverse	432	10,000	15,000	25,000	45,000	110,000
1797	427	9,500	12,500	16,000	32,000	70,000
1798	1,094	3,750	5,000	7,500	20,000	40,000
1802, 2 over 1	3,035	3,250	4,250	5,500	8,500	18,000
1804, 13-Star reverse	} 3,327	20,000	30,000	60,000	100,000	150,000
1804, 14-Star reverse		3,300	5,000	6,500	10,000	22,000
1805	1,781	3,100	4,250	5,500	8,000	20,000
1806, 6 over 4, stars 8 left, 5 right	1,136	3,100	4,250	5,500	8,000	20,000
1806, 6 over 5, stars 7 left, 6 right	480	6,000	9,500	14,000	30,000	60,000
1807	6,812	3,000	4,000	5,500	8,000	18,000

CAPPED BUST TO LEFT, Large Size 1808

Designer John Reich. Standards same as previous issue.

F-12 FINE—*E PLURIBUS UNUM on reverse, and LIBERTY on headband readable but weak.*
VF-20 VERY FINE—*Motto and LIBERTY clear.*
EF-40 EXTREMELY FINE—*All details of hair are plain.*
AU-50 ABOUT UNCIRCULATED—*Trace of wear above eye, on top of cap, cheek and hair.*
MS-60 UNCIRCULATED—*No trace of wear. Light blemishes.*

1808	2,710	9,000	14,500	21,000	35,000	55,000

CAPPED HEAD TO LEFT 1821-1834

Those dated 1829 through 1834 are smaller in diameter than the 1821-1827 pieces. They also have smaller letters, dates and stars.

Standards same as previous issue. Diameter changed to approximately 18.5 mm.

1821	6,448	3,200	4,000	5,000	7,500	17,500
1824, 4 over 1	2,600	3,500	4,000	5,000	6,500	15,000
1825	4,434	3,000	3,650	5,000	6,000	15,000
1826, 6 over 5	760	3,700	4,250	6,000	8,500	30,000
1827	2,800	3,700	4,250	6,000	8,000	17,000

QUARTER EAGLES ($2.50 GOLD PIECES)
Reduced Size 1829-1834

	Quan. Minted	F-12	VF-20	EF-40	AU-50	MS-60
1829	3,403	$3,000	$3,750	$4,500	$6,500	$10,000
1830	4,540	3,200	3,800	4,750	7,000	10,500
1831	4,520	3,200	3,800	4,750	7,000	10,500
1832	4,400	3,200	3,800	4,750	7,000	10,500
1833	4,160	3,200	3,800	4,750	7,000	12,000
1834 (Motto)	4,000	7,000	10,500	16,000	28,000	35,000

CLASSIC HEAD TYPE, No Motto on Reverse 1834-1839

In 1834 the quarter eagle was redesigned. A ribbon binding the hair, bearing the word LIBERTY, replaces the Liberty cap. The motto was omitted from the reverse. In 1840 a coronet and smaller head were designed to conform in appearance with that of the larger gold coins.

Designer William Kneass; weight 4.18 grams; composition: .8992 gold, .1008 silver and copper changed to .900 gold in 1837; diameter 18.2 mm; reeded edge; mints: Philadelphia, Charlotte, Dahlonega, New Orleans.

F-12 FINE—LIBERTY *readable and complete. Curl under ear outlined but no detail.*
VF-20 VERY FINE—*LIBERTY plain. Hair curl has detail.*
EF-40 EXTREMELY FINE—*Small amount of wear on top of hair and below L in LIBERTY. Wear evident on wing.*
AU-50 ABOUT UNCIRCULATED—*Trace of wear on coronet and hair above ear.*
MS-60 UNCIRCULATED—*No trace of wear. Light blemishes.*

Mint mark location.

	Quan. Minted	F-12	VF-20	EF-40	AU-50	MS-60
1834 No motto	112,234	$210.00	$275.00	$450.00	$700.00	$1,800
1835	131,402	210.00	275.00	450.00	700.00	2,150
1836 Script 8	} 547,986	210.00	275.00	450.00	750.00	1,800
1836 Block 8		210.00	275.00	450.00	750.00	1,800
1837	45,080	210.00	275.00	450.00	800.00	2,500
1838	47,030	210.00	275.00	450.00	750.00	1,800
1838C	7,880	600.00	1,150	2,750	6,500	28,000
1839	27,021	250.00	400.00	800.00	1,900	5,000
1839C	18,140	500.00	850.00	2,400	3,800	21,000
1839D	13,674	525.00	1,100	2,750	5,750	23,000
1839O	17,781	350.00	525.00	1,000	1,850	5,500

1839, So-called "9 over 8" varieties for P, C and D mints are made from defective punches.

CORONET TYPE 1840-1907

Mint mark location.

QUARTER EAGLES ($2.50 GOLD PIECES)

Designer Christian Gobrecht; weight 4.18 grams; composition .900 gold, .100 copper; diameter 18 mm; reeded edge. Net weight .12094 oz. pure gold.

	Quan. Minted	VF-20	EF-40	AU-50	MS-60
1840	18,859	$300.00	$700.00	$3,000	$6,000
1840C	12,822	700.00	1,650	5,000	15,500
1840D	3,532	2,150	6,000	16,000	35,000
1840O	33,580	350.00	850.00	2,000	10,000
1841 Proofs only		30,000	60,000	85,000	130,000
1841C	10,281	625.00	1,400	3,500	20,000
1841D	4,164	1,600	3,000	8,000	25,000
1842	2,823	750.00	2,850	7,000	20,000
1842C	6,729	1,350	3,250	8,500	23,000
1842D	4,643	1,350	2,850	11,000	27,500
1842O	19,800	400.00	1,500	2,500	12,000
1843	100,546	160.00	235.00	375.00	1,650
1843C Small date, crosslet 4	2,988	2,100	4,750	8,500	22,000
1843C Large date, plain 4	23,076	700.00	1,300	3,200	8,500
1843D Small date, crosslet 4	36,209	650.00	1,250	2,750	8,700
1843O Small date, crosslet 4	288,002	200.00	275.00	425.00	1,700
1843O Large date, plain 4	76,000	275.00	650.00	1,500	6,000
1844	6,784	375.00	700.00	2,100	7,200
1844C	11,622	750.00	1,600	5,250	18,000
1844D	17,332	675.00	1,350	2,000	8,500
1845	91,051	220.00	300.00	525.00	1,300
1845D	19,460	700.00	1,500	3,000	12,000
1845O	4,000	1,100	2,350	5,500	16,000
1846	21,598	300.00	700.00	1,350	6,000
1846C	4,808	1,000	2,300	7,000	18,000
1846D	19,303	725.00	1,350	2,750	11,000
1846O	62,000	250.00	500.00	1,150	5,500
1847	29,814	215.00	350.00	850.00	4,000
1847C	23,226	650.00	1,150	2,000	7,000
1847D	15,784	675.00	1,200	2,450	9,500
1847O	124,000	225.00	425.00	1,050	4,000
1848	7,497	500.00	1,100	2,000	6,500

CAL. Above Eagle on Reverse

California Gold Quarter Eagle

In 1848 about two hundred and thirty ounces of gold were sent to Secretary of War Marcy by Col. R. B. Mason, Military Governor of California. The gold was turned over to the mint and made into quarter eagles. The distinguishing mark "CAL." was punched above the eagle on the reverse side, while the coins were in the die. Two specimens with proof surface are known.

	Quan. Minted	VF-20	EF-40	AU-50	MS-60
1848 CAL. above eagle	1,389	9,500	16,000	24,000	35,000
1848C	16,788	700.00	1,500	2,650	13,000
1848D	13,771	675.00	1,250	2,500	10,000
1849	23,294	235.00	500.00	1,000	3,000
1849C	10,220	675.00	2,000	5,000	18,000
1849D	10,945	700.00	1,600	4,000	15,000
1850	252,923	160.00	200.00	325.00	1,100
1850C	9,148	700.00	1,650	3,250	17,000
1850D	12,148	700.00	1,600	3,000	15,000
1850O	84,000	225.00	450.00	1,400	4,500
1851	1,372,748	140.00	180.00	235.00	375.00
1851C	14,923	650.00	1,500	4,000	14,000
1851D	11,264	700.00	1,350	2,900	13,000

QUARTER EAGLES ($2.50 GOLD PIECES)

	Quan. Minted	VF-20	EF-40	AU-50	MS-60	Proof-63
1851O	148,000	$175.00	$300.00	$900.00	$5,000	
1852	1,159,681	140.00	165.00	200.00	375.00	
1852C	9,772	600.00	1,650	3,450	16,500	
1852D	4,078	875.00	2,700	6,000	20,000	
1852O	140,000	200.00	300.00	900.00	5,000	
1853	1,404,668	140.00	165.00	200.00	375.00	
1853D	3,178	1,300	2,400	4,750	18,000	
1854	596,258	140.00	165.00	200.00	375.00	
1854C	7,295	700.00	2,250	4,750	17,000	
1854D	1,760	2,700	5,850	12,500	27,500	
1854O	153,000	175.00	275.00	600.00	1,700	
1854S	246	40,000	60,000	125,000	—	
1855	235,480	160.00	180.00	225.00	400.00	
1855C	3,677	1,400	4,000	7,000	24,000	
1855D	1,123	3,800	8,000	16,000	37,500	
1856	384,240	140.00	165.00	200.00	400.00	$37,500
1856C	7,913	850.00	2,000	4,250	15,000	
1856D	874	6,250	11,000	22,000	45,000	
1856O	21,100	275.00	750.00	1,500	7,500	
1856S	72,120	200.00	375.00	1,000	5,500	
1857	214,130	140.00	165.00	200.00	400.00	23,000
1857D	2,364	1,150	2,250	4,000	13,000	
1857O	34,000	175.00	350.00	1,400	5,000	
1857S	69,200	175.00	375.00	1,100	5,500	
1858	47,377	150.00	225.00	450.00	1,350	22,000
1858C	9,056	750.00	1,600	3,000	9,500	

A modified reverse design (smaller letters and arrowheads) was used on Philadelphia issues from 1859 through 1907, and on San Francisco issues of 1877 through 1879. A few Philadelphia Mint pieces were made in 1859, 1860 and 1861 with the old large letters reverse design.

1859 New rev. ....(80)	39,444	160.00	250.00	500.00	1,300	18,000
1859 Old reverse		200.00	400.00	850.00	3,500	
1859D	2,244	1,300	3,000	5,000	21,500	
1859S	15,200	400.00	1,100	2,400	7,000	
1860 New rev. ...(112)	22,675	150.00	225.00	450.00	1,100	12,500
1860 Old reverse		2,100	3,450	5,500	10,500	
1860C	7,469	750.00	2,000	4,200	20,000	
1860S	35,600	250.00	650.00	1,300	4,250	

1862, 2 Over 1

1861 New rev .....(90)	1,283,878	140.00	165.00	200.00	400.00	10,000
1861 Old reverse		500.00	1,100	2,100	4,500	
1861S	24,000	375.00	1,000	3,250	7,000	
1862, 2 over 1 .... }	98,543	825.00	1,950	4,000	9,000	
1862 ....(35)		185.00	275.00	450.00	1,350	10,000
1862S	8,000	875.00	2,000	4,500	17,000	
1863 Proofs only (30)	30					32,000
1863S	10,800	425.00	1,500	3,500	16,500	
1864 ....(50)	2,874	5,500	11,000	20,000	35,000	15,000
1865 ....(25)	1,545	4,250	10,000	20,000	35,000	15,000
1865S	23,376	300.00	675.00	1,350	5,000	
1866 ....(30)	3,110	1,100	3,500	6,500	15,000	12,000
1866S	38,960	325.00	850.00	1,800	7,500	

QUARTER EAGLES ($2.50 GOLD PIECES)

	Quan. Minted	VF-20	EF-40	AU-50	MS-60	Proof-63
1867.................(50)	3,250	$350.00	$700.00	$1,500	$4,750	$9,000
1867S	28,000	350.00	800.00	1,750	5,000	
1868.................(25)	3,625	225.00	550.00	875.00	2,650	10,000
1868S............................	34,000	225.00	500.00	1,100	5,100	
1869.................(25)	4,345	225.00	375.00	800.00	3,250	8,500
1869S............................	29,500	300.00	550.00	1,000	5,150	
1870.................(35)	4,555	225.00	375.00	750.00	3,500	8,500
1870S............................	16,000	225.00	450.00	1,000	5,000	
1871.................(30)	5,350	225.00	400.00	650.00	2,500	8,250
1871S............................	22,000	200.00	325.00	650.00	2,500	
1872.................(30)	3,030	350.00	800.00	1,500	5,500	8,000
1872S............................	18,000	225.00	400.00	1,000	4,500	
1873 Closed 3.....(25)	55,225	165.00	200.00	300.00	800.00	7,500
1873 Open 3	122,800	130.00	160.00	200.00	400.00	
1873S............................	27,000	230.00	450.00	1,100	2,850	
1874.................(20)	3,940	250.00	400.00	800.00	2,650	9,000
1875.................(20)	420	3,600	5,000	8,000	16,000	24,000
1875S............................	11,600	200.00	400.00	800.00	4,250	
1876.................(45)	4,221	250.00	650.00	1,100	3,500	7,000
1876S............................	5,000	250.00	700.00	1,300	4,000	
1877.................(20)	1,652	375.00	700.00	1,000	3,000	9,000
1877S............................	35,400	150.00	175.00	225.00	625.00	
1878.................(20)	286,260	145.00	165.00	200.00	375.00	9,000
1878S............................	178,000	145.00	165.00	200.00	450.00	
1879.................(30)	88,990	145.00	165.00	200.00	300.00	7,500
1879S............................	43,500	160.00	250.00	600.00	2,000	
1880.................(36)	2,996	225.00	325.00	600.00	1,400	8,000
1881.................(51)	691	1,600	3,000	4,500	8,500	7,500
1882.................(67)	4,067	225.00	300.00	400.00	850.00	6,000
1883.................(82)	2,002	225.00	350.00	650.00	2,200	6,000
1884.................(73)	2,023	225.00	350.00	600.00	1,650	6,000
1885.................(87)	887	800.00	1,500	2,500	4,000	6,000
1886.................(88)	4,088	200.00	275.00	475.00	1,300	6,000
1887.................(122)	6,282	200.00	250.00	375.00	1,000	6,000
1888.................(97)	16,098	160.00	200.00	250.00	450.00	6,000
1889.................(48)	17,648	160.00	200.00	250.00	450.00	6,500
1890.................(93)	8,813	175.00	200.00	275.00	500.00	6,500
1891.................(80)	11,040	170.00	235.00	275.00	425.00	6,000
1892.................(105)	2,545	180.00	275.00	400.00	825.00	5,500
1893.................(106)	30,106	140.00	165.00	225.00	375.00	5,500
1894.................(122)	4,122	160.00	225.00	350.00	700.00	5,500
1895.................(119)	6,119	140.00	175.00	210.00	350.00	5,500
1896.................(132)	19,202	135.00	155.00	180.00	300.00	5,500
1897.................(136)	29,904	135.00	155.00	180.00	300.00	5,500
1898.................(165)	24,165	135.00	155.00	180.00	300.00	5,500
1899.................(150)	27,350	135.00	155.00	180.00	300.00	5,500
1900.................(205)	67,205	130.00	155.00	170.00	300.00	5,000
1901.................(223)	91,323	130.00	155.00	170.00	285.00	5,000
1902.................(193)	133,733	130.00	155.00	170.00	285.00	5,000
1903.................(197)	201,257	130.00	155.00	170.00	285.00	5,000
1904.................(170)	160,960	130.00	155.00	170.00	285.00	5,000
1905*...............(144)	217,944	130.00	155.00	170.00	285.00	5,000
1906.................(160)	176,490	130.00	155.00	170.00	285.00	5,000
1907.................(154)	336,448	130.00	155.00	170.00	285.00	5,000

*Pieces dated 1905S are counterfeit.

Values of common gold coins have been based on the current bullion price of gold and may vary with the prevailing spot price.

QUARTER EAGLES ($2.50 GOLD PIECES)
INDIAN HEAD TYPE 1908-1929

The new type represents a departure from all preceding coin types in the United States series. Bela Lyon Pratt was the designer of this and the similar half eagle piece. The coin has no raised edge and the main devices and legends are incuse.

Designer Bela Lyon Pratt; weight 4.18 grams; composition: .900 gold, .100 copper; diameter 18 mm; reeded edge; mints: Philadelphia, Denver. Net weight: .12094 oz. pure gold.

VF-20 VERY FINE—Hair cord knot distinct. Feathers at top of head clear. Cheekbone worn.
EF-40 EXTREMELY FINE—Cheekbone, war bonnet and headband feathers slightly worn.
AU-50 ABOUT UNCIRCULATED—Trace of wear on cheekbone and headdress.
MS-60 UNCIRCULATED—No trace of wear. Light blemishes.

Mint mark location is on reverse left of arrows.

	Quan. Minted	VF-20	EF-40	AU-50	MS-60	Matte Proof-63
1908 ....(236)	565,057	$150.00	$165.00	$180.00	$250.00	$6,000
1909 ....(139)	441,899	150.00	165.00	180.00	265.00	6,000
1910 ....(682)	492,682	150.00	165.00	180.00	265.00	6,000
1911 ....(191)	704,191	150.00	165.00	180.00	250.00	6,500
1911D* 55,680		650.00	1,100	1,600	2,750	
1912 ....(197)	616,197	150.00	165.00	180.00	265.00	6,000
1913 ....(165)	722,165	150.00	165.00	180.00	250.00	6,500
1914 ....(117)	240,117	150.00	190.00	225.00	400.00	6,250
1914D...................448,000		150.00	170.00	190.00	285.00	
1915 ....(100)	606,100	150.00	165.00	180.00	250.00	6,250
1925D...................578,000		150.00	165.00	180.00	235.00	
1926 446,000		150.00	165.00	180.00	235.00	
1927 388,000		150.00	165.00	180.00	235.00	
1928 416,000		150.00	165.00	180.00	235.00	
1929 532,000		150.00	165.00	180.00	235.00	

*Values for coins with bold mint mark; weak D pieces are worth less. Beware of counterfeits.

THREE DOLLAR GOLD PIECES—1854-1889

The three dollar gold piece was authorized by the Act of February 21, 1853. The coin was first struck in 1854. It was never popular and saw very little circulation.

The coin weighs 77.4 grains, .900 fine. The head on the obverse represents an Indian princess with hair tightly curling over the neck, head crowned with a circle of feathers, the band of which is inscribed LIBERTY. A wreath of tobacco, wheat, corn and cotton occupies the field of the reverse, with the denomination and date within it.

Restrikes of some years were made at the Mint; particularly 1873 and 1876.

In the year 1854 only, the word DOLLARS is in much smaller letters than in years 1855 through 1889. The 1856 proof has DOLLARS in large letters cut over the same word in small letters.

+ or − indicates change from previous year	TYPE COIN VALUES									
	F-12	VF-20	EF-40	AU-50	MS-60	MS-63	MS-65	PF-60	PF-63	PF-65
Indian Head 1854-1889..........	350.00	500.00+	650.00+	850.00+	1,700	4,500-	12,000	3,500	9,000	25,000

Designer James B. Longacre, weight 5.015 grams; composition: .900 gold, .100 copper; diameter 20.5 mm; reeded edge; mints: Philadelphia, Dahlonega, New Orleans, San Francisco. Net weight: .14512 oz. pure gold.

THREE DOLLAR GOLD PIECES

VF-20 VERY FINE—*Eyebrow, hair about forehead and ear and bottom curl are worn smooth. Curled feather-ends have faint details showing.*

EF-40 EXTREMELY FINE—*Light wear above and to right of eye. and on top of curled feathers.*

AU-50 ABOUT UNCIRCULATED—*Trace of wear on top of curled feathers and in hair above and to right of eye.*

MS-60 UNCIRCULATED—*No traces of wear. Light blemishes.*

Mint mark location is on reverse below wreath.

	Quan. Minted	VF-20	EF-40	AU-50	MS-60	Proof-63
1854	138,618	$500.00	$650.00	$850.00	$1,800	$45,000
1854D	1,120	7,000	12,500	22,000	70,000	
1854O	24,000	750.00	1,200	3,000	16,500	
1855	50,555	500.00	650.00	850.00	2,000	35,000
1855S	6,600	875.00	2,000	5,000	21,000	
1856	26,010	550.00	700.00	900.00	2,100	20,000
1856S‡	34,500	650.00	1,100	2,100	8,000	
1857	20,891	525.00	675.00	1,000	2,600	17,500
1857S	14,000	800.00	1,750	4,000	15,000	
1858	2,133	700.00	1,300	2,450	6,000	17,500
1859 ....(80)	15,638	525.00	750.00	1,000	2,150	15,000
1860 ....(119)	7,155	575.00	850.00	1,200	2,500	11,500
1860S ..(2,592 melted at mint)	7,000	750.00	1,650	5,000	—	
1861 ....(113)	6,072	600.00	850.00	1,350	3,000	11,500
1862 ....(35)	5,785	600.00	850.00	1,300	3,000	11,500
1863 ....(39)	5,039	650.00	850.00	1,350	3,000	11,500
1864 ....(50)	2,680	700.00	850.00	1,350	3,250	11,500
1865 ....(25)	1,165	1,100	2,000	4,200	7,500	16,500
1866 ....(30)	4,030	700.00	900.00	1,350	3,000	12,000
1867 ....(50)	2,650	700.00	900.00	1,350	3,000	12,000
1868* ....(25)	4,875	700.00	900.00	1,300	2,750	12,000
1869* ....(25)	2,525	650.00	900.00	1,600	3,500	12,000
1870 ....(35)	3,535	625.00	950.00	1,600	3,750	12,000
1870S *(Unique)*	1	1,000,000				
1871 ....(30)	1,330	650.00	900.00	1,600	3,250	12,000
1872 ....(30)	2,030	650.00	850.00	1,500	3,250	11,500
1873 Open 3 (Original) .....(25)	25		5,000	8,000		27,500
1873 Closed 3		3,000	4,500	7,500	21,500	25,000
1874 ....(20)	41,820	500.00	600.00	850.00	1,700	16,000
1875 Proofs only ....(20)	20			40,000		85,000
1876 Proofs only ....(45)	45			13,000		27,500
1877 ....(20)	1,488	1,200	2,500	5,000	11,000	15,000
1878* ....(20)	82,324	500.00	650.00	850.00	1,700	14,500
1879 ....(30)	3,030	550.00	750.00	1,200	2,100	11,000
1880 ....(36)	1,036	650.00	1,300	1,900	2,650	11,000
1881 ....(54)	554	1,000	1,900	3,600	5,200	11,000
1882 ....(76)	1,576	700.00	900.00	1,600	2,650	9,000
1883 ....(89)	989	675.00	1,250	1,800	2,850	9,000
1884 ....(106)	1,106	875.00	1,400	1,800	2,850	9,000
1885 ....(109)	910	875.00	1,400	2,000	3,500	9,000
1886 ....(142)	1,142	875.00	1,400	2,000	3,500	9,000
1887 ....(160)	6,160	525.00	700.00	1,350	2,100	9,000
1888 ....(291)	5,291	525.00	700.00	1,000	1,950	9,000
1889 ....(129)	2,429	525.00	675.00	1,000	1,950	9,000

‡Small and medium S varieties exist.
* Varieties showing traces of overdating include: 1868/7, 1869/8 and 1878/7.

FOUR DOLLAR GOLD OR "STELLA"

These pattern coins were first suggested by the Hon. John A. Kasson, then U.S. Minister to Austria; and it was through the efforts of Dr. W. W. Hubbell, who patented the goloid metal used in making the goloid metric dollars, that we have these beautiful and interesting pieces.

There are two distinct types in both years of issue. Charles E. Barber designed the flowing hair type, and George T. Morgan the coiled hair. They were struck as patterns in gold, aluminum, copper and white metal. Only those struck in gold are listed.

	Quan. Minted	EF-40	AU-50	Proof-60	Proof-63	Proof-65
1879 Flowing hair	(425)	$20,000	$25,000	$40,000	$50,000	$90,000
1879 Coiled hair	(10)			110,000	175,000	250,000
1880 Flowing hair	(15)			45,000	80,000	145,000
1880 Coiled hair	(10)			145,000	185,000	350,000

HALF EAGLES — 1795-1929
($5.00 GOLD PIECES)

The half eagle was the first gold coin actually struck for the United States. The $5.00 piece was authorized to be coined by the Act of April 2, 1792, and the first type weighed 135 grains, 916 2/3 fine. The Act of June 28, 1834 changed the weight to 129 grains, 899.225 fine. Fineness became .900 by the Act of January 18, 1837.

There are many varieties among the early dates caused by changes in the number of stars, style of eagle, overdates, and differences in the size of figures in the dates. Those dated prior to 1807 do not bear any mark of value. The 1822 half eagle is considered the most valuable regular issue coin of the entire United States series. Proofs of some dates prior to 1855 are known to exist, and all are rare. Commemorative and Bullion $5 coins have been made at West Point since 1986 and 1994 respectively, thus this is the only U.S. denomination made at each of the eight mints.

+ or – indicates change from previous year	TYPE COIN VALUES									
	F-12	VF-20	EF-40	AU-50	MS-60	MS-63	MS-65	PF-60	PF-63	PF-65
Cap Bust-Sm. Eag. 1795-1798	6,000	9,000	12,500	18,000-	35,000-	100,000	250,000			
Cap Bust-Lg. Eag. 1795-1807	1,300	1,650	2,350	3,200	6,000	14,000	80,000			
Cap Draped Bust 1807-1812	1,250	1,650	2,350	3,000	5,750	13,500	85,000			
Cap Head 1813-1834	1,500	1,900	2,400	3,250	6,500	13,500	80,000			
Classic Head 1834-1838	225.00	300.00	450.00	750.00	2,500	6,500	50,000			
Lib Coronet-NM 1839-1866	115.00	165.00	200.00	275.00	1,300	6,000	35,000	6,000	17,500	45,000
Lib Coronet 1866-1908	110.00	140.00-	150.00-	165.00-	200.00	700.00-	3,000-	2,500	8,500	28,000
Indian Head 1908-1929	135.00	185.00	200.00	235.00	300.00	1,100	12,000	3,500	8,750	24,000

CAPPED BUST TO RIGHT, SMALL EAGLE 1795-1798

This type was struck from mid-1795 to early 1798, when the small eagle reverse was changed to the large or "heraldic" eagle. Note that the 1795 and 1797 dates exist for both types, but the heraldic reverses of these dates were probably struck under emergency conditions in late 1798.

Designer Robert Scot; weight 8.75 grams; composition: .9167 gold, .0833 silver and copper; approx. diameter 25 mm; reeded edge.

HALF EAGLES ($5.00 GOLD PIECES)

F-12 FINE—*Hair worn smooth but with distinct outline. For heraldic type, E PLURIBUS UNUM is faint but readable.*
VF-20 VERY FINE—*Slight to noticeable wear on high spots such as hair, turban, eagle's head and wings.*
EF-40 EXTREMELY FINE—*Slight wear on hair and highest part of cheek.*
AU-50 ABOUT UNCIRCULATED—*Trace of wear on cap, hair, cheek and drapery.*
MS-60 UNCIRCULATED—*No trace of wear. Light blemishes.*

	Quan. Minted	F-12	VF-20	EF-40	AU-50	MS-60
1795 Small eagle*	8,707	$6,000	$9,000	$12,500	$18,000	$35,000

*One variety has the final S in STATES punched over an erroneous D.

1796, 6 over 5	**1797, 15 Stars**	**1797, 16 Stars**

	Quan. Minted	F-12	VF-20	EF-40	AU-50	MS-60
1796, 6 over 5	6,196	6,500	9,000	15,000	25,000	60,000
1797, 15 stars	} 3,609	9,000	14,000	27,000	50,000	90,000
1797, 16 stars		7,500	13,000	25,000	40,000	85,000
1798 Small eagle *(7 known)*		—	80,000	150,000	275,000	—

CAPPED BUST TO RIGHT, HERALDIC EAGLE 1795-1807

	Quan. Minted	F-12	VF-20	EF-40	AU-50	MS-60
1795 Heraldic eagle*		7,000	10,000	19,000	37,000	80,000
1797, 7 over 5*		6,500	7,500	18,000	35,000	60,000
1797, 16 star obverse* *(Unique)*				—		
1797, 15 star obverse* *(Unique)*				—		
1798 Small 8		1,800	2,600	4,200	7,000	17,000
1798 Large 8, 13 star reverse	} 24,867	1,500	2,200	3,800	5,500	12,000
1798 Large 8, 14 star reverse.		1,900	3,500	6,750	15,000	26,500
1799	7,451	1,500	2,500	4,500	7,500	16,500

*These four pieces are thought to have been struck in 1798 and included in the mintage figure for that year.

HALF EAGLES ($5.00 GOLD PIECES)

1802 over 1

1803 over 2

Small 8 over Large 8

	Quan. Minted	F-12	VF-20	EF-40	AU-50	MS-60
1800	37,628	$1,300	$1,750	$2,500	$3,250	$6,850
1802, 2 over 1	53,176	1,300	1,750	2,500	3,450	6,350
1803, 3 over 2	33,506	1,300	1,750	2,500	3,450	6,350
1804 Small 8	} 30,475	1,300	1,750	2,650	3,750	7,500
1804 Small 8 over large 8..		1,300	1,750	2,650	3,750	7,500
1805	33,183	1,300	1,750	2,500	3,450	6,350

Pointed 6, Stars 8 and 5   Round Top 6, Stars 7 and 6

1806 Pointed top 6	9,676	1,300	1,850	2,500	3,550	7,750
1806 Round top 6	54,417	1,300	1,650	2,350	3,200	6,000
1807	32,488	1,300	1,650	2,350	3,200	6,250

CAPPED BUST TO LEFT 1807-1812

Designer John Reich. Standards same as previous issue.

F-12 FINE—*LIBERTY readable but partly weak.*
VF-20 VERY FINE—*Headband edges slightly worn. LIBERTY is bold.*
EF-40 EXTREMELY FINE—*Slight wear on highest portions of hair. 80% of major curls are plain.*
AU-50 ABOUT UNCIRCULATED— *Trace of wear above eye, on top of cap, cheek and hair.*
MS-60 UNCIRCULATED—*No trace of wear. Light blemishes.*

	Quan. Minted	F-12	VF-20	EF-40	AU-50	MS-60
1807	51,605	$1,350	$1,750	$2,350	$3,150	$5,500

1808, 8 over 7   Normal Date   1809, 9 over 8

[208]

HALF EAGLES ($5.00 GOLD PIECES)

	Quan. Minted	F-12	VF-20	EF-40	AU-50	MS-60
1808, 8 over 7	} 55,578	$1,500	$1,850	$2,800	$6,000	$9,000
1808		1,250	1,750	2,300	3,000	5,650
1809, 9 over 8	33,875	1,250	1,750	2,300	3,000	5,650

Small Date

Large Date

Large 5

Tall 5

		F-12	VF-20	EF-40	AU-50	MS-60
1810 All kinds	100,287					
1810 Small date, small 5		8,000	15,000	28,000	—	
1810 Small date, tall 5		1,500	1,800	2,450	3,400	6,000
1810 Large date, small 5		8,000	12,000	20,000	27,500	45,000
1810 Large date, large 5		1,250	1,650	2,350	3,000	5,750
1811 Small 5	} 99,581	1,250	1,650	2,350	3,000	5,750
1811 Tall 5		1,250	1,650	2,350	3,000	5,750
1812	58,087	1,250	1,650	2,350	3,000	5,750

CAPPED HEAD TO LEFT (large diameter) 1813-1829

		F-12	VF-20	EF-40	AU-50	MS-60
1813	95,428	1,500	1,900	2,400	3,250	6,500
1814, 4 over 3	15,454	1,600	2,250	3,000	4,500	8,500
1815	635			65,000	95,000	150,000
1818 All kinds	48,588					
1818 Normal dies		1,600	2,200	2,750	3,850	8,000
1818 STATESOF one word		1,700	2,250	3,350	5,250	13,500
1818, 5D over 50		—	2,750	4,000	9,000	15,000
1819	} 51,723		—	30,000	40,000	50,000
1819, 5D over 50			20,000	35,000	45,000	

Curved Base 2

Square Base 2

Small Letters

Large Letters

		F-12	VF-20	EF-40	AU-50	MS-60
1820 All kinds	263,806					
1820 Curved-base 2, small letters		1,700	2,400	4,000	5,500	10,500
1820 Curved-base 2, large letters		1,700	2,400	4,000	5,750	10,500
1820 Square-base 2		1,700	2,400	3,550	5,250	9,500
1821	34,641	3,250	6,000	11,000	20,000	35,000

HALF EAGLES ($5.00 GOLD PIECES)

1825, 5 over 1

1825, 5 over 4

	Quan. Minted	F-12	VF-20	EF-40	AU-50	MS-60
1822 *(3 known)*	17,796		—	$1,000,000	—	
1823	14,485	$1,700	$2,750	3,750	$6,000	$15,000
1824	17,340	4,000	8,000	12,000	16,500	30,000
1825, 5 over 1	} 29,060	4,000	6,500	8,500	14,000	27,500
1825, 5 over 4 *(2 known)*				200,000		250,000
1826	18,069	3,250	6,500	8,500	11,500	23,500
1827	24,913	5,000	8,250	12,000	15,000	28,500

Large Date

Small Date

1828, 8 over 7	} 28,029	6,500	10,000	20,000	33,500	70,000
1828		6,500	9,500	18,000	30,000	60,000
1829 Large date	57,442	—	—	—	—	150,000

CAPPED HEAD TO LEFT (reduced diameter) 1829-1834

The half eagles dated 1829 (small date) through 1834 are smaller in diameter than the earlier pieces. They also have smaller letters, dates and stars.

Standards as before. Modified design by William Kneass. Diameter 23.8 mm.

Large 5D

Small 5D

**13 Stars
Square Base 2**

1829 Small date	incl. above		38,500	60,000	90,000	150,000
1830 Small or large 5 D	126,351	3,500	5,500	6,500	8,500	17,000
1831 Small or large 5 D	140,594	3,500	5,500	6,500	8,500	17,000
1832 Curved-base 2, 12 stars *(6 known)*	} 157,487	—	60,000	100,000	—	—
1832 Square-base 2, 13 stars		3,500	5,500	7,000	10,000	17,500

HALF EAGLES ($5.00 GOLD PIECES)

	Quan. Minted	F-12	VF-20	EF-40	AU-50	MS-60
1833 Large date	} 193,630	$3,500	$5,000	$6,000	$7,500	$14,500
1833 Small date		6,000	8,000	9,000	11,000	20,000

 Plain 4   Crosslet 4

	Quan. Minted	F-12	VF-20	EF-40	AU-50	MS-60
1834 Plain 4	} 50,141	3,300	5,250	6,500	9,000	17,500
1834 Crosslet 4		3,500	5,500	7,000	10,000	23,000

CLASSIC HEAD TYPE 1834-1838

As on the quarter eagle of 1834, the motto E PLURIBUS UNUM was omitted from the new, reduced size half eagle in 1834, to distinguish the old coins which had become worth more than face value.

Designer William Kneass; weight 8.36 grams; composition: .8992 gold, .1008 silver and copper, changed to .900 gold in 1837; diameter 22.5 mm; reeded edge; mints: Philadelphia, Charlotte, Dahlonega.

Mint mark above date. See page 200.

	Quan. Minted	F-12	VF-20	EF-40	AU-50	MS-60
1834 Plain 4‡	} 657,460	225.00	300.00	450.00	750.00	2,500
1834 Crosslet 4		750.00	1,500	2,650	5,000	14,000
1835‡	371,534	225.00	300.00	475.00	750.00	2,650
1836	553,147	225.00	300.00	475.00	750.00	2,500
1837‡	207,121	250.00	325.00	550.00	900.00	3,000
1838	286,588	250.00	325.00	500.00	850.00	3,000
1838C	17,179	1,000	1,750	4,500	10,000	30,000
1838D	20,583	900.00	1,650	3,750	6,500	22,000

‡Varieties have either script 8 or block style 8 in date.

CORONET TYPE, No Motto Above Eagle 1839-1866

Designer Christian Gobrecht; weight 8.359 grams; composition: .900 gold, .100 copper; diameter (1839-40) 22.5 mm. (1840-1929) 21.6 mm; reeded edge. Net weight: .24187 oz. pure gold.

VF-20 VERY FINE—*LIBERTY bold. Major lines show in neck hair.*
EF-40 EXTREMELY FINE—*Neck hair details clear. Slight wear on top and lower part of coronet, and hair.*
AU-50 ABOUT UNCIRCULATED—*Trace of wear on coronet and hair above eye.*
MS-60 UNCIRCULATED—*No trace of wear. Light blemishes.*

Mint mark above date 1839 only, below eagle 1840-1908.

	Quan. Minted	VF-20	EF-40	AU-50	MS-60
1839	118,143	$275.00	$425.00	$1,200	$3,500
1839C	17,205	1,100	2,350	6,000	20,000
1839D	18,939	1,100	2,500	5,500	15,000
1840*	137,382	250.00	400.00	1,250	3,750
1840C*	18,992	900.00	2,200	6,000	20,000
1840D*	22,896	900.00	1,950	5,750	16,000
1840O*	40,120	425.00	950.00	1,750	8,250
1841	15,833	400.00	950.00	1,800	5,750
1841C	21,467	800.00	1,500	3,250	15,000
1841D	29,392	850.00	1,500	3,250	13,500
1841O (Unconfirmed in any collection)	50				

*Scarce varieties of the 1840 coins have the fine edge reeding and wide rims of the 1839 issues.

HALF EAGLES ($5.00 GOLD PIECES)

1847

1842 Large Date	Large Letters	Small Letters	Extra 7 at border

	Quan. Minted	VF-20	EF-40	AU-50	MS-60
1842 Small letters	} 27,578	$375.00	$1,200	$3,250	$10,500
1842 Large letters		700.00	1,800	8,000	12,000
1842C Small date	} 27,432	5,500	16,500	40,000	80,000
1842C Large date		750.00	1,500	3,300	16,000
1842D Small date	} 59,608	750.00	1,350	3,100	14,500
1842D Large date		2,300	5,000	12,000	28,000
1842O	16,400	900.00	3,000	9,000	17,500
1843	611,205	175.00	220.00	350.00	1,650
1843C	44,277	750.00	1,450	4,250	14,500
1843D	98,452	650.00	1,300	2,500	7,500
1843O Small letters	19,075	600.00	1,650	3,250	17,500
1843O Large letters	82,000	250.00	1,150	2,500	11,500
1844	340,330	165.00	225.00	325.00	1,800
1844C	23,631	1,000	2,500	6,000	19,000
1844D	88,982	650.00	1,200	2,600	11,000
1844O	364,600	275.00	400.00	900.00	4,250
1845	417,099	200.00	225.00	350.00	1,800
1845D	90,629	650.00	1,200	2,400	12,000
1845O	41,000	350.00	700.00	3,250	11,000
1846 Large date	} 395,942	165.00	300.00	400.00	2,350
1846 Small date		165.00	300.00	400.00	2,350
1846C	12,995	1,150	2,500	5,500	19,000
1846D	} 80,294	650.00	1,300	3,450	10,000
1846D High second D over D		650.00	1,300	3,500	10,500
1846O	58,000	400.00	900.00	3,500	10,500
1847	915,981	165.00	220.00	300.00	1,300
1847 Top of extra very low 7 at border		190.00	250.90	400.00	1,750
1847C	84,151	700.00	1,300	3,250	13,000
1847D	64,405	600.00	1,200	2,750	8,500
1847O	12,000	1,400	5,200	11,000	22,000
1848	260,775	180.00	250.00	450.00	1,400
1848C	64,472	700.00	1,300	2,900	15,000
1848D	47,465	700.00	1,300	2,850	13,000
1849	133,070	175.00	275.00	600.00	2,500
1849C	64,823	650.00	1,200	2,500	10,500
1849D	39,036	700.00	1,300	3,150	13,500
1850	64,491	300.00	650.00	1,200	3,650
1850C	63,591	650.00	1,150	2,500	12,500
1850D	43,984	800.00	1,550	3,800	18,000
1851	377,505	165.00	225.00	350.00	2,200
1851C	49,176	675.00	1,250	3,400	13,000
1851D	62,710	675.00	1,500	3,000	12,500
1851O	41,000	600.00	1,300	3,750	11,500
1852	573,901	165.00	200.00	275.00	1,300
1852C	72,574	650.00	1,150	2,700	7,500
1852D	91,584	650.00	1,200	2,600	10,000
1853	305,770	165.00	200.00	275.00	1,400
1853C	65,571	650.00	1,150	2,350	8,000

HALF EAGLES ($5.00 GOLD PIECES)

	Quan. Minted	VF-20	EF-40	AU-50	MS-60	Proof-63
1853D	89,678	$575.00	$1,000	$2,100	$6,250	
1854	160,675	200.00	275.00	450.00	2,000	
1854C	39,283	725.00	1,350	3,500	14,000	
1854D	56,413	625.00	1,200	2,500	11,000	
1854O	46,000	300.00	600.00	1,500	7,500	
1854S	268		—	325,000	—	
1855	117,098	165.00	225.00	350.00	1,600	—
1855C	39,788	800.00	1,600	3,200	14,000	
1855D	22,432	800.00	1,400	3,100	16,000	
1855O	11,100	700.00	1,900	4,500	17,000	
1855S	61,000	375.00	1,100	2,250	13,000	
1856	197,990	165.00	220.00	325.00	1,750	—
1856C	28,457	700.00	1,450	3,500	16,000	
1856D	19,786	700.00	1,350	3,250	12,000	
1856O	10,000	650.00	1,400	5,000	16,000	
1856S	105,100	285.00	700.00	1,350	6,000	
1857	98,188	165.00	220.00	350.00	1,500	—
1857C	31,360	625.00	1,200	2,850	11,000	
1857D	17,046	650.00	1,300	3,350	12,000	
1857O	13,000	625.00	1,300	4,500	16,000	
1857S	87,000	275.00	600.00	1,200	7,500	
1858	15,136	275.00	500.00	800.00	3,500	—
1858C	38,856	650.00	1,250	3,000	12,000	
1858D	15,362	650.00	1,250	3,000	12,500	
1858S	18,600	750.00	2,250	6,000	24,000	
1859	(80) 16,814	275.00	450.00	850.00	5,250	$25,000
1859C	31,847	750.00	1,500	3,250	13,500	
1859D	10,366	725.00	1,600	2,750	12,000	
1859S	13,220	1,300	3,750	7,000	25,000	
1860	(62) 19,825	250.00	400.00	850.00	3,650	23,500
1860C	14,813	850.00	1,800	4,250	13,000	
1860D	14,635	850.00	1,800	4,000	15,000	
1860S	21,200	900.00	1,800	7,500	21,000	
1861	(66) 688,150	165.00	220.00	300.00	1,200	23,500
1861C	6,879	1,850	3,750	9,000	27,500	
1861D	1,597	4,250	7,500	17,000	42,500	
1861S	18,000	900.00	3,500	8,000	30,000	
1862	(35) 4,465	700.00	1,750	3,000	20,000	19,500
1862S	9,500	2,950	5,500	16,500	50,000	
1863	(30) 2,472	1,000	3,000	6,200	21,000	21,500
1863S	17,000	1,150	3,500	10,000	27,500	
1864	(50) 4,220	550.00	1,700	3,750	12,500	17,500
1864S	3,888	5,000	12,000	30,000	—	
1865	(25) 1,295	1,200	3,650	9,500	22,500	18,000
1865S	27,612	1,250	2,500	5,750	15,000	
1866S	9,000	1,600	3,850	11,500	32,500	

Variety 2 — Motto Above Eagle 1866-1908

Designer Christian Gobrecht; weight 8.359 grams; composition: .900 gold, .100 copper; diameter 21.6 mm; reeded edge; mints: Philadelphia, Carson City, Denver, New Orleans, San Francisco. Net weight: .24187 oz. pure gold.

VF-20 VERY FINE—*Half of hairlines above coronet missing. Hair curls under ear evident, but worn. Motto and its ribbon sharp.*
EF-40 EXTREMELY FINE—*Small amount of wear on top of hair and below L in LIBERTY. Wear evident on wing tips and neck of eagle.*
AU-50 ABOUT UNCIRCULATED—*Trace of wear on tip of coronet and hair above eye.*
MS-60 UNCIRCULATED—*No trace of wear. Light blemishes.*

HALF EAGLES ($5.00 GOLD PIECES)

	Quan. Minted	VF-20	EF-40	AU-50	MS-60	Proof-63
1866.....................(30)	6,730	$625.00	$1,400	$3,250	$12,500	$16,500
1866S	34,920	800.00	2,750	7,650	19,500	
1867.....................(50)	6,920	500.00	1,500	3,500	8,500	15,000
1867S	29,000	1,000	3,000	9,000	25,000	
1868.....................(25)	5,725	550.00	1,000	3,250	8,750	19,500
1868S	52,000	450.00	1,600	4,800	20,000	
1869.....................(25)	1,785	800.00	2,000	3,650	17,500	20,000
1869S	31,000	600.00	1,800	4,250	20,000	
1870.....................(35)	4,035	550.00	1,600	3,350	14,000	21,500
1870CC	7,675	4,500	12,000	24,000		
1870S	17,000	1,000	2,000	8,000	22,500	
1871.....................(30)	3,230	700.00	1,600	3,750	16,000	17,500
1871CC	20,770	1,100	3,000	11,000	20,000	
1871S	25,000	500.00	1,000	3,350	13,000	
1872.....................(30)	1,690	750.00	1,500	3,000	12,000	16,000
1872CC	16,980	950.00	4,000	8,000	17,500	
1872S	36,400	500.00	1,000	3,150	10,000	
1873 Closed 3........(25) ⎫	112,505	165.00	225.00	400.00	1,000	19,500
1873 Open 3 .... ⎭		165.00	225.00	375.00	750.00	
1873CC	7,416	2,200	9,000	16,000	25,000	
1873S	31,000	650.00	1,400	4,000	18,000	
1874.....................(20)	3,508	550.00	1,200	2,350	12,000	16,000
1874CC	21,198	700.00	2,000	7,500	14,000	
1874S	16,000	650.00	2,000	5,750	16,000	
1875.....................(20)	220	35,000	45,000	60,000	—	70,000
1875CC	11,828	1,350	4,000	10,000	25,000	
1875S	9,000	675.00	2,250	6,000	19,000	
1876.....................(45)	1,477	700.00	1,900	3,500	10,000	12,500
1876CC	6,887	1,200	4,500	12,000	21,000	
1876S	4,000	1,300	3,500	11,000	23,500	
1877.....................(20)	1,152	850.00	2,250	3,850	10,000	16,500
1877CC	8,680	1,100	3,000	8,000	18,000	
1877S	26,700	300.00	650.00	1,900	7,250	
1878.....................(20)	131,740	150.00	165.00	200.00	425.00	16,500
1878CC	9,054	2,750	7,000	20,000		
1878S	144,700	165.00	185.00	250.00	750.00	
1879.....................(30)	301,950	165.00	180.00	225.00	275.00	14,000
1879CC	17,281	600.00	1,200	2,750	12,000	
1879S	426,200	160.00	200.00	250.00	750.00	
1880.....................(36)	3,166,436	140.00	150.00	165.00	210.00	11,500
1880CC	51,017	350.00	700.00	1,600	9,000	
1880S	1,348,900	150.00	165.00	185.00	225.00	
1881, 1 over 0 .... ⎫	5,708,802	225.00	450.00	675.00	1,350	
1881.....................(42) ⎭		140.00	150.00	165.00	210.00	11,500
1881CC	13,886	525.00	1,600	5,500	15,000	
1881S	969,000	140.00	150.00	165.00	210.00	
1882.....................(48)	2,514,568	140.00	150.00	165.00	210.00	11,500
1882CC	82,817	325.00	500.00	850.00	5,750	

HALF EAGLES ($5.00 GOLD PIECES)

	Quan. Minted	VF-20	EF-40	AU-50	MS-60	Proof-63
1882S 969,000		$140.00	$150.00	$165.00	$210.00	
1883....................(61) 233,461		140.00	105.00	200.00	300.00	$11,500
1883CC 12,958		400.00	900.00	3,000	15,000	
1883S 83,200		160.00	200.00	300.00	800.00	
1884....................(48) 191,078		140.00	175.00	225.00	650.00	11,500
1884CC 16,402		450.00	900.00	2,700	14,000	
1884S 177,000		175.00	200.00	250.00	325.00	
1885....................(66) 601,506		140.00	150.00	165.00	210.00	11,500
1885S 1,211,500		140.00	150.00	165.00	210.00	
1886....................(72) 388,432		140.00	150.00	185.00	225.00	11,500
1886S 3,268,000		140.00	150.00	165.00	210.00	
1887 Proofs only ...(87) 87						50,000
1887S 1,912,000		140.00	150.00	165.00	210.00	
1888....................(95) 18,296		170.00	210.00	250.00	475.00	9,500
1888S 293,900		170.00	200.00	375.00	1,100	
1889....................(45) 7,565		250.00	400.00	550.00	1,000	10,500
1890....................(88) 4,328		300.00	500.00	700.00	1,700	10,500
1890CC 53,800		250.00	325.00	550.00	1,100	
1891....................(53) 61,413		160.00	175.00	225.00	425.00	9,000
1891CC 208,000		225.00	300.00	475.00	700.00	
1892....................(92) 753,572		140.00	150.00	165.00	210.00	11,000
1892CC 82,968		250.00	350.00	600.00	1,500	
1892O 10,000		475.00	850.00	1,350	2,750	
1892S 298,400		140.00	150.00	200.00	600.00	
1893....................(77) 1,528,197		140.00	150.00	165.00	210.00	10,500
1893CC 60,000		275.00	350.00	650.00	1,500	
1893O 110,000		200.00	250.00	375.00	800.00	
1893S 224,000		150.00	175.00	215.00	300.00	
1894....................(75) 957,955		140.00	150.00	165.00	210.00	10,500
1894O 16,600		200.00	275.00	425.00	1,200	
1894S 55,900		225.00	300.00	500.00	2,500	
1895....................(81) 1,345,936		140.00	150.00	165.00	200.00	9,500
1895S 112,000		200.00	300.00	500.00	2,850	
1896....................(103) 59,063		140.00	165.00	200.00	275.00	9,250
1896S 155,400		200.00	250.00	400.00	1,250	
1897....................(83) 867,883		140.00	150.00	165.00	225.00	9,250
1897S 354,000		165.00	180.00	300.00	850.00	
1898....................(75) 633,495		140.00	150.00	165.00	225.00	9,250
1898S 1,397,400		140.00	150.00	165.00	250.00	
1899....................(99) 1,710,729		140.00	150.00	165.00	200.00	9,250
1899S 1,545,000		140.00	150.00	165.00	225.00	
1900....................(230) 1,405,730		140.00	150.00	165.00	200.00	8,750
1900S 329,000		140.00	185.00	210.00	275.00	
1901....................(140) 616,040		140.00	150.00	165.00	200.00	8,500
1901S, 1 over 0............ } 3,648,000		140.00	185.00	225.00	325.00	
1901S........................		140.00	150.00	165.00	200.00	
1902....................(162) 172,562		140.00	150.00	165.00	210.00	8,500
1902S 939,000		140.00	150.00	165.00	200.00	
1903....................(154) 227,024		140.00	150.00	165.00	200.00	8,500
1903S 1,855,000		140.00	150.00	165.00	200.00	
1904....................(136) 392,136		140.00	150.00	165.00	200.00	8,500
1904S 97,000		170.00	190.00	275.00	800.00	
1905....................(108) 302,308		140.00	150.00	165.00	210.00	9,000
1905S 880,700		140.00	150.00	225.00	450.00	

Values of common gold coins have been based on the current bullion price
of gold and may vary with the prevailing spot price.

HALF EAGLES ($5.00 GOLD PIECES)

	Quan. Minted	VF-20	EF-40	AU-50	MS-60	Proof-63
1906.....................(85)	348,820	$140.00	$150.00	$165.00	$200.00	$8,500
1906D.................................320,000		140.00	150.00	165.00	200.00	
1906S.................................598,000		140.00	150.00	165.00	250.00	
1907.....................(92)	626,192	140.00	150.00	165.00	200.00	8,500
1907D.................................888,000		140.00	150.00	165.00	200.00	
1908.....................................421,874		140.00	150.00	165.00	200.00	

INDIAN HEAD TYPE 1908-1929

This type conforms to the quarter eagle of the same date. The sunken (incuse) designs and lettering make these two series unique in our United States coinage.

Designer Bela Lyon Pratt; weight 8.359 grams; composition: .900 gold, .100 copper; diameter 21.6 mm; reeded edge; mints: Philadelphia, Denver, New Orleans, San Francisco. Net weight: .24187 oz. pure gold.

    →

Mint mark location.

VF-20 VERY FINE—*Noticeable wear on large middle feathers and tip of eagle's wing.*
EF-40 EXTREMELY FINE—*Cheekbone, war bonnet and headband feathers slightly worn. Feathers on eagle's upper wing show considerable wear.*
AU-50 ABOUT UNCIRCULATED—*Trace of wear on cheekbone and headdress.*
MS-60 UNCIRCULATED—*No trace of wear. Light blemishes.*

Scarcer coins with well struck mint marks command higher prices.

						Matte Proof-63
1908.....................(167)	578,012	185.00	200.00	235.00	325.00	$8,750
1908D.................................148,000		185.00	200.00	235.00	325.00	
1908S 82,000		235.00	400.00	550.00	1,100	
1909.....................(78)	627,138	185.00	200.00	235.00	325.00	9,500
1909D.................................3,423,560		185.00	200.00	235.00	300.00	
1909O*.................................34,200		650.00	1,200	1,700	6,000	
1909S 297,200		210.00	245.00	350.00	1,200	
1910.....................(250)	604,250	185.00	200.00	235.00	300.00	9,500
1910D.................................193,600		185.00	200.00	235.00	350.00	
1910S 770,200		210.00	250.00	350.00	1,000	
1911.....................(139)	915,139	185.00	200.00	235.00	300.00	9,000
1911D.................................72,500		325.00	500.00	650.00	3,150	
1911S 1,416,000		200.00	250.00	300.00	525.00	
1912.....................(144)	790,144	185.00	200.00	245.00	310.00	9,000
1912S 392,000		210.00	265.00	325.00	1,500	
1913.....................(99)	916,000	185.00	200.00	235.00	300.00	9,750
1913S 408,000		200.00	250.00	375.00	1,400	
1914.....................(125)	247,125	185.00	210.00	245.00	325.00	9,500
1914D.................................247,000		185.00	200.00	235.00	350.00	
1914S 263,000		185.00	225.00	350.00	1,250	
1915‡ ....(75)	588,075	185.00	200.00	235.00	300.00	13,000
1915S 164,000		220.00	285.00	450.00	1,800	
1916S 240,000		185.00	210.00	350.00	550.00	
1929.....................................662,000		3,750	4,500	5,000	5,850	

*Beware spurious "O" mint mark.
‡Pieces dated 1915D are counterfeit.

EAGLES ($10.00 GOLD PIECES) — 1795-1933

Coinage authority including specified weights and fineness of the eagle conforms to that of the half eagle. The small eagle reverse was used until 1797 when the large, heraldic eagle replaced it. The early dates have variations in the number of stars, the rarest date being 1798. Many of these early pieces show file scratches from the mint's practice of adjusting weight. No eagles were struck dated 1805 to 1837. Proofs of some dates prior to 1855 are known to exist, and all are rare.

+ or – indicates change from previous year	TYPE COIN VALUES									
	F-12	VF-20	EF-40	AU-50	MS-60	MS-63	MS-65	PF-60	PF-63	PF-65
Cap Bust-Sm. Eag. 1795-1797	6,500	9,000	15,000	23,000	48,000	*90,000*	*300,000*			
Cap Bust-Lg. Eag. 1797-1804 .	2,300	3,000	4,250	6,000	10,000	*25,000*	*140,000*			
Lib Coronet-NM 1838-1866	220.00	250.00	300.00	550.00	3,250	*13,000*	*50,000*	7,500	30,000	*130,000*
Lib Coronet 1866-1907	180.00	200.00	225.00	240.00	285.00	600.00	3,500	2,750	11,000	*40,000*
Indian Head-NM 1907-1908....	300.00	335.00	385.00	425.00	475.00	1,600	7,000			
Indian Head 1908-1933	260.00	285.00	300.00	330.00	400.00	650.00	3,500	3,650	13,500	30,000

CAPPED BUST TO RIGHT, SMALL EAGLE 1795-1797

Designer Robert Scot; weight 17.50 grams; composition: .9167 gold, .0833 silver and copper; approx. diameter 33 mm; reeded edge.

F-12 FINE—*Details on turban and head obliterated.*

VF-20 VERY FINE—*Neck hair lines and details under turban and over forehead are worn but distinguishable.*

EF-40 EXTREMELY FINE—*Definite wear on hair to left of eye and strand of hair across and around turban, also on eagle's wing tips.*

AU-50 ABOUT UNCIRCULATED—*Trace of wear on cap, hair, cheek and drapery.*

MS-60 UNCIRCULATED—*No trace of wear. Light blemishes.*

	Quan. Minted	F-12	VF-20	EF-40	AU-50	MS-60
1795, 13 leaves below eagle..........	} 5,583	$6,500	$9,000	$15,000	$23,000	$48,000
1795, 9 leaves below eagle............		16,000	27,000	45,000	67,500	140,000
1796	4,146	6,750	9,500	16,000	25,000	60,000
1797 Small eagle............................	3,615	7,200	12,000	22,000	35,000	70,000

CAPPED BUST TO RIGHT, HERALDIC EAGLE 1797-1804

	Quan. Minted	F-12	VF-20	EF-40	AU-50	MS-60
1797 Large eagle	10,940	$2,400	$3,750	$5,500	$8,200	$18,000
1798, 8 over 7, 9 stars left, 4 right	900	5,500	10,000	18,000	30,000	60,000
1798, 8 over 7, 7 stars left, 6 right	842	12,000	22,000	50,000	95,000	—
1799 Small obverse stars	} 37,449	2,300	3,100	4,750	7,250	11,000
1799 Large obverse stars		2,400	3,000	4,500	6,500	10,000
1800	5,999	2,500	3,750	5,000	7,250	15,000

EAGLES ($10.00 GOLD PIECES)

	Quan. Minted	F-12	VF-20	EF-40	AU-50	MS-60
1801	44,344	$2,300	$3,000	$4,250	$6,000	$11,000
1803 Small reverse stars	} 15,017	2,400	3,250	4,500	6,250	12,500
1803 Large reverse stars		2,400	3,250	4,750	6,500	12,500
1804	3,757	3,250	4,150	6,250	12,500	26,000
1804 Plain 4. Proof restrike. *(4 known)*						150,000

CORONET TYPE, No Motto Above Eagle 1838-1866

In 1838 the weight and diameter of the eagle were reduced and the obverse and reverse were redesigned. Liberty now faces left and the word LIBERTY is placed on the coronet. A more natural appearing eagle is used on the reverse. The value, TEN D., is shown for the first time on this denomination.

Designer Christian Gobrecht; weight 16.718 grams; composition: .900 gold, .100 copper, diameter 27 mm; reeded edge; mints: Philadelphia, New Orleans, San Francisco. Net weight: .48375 oz. pure gold.

VF-20 VERY FINE—*Hairlines above coronet partly worn. Curls under ear worn but defined.*
EF-40 EXTREMELY FINE—*Small amount of wear on top of hair and below L in LIBERTY. Wear evident on wing tips and neck of eagle.*
AU-50 ABOUT UNCIRCULATED—*Trace of wear on tip of coronet and hair above eye.*
MS-60 UNCIRCULATED—*No trace of wear. Light blemishes.*

Mint mark location on reverse below eagle.

	Quan. Minted	VF-20	EF-40	AU-50	MS-60	Proof-63
1838	7,200	$975.00	$2,500	$5,750	$27,000	
1839 Large letters	25,801	800.00	1,800	4,350	20,000	

The Liberty head style of 1838 and 1839 (large letters) differs from that used for subsequent issues.

	Quan. Minted	VF-20	EF-40	AU-50	MS-60	Proof-63
1839 Small letters	12,447	1,500	3,500	6,000	24,000	
1840	47,338	350.00	600.00	1,500	11,000	
1841	63,131	300.00	500.00	1,300	8,000	
1841O	2,500	2,000	4,500	11,500	28,000	
1842 Small date	18,623	300.00	550.00	1,750	10,000	
1842 Large date	62,884	300.00	550.00	1,750	10,000	
1842O	27,400	300.00	650.00	2,500	16,000	
1843	75,462	300.00	600.00	1,750	10,000	
1843O	175,162	275.00	450.00	1,200	10,500	
1844	6,361	1,000	2,500	5,000	16,000	
1844O	118,700	285.00	500.00	1,500	14,000	
1845	26,153	500.00	900.00	2,250	13,500	
1845O	47,500	400.00	875.00	1,900	13,000	
1846	20,095	700.00	1,150	4,650	17,000	

EAGLES ($10.00 GOLD PIECES)

	Quan. Minted	VF-20	EF-40	AU-50	MS-60	Proof-63
1846O	} 81,780	$450.00	$850.00	$2,850	$14,000	
1846O, "6 over 5".........		450.00	850.00	2,850	14,000	
1847................................862,258		250.00	300.00	550.00	3,250	
1847O................................571,500		250.00	375.00	700.00	5,000	
1848................................145,484		280.00	475.00	850.00	4,750	
1848O................................35,850		450.00	1,000	3,750	14,000	
1849................................653,618		250.00	325.00	600.00	3,250	
1849O................................23,900		600.00	1,900	5,500	18,000	
1850 Large date	} 291,451	250.00	400.00	650.00	3,750	
1850 Small date		450.00	1,000	2,000	10,000	
1850O................................57,500		350.00	800.00	3,500	13,500	
1851................................176,328		250.00	400.00	800.00	5,000	
1851O................................263,000		275.00	475.00	1,050	6,500	
1852................................263,106		250.00	350.00	800.00	4,200	
1852O................................18,000		600.00	1,200	4,000	20,000	

1853,
3 over 2

	Quan. Minted	VF-20	EF-40	AU-50	MS-60	Proof-63
1853, 3 over 2	} 201,253	425.00	900.00	1,700	13,500	
1853		250.00	300.00	550.00	3,500	
1853O................................51,000		300.00	600.00	1,200	10,000	
1854................................54,250		300.00	500.00	1,000	5,000	
1854O Large or small date .52,500		300.00	750.00	1,800	9,500	
1854S 123,826		300.00	500.00	1,500	8,000	
1855................................121,701		250.00	350.00	650.00	3,750	—
1855O................................18,000		600.00	1,400	4,750	17,000	
1855S 9,000		1,300	2,200	6,250	21,000	—
1856................................60,490		250.00	325.00	700.00	3,650	
1856O................................14,500		650.00	1,900	4,000	14,000	
1856S 68,000		275.00	500.00	1,250	8,000	
1857................................16,606		350.00	800.00	1,900	10,000	—
1857O................................5,500		950.00	2,000	3,500	18,000	
1857S 26,000		400.00	700.00	2,000	9,000	
1858*................................2,521		4,500	7,500	13,000	33,000	—
1858O................................20,000		275.00	700.00	1,500	9,000	
1858S 11,800		1,700	3,750	6,000	27,000	
1859......................(80)	16,093	325.00	750.00	1,600	8,500	$40,000
1859O................................2,300		3,650	7,500	15,000	40,000	
1859S 7,000		2,000	5,000	12,000	30,000	
1860......................(50)	15,105	350.00	800.00	1,600	7,500	32,500
1860O................................11,100		500.00	1,300	2,600	14,000	
1860S 5,000		2,500	6,000	13,000	37,500	
1861......................(69)	113,233	250.00	325.00	650.00	3,250	30,000
1861S 15,500		1,300	2,850	6,750	28,500	
1862......................(35)	10,995	450.00	1,150	2,400	11,000	30,000
1862S 12,500		1,500	3,200	6,000	29,000	
1863......................(30)	1,248	4,000	7,500	17,000	45,000	35,000
1863S 10,000		1,500	3,250	8,000	24,000	
1864......................(50)	3,580	1,700	3,500	7,500	15,500	32,500
1864S 2,500		4,250	13,000	24,000		

*Beware removed mint mark.

EAGLES ($10.00 GOLD PIECES)

	Quan. Minted	VF-20	EF-40	AU-50	MS-60	Proof-63
1865 ....(25)	4,005	$1,500	$3,650	$6,750	$25,000	$30,000
1865S	} 16,700	4,250	9,500	14,000	33,000	
1865S, 865 over inverted 186		3,500	6,000	12,000		
1866S....................................8,500		2,750	3,750	11,000	30,000	

Variety 2 — Motto Above Eagle 1866-1907

Standards as before. Mints: Philadelphia, Carson City, Denver, New Orleans, San Francisco.

VF-20 VERY FINE — *Half of hairlines over coronet visible. Curls under ear worn but defined. IN GOD WE TRUST and its ribbon are sharp.*

EF-40 EXTREMELY FINE — *Small amount of wear on top of hair and below L in LIBERTY. Wear evident on wing tips and neck of eagle.*

AU-50 ABOUT UNCIRCULATED — *Trace of wear on hair above eye and on coronet.*

MS-60 UNCIRCULATED — *No trace of wear. Light blemishes.*

Mint mark location is on the reverse below the eagle.

		VF-20	EF-40	AU-50	MS-60	Proof-63
1866 ....(30)	3,780	750.00	2,000	4,250	17,000	24,000
1866S..11,500		1,500	3,500	6,500	18,500	
1867 ....(50)	3,140	1,500	3,000	5,000	22,000	21,000
1867S....................................9,000		2,500	6,000	8,500	30,000	
1868 ....(25)	10,655	550.00	800.00	2,000	14,000	22,500
1868S..13,500		1,200	2,250	4,500	22,000	
1869 ....(25)	1,855	1,500	3,000	5,500	25,000	21,000
1869S....................................6,430		1,300	2,600	5,750	24,000	
1870 ....(35)	4,025	800.00	1,250	2,500	12,000	22,500
1870CC..5,908		7,750	25,000	40,000		
1870S....................................8,000		1,200	2,500	6,250	23,000	
1871 ....(30)	1,820	1,300	2,500	4,000	15,000	27,000
1871CC..8,085		2,500	6,000	16,000	—	
1871S..16,500		1,200	2,250	6,000	18,000	
1872 ....(30)	1,650	2,200	4,000	9,500	22,000	20,000
1872CC..4,600		2,400	8,000	18,000	—	
1872S..17,300		600.00	1,150	2,500	16,000	
1873 ....(25)	825	4,000	8,500	20,000	36,000	30,000
1873CC..4,543		3,000	8,000	25,000	—	
1873S..12,000		1,000	2,250	4,500	17,000	
1874 ....(20)	53,160	225.00	300.00	400.00	1,800	25,000
1874CC..16,767		1,000	2,750	8,000	23,000	
1874S..10,000		1,100	3,300	8,000	23,000	
1875 ....(20)	120	37,500	55,000	75,000		—
1875CC..7,715		3,000	8,000	21,000	—	
1876 ....(45)	732	2,750	7,500	12,500	38,000	25,000
1876CC..4,696		3,000	6,750	15,000	39,000	
1876S....................................5,000		1,250	2,500	6,000	22,000	
1877 ....(20)	817	2,500	5,000	8,000	24,000	27,000
1877CC..3,332		2,500	5,000	12,000	26,000	
1877S..17,000		450.00	650.00	2,000	17,000	
1878 ....(20)	73,800	210.00	250.00	300.00	1,000	22,000

EAGLES ($10.00 GOLD PIECES)

	Quan. Minted	VF-20	EF-40	AU-50	MS-60	Proof-63
1878CC	3,244	$3,250	$7,000	$16,000	$32,000	
1878S	26,100	375.00	650.00	1,850	12,000	
1879 ......(30)	384,770	225.00	250.00	325.00	500.00	$20,000
1879CC	1,762	5,500	10,000	21,000	36,000	
1879O	1,500	2,000	4,250	9,000	22,500	
1879S	224,000	225.00	250.00	300.00	900.00	
1880 ......(36)	1,644,876	225.00	250.00	275.00	300.00	18,000
1880CC	11,190	400.00	700.00	1,500	8,000	
1880O	9,200	325.00	600.00	1,200	7,250	
1880S	506,250	225.00	250.00	275.00	300.00	
1881 ......(40)	3,877,260	200.00	225.00	240.00	285.00	19,000
1881CC	24,015	375.00	550.00	1,100	5,200	
1881O	8,350	325.00	650.00	1,100	5,000	
1881S	970,000	200.00	225.00	240.00	285.00	
1882 ......(40)	2,324,480	200.00	225.00	240.00	285.00	18,500
1882CC	6,764	525.00	1,000	3,000	11,000	
1882O	10,820	285.00	550.00	1,300	5,000	
1882S	132,000	220.00	245.00	285.00	500.00	
1883 ......(40)	208,740	210.00	225.00	250.00	285.00	20,000
1883CC	12,000	400.00	650.00	2,250	10,000	
1883O	800	2,500	6,500	10,500	28,500	
1883S	38,000	200.00	225.00	240.00	800.00	
1884 ......(45)	76,905	200.00	235.00	250.00	600.00	26,000
1884CC	9,925	450.00	1,000	2,600	10,000	
1884S	124,250	210.00	230.00	275.00	550.00	
1885 ......(65)	253,527	200.00	225.00	240.00	325.00	17,000
1885S	228,000	200.00	225.00	240.00	285.00	
1886 ......(60)	236,160	200.00	225.00	240.00	310.00	16,000
1886S	826,000	200.00	225.00	240.00	285.00	
1887 ......(80)	53,680	200.00	225.00	275.00	700.00	15,000
1887S	817,000	200.00	225.00	240.00	285.00	
1888 ......(75)	132,996	200.00	225.00	275.00	575.00	14,000
1888O	21,335	200.00	250.00	300.00	500.00	
1888S	648,700	200.00	225.00	240.00	285.00	
1889 ......(45)	4,485	250.00	350.00	800.00	2,000	18,000
1889S	425,400	200.00	225.00	240.00	285.00	
1890 ......(63)	58,043	200.00	225.00	275.00	600.00	15,000
1890CC	17,500	300.00	425.00	625.00	1,700	
1891 ......(48)	91,868	200.00	240.00	265.00	310.00	12,000
1891CC	103,732	275.00	350.00	500.00	800.00	
1892 ......(72)	797,552	200.00	230.00	240.00	285.00	13,500
1892CC	40,000	325.00	450.00	700.00	2,850	
1892O	28,688	200.00	230.00	275.00	400.00	
1892S	115,500	225.00	245.00	275.00	350.00	
1893 ......(55)	1,840,895	225.00	245.00	275.00	310.00	13,500
1893CC	14,000	350.00	625.00	1,600	4,500	
1893O	17,000	225.00	250.00	300.00	600.00	
1893S	141,350	225.00	250.00	275.00	400.00	
1894 ......(43)	2,470,778	200.00	225.00	240.00	285.00	13,500
1894O	107,500	200.00	225.00	300.00	850.00	
1894S	25,000	200.00	250.00	700.00	3,200	
1895 ......(56)	567,826	200.00	225.00	240.00	285.00	12,000
1895O	98,000	225.00	250.00	300.00	500.00	
1895S	49,000	235.00	235.00	650.00	2,350	
1896 ......(78)	76,348	200.00	225.00	240.00	285.00	12,000
1896S	123,750	225.00	275.00	550.00	2,350	
1897 ......(69)	1,000,159	200.00	225.00	240.00	285.00	12,000

EAGLES ($10.00 GOLD PIECES)

	Quan. Minted	VF-20	EF-40	AU-50	MS-60	Proof-63
1897O	42,500	$200.00	$225.00	$300.00	$600.00	
1897S	234,750	200.00	225.00	300.00	800.00	
1898 ....(67)	812,197	200.00	225.00	240.00	285.00	$12,000
1898S	473,600	200.00	225.00	275.00	400.00	
1899 ....(86)	1,262,305	200.00	225.00	240.00	285.00	11,000
1899O	37,047	200.00	225.00	275.00	600.00	
1899S	841,000	200.00	225.00	240.00	285.00	
1900 ....(120)	293,960	200.00	225.00	240.00	285.00	11,000
1900S	81,000	225.00	265.00	325.00	750.00	
1901 ....(85)	1,718,825	200.00	225.00	240.00	285.00	11,000
1901O	72,041	200.00	225.00	275.00	400.00	
1901S	2,812,750	200.00	225.00	240.00	285.00	
1902 ....(113)	82,513	200.00	225.00	240.00	285.00	11,000
1902S	469,500	200.00	225.00	240.00	285.00	
1903 ....(96)	125,926	200.00	225.00	240.00	285.00	11,000
1903O	112,771	200.00	225.00	275.00	375.00	
1903S	538,000	200.00	225.00	275.00	325.00	
1904 ....(108)	162,038	200.00	225.00	240.00	285.00	11,000
1904O	108,950	200.00	225.00	275.00	375.00	
1905 ....(86)	201,078	200.00	225.00	240.00	285.00	11,000
1905S	369,250	200.00	225.00	300.00	1,100	
1906 ....(77)	165,497	200.00	225.00	240.00	285.00	11,000
1906D	981,000	200.00	225.00	240.00	285.00	
1906O	86,895	200.00	225.00	275.00	400.00	
1906S	457,000	200.00	225.00	275.00	525.00	
1907 ....(74)	1,203,973	200.00	225.00	240.00	285.00	11,000
1907D	1,030,000	200.00	225.00	240.00	285.00	
1907S	210,500	200.00	225.00	300.00	550.00	

Values of common gold coins have been based on the current bullion price of gold and may vary with the prevailing spot price.

INDIAN HEAD TYPE 1907-1933

Augustus Saint-Gaudens, considered by many the greatest of modern sculptors, introduced a new high standard of art in United States coins evidenced by his eagle and double eagle types of 1907. The obverse of the eagle shows the head of Liberty crowned with an Indian war bonnet while an impressively majestic eagle dominates the reverse side. A departure from older standards is found on the edge of the piece, where 46 raised stars are arranged signifying the states of the Union, instead of a lettered or reeded edge (48 stars 1912 and later).

The first eagles struck had no motto IN GOD WE TRUST as did the later issues starting in 1908. President Theodore Roosevelt personally objected to the use of the Deity's name on coins. The motto was restored to the coins by an Act of Congress in 1908.

Designer Augustus Saint-Gaudens. Standards same as previous issue. Edge 1907-1911: 46 raised stars; 1912-1933: 48 raised stars. Net weight: .48375 oz. pure gold; mints: Philadelphia, Denver, San Francisco.

VF-20 VERY FINE — *Bonnet feathers worn near band. Hair high points show wear.*
EF-40 EXTREMELY FINE — *Slight wear on cheekbone and headdress feathers. Eagle's eye and left wing will show slight wear.*
AU-50 ABOUT UNCIRCULATED — *Trace of wear on hair above eye and on forehead.*
MS-60 UNCIRCULATED — *No trace of wear. Light blemishes.*

EAGLES ($10.00 GOLD PIECES)
Variety 1 — No Motto on Reverse 1907-1908

No Motto

Mint mark location is above left tip of branch on 1908-D no motto, and at left of arrow points thereafter.

Choice uncirculated (MS-65) coins are rare and worth substantial premiums.

	Quan. Minted	VF-20	EF-40	AU-50	MS-60	Proof-63
1907 Wire rim, periods 500			$6,000	$7,000	$9,500	
1907 Rounded rim, periods before and						
after ●E●PLURIBUS●UNUM● *42			16,500	23,000	28,000	—
1907 No periods 239,406		$335.00	385.00	425.00	475.00	
1908 No motto.............................33,500		350.00	400.00	450.00	800.00	
1908D No motto 210,000		375.00	425.00	475.00	650.00	

*19,958 melted at Mint.

Variety 2 — Motto on Reverse 1908-1933

With Motto
IN GOD WE TRUST

						Matte Proof-63
1908......................(116)	341,486	325.00	335.00	400.00	485.00	$14,000
1908D 836,500		350.00	400.00	450.00	650.00	
1908S...59,850		425.00	500.00	625.00	1,500	
1909......................(74)	184,863	285.00	325.00	385.00	525.00	13,500
1909D 121,540		325.00	375.00	400.00	650.00	
1909S...292,350		325.00	375.00	425.00	650.00	
1910......................(204)	318,704	285.00	300.00	330.00	400.00	13,500
1910D 2,356,640		285.00	300.00	330.00	450.00	
1910S...811,000		325.00	350.00	400.00	700.00	
1911......................(95)	505,595	285.00	300.00	330.00	425.00	13,500
1911D 30,100		450.00	600.00	850.00	3,850	
1911S...51,000		390.00	425.00	550.00	1,100	
1912......................(83)	405,083	285.00	300.00	330.00	425.00	13,500
1912S...300,000		325.00	375.00	450.00	850.00	
1913......................(71)	442,071	285.00	300.00	330.00	425.00	13,500
1913S...66,000		400.00	475.00	750.00	3,750	
1914......................(50)	151,050	285.00	300.00	350.00	450.00	14,000
1914D 343,500		315.00	350.00	385.00	450.00	
1914S...208,000		335.00	375.00	425.00	675.00	
1915......................(75)	351,075	285.00	300.00	330.00	400.00	15,000

EAGLES ($10.00 GOLD PIECES)

	Quan. Minted	VF-20	EF-40	AU-50	MS-60	Matte Proof-63
1915S	59,000	$350.00	$500.00	$800.00	$2,750	
1916S	138,500	335.00	375.00	450.00	650.00	
1920S	126,500	5,000	7,000	8,750	16,000	
1926	1,014,000	285.00	300.00	330.00	400.00	
1930S	96,000	3,750	5,000	7,000	9,000	
1932	4,463,000	285.00	300.00	330.00	400.00	
1933	312,500				70,000	

DOUBLE EAGLES ($20.00 GOLD PIECES) — 1850-1933

This largest denomination of all regular United States issues was authorized to be coined by the Act of March 3, 1849. Its weight was 516 grains, .900 fine. The 1849 double eagle is a unique pattern and reposes in the Smithsonian. The rarest date obtainable is 1884. The 1861 reverse design by Anthony C. Paquet was withdrawn soon after striking. Very few specimens are known.

+ or – indicates change from previous year	TYPE COIN VALUES									
	F-12	VF-20	EF-40	AU-50	MS-60	MS-63	MS-65	PF-60	PF-63	PF-65
Lib Coronet-NM 1849-1866	450.00	575.00	625.00	750.00	2,100	8,000-	25,000-	10,000	45,000	175,000
Lib (Twenty D.) 1866-1876	435.00	475.00	525.00	575.00	700.00	8,000	50,000-	6,500	26,000	120,000
Lib 1877-1907	360.00	375.00	400.00-	425.00-	475.00-	600.00-	2,750-	5,000	16,000	52,000
Saint-Gaudens-RN, HR 1907	2,500	4,000	5,000+	6,000+	7,750	14,000	35,000			
Saint-Gaudens 1907-1933	360.00	375.00	400.00	425.00	475.00	500.00	1,000	6,000	16,500	40,000

Designer James B. Longacre; weight 33.436 grams; composition: .900 gold, .100 copper; diameter 34 mm; reeded edge; mints: Philadelphia, Carson City, Denver, New Orleans, San Francisco. Net weight: .96750 oz. pure gold.

VF-20 VERY FINE—*LIBERTY is bold. Prongs on crown defined. Lower half worn flat. Hair worn about ear.*
EF-40 EXTREMELY FINE—*Trace of wear on rounded prongs of crown and down hair curls. Minor bag marks.*
AU-50 ABOUT UNCIRCULATED—*Trace of wear on hair over eye and on coronet.*
MS-60 UNCIRCULATED—*No trace of wear. Light blemishes.*

Mint mark location is below the eagle.

1853, 3 over 2

Without Motto on Reverse 1849-1866

See page 6 for information on gold coins as an investment.

	Quan. Minted	VF-20	EF-40	AU-50	MS-60	Proof-63
1849	1		Smithsonian collection			
1850	1,170,261	$650.00	$800.00	$1,800	$5,000	
1850O	141,000	750.00	1,200	5,500	27,500	
1851	2,087,155	525.00	625.00	850.00	2,650	
1851O	315,000	650.00	800.00	1,750	14,000	
1852	2,053,026	575.00	650.00	800.00	2,750	
1852O	190,000	625.00	750.00	1,700	15,000	
1853, 3 over 2	} 1,261,326	675.00	1,200	2,750	27,000	
1853		600.00	675.00	850.00	4,500	

DOUBLE EAGLES ($20.00 GOLD PIECES)

	Quan. Minted	VF-20	EF-40	AU-50	MS-60	Proof-63
1853O 71,000		$650.00	$1,000	$2,500	$24,000	
1854 Small date .... }	757,899	600.00	650.00	800.00	5,000	
1854 Large date .... }		600.00	750.00	1,600	6,000	
1854O 3,250		25,000	45,000	85,000	160,000	
1854S 141,468		625.00	650.00	1,100	3,100	
1855 364,666		600.00	675.00	1,000	7,000	
1855O...................................8,000		2,600	5,750	18,000	—	
1855S 879,675		600.00	675.00	850.00	6,800	
1856 329,878		600.00	675.00	850.00	7,500	
1856O...................................2,250		33,000	62,000	110,000		
1856S 1,189,750		600.00	675.00	850.00	3,500	
1857 439,375		600.00	675.00	850.00	3,500	
1857O...................................30,000		950.00	1,500	4,000	22,000	
1857S 970,500		600.00	675.00	850.00	3,500	
1858 211,714		675.00	800.00	1,300	4,250	
1858O...................................35,250		1,100	1,850	4,750	22,000	
1858S 846,710		600.00	675.00	1,000	7,500	
1859.................(80)	43,677	875.00	2,000	3,850	35,000	—
1859O...................................9,100		3,000	6,000	15,000	52,500	
1859S 636,445		575.00	625.00	850.00	5,000	
1860.................(59)	577,729	600.00	675.00	750.00	3,650	—
1860O...................................6,600		3,200	5,750	14,500	48,000	
1860S 544,950		600.00	675.00	1,100	5,500	
1861.................(66)	2,976,519	575.00	625.00	750.00	2,100	$50,000
1861O...................................17,741		1,650	3,250	6,500	25,000	
1861S 768,000		575.00	650.00	1,400	7,500	

1861S Normal Obverse

1861S Paquet Reverse

		VF-20	EF-40	AU-50	MS-60	Proof-63
1861 — A.C. Paquet rev. (Tall letters)					850,000	
1861S—A.C. Paquet rev. (Tall letters)		6,000	12,000	24,000	55,000	
1862 ....(35)	92,168	725.00	1,250	2,500	10,000	45,000
1862S...........................854,173		600.00	675.00	1,500	11,000	
1863 ....(30)	142,820	600.00	700.00	1,600	13,000	45,000
1863S...........................966,570		650.00	675.00	1,150	6,000	
1864 ....(50)	204,285	600.00	775.00	1,600	8,500	45,000
1864S...........................793,660		600.00	675.00	1,600	7,250	
1865 ....(25)	351,200	600.00	675.00	850.00	5,500	45,000
1865S...........................1,042,500		600.00	675.00	1,200	4,500	
1866S...................................Est. 12,000		1,500	2,800	8,000	—	

DOUBLE EAGLES ($20.00 GOLD PIECES)
Motto Above Eagle, Value TWENTY D. 1866-1876

	Quan. Minted	VF-20	EF-40	AU-50	MS-60	Proof-63
1866 ....(30)	698,775	$575.00	$650.00	$1,200	$4,800	$26,000
1866S (see preceding page)....842,250		550.00	700.00	1,500	14,500	
1867 ....(50)	251,065	500.00	550.00	650.00	1,700	26,000
1867S 920,750		550.00	700.00	1,300	13,000	
1868 ....(25)	98,600	700.00	850.00	1,600	8,000	26,000
1868S 837,500		525.00	675.00	1,200	8,000	
1869 ....(25)	175,155	650.00	750.00	1,000	4,500	31,000
1869S 686,750		500.00	600.00	900.00	4,250	
1870 ....(35)	155,185	650.00	750.00	1,400	7,000	31,000
1870CC 3,789		60,000	90,000	—	—	
1870S 982,000		500.00	575.00	800.00	4,500	
1871 ....(30)	80,150	625.00	800.00	1,300	3,500	31,000
1871CC 17,387		3,000	5,000	14,000		
1871S 928,000		500.00	575.00	675.00	3,250	
1872 ....(30)	251,880	500.00	575.00	650.00	2,500	31,000
1872CC 26,900		1,100	1,600	4,500	23,000	
1872S 780,000		500.00	550.00	625.00	2,200	
1873 Closed 3 ....(25) ⎫	1,709,825	550.00	650.00	900.00	2,300	31,000
1873 Open 3 ....⎭		500.00	550.00	600.00	700.00	
1873CC Closed 3 22,410		850.00	1,750	4,250	23,000	
1873S Closed 3 .... ⎫	1,040,600	500.00	550.00	600.00	1,450	
1873S Open 3...............⎭		550.00	700.00	1,000	3,750	
1874 ....(20)	366,800	475.00	525.00	575.00	1,100	31,000
1874CC 115,085		700.00	850.00	1,700	7,500	
1874S 1,214,000		525.00	575.00	625.00	1,400	
1875 ....(20)	295,740	500.00	550.00	600.00	700.00	—
1875CC 111,151		650.00	750.00	1,000	2,200	
1875S 1,230,000		475.00	525.00	575.00	800.00	
1876 ....(45)	583,905	475.00	525.00	575.00	750.00	*26,000
1876CC 138,441		700.00	800.00	1,200	3,850	
1876S 1,597,000		475.00	525.00	575.00	700.00	

*A transitional proof pattern also exists dated 1876 but of the type of 1877.

Value spelled TWENTY DOLLARS, 1877-1907

DOUBLE EAGLES ($20.00 GOLD PIECES)

	Quan. Minted	VF-20	EF-40	AU-50	MS-60	Proof-63
1877................(20)	397,670	$475.00	$525.00	$575.00	$700.00	$22,000
1877CC 42,565		850.00	950.00	1,700	12,000	
1877S 1,735,000		475.00	525.00	575.00	700.00	
1878................(20)	543,645	475.00	525.00	575.00	700.00	22,000
1878CC 13,180		900.00	1,500	3,750	16,500	
1878S 1,739,000		475.00	500.00	550.00	750.00	
1879................(30)	207,630	475.00	525.00	575.00	900.00	23,000
1879CC 10,708		1,000	1,700	4,500	17,000	
1879O 2,325		2,750	4,250	9,500	27,500	
1879S 1,223,800		475.00	500.00	600.00	1,200	
1880................(36)	51,456	475.00	550.00	650.00	2,900	23,000
1880S 836,000		475.00	525.00	600.00	1,100	
1881................(61)	2,260	3,750	6,500	12,500	32,000	36,000
1881S 727,000		475.00	500.00	550.00	900.00	
1882................(59)	630	7,000	15,000	25,000	46,000	36,000
1882CC 39,140		700.00	800.00	1,200	5,250	
1882S 1,125,000		435.00	475.00	500.00	725.00	
1883 Proofs only ...(92)	92					50,000
1883CC 59,962		750.00	850.00	1,000	4,000	
1883S 1,189,000		435.00	475.00	500.00	600.00	
1884 Proofs only ...(71)	71					50,000
1884CC 81,139		700.00	850.00	1,000	2,450	
1884S 916,000		425.00	450.00	500.00	575.00	
1885................(77)	828	6,000	7,000	11,000	32,000	30,000
1885CC 9,450		1,000	1,750	3,000	10,000	
1885S 683,500		475.00	525.00	550.00	625.00	
1886................(106)	1,106	6,000	11,000	19,500	37,500	36,000
1887 Proofs only .(121)	121					36,000
1887S 283,000		475.00	525.00	550.00	675.00	
1888................(105)	226,266	475.00	525.00	550.00	750.00	21,000
1888S 859,600		475.00	525.00	550.00	650.00	
1889................(41)	44,111	425.00	450.00	525.00	650.00	21,000
1889CC 30,945		750.00	900.00	1,300	3,600	
1889S 774,700		425.00	450.00	475.00	550.00	
1890................(55)	75,995	425.00	450.00	500.00	600.00	21,000
1890CC 91,209		700.00	775.00	1,100	2,500	
1890S 802,750		375.00	425.00	475.00	550.00	
1891................(52)	1,442	2,850	4,500	7,500	22,000	21,000
1891CC 5,000		1,600	2,600	5,000	12,000	
1891S 1,288,125		375.00	400.00	425.00	500.00	
1892................(93)	4,523	950.00	1,400	2,250	5,000	21,000
1892CC 27,265		700.00	850.00	1,200	3,000	
1892S 930,150		375.00	400.00	425.00	475.00	
1893................(59)	344,339	375.00	400.00	425.00	475.00	20,000
1893CC 18,402		800.00	850.00	1,100	2,350	
1893S 996,175		375.00	400.00	425.00	475.00	
1894................(50)	1,368,990	375.00	400.00	425.00	475.00	19,000
1894S 1,048,550		375.00	400.00	425.00	475.00	
1895................(51)	1,114,656	375.00	400.00	425.00	475.00	19,000
1895S 1,143,500		375.00	400.00	425.00	475.00	
1896................(128)	792,663	375.00	400.00	425.00	475.00	18,000
1896S 1,403,925		375.00	400.00	425.00	475.00	
1897................(86)	1,383,261	375.00	400.00	425.00	475.00	18,000
1897S 1,470,250		375.00	400.00	425.00	475.00	
1898................(75)	170,470	375.00	400.00	500.00	600.00	18,000
1898S 2,575,175		375.00	400.00	425.00	475.00	
1899................(84)	1,669,384	375.00	400.00	425.00	475.00	18,000

DOUBLE EAGLES ($20.00 GOLD PIECES)

	Quan. Minted	VF-20	EF-40	AU-50	MS-60	Proof-63
1899S	2,010,300	$375.00	$400.00	$425.00	$475.00	
1900 (124)	1,874,584	375.00	400.00	425.00	550.00	$17,000
1900S	2,459,500	375.00	400.00	425.00	475.00	
1901 (96)	111,526	375.00	400.00	425.00	475.00	
1901S	1,596,000	375.00	400.00	425.00	525.00	
1902 (114)	31,254	450.00	500.00	550.00	850.00	17,000
1902S	1,753,625	375.00	400.00	425.00	550.00	
1903 (158)	287,428	375.00	400.00	425.00	475.00	16,000
1903S	954,000	375.00	400.00	425.00	550.00	
1904 (98)	6,256,797	375.00	400.00	425.00	475.00	16,000
1904S	5,134,175	375.00	400.00	425.00	475.00	
1905 (92)	59,011	450.00	500.00	575.00	1,000	16,000
1905S	1,813,000	375.00	400.00	425.00	550.00	
1906 (94)	69,690	375.00	400.00	500.00	600.00	16,000
1906D	620,250	375.00	400.00	425.00	475.00	
1906S	2,065,750	375.00	400.00	425.00	475.00	
1907 (78)	1,451,864	375.00	400.00	425.00	475.00	16,000
1907D	842,250	375.00	400.00	425.00	475.00	
1907S	2,165,800	375.00	400.00	425.00	475.00	

> Values of common gold coins are based on the current bullion price of gold and may vary with the prevailing spot price.

SAINT-GAUDENS TYPE 1907-1933

The $20 gold piece designed by Augustus Saint-Gaudens is considered to be the most beautiful United States coin. The first coins issued were 11,250 high relief pieces struck for general circulation. The relief is much higher than later issues and the date 1907 is in Roman numerals. A few of the proof coins were made using the lettered edge collar from the extremely high relief version. These can be distinguished by a pronounced bottom left serif on the N in UNUM, and other minor differences. High-relief proofs are trial or experimental pieces. Flat-relief double eagles were issued later in 1907 with Arabic numerals, and continued through 1933.

The field of the rare extremely high relief experimental pieces is excessively concave and connects directly with the edge without any border, giving it a sharp knifelike appearance; Liberty's skirt shows two folds on the side of her right leg; the Capitol building in the background at left is very small; the sun, on the reverse side, has 14 rays, as opposed to the regular high relief coins that have only 13 rays extending from the sun.

Designer Augustus Saint-Gaudens. Standards same as previous issue. Mints: Philadelphia, Denver, San Francisco. Edge: E PLURIBUS UNUM with words divided by stars. One specimen of the high relief variety with plain edge is known.

VF-20 VERY FINE—*Minor wear on legs and toes. Eagle's left wing and breast feathers worn.*
EF-40 EXTREMELY FINE—*Drapery lines on chest visible. Wear on left breast, knee and below. Eagle's feathers on breast and right wing are bold.*
AU-50 ABOUT UNCIRCULATED—*Trace of wear on nose, breast and knee. Wear visible on eagle's wings.*
MS-60 UNCIRCULATED—*No trace of wear. Light marks or blemishes.*

See page 6 for information on investment grade coins.

Extremely High Relief Patterns of 1907

	Proof
1907 Ex. high relief, plain edge *(Unique)*	—
1907 Ex. high relief, lettered edge ....1996 Sotheby Auction	$825,000

DOUBLE EAGLES ($20.00 GOLD PIECES)

	Quan. Minted	VF-20	EF-40	AU-50	MS-60	Proof
1907 High relief, Roman numerals (MCMVII), wire rim.......	} 11,250	$4,000	$5,000	$6,000	$7,750	—
1907 Same, flat rim.................		4,000	5,000	6,000	7,750	—

Arabic Numerals

No Motto

	Quan. Minted	VF-20	EF-40	AU-50	MS-60
1907 Arabic numerals.............	361,667	375.00	420.00	500.00	550.00
1908..4,271,551		375.00	400.00	475.00	525.00
1908D......................................	663,750	375.00	420.00	500.00	550.00

Mint mark location is on obverse above date.

With Motto IN GOD WE TRUST, 1908-1933

		VF-20	EF-40	AU-50	MS-60	Matte Proof-63
1908 ....(101)	156,359	375.00	400.00	425.00	525.00	$16,500
1908D...349,500		375.00	400.00	425.00	525.00	
1908S 22,000		650.00	875.00	1,500	4,200	

DOUBLE EAGLES ($20.00 GOLD PIECES)

Double eagles from 1907 to 1911 have 46 stars on the obverse and 48 stars from 1912 to 1933.

1909, 9 over 8

	Quan. Minted	VF-20	EF-40	AU-50	MS-60	Matte Proof-63
1909, 9 over 8	} 161,282	$450.00	$550.00	$675.00	$1,000	
1909......................(67)		475.00	550.00	600.00	700.00	$18,000
1909D................................52,500		500.00	575.00	650.00	1,250	
1909S 2,774,925		375.00	400.00	425.00	475.00	
1910.....................(167) 482,167		375.00	400.00	425.00	475.00	16,500
1910D................................429,000		375.00	400.00	425.00	475.00	
1910S 2,128,250		375.00	400.00	425.00	475.00	
1911.....................(100) 197,350		375.00	400.00	425.00	575.00	17,000
1911D................................846,500		375.00	400.00	425.00	475.00	
1911S 775,750		375.00	400.00	425.00	550.00	
1912......................(74) 149,824		375.00	400.00	425.00	575.00	17,500
1913......................(58) 168,838		375.00	400.00	425.00	550.00	17,500
1913D................................393,500		375.00	400.00	425.00	475.00	
1913S 34,000		525.00	600.00	700.00	1,100	
1914......................(70) 95,320		375.00	400.00	425.00	500.00	17,000
1914D................................453,000		375.00	400.00	425.00	475.00	
1914S 1,498,000		375.00	400.00	425.00	475.00	
1915......................(50) 152,050		375.00	400.00	425.00	475.00	18,000
1915S 567,500		375.00	400.00	425.00	475.00	
1916S 796,000		375.00	400.00	425.00	475.00	
1920....................................228,250		375.00	400.00	425.00	475.00	
1920S 558,000		6,500	8,500	12,000	26,000	
1921....................................528,500		8,000	10,500	16,500	35,000	
1922.................................1,375,500		375.00	400.00	425.00	475.00	
1922S 2,658,000		525.00	600.00	675.00	800.00	
1923....................................566,000		375.00	400.00	425.00	475.00	
1923D.............................1,702,250		375.00	400.00	425.00	475.00	
1924.................................4,323,500		375.00	400.00	425.00	475.00	
1924D.............................3,049,500		800.00	1,000	1,200	1,800	
1924S 2,927,500		800.00	1,050	1,250	2,200	
1925.................................2,831,750		375.00	400.00	425.00	475.00	
1925D.............................2,938,500		1,000	1,400	1,750	3,100	
1925S 3,776,500		850.00	1,200	1,600	5,000	
1926....................................816,750		375.00	400.00	425.00	475.00	
1926D................................481,000		1,500	2,500	3,000	7,000	
1926S 2,041,500		800.00	1,000	1,300	1,800	
1927.................................2,946,750		375.00	400.00	425.00	475.00	
1927D................................180,000					300,000	
1927S 3,107,000			4,000	6,000	12,000	
1928.................................8,816,000		375.00	400.00	425.00	475.00	
1929.................................1,779,750			6,250	7,500	9,000	
1930S 74,000			9,000	12,500	18,500	
1931.................................2,938,250			8,000	11,000	15,000	
1931D................................106,500			7,500	9,000	15,000	
1932.................................1,101,750			9,000	11,500	16,500	
1933....................................445,500		None placed in circulation				

COMMEMORATIVE COINS

Commemorative coins have been popular since the days of the Greeks and Romans. In the beginning they served to record and honor important events and in the absence of newspapers they proved highly useful in passing along news of the day.

Many modern nations have issued commemorative coins and such pieces are highly esteemed by collectors. Yet no nation has surpassed our own country when it comes to commemorative coins and in this we have reason to be proud.

The unique position occupied by commemoratives in United States coinage is largely due to the fact that with few exceptions all commemorative coins have a real historical significance. The progress and advance of people in the New World are presented in an interesting and instructive manner on the commemorative issues. Such a record of facts artistically presented on our gold and silver memorial issues appeals strongly to the collector who favors the historical side of numismatics. It is the historical features of the commemoratives, in fact, that create interest among many people who would otherwise have little interest in coins.

Commemorative issues are considered for coinage by two committees of Congress — The Committee on Banking, Housing and Urban Affairs, and the Committee on Banking and Financial Services of the House, as well as the Citizens Commemorative Coin Advisory Committee. Congress is guided to a great extent by the reports of these committees when passing upon bills authorizing commemorative coins.

These special coins are usually issued either to commemorate events or to help pay for monuments or celebrations that commemorate historical persons, places or things. The commemorative coins are offered in most instances by a commission in charge of the event to be commemorated, and sold at a price in advance of the face value of the piece. All are of the standard weight and fineness of traditional gold, silver, or clad coins, and all are legal tender.

Commemorative coins are popularly collected either by major types or in sets with mint mark varieties. In many years no special commemorative coins were issued. Some regular coins such as the Lincoln cent of 1909, Washington quarter of 1932, and Bicentennial issues of 1976 are also commemorative in nature.

Unless otherwise stated, the coinage figures given represent the total outstanding coinage. In many cases, larger quantities were minted but were not all sold. The unsold coins were usually returned to the mint and melted, although some were placed in circulation at face value.

Note: The commemorative coins listed on pages 233-254 are arranged alphabetically and by denomination. The modern commemorative coin section on page 254 and beyond is arranged chronologically.

COMMEMORATIVE COINS

High quality brilliant uncirculated commemoratives (MS-65) are worth far more than uncirculated (MS-60) pieces, which are often dull, cleaned, or blemished by contact marks.

A limited number of proof strikings or presentation pieces were made for some of the 1892-1954 issues. All are very rare and valuable.

PRICE PERFORMANCE

Few people would ever guess, or even believe, that this country once issued an official half dollar bearing the portrait of P. T. Barnum, the famous con man who is credited with the saying "There's a sucker born every minute." He had nothing to do with the coins, which were made in 1936 long after his death, but the exceptional honor and the fact that the 50c coins were sold to the public for $2.00 each would have made him smile about bilking the public one last time.

Barnum did not have the last laugh in this matter. Those people who were fortunate enough to buy one of the original coins in 1936, and save it in perfect condition, find that today their treasure is worth over $300.00! Only 25,000 of the pieces were made, and at the time they were not very popular even with the few people who ever heard about them.

The Bridgeport commemorative half dollar with P. T. Barnum's portrait is but one of many different designs that have been used on special coins made for collectors since 1892. During that time commemorative coins have been issued to celebrate the founding of cities, mark expositions, honor famous citizens and presidents, and even to promote the Olympic contests in recent years. These coins are not normally placed in circulation, and are usually distributed by some agency at a price over face value with the surplus going to fund the event being celebrated. All commemorative coins made since 1982 have been distributed through the Mint with proceeds going directly to the government, and from there, to the various sponsoring organizations.

It has only been in recent years that the general public has learned about commemorative coins. They have long been popular with coin collectors who enjoy the artistry and history associated with them, as well as the tremendous profit that they have made from owning these rare pieces. Very few of them ever reached circulation because they were all originally sold above face value, and because they are all so rare. Most of the early issues were of the half dollar denomination, and were usually made in quantities of less than 20,000 pieces. This is miniscule when compared to the regular half dollar pieces which are made by the millions each year, and still rarely seen in circulation.

At the beginning of 1988 prices of commemoratives in MS-65 condition had risen so high that most collectors had to content themselves with pieces in lower grades. Investors continued to apply pressure to the high quality pieces and drive prices even higher, while the collector community went after coins in grades from About Uncirculated to MS-63. For several months the pressure from both influences caused prices to rise very rapidly for all issues and grades of commemoratives without even taking the price adjustment breather that usually goes along with such activity.

By 1990 prices dropped to the point where several of the commemoratives began to look like bargains once again. Many of the MS-65 pieces held firm at price levels above the $3,000.00 mark, but others were still available at under $500.00 even for coins of similar mintage. Coins in MS-63 or MS-64 were priced at but a fraction of the MS-65 pieces which would seem to make them reasonably priced because the demand for these pieces is universal, and not simply keyed to grade, rarity or speculator pressure.

Historically, the entire series of commemorative coins has frequently undergone a roller coaster cycle of price adjustments. These cycles have usually been of short duration, lasting from a month to a year, with prices always recovering and eventually exceeding previous levels.

ISABELLA QUARTER DOLLAR

In 1893 the Board of Lady Managers of the Columbian Exposition petitioned for a souvenir quarter dollar. Authority was granted March 3, 1893. The coin known as the Isabella quarter was designed by C. E. Barber. These souvenir quarters were sold for $1.00. The obverse has the crowned bust of Queen Isabella of Spain. The kneeling female on the reverse with distaff and spindle is emblematic of women's industry.

	Quan. Issued	AU-50	MS-60	MS-63	MS-65
1893 Columbian Exposition, Chicago	24,214	$415.00	$640.00	$685.00	$2,900

ALABAMA CENTENNIAL

The Alabama half dollars were authorized in 1920 for the centennial, which was celebrated in 1919, but they were not struck until 1921. The coins, designed by Laura Gardin Fraser, were offered first during President Harding's visit to Birmingham, October 26, 1921. The St. Andrews cross, an emblem on the state flag, appears on a part of the issue between the figures 2 x 2 indicating the twenty-second state of the Union. The obverse has busts of William Wyatt Bibb, first governor of Alabama, and T. E. Kilby, governor at the time of the centennial. This is the first instance of the use of a living person's portrait on a United States coin.

2 x 2 in Field

		AU-50	MS-60	MS-63	MS-65
1921 Alabama Centennial, with 2 x 2 in field of obverse	6,006	180.00	300.00	500.00	2,500
1921 Alabama Centennial, no 2 x 2	59,038	110.00	210.00	430.00	2,375

ALBANY, NEW YORK CHARTER

The 250th anniversary of the granting of a charter to the city of Albany was the occasion for a commemorative half dollar. The reverse design shows Governor Dongan, Peter Schuyler and Robert Livingston. The obverse depicts a beaver gnawing on a maple branch. Gertrude K. Lathrop of Albany was the designer.

		AU-50	MS-60	MS-63	MS-65
1936 Albany, New York	17,671	190.00	200.00	225.00	315.00

COMMEMORATIVE SILVER — Antietam, Arkansas

BATTLE OF ANTIETAM

A souvenir half dollar was designed by William Marks Simpson and struck in 1937 to commemorate the seventy-fifth anniversary of the famous Civil War battle to thwart Lee's invasion of Maryland. The opposing generals McClellan and Lee are featured on the obverse while the Burnside Bridge, an important tactical objective, is shown on the reverse. The Battle of Antietam, on September 17, 1862, was one of the bloodiest single-day battles of the war with total losses of about 25,000 men.

	Quan. Issued	AU-50	MS-60	MS-63	MS-65
1937 Battle of Antietam 1862-1937	18,028	$380.00	$420.00	$430.00	$660.00

ARKANSAS CENTENNIAL

This souvenir issue marked the one hundredth anniversary of the admission of Arkansas into the Union. Edward Everett Burr designed the piece and models were prepared by Emily Bates of Arkansas. Although 1936 was the centennial year the first of several issues was brought out in 1935 from all three mints. The 1937 and 1938 issues were the same as those of 1935 except for the dates. They were sold by the distributors at $8.75 per set of three coins. The reverse shows accolated heads of an Indian chief of 1836 and an American girl of 1936. During 1936 a second design was authorized by Congress. Senator Joseph T. Robinson consented to have his portrait placed on the reverse side of the coins which were struck at the Philadelphia Mint. (See listing on page 247).

	Quan. Issued		MS-60	MS-63	MS-65
1935 Arkansas Centennial	13,012				
1935D Same type D mint	5,505	Set	$200.00	$225.00	$710.00
1935S Same type S mint	5,506				
1936 Arkansas Centennial, same as 1935— date 1936 on rev	9,660				
1936D Same type D mint	9,660	Set	200.00	225.00	760.00
1936S Same type S mint	9,662				
1937 Arkansas Centennial (same as 1935)	5,505				
1937D Same type D mint	5,505	Set	230.00	300.00	950.00
1937S Same type S mint	5,506				
1938 Arkansas Centennial (same as 1935)	3,156				
1938D Same type D mint	3,155	Set	330.00	425.00	1,725
1938S Same type S mint	3,156				
1939 Arkansas Centennial (same as 1935)	2,104				
1939D Same type D mint	2,104	Set	600.00	800.00	2,900
1939S Same type S mint	2,105				
Single, type coin	Abt. Unc.	$57.50	57.50	70.00	205.00

COMMEMORATIVE SILVER — Bay Bridge, Boone

BAY BRIDGE
SAN FRANCISCO-
OAKLAND

The opening of the San Francisco Bay Bridge was the occasion for a special souvenir fifty-cent piece. The designs were the work of Jacques Schnier, a San Francisco artist. A California grizzly bear domi-nates the obverse. The famous landmark bridge is shown on the reverse. The coins were struck at the San Francisco Mint in November, 1936. The bear depicted was a composite of animals in local zoos.

	Quan. Issued	AU-50	MS-60	MS-63	MS-65
1936S San Francisco-Oakland Bay Bridge...71,424		$90.00	$115.00	$125.00	$260.00

DANIEL BOONE BICENTENNIAL

Date added in field.

This coin type, which was minted for five years, was struck in 1934 to commemorate the two hundredth anniversary of the famous frontiersman's birth. The change of date to 1935 for the second year's coinage brought about the addition of the commemorative date 1934 above the words PIONEER YEAR. Coinage covered several years similar to the schedule for the Texas issues. The models for this coin were prepared by Augustus Lukeman. The obverse bears a portrait of Daniel Boone. The reverse shows Boone with Chief Black Fish.

	Quan. Issued	AU-50	MS-60	MS-63	MS-65
1934 Daniel Boone Bicentennial 10,007		$60.00	$68.00	$80.00	$170.00
1935 Same type 10,010					
1935D Same type D mint..................................5,005	Set		225.00	275.00	520.00
1935S Same type S mint....................................5,005					
1935 Daniel Boone same as 1934					
sm. 1934 on rev 10,008					
1935D Same type D mint..................................2,003	Set		610.00	750.00	1,700
1935S Same type S mint....................................2,004					
1936 Daniel Boone (same as 1934)..................12,012					
1936D Same type D mint..................................5,005	Set		210.00	265.00	500.00
1936S Same type S mint....................................5,006					
1937 Daniel Boone (same as 1934)....................9,810					
1937D Same type D mint..................................2,506	Set		585.00	660.00	1,000
1937S Same type S mint....................................2,506					
1938 Daniel Boone (same as 1934)....................2,100					
1938D Same type D mint..................................2,100	Set		750.00	940.00	1,375
1938S Same type S mint....................................2,100					
Single, type coin		60.00	68.00	80.00	170.00

COMMEMORATIVE SILVER
Bridgeport, California, Carver-Washington

BRIDGEPORT, CONNECTICUT CENTENNIAL

In commemoration of the one hundredth anniversary of the incorporation of the city of Bridgeport a special fifty-cent piece was authorized May 15, 1936. Henry Kreis designed this coin. The head of P. T. Barnum, who was Bridgeport's best known citizen, occupies the obverse. An ultra-modernistic eagle dominates the reverse.

	Quan. Issued	AU-50	MS-60	MS-63	MS-65
1936 Bridgeport, Conn., Centennial	25,015	$110.00	$120.00	$150.00	$225.00

CALIFORNIA DIAMOND JUBILEE

The California half dollar was designed by Jo Mora, a noted California sculptor. The obverse bears a kneeling figure of a forty-niner. The reverse shows a walking grizzly bear, the state emblem. The celebration for which these coins were struck marked the seventy-fifth anniversary of the admission of California into the Union. The jubilee was held in 1925.

1925S California Diamond Jubilee	86,394	100.00	115.00	165.00	880.00

CARVER-WASHINGTON

Designed by Isaac Scott Hathaway, this coin portrays the conjoined busts of two prominent black Americans. Booker T. Washington was a lecturer, educa-

tor, and principal of Tuskegee Institute. He urged training to advance independence and efficiency for his race. George Washington Carver was an agricultural chemist who worked to improve the economy of the south. He spent his life teaching crop improvement and new uses for soybeans, peanuts, sweet potatoes and cotton waste. Money obtained from the sale of these commemoratives was to be used "to oppose the spread of communism among Negroes in the interest of national defense."

1951 Carver-Washington	110,018			
1951D Same type D mint	10,004	Set 77.00	85.00	525.00
1951S Same type S mint	10,004			

COMMEMORATIVE SILVER
Carver-Washington, Cincinnati, Cleveland

	Quan. Issued	AU-50	MS-60	MS-63	MS-65
1952 Same type as 1951	2,006,292				
1952D Same type D mint	8,006	Set	$75.00	$110.00	$340.00
1952S Same type S mint	8,006				
1953 Same type as 1951	8,003				
1953D Same type D mint	8,003	Set	75.00	110.00	480.00
1953S Same type S mint	108,020				
1954 Same type as 1951	12,006				
1954D Same type D mint	12,006	Set	75.00	85.00	360.00
1954S Same type S mint	122,024				
Single, type coin		$12.00	14.00	18.00	47.50

CINCINNATI MUSIC CENTER

Although the head of Stephen Foster, "America's Troubadour," dominates the obverse of this special issue, the anniversary celebrated bears no relation to him. The coins, designed by Constance Ortmayer of Washington, D. C., were supposedly struck to commemorate the fiftieth anniversary in 1936 of Cincinnati as a center of music. The coins were struck at the three mints and were sold only in sets at $7.75, the highest initial cost of a new type.

1936 Cincinnati Music Center	5,005			
1936D Same type D	5,005	Set	650.00	725.00	2,250
1936S Same type S	5,006			
Single, type coin		190.00	210.00	230.00	600.00

CLEVELAND GREAT LAKES EXPOSITION

A special coinage of fifty-cent pieces was authorized in commemoration of the centennial celebration of Cleveland, Ohio on the occasion of the Great Lakes Exposition held there in 1936. The designs were prepared by Brenda Putnam.
Although half the coinage was struck in 1937 all were dated 1936. The obverse has a bust of Moses Cleaveland and the reverse displays a map of the Great Lakes region with a compass pointed at Cleveland. Nine Great Lakes cities are marked by stars.

1936 Cleveland, Great Lakes Exposition	50,030	55.00	63.00	74.00	225.00

COMMEMORATIVE SILVER
Columbia, South Carolina, Columbian, Connecticut

COLUMBIA, SOUTH CAROLINA SESQUICENTENNIAL

Souvenir half dollars were authorized to help finance the extensive celebrations marking the sesquicentennial of the founding of Columbia in 1786. A. Wolfe Davidson designed the coin which was struck at all three mints and sold in sets. The obverse bears the figure of Justice with sword and scales. At the left is the Capital of 1786 and at the right the Capital of 1936. A palmetto tree, the state emblem, is the reverse device.

	Quan. Issued	AU-50	MS-60	MS-63	MS-65
1936 Columbia, S.C., Sesquicentennial	9,007				
1936D Same type D mint	8,009 } Set		$500.00	$520.00	$675.00
1936S Same type S mint	8,007				
Single, type coin		$155.00	175.00	190.00	210.00

COLUMBIAN EXPOSITION HALF DOLLAR

The first United States commemorative coin was the Columbian half dollar designed by Olin Lewis Warner. C. E. Barber engraved the obverse showing the bust of Columbus; and G. T. Morgan engraved

the reverse having a representation of Columbus' flagship the Santa Maria above two hemispheres. The coins were sold for $1.00 each at the World's Columbian Exposition in Chicago during 1893. A great many remained unsold and a substantial quantity was later released for circulation at face value. Approximately 100 brilliant proofs were struck for each date.

1892 Columbian Exp. Chicago	950,000	16.00	30.00	85.00	700.00
1893 Same type	1,550,405	15.00	30.00	85.00	860.00

CONNECTICUT TERCENTENARY

In commemoration of the three hundredth anniversary of the founding of the Colony of Connecticut, a souvenir half dollar was struck. Henry Kreis designed the coin. The famous "Charter Oak" is the main device on the reverse. According to tradition the Royal Charter was secreted in the tree during the reign of James II who wished to revoke it. The Charter was produced after the king's overthrow in 1688 and the Colony continued under its protection.

1935 Connecticut Tercentenary	25,018	160.00	180.00	200.00	500.00

COMMEMORATIVE SILVER
Delaware, Elgin, Gettysburg

DELAWARE TERCENTENARY

The three hundredth anniversary of the landing of the Swedes in Delaware was the occasion for a souvenir issue of half dollars. The colonists landed on a spot which is now Wilmington and established a church which is the oldest Protestant church still used for worship. Their ship "Kalmar Nyckel" is shown on the reverse of the coin and the Old Swedes Church is on the obverse. Designs were chosen from a competition that was won by Carl L. Schmitz. This coin was authorized in 1936, struck in 1937 and dated 1938 on the reverse and 1936 on the obverse. The anniversary was celebrated in 1938 both in Sweden and America. A two kronor coin was issued in Sweden to commemorate the same event.

	Quan. Issued	AU-50	MS-60	MS-63	MS-65
1936 Delaware Tercentenary	20,993	$200.00	$220.00	$230.00	$330.00

ELGIN, ILLINOIS CENTENNIAL

The one hundredth anniversary of the founding of Elgin was marked by a special issue of half dollars in 1936. The proceeds were devoted to financing a Pioneer Memorial statue, which is depicted on the reverse of the coin. The year 1673 bears no relation to the event but refers to the year in which Joliet and Marquette entered Illinois Territory. The designs were prepared by Trygve Rovelstad who also designed the Memorial, which was not dedicated until 2001.

1936 Elgin, Illinois, Centennial	20,015	145.00	160.00	170.00	240.00

BATTLE OF GETTYSBURG

On June 16, 1936 Congress authorized a coinage of fifty-cent pieces in commemoration of the 1863 Battle of Gettysburg. The models were prepared by Frank Vittor, a Pittsburgh sculptor. Portraits of a Union and a Confederate veteran are shown on the obverse. Two shields representing the Union and Confederate armies separated by a double-bladed fasces are on the reverse.

1936 Battle of Gettysburg 1863-1938	26,928	260.00	275.00	300.00	600.00

COMMEMORATIVE SILVER
Grant, Hawaiian, Hudson
GRANT MEMORIAL

This coin was struck during 1922 as a centenary souvenir of Ulysses S. Grant's birth. A star which appeared on the first issues was later removed, creating a second variety. The star has no particular significance. Laura Gardin Fraser designed both the Grant half dollar and gold dollar. The reverse shows the frame house in Point Pleasant, Ohio, where Grant was born April 27, 1822.

Star in obverse field
(Fake stars usually have
flattened spot on reverse.)

	Quan. Issued	AU-50	MS-60	MS-63	MS-65
1922 Grant Memorial. Star in obv. field	4,256	$625.00	$875.00	$1,500	$7,000
1922 Same, no star	67,405	75.00	90.00	150.00	875.00

HAWAIIAN SESQUICENTENNIAL

This small issue was struck to commemorate the 150th anniversary of the arrival on the Hawaiian Islands of Captain James Cook in 1778. The design was sketched by Juliette May Fraser of Honolulu and executed by Chester Beach. Captain Cook is shown on the obverse and a native chief on the reverse. The coins were distributed in 1928 and sold for $2.00 each, the highest initial sale price up to that time.

1928 Hawaiian Sesquicentennial	9,958	1,000	1,200	1,700	4,800
1928 Hawaiian Sesquicentennial — sandblast proof presentation piece	50				22,000

HUDSON, NEW YORK SESQUICENTENNIAL

This souvenir half dollar marked the one hundred and fiftieth anniversary of the founding of Hudson, New York, which was named after the explorer Hendrik Hudson. The designs by Chester Beach show Hudson's flagship the "Half Moon" on the obverse and the seal of the City of Hudson on the reverse. Details of the seal include representations of Neptune with trident on a spouting whale and a mermaid blowing a conch shell.

1935 Hudson, N.Y. Sesquicentennial	10,008	410.00	460.00	485.00	1,325

COMMEMORATIVE SILVER
Huguenot, Illinois, Iowa

HUGUENOT-WALLOON TERCENTENARY

Settling of the Huguenots and Walloons in the New World was the occasion commemorated by this issue. New Netherlands, now New York, was founded in 1624 by a group of Dutch colonists. The persons represented on the obverse were not directly concerned with the occasion, however. They are Admiral Coligny and William the Silent. The reverse shows the vessel "Nieuw Nederland." G. T. Morgan prepared the models for this coin.

	Quan. Issued	AU-50	MS-60	MS-63	MS-65
1924 Huguenot-Walloon Tercentenary	142,080	$90.00	$110.00	$135.00	$480.00

ILLINOIS CENTENNIAL

The obverse was designed by G. T. Morgan and the reverse by J. R. Sinnock. The obverse shows the head of Lincoln taken from the statue by Andrew O'Connor in Springfield, Illinois. The reverse is based on the Illinois State Seal. This coin was authorized to commemorate the one hundredth anniversary of the admission of Illinois into the Union, the first souvenir piece for such an event.

1918 Illinois Centennial	100,058	75.00	100.00	115.00	450.00

IOWA CENTENNIAL

This half dollar, commemorating the one hundredth anniversary of Iowa's statehood, was designed by Adam Pietz of Philadelphia. The reverse shows the Iowa state seal, and the obverse has the first stone capitol building at Iowa City. This issue was sold first to the residents of Iowa and only a small remainder to others. The entire issue was disposed of within several months.

1946 Iowa Centennial	100,057	60.00	65.00	75.00	110.00

COMMEMORATIVE SILVER
Lexington, Long Island, Lynchburg

LEXINGTON-CONCORD SESQUICENTENNIAL

The two famous battles fought in 1775 are commemorated on this coin. A statue of the familiar Minute Man is depicted on the obverse, and the Old Belfry at Lexington is the reverse device. Chester Beach designed the coin. The famous statue by Daniel Chester French located in Concord was used for the design.

	Quan. Issued	AU-50	MS-60	MS-63	MS-65
1925 Lexington-Concord Sesquicentennial	162,013	$60.00	$75.00	$100.00	$600.00

LONG ISLAND TERCENTENARY

This souvenir issue was authorized to commemorate the three hundredth anniversary of the first white settlement on Long Island which was at Jamaica Bay by Dutch colonists. The design was prepared by Howard Kenneth Weinman, son of the sculptor A. A. Weinman who designed the regular Liberty walking type half dollar. Accolated heads depicting a Dutch settler and an Indian are shown on the obverse, while a Dutch sailing vessel is the reverse device. This was the first issue for which a date was specified (1936) irrespective of the year minted or issued, as a safeguard against extending the coinage over a period of years.

1936 Long Island Tercentenary	81,826	60.00	65.00	80.00	400.00

LYNCHBURG, VIRGINIA SESQUICENTENNIAL

The issuance of a charter to the city of Lynchburg in 1786 was commemorated in 1936 by a special coinage of half dollars. The models for the coin were prepared by Charles Keck. The obverse bears a portrait of Senator Carter Glass, a native of Lynchburg and former Secretary of the Treasury, who objected to the idea of using portraits of living men on coins. Despite his protests, his likeness was incorporated on the coin. The reverse shows Liberty standing, with the old Lynchburg courthouse in the background.

1936 Lynchburg, Va., Sesquicentennial	20,013	140.00	160.00	175.00	260.00

COMMEMORATIVE SILVER
Maine, Maryland, Missouri

MAINE
CENTENNIAL

Congress authorized the Maine Centennial half dollar May 10, 1920, to be sold at the Centennial celebration at Portland. They were received too late for this event and were sold by the state Treasurer for many years. Anthony de Francisci modeled this coin according to specifications furnished him. The obverse device is the arms of the state of Maine; the latin word DIRIGO means: I direct.

	Quan. Issued	AU-50	MS-60	MS-63	MS-65
1920 Maine Centennial	50,028	$87.50	$125.00	$160.00	$550.00

MARYLAND
TERCENTENARY

The three hundredth anniversary of the founding of the Maryland Colony by Cecil Calvert (known as Lord Baltimore) was the occasion for this special coin. The profits from the sale of this issue were used to finance the celebration in Baltimore during 1934. Hans Schuler designed the coin which shows the facing head of Lord Baltimore on the obverse and the arms of Maryland on the reverse, reminiscent of the Maryland colonial pieces.

1934 Maryland Tercentenary	25,015	120.00	135.00	175.00	310.00

MISSOURI CENTENNIAL

The one hundredth anniversary of the admission of Missouri to the Union was celebrated at Sedalia during August, 1921. To mark the occasion Congress authorized the coinage of a fifty-cent piece. Robert Aitken designed the piece that shows the bust of a frontiersman on the obverse, and another frontiersman and Indian on the reverse. The first coins struck show 2★4 incused, indicating that Missouri was the twenty-fourth star in the flag. The type without this marking was struck later, but was the first to be sold.

2 ★ 4 in field

1921 Missouri Centennial 2★4 in field	5,000	390.00	470.00	875.00	5,000
1921 Missouri Centennial, no 2★4	15,428	215.00	400.00	735.00	5,100

COMMEMORATIVE SILVER
Monroe, New Rochelle, Norfolk

MONROE DOCTRINE CENTENNIAL

The motion picture industry promoted this issue in conjunction with a motion picture exposition in June, 1923. The obverse shows the heads of James Monroe and John Quincy Adams who were identified with the Monroe Doctrine. The Western Hemisphere is portrayed on the reverse by two female figures. Chester Beach prepared the models for this coin.

	Quan. Issued	AU-50	MS-60	MS-63	MS-65
1923S Monroe Doctrine Centennial	274,077	$27.50	$47.50	$175.00	$2,750

NEW ROCHELLE, NEW YORK

To observe the founding of New Rochelle in 1688 by French Huguenots, a special half dollar was issued in 1938. The title to the land that the Huguenots purchased from John Pell provided that a fattened calf be given away every year on June 20th. This is represented by a calf and figure of John Pell on the obverse of the coin. The fleur-de-lis, which is shown on the reverse, is adopted from the Seal of the city. Both sides of the coin were designed by Gertrude K. Lathrop.

1938 New Rochelle, N.Y. 1688-1938	15,266	245.00	265.00	280.00	360.00

NORFOLK, VIRGINIA BICENTENNIAL

To provide funds for the celebration of Norfolk's anniversary of its growth from a township in 1682 to a royal borough in 1736, Congress first passed a law for the striking of medals. The proponents, however, being dissatisfied finally succeeded in winning authority for half dollars commemorating the 300th anniversary of the original Norfolk land grant and the 200th anniversary of the establishment of the borough. William Marks Simpson and his wife Marjorie Emory Simpson designed the piece. The obverse shows the Seal of the City of Norfolk with a three-masted ship as the central device. The reverse features the Royal Mace of Norfolk presented by Lieutenant Governor Dinwiddie in 1753.

1936 Norfolk, Va. Bicentennial	16,936	340.00	370.00	380.00	430.00

COMMEMORATIVE SILVER
Oregon, Panama-Pacific

OREGON TRAIL MEMORIAL

This memorial coin was struck in commemoration of the Oregon trail and in memory of the pioneers, many of whom lie buried along fhe famous 2,000 mile highway of history. James Earle Fraser and his wife, Laura Gardin Fraser, prepared the designs. The original issue was struck at Philadelphia and San Francisco in 1926. Coinage was resumed in 1928 (released in 1933), 1933, 1934, and 1936 to 1939. The 1933 half dollar was the first commemorative coin struck at the Denver Mint.

	Quan. Issued	AU-50	MS-60	MS-63	MS-65
1926 Oregon Trail Memorial	47,955	$90.00	$100.00	$110.00	$210.00
1926S Same type S mint	83,055	95.00	100.00	115.00	210.00
1928 Oregon Trail Mem. (same as 1926)	6,028	140.00	160.00	170.00	260.00
1933D Oregon Trail Mem. (same), D mint	5,008	210.00	230.00	260.00	420.00
1934D Oregon Trail Mem. (same), D mint	7,006	130.00	145.00	160.00	270.00
1936 Oregon Trail Mem. (same as 1926)	10,006	100.00	115.00	125.00	200.00
1936S Same type S mint	5,006	115.00	130.00	160.00	250.00
1937D Oregon Trail Memorial, D mint	12,008	115.00	130.00	150.00	200.00
1938 Oregon Trail Mem. (same as 1926)	6,006 }				
1938D Same type D mint	6,005 } Set		500.00	590.00	620.00
1938S Same type S mint	6,006 }				
1939 Oregon Trail Mem. (same as 1926)	3,004 }				
1939D Same type D mint	3,004 } Set		1,150	1,250	1,600
1939S Same type S mint	3,005 }				
Single, type coin		90.00	100.00	110.00	210.00

PANAMA-PACIFIC EXPOSITION

This half dollar was designed by C. E. Barber (obv.) and George T. Morgan. The exposition held in San Francisco in 1915 celebrated the opening of the Panama Canal. The coins were struck at the San Francisco Mint and were sold at $1.00 each during the exposition. A representation of Columbia with the golden gate in the background is the principal feature of the obverse. The Panama-Pacific coins have the distinction of being the first commemorative coins to carry the motto IN GOD WE TRUST which appears above the eagle.

1915S Panama-Pacific Exposition	27,134	210.00	315.00	630.00	2,450

COMMEMORATIVE SILVER
Pilgrim, Rhode Island

PILGRIM TERCENTENARY

To commemorate the landing of the Pilgrims at Plymouth, Massachusetts in 1620, Congress authorized a special half dollar May 12, 1920. Cyrus E. Dallin, a Boston sculptor, executed the designs furnished him by the Commission. His initial D is placed below Bradford's elbow. The obverse has a portrait of Governor Bradford. The reverse shows the "Mayflower." The first issue had no date on the obverse. The coins struck in 1921 show that date in addition to 1620-1920. There was a large coinage of both issues and not all were sold. A total of 128,000 were returned to the mint and melted.

	Quan. Issued	AU-50	MS-60	MS-63	MS-65
1920 Pilgrim Tercentenary	152,112	$52.50	$70.00	$90.00	$500.00

→ **With 1921 Date Added in Field on Obverse.**

1921 Same type	20,053	100.00	125.00	160.00	660.00

PROVIDENCE, RHODE ISLAND TERCENTENARY

The three hundredth anniversary of Roger Williams' founding of Providence was the occasion for this special half dollar in 1936. The designs were the work of Arthur Graham Carey and John Howard Benson. The obverse shows Roger Williams in a canoe being welcomed by an Indian. The reverse has the anchor of Hope with a shield and mantling in the background. Although the founding of Providence was being celebrated, no mention of the city is to be found on the coin.

1936 Rhode Island Tercentenary	20,013				
1936D Same type D mint	15,010	Set	210.00	250.00	680.00
1936S Same type S mint	15,011				
Single, type coin		60.00	70.00	85.00	215.00

COMMEMORATIVE SILVER
Roanoke, Robinson, San Diego

ROANOKE ISLAND, NORTH CAROLINA

A celebration was held in Old Fort Raleigh in 1937 to commemorate the 350th anniversary of Sir Walter Raleigh's "Lost Colony" and the birth of Virginia Dare, the first white child born in British North America. A special half dollar for the occasion was designed by William Marks Simpson of Baltimore. The obverse bears a portrait of Sir Walter Raleigh and the reverse has a figure representing Ellinor Dare holding the child Virginia Dare.

	Quan. Issued	AU-50	MS-60	MS-63	MS-65
1937 Roanoke Island, N.C., 1587-1937	29,030	$140.00	$200.00	$215.00	$240.00

ROBINSON-ARKANSAS CENTENNIAL

A new reverse design for the Arkansas Centennial coin was authorized by the Act of June 26, 1936. Senator Joseph T. Robinson is the subject for the new issue engraved by Henry Kreis. The obverse, designed by Everett Burr, was unchanged. The law specified a change in the reverse, because of the fact that the obverse side is that which bears the date. From a numismatic viewpoint, however, the side which has the portrait is usually considered the obverse. Thus in this instance, the side with the eagle device is often considered the reverse.

1936 Arkansas Centennial (Robinson)	25,265	90.00	100.00	115.00	300.00

SAN DIEGO-CALIFORNIA-PACIFIC EXPOSITION

Congress approved the coinage of souvenir half dollars for the exposition on May 3, 1935. Robert Aitken designed the coin which was struck at the San Francisco Mint. The same type with date 1936 was struck at the Denver Mint, under authority of the special Recoinage Act of May 6, 1936, which specified that 180,000 pieces could be recoined with the date 1936 irrespective of the year of issue. The obverse displays a seated female with spear and a bear in the left background. The reverse shows the observation tower and the State of California building at the Exposition.

1935S San Diego, California-Pacific Exp.	70,132	50.00	60.00	65.00	110.00
1936D, D mint (same as 1935)	30,092	55.00	65.00	75.00	140.00

COMMEMORATIVE SILVER
Sesquicentennial, Old Spanish Trail, Stone Mountain
SESQUICENTENNIAL OF AMERICAN INDEPENDENCE

The one hundred and fiftieth anniversary of the signing of the Declaration of Independence was the occasion for an International Fair held in Philadelphia in 1926. To help raise funds for financing the fair, special issues of half dollars and quarter-eagles were authorized by Congress. For the first time a portrait of a president appeared on a coin struck during his lifetime. Presidents Coolidge and Washington are depicted on the obverse of the half dollar. The reverse bears an accurate model of the Liberty Bell. John R. Sinnock, Chief Engraver of the United States mint, modeled the sesquicentennial coins from designs by John Frederick Lewis. The dies were in very low relief causing much loss of detail.

	Quan. Issued	AU-50	MS-60	MS-63	MS-65
1926 Sesquicentennial of American Independence	141,120	$60.00	$75.00	$160.00	$5,250

OLD SPANISH TRAIL

This coin commemorated the four hundredth anniversary of the overland trek of the Cabeza de Vaca Expedition through the gulf states in 1535. L. W. Hoffecker designed the coin, and models were prepared by Edmund J. Senn. The explorer's name literally translated means "head of a cow;" therefore this device was chosen for the obverse. The reverse bears a yucca tree and a map showing the Old Spanish Trail.

1935 Old Spanish Trail 1535-1935	10,008	725.00	800.00	830.00	1,100

STONE MOUNTAIN MEMORIAL

The models for this coin were prepared by Gutzon Borglum. The first coins were struck at Philadelphia January 21, 1925, General Thomas "Stonewall" Jackson's birthday. Generals Robert E. Lee and Jackson, mounted, are shown on the obverse. The funds received from the sale of this large issue of half dollars were devoted to the expense of carving figures of Confederate leaders and soldiers on Stone Mountain in Georgia. The carving was completed and dedicated in 1970. Some of these coins were privately counterstamped on the reverse with letters and numbers by individual state sales agencies. These are generally valued much higher than normal coins.

1925 Stone Mountain Memorial	1,314,709	32.50	45.00	62.50	205.00

COMMEMORATIVE SILVER
Texas, Vancouver

TEXAS
CENTENNIAL

This issue commemorated the independence of Texas in 1836. The first of several dates was offered in 1934. The later dates were struck at all three mints. The models were prepared by Pompeo Coppini. The reverse shows the kneeling figure of winged Victory, and on each side, medallions with portraits of General Sam Houston and Stephen Austin, founders of the Republic and State of Texas. The large five-pointed star behind the eagle on the obverse carries out the "Lone star" tradition.

	Quan. Issued	AU-50	MS-60	MS-63	MS-65
1934 Texas Centennial	61,463	$85.00	$90.00	$100.00	$160.00
1935 Texas Centennial (same as 1934)	9,996				
1935D Same type D mint	10,007 } Set		275.00	300.00	485.00
1935S Same type S mint	10,008				
1936 Texas Centennial (same as 1934)	8,911				
1936D Same type D mint	9,039 } Set		275.00	300.00	475.00
1936S Same type S mint	9,055				
1937 Texas Centennial (same as 1934)	6,571				
1937D Same type D mint	6,605 } Set		275.00	300.00	475.00
1937S Same type S mint	6,637				
1938 Texas Centennial (same as 1934)	3,780				
1938D Same type D mint	3,775 } Set		600.00	700.00	1,000
1938S Same type S mint	3,814				
Single, type coin		85.00	90.00	100.00	160.00

FORT VANCOUVER CENTENNIAL

Dr. John McLoughlin, shown on the obverse of this coin, built Fort Vancouver (Washington) on the Columbia River in 1825. The sale of the coins at $1.00 each helped to finance the pageant staged for the celebration. Laura Gardin Fraser prepared the models for this coin which was minted in San Francisco. The S mint mark was omitted. The reverse has a pioneer settler in buckskin suit with a musket in his hands. Fort Vancouver is in the background.

1925 Fort Vancouver Centennial	14,994	230.00	300.00	375.00	1,350

COMMEMORATIVE SILVER
Vermont, B. T. Washington
VERMONT SESQUICENTENNIAL

This souvenir issue commemorates the 150th Anniversary of the Battle of Bennington and the Independence of Vermont. Authorized in 1925, it was not coined until 1927. The models were prepared by Charles Keck. The obverse shows the head of Ira Allen, founder of Vermont. The reverse bears a catamount on a pedestal.

	Quan. Issued	AU-50	MS-60	MS-63	MS-65
1927 Vermont Sesquicentennial (Bennington)	28,142	$145.00	$160.00	$175.00	$800.00

BOOKER T. WASHINGTON MEMORIAL

This commemorative coin was issued to perpetuate the ideals and teachings of Booker T. Washington and to construct memorials to his memory. Issued from all mints, it received wide distribution from the start. The reverse has the legend FROM SLAVE CABIN TO HALL OF FAME. His log cabin birthplace is shown beneath.

This coin was designed by Isaac Scott Hathaway, as was the Carver-Washington half dollar issued under the same authority.

1946 Booker T. Washington *1,000,546				
1946D Same type D mint .... 200,113 } Set	$40.00	$50.00	$115.00
1946S Same type S mint 500,279				
1947 Same type as 1946 100,017				
1947D Same type D mint .... 100,017 } Set	70.00	80.00	250.00
1947S Same type S mint 100,017				
1948 Same type as 1946 8,005				
1948D Same type D mint .... 8,005 } Set	130.00	140.00	175.00
1948S Same type S mint 8,005				
1949 Same type as 1946 6,004				
1949D Same type D mint .... 6,004 } Set	200.00	220.00	300.00
1949S Same type S mint 6,004				
1950 Same type as 1946 6,004				
1950D Same type D mint .... 6,004 } Set	115.00	125.00	160.00
1950S Same type S mint 512,091				
1951 Same type as 1946 510,082				
1951D Same type D mint .... 7,004 } Set	100.00	125.00	160.00
1951S Same type S mint 7,004				
Single, type coin $12.00	14.00	16.00	37.50

*Minted; quantity melted unknown.

COMMEMORATIVE SILVER — Wisconsin, York County, Lafayette Dollar

WISCONSIN TERRITORIAL CENTENNIAL

The one hundredth anniversary of the Wisconsin Territorial government was the occasion for this issue. The original design was made by David Parsons, a University of Wisconsin student. Benjamin Hawkins, a New York artist, made changes to conform with technical requirements. The reverse has the Territorial Seal, which includes a forearm holding a pickaxe over a mound of lead ore, and the inscription 4th DAY OF JULY ANNO DOMINI 1836. The obverse shows a badger on a log, the state emblem, and arrows representing the Black Hawk War of the 1830's.

	Quan. Issued	AU-50	MS-60	MS-63	MS-65
1936 Wisconsin Centennial	25,015	$145.00	$155.00	$165.00	$225.00

YORK COUNTY, MAINE TERCENTENARY

A souvenir half dollar was authorized by Congress upon the three hundredth anniversary of the founding of York County, Maine. Brown's Garrison on the Saco River was the site of a town that was settled in 1636. The designs were made by Walter H. Rich of Portland. The obverse design shows a stockade, and the reverse has an adaptation of the York County seal.

1936 York County, Maine Tercentenary	25,015	135.00	145.00	155.00	175.00

LAFAYETTE DOLLAR

The heads of Washington and Lafayette appear on this issue, which was the first commemorative coin of one dollar denomination, and the first authorized United States coin to bear a portrait of one of our presidents. The dies were prepared by C. E. Barber. The statue on the reverse is similar to the monument of General Lafayette that was erected in Paris as a gift of the American people. The coins were sold by the Lafayette Memorial Commission for $2.00 each.

1900 Lafayette Dollar	36,026	325.00	570.00	1,325	8,800

COMMEMORATIVE GOLD — Grant, Lewis & Clark, Louisiana Purchase, McKinley

GRANT MEMORIAL GOLD DOLLARS

Like the half-dollar commemorative coins, the gold dollars were first issued with a star which was removed for the later issues. The designs by Laura Gardin Fraser are the same as for the half-dollar coinage.

	Quan.Issued	AU-50	MS-60	MS-63	MS-65
1922 Grant Memorial Dollar with star	5,016	$1,100	$1,275	$1,675	$3,300
1922 Grant Memorial Dollar no star	5,000	1,025	1,150	1,500	3,250

LEWIS AND CLARK EXPOSITION

The Lewis and Clark Centennial Exposition was held in Portland, Oregon in 1905. A souvenir issue of gold dollars was struck to mark the event with the dates 1904 and 1905. The two famous explorers are represented on either side of the coin which was designed by C. E. Barber. A bronze memorial of the Indian guide, Sacagawea, who assisted in the famous expedition, was erected in Portland, Oregon and financed by the sale of these coins.

1904 Lewis and Clark Dollar	10,025	485.00	750.00	1,800	8,000
1905 Lewis and Clark Dollar	10,041	485.00	825.00	2,100	16,100

LOUISIANA PURCHASE EXPOSITION

The first souvenir gold coins were authorized for the Louisiana Purchase Exposition held in St. Louis in 1904. There are two varieties of gold dollars — one with the head of Jefferson who was president when the Louisiana Territory was purchased from France; and the other President William McKinley who sanctioned the Exposition. The reverse is the same for each variety. The designs were by C. E. Barber.

*1903 Louisiana Pur. Jefferson Dol	17,500	300.00	415.00	630.00	2,650
*1903 Louisiana Pur. McKinley Dol	17,500	300.00	375.00	600.00	2,750

*Proofs exist of each type.

McKINLEY MEMORIAL GOLD DOLLARS

The sale of the McKinley dollars aided in paying for a memorial building at Niles, Ohio, the martyred president's birthplace. The obverse showing a pro-

COMMEMORATIVE GOLD
McKinley, Panama-Pacific

file of McKinley was designed by C. E. Barber; the reverse with the memorial building was designed by G. T. Morgan.

	Quan. Issued	AU-50	MS-60	MS-63	MS-65
1916 McKinley Memorial Dollar	15,000	$250.00	$350.00	$500.00	$2,550
1917 McKinley Memorial Dollar	5,000	330.00	490.00	875.00	3,300

PANAMA-PACIFIC INTERNATIONAL EXPOSITION

Charles Keck designed the gold dollar, the obverse of which has the head of a man representing a Panama Canal laborer. Two dolphins encircle ONE DOLLAR on the reverse.

The quarter eagle was the work of Charles E. Barber and George T. Morgan. It was the first commemorative coin of this denomination. The obverse shows Columbia with a caduceus in her left hand seated on a hippocampus typifying the use of the Panama Canal. An American eagle with raised wings is shown on the reverse.

The fifty-dollar gold piece was designed by Robert Aitken and was issued in both round and octagonal form. The obverse bears a helmeted head of Minerva; the owl, symbol of wisdom, is on the reverse. The octagonal issue has eight dolphins in the angles on both sides. Other devices are smaller on the octagonal variety.

1915S Panama-Pacific Exposition Dollar...15,000	310.00	340.00	475.00	2,600
1915S Panama-Pacific Exposition $2.50 6,749	1,150	1,375	2,650	5,700

1915S Panama-Pacific $50 Round 483	23,000	26,000	37,000	120,000

COMMEMORATIVE GOLD — Panama-Pacific,
United States Sesquicentennial

	Quan. Issued	AU-50	MS-60	MS-63	MS-65
1915S Panama-Pacific $50 Octagonal 645		$20,000	$23,000	$33,000	$95,000

SESQUICENTENNIAL OF AMERICAN INDEPENDENCE

The obverse of this special gold quarter eagle has a standing female figure symbolic of Liberty, holding in one hand a scroll representing the Declaration of Independence and in the other the Torch of Freedom. The reverse bears a representation of Independence Hall in Philadelphia. The coin was designed by John R. Sinnock.

1926 U.S. Sesquicentennial $2.50...............46,019	270.00	300.00	525.00	3,575

MODERN COMMEMORATIVES — Washington

GEORGE WASHINGTON

This coin, the first commemorative half dollar issued since 1954, commemorated the 250th anniversary of the birth of George Washington. It was also the first 90% silver coin produced by the U.S. Mint since 1964. Designed by Elizabeth Jones, Chief Sculptor and Engraver of the United States, the obverse features George Washington astride a horse. The reverse depicts the eastern facade of Mount Vernon. The uncirculated version was struck at Denver and the proof at San Francisco.

	Quan. Issued	MS-65	Proof-65
1982D Geo. Washington-250th Anniversary 2,210,458		$5.00	
1982S Same, proof..4,894,044			$5.25

MODERN COMMEMORATIVES
Los Angeles Olympiad

LOS ANGELES XXIII OLYMPIAD

Three distinctive coins were issued to commemorate the 1984 Los Angeles Summer Olympic Games. The silver dollar dated 1983 was designed by Elizabeth Jones, Chief Engraver of the Mint. On the obverse is a representation of the traditional Greek discus thrower inspired by the ancient work of the sculptor Myron. The reverse depicts the head and upper body of an American eagle.

	Quan. Issued		MS-65	Proof-65
1983P Discus Thrower Silver Dollar 294,543			$12.00	
1983D Same type D mint 174,014			12.00	
1983S Same type S mint 174,014	(1,577,025)		12.00	$13.00

The 1984 Olympic silver dollar was designed by Robert Graham, an American sculptor who created the sculpture placed at the entrance to the Los Angeles Memorial Coliseum. The obverse depicts Graham's sculpture with the Coliseum in the background. The reverse features an American eagle.

1984P Olympic Coliseum Silver Dollar 217,954			15.00	
1984D Same type D mint 116,675			23.00	
1984S Same type S mint 116,675	(1,801,210)		25.00	13.00

Mintage of a commemorative gold coin for the 1984 Olympics was the first U.S. gold piece issued in over 50 years. The weight, size and fineness are the same as the last ten dollar coin issued in 1933. It is the first coin ever to bear the W mint mark for West Point.

The obverse depicts two runners bearing the Olympic torch aloft, and was designed by John Mercanti from a concept by James Peed, an artist at the Mint. The eagle on the reverse is modeled after the Great Seal.

	Quan. Issued	MS-65	Proof-65
1984P Olympic Gold Eagle...	(33,309)		$255.00
1984D Olympic Gold Eagle	(34,533)		255.00
1984S Olympic Gold Eagle...	(48,551)		200.00
1984W Olympic Gold Eagle 75,886	(381,085)	$200.00	200.00

STATUE OF LIBERTY

The first copper-nickel clad half dollar commemorative depicts this country's heritage as a nation of immigrants. The obverse, designed by Edgar Steever, pictures a ship of immigrants steaming into New York harbor, with the Statue of Liberty greeting them in the foreground and the New York skyline in the distance. The reverse, designed by Sherl Joseph Winter, has a scene of an immigrant family with their belongings on the threshold of America. Weight and composition are the same as that of regular issue clad half dollars.

1986D Statue of Liberty Half Dollar	928,008	5.00	
1986S Same type S mint proof..	(6,925,627)		5.00

Designed by Mint artist John Mercanti, this .900 fine silver dollar commemorates Ellis Island as the "Gateway to America." The obverse features a classic pose of Liberty in the foreground, with the Ellis Island Immigration Center standing behind her. On the reverse is a depiction of Liberty's torch, along with the words "Give me your tired, your poor, your huddled masses yearning to breathe free." Matthew Peloso assisted in the model work on the reverse.

MODERN COMMEMORATIVES — Statue of Liberty
(Cont'd), Constitution

	Quan. Issued	MS-65	Proof-65
1986P Statue of Liberty Silver Dollar	723,635	$12.00	
1986S Same type S mint proof	(6,414,638)		$12.00

The commemorative half eagle is also the first of this denomination to be minted in over fifty years. Standards for weight and size are the same as previous half eagle gold coins. The design is the creation of the Mint's chief engraver, Elizabeth Jones. The obverse features a compelling close-up view of Liberty's face in sharp relief with the inscription 1986 LIBERTY. An eagle in flight adorns the reverse. All were minted at West Point and bear the W mint mark.

1986W Statue of Liberty Gold $5	95,248	(404,013)	100.00	100.00

CONSTITUTION BICENTENNIAL

The silver dollar commemorating the 200th anniversary of the United States Constitution was designed by Patricia Lewis Verani using standard weight, size and fineness. A quill pen, a sheaf of parchment and the words WE THE PEOPLE are depicted on the obverse. The reverse portrays a cross section of Americans from various periods representing contrasting lifestyles.

1987P U.S. Constitution Silver Dollar	451,629	12.00	
1987S Same type S mint proof	(2,747,116)		11.00

A modernistic design by Marcel Jovine was selected for the $5 gold coin of standard weight, size and fineness commemorating the bicentennial of the United States Consitition. The obverse portrays a stylized eagle holding a massive quill pen. Another large quill pen is featured on the reverse. To the left are nine stars signifying the first colonies that ratified the Constitution. Four stars to the right represent the remaining original states. Both uncirculated and proof versions were minted at West Point.

1987W U.S. Constitution Gold $5	214,225	(651,659)	100.00	100.00

MODERN COMMEMORATIVES — Olympiad, Congress

OLYMPIAD 1988

The 1988 Olympic silver dollar commemorates the U.S. participation in the Seoul Olympiad. Its size and weight are identical to other silver dollars. Design of the obverse is by Patricia Lewis Verani. The reverse is by Mint Sculptor Engraver Sherl Joseph Winter.

	Quan. Issued	MS-65	Proof-65
1988D Olympic Silver Dollar	191,368	$11.00	
1988S Same type S mint proof	(1,359,366)		$11.00

The 1988 $5 gold Olympic coin was designed by Elizabeth Jones, Chief Sculptor and Engraver of the U.S. Mint. The obverse features Nike, goddess of Victory, wearing a crown of olive leaves. The reverse features Marcel Jovine's stylized Olympic flame, evoking the spectacle of the Games and the renewal of the Olympic spirit every four years.

1988W Olympic Gold $5	62,913	(281,465)	100.00	100.00

CONGRESS BICENTENNIAL

The obverse is designed by sculptor Patricia L. Verani and features a detailed bust of the Statue of Freedom. The reverse, designed by William Woodward offers a full view of the Capitol Building accented by a wreath of stars. The clad composition is approximately 92% copper, 8% nickel.

1989D Congress Bicentennial Half Dollar	163,753	8.00	
1989S Same type S mint proof	(767,897)		5.50

Designed by muralist William Woodward, the obverse of the dollar features the Statue of Freedom which towers atop the Capitol dome. The reverse shows the Mace of

MODERN COMMEMORATIVES — Congress,
Eisenhower

the House of Representatives which resides in the House Chamber whenever the House is in session. The Mace's staff is topped by an eagle astride a world globe. A scarce variety of the 1989D dollar shows the dies rotated 360° rather than the normal "coin turn" of 180°.

	Quan. Issued	MS-65	Proof-65
1989D Congress Silver Dollar	135,203	$14.00	
1989S Same type S mint proof	(762,198)		$13.00

  The Capitol Dome is depicted on the obverse of the $5.00 gold coin and is the work of Mint Engraver John Mercanti. The reverse features a majestic eagle atop the canopy overlooking the Old Senate Chamber.

1989W Congress Gold $5.00	46,899	(164,690)	110.00	100.00

EISENHOWER CENTENNIAL

The unusual design on this coin features the profile of President Eisenhower facing right, which is superimposed over his own left-facing profile as a five-star general. It is the creation of Mint Engraver John Mercanti. The reverse shows the Eisenhower home at Gettysburg, a National Historic Site, and was designed by Marcel Jovine. The coin was issued to celebrate the 100th anniversary of the birth of the 34th president.

1990W Eisenhower Silver Dollar	241,669	16.00	
1990P Same type P mint proof	(1,144,461)		15.00

MODERN COMMEMORATIVES — Mount Rushmore
MOUNT RUSHMORE GOLDEN ANNIVERSARY

The 50th anniversary of the Mount Rushmore National Memorial was commemorated on three coins. Surcharges from the sale of these pieces were divided between the Treasury Department and the Mount Rushmore National Memorial Society of Black Hills, South Dakota, with money going to finance restoration work on the national landmark. The obverse of the copper-nickel half dollar was designed by New Jersey artist Marcel Jovine, and features a view of the famous carving by Gutzon Borglum. The reverse designed by Mint Sculptor-Engraver James Ferrell shows an American bison with the words GOLDEN ANNIVERSARY.

	Quan. Issued	MS-65	Proof-65
1991D Mount Rushmore Half Dollar 172,754		$11.00	
1991S Same type S mint proof.......................................(753,257)			$11.00

The Mount Rushmore Golden Anniversary silver dollar obverse was designed by Marika Somogyi. It displays the traditional portraits of Presidents George Washington, Thomas Jefferson, Theodore Roosevelt and Abraham Lincoln as sculptured on the mountain by Gutzon Borglum, who earlier had modeled the figures shown on the Stone Mountain Commemorative coin. The reverse which was designed by former Chief Sculptor-Engraver of the Mint, Frank Gasparro, features a small outline map of the United States with the great seal above.

1991P Mount Rushmore Silver Dollar 133,139		30.00	
1991S Same type S mint proof.......................................(738,419)			30.00

The $5 gold coin commemorating the 50th anniversary of the Mount Rushmore National Memorial features an American eagle flying above the monument with LIBERTY and the date in the field. The obverse was designed by Mint Sculptor-Engraver John Mercanti, and the reverse was designed by Rhode Island artist Robert Lamb, and engraved by Mint Sculptor-Engraver William Cousins. The size, weight and fineness is the same as for all other half eagle coins.

	Quan. Issued	MS-65	Proof-65
1991W Mount Rushmore Gold $5.00.....................31,959	(111,991)	$127.50	$120.00

KOREAN WAR MEMORIAL

The 38th anniversary of the end of the Korean War was the occasion for striking this coin which honors the end of the conflict and those who served in combat. The design has been criticized as being cluttered, and the occasion no more than a fund raising opportunity for the creation of a national monument in Washington. The obverse, designed by Sculptor-Engraver of the U.S. Mint, John Mercanti, features an Army Infantryman in full gear. On the reverse is an outline map of Korea with North and South divided at the 38th parallel, designed by Mint Sculptor-Engraver James Ferrell.

1991D Korean War Silver Dollar..213,049	16.00	
1991P Same type P mint proof..(618,488)		16.00

UNITED SERVICE ORGANIZATIONS

A special commemorative silver dollar was struck to honor the 50th anniversary of United Service Organizations. The group was founded in 1941 to supply social, recreational, welfare and spiritual facilities to armed services personnel. Surcharges on sales of the coins were divided equally between the USO and the Department of the Treasury. The coins were launched on Flag Day, June 14, using designs selected in a limited competition between Mint staff and five outside invited artists. The obverse uses a banner inscribed USO designed by Rhode Island artist Robert Lamb. On the reverse is a globe with an eagle on top, and is the work of Mint Sculptor-Engraver John Mercanti.

	Quan. Issued	MS-65	Proof-65
1991D USO Silver Dollar	124,958	$17.00	
1991S Same type S mint proof	(321,275)		$20.00

XXV OLYMPIAD 1992

The XXV Olympiad held Winter Olympic games in Albertville and Savoie, France, and Summer Olympic games in Barcelona, Spain. United States commemorative coins were issued to honor the participation of American athletes and finance the training of the athletes. Competitive designs were selected from 1,107 entries.

The clad half dollar obverse designed by Mint Sculptor-Engraver William Cousins depicts a gymnast in motion. The reverse, by Steven M. Bieda, has the inscription "Citius, Altius, Fortius" (the Olympic motto: Faster, Higher, Stronger) with an olive branch crossing the Olympic torch.

1992P Olympic Clad Half Dollar	161,619	6.00	
1992S Same type S mint proof	(519,699)		8.00

The 1992 Olympic silver dollar obverse is a rendering by John R. Deecken of a pitcher firing a ball to home plate. The reverse, by sculptor Marcel Jovine, combines the Olympic rings, olive branches, stars and stripes, with a bold USA. Uncirculated dollars minted at Denver have the phrase XXV OLYMPIAD impressed four times around the edge, alternately inverted, on a reeded background.

MODERN COMMEMORATIVES — Olympiad, White House

	Quan. Issued	MS-65	Proof-65
1992D Olympic Silver Dollar	187,552	$20.00	
1992S Same type S mint proof	(504,505)		$25.00

The obverse of the 1992 Olympic $5 gold was designed by James Sharpe, and modeled by T. James Ferrell. It depicts a sprinter in a burst of speed. The reverse, by James Peed, unites two impressive symbols, the Olympic rings and the American bald eagle. Size and fineness of these coins is the same as for other United States commemorative issues.

1992W Olympic Gold $5.00	27,732 (77,313)	127.50	115.00

White House 200th Anniversary

The obverse of this coin, designed by Mint Sculptor Edgar Z. Steever IV, depicts the north portico of the White House. The reverse, by Mint Sculptor Chester Y. Martin, features a bust of James Hoban, the original architect, and the main entrance he designed.

1992D White House Silver Dollar	123,803	33.00	
1992W Same type W mint proof	(375,849)		28.00

MODERN COMMEMORATIVES —
Columbus
Christopher Columbus Quincentenary

The copper-nickel half dollar, designed by Mint Sculptor T. James Ferrell, depicts Columbus landing in the New World on the obverse, and his three ships on the reverse.

	Quan. Issued	MS-65	Proof-65
1992D Columbus Half Dollar	135,718	$12.00	
1992S Same type S mint proof	(390,255)		$13.00

Mint Sculptor John Mercanti designed this silver dollar obverse which features a full-length figure of Columbus beside a globe, with his ships above. The reverse, by Mint Sculptor Thomas D. Rogers, Sr., is a split image of the Santa Maria and the U.S. Space Shuttle Discovery.

1992D Columbus Silver Dollar	106,949	25.00	
1992P Same type P mint proof	(385,241)		29.00

The five dollar gold coin obverse, designed by Mint Sculptor T. James Ferrell, bears a portrait of Columbus facing a map of the New World. The reverse, by Mint Sculptor Thomas D. Rogers, Sr., shows the Crest of the Admiral of the Ocean Sea.

1992W Columbus Gold $5.00	24,329	(79,730)	140.00	130.00

MODERN COMMEMORATIVES —
Bill of Rights
BILL OF RIGHTS

The silver half dollar in this series depicts James Madison penning the Bill of Rights. It was designed by Mint Sculptor T. James Ferrell. The reverse, by Dean McMullen, displays the torch of freedom. 9,656 of the Uncirculated version were privately marked on the edge with a serial number and the initials of the Madison Foundation and the American Numismatic Association.

	Quan. Issued	MS-65	Proof-65
1993W Bill of Rights Silver Half Dollar	173,224	$13.00	
1993S Same type S mint proof	(559,758)		$13.00

A portrait of James Madison is shown on the obverse of this silver dollar designed by William Krawczewicz. Dean McMullen designed the reverse which shows Montpelier, the Virginia home of James and Dolley Madison.

1993D Bill of Rights Silver Dollar	98,383	18.00	
1993S Same type S mint proof	(534,001)		18.00

The obverse of the five dollar gold coin was designed by Scott R. Blazek. It features Madison studying the Bill of Rights. On the reverse, by Joseph D. Peña, is a quotation by Madison, accented by an eagle, torch and laurel branch.

1993W Bill of Rights Gold $5.00	23,266	(78,651)	150.00	120.00

MODERN COMMEMORATIVES —
World War II
50TH ANNIVERSARY OF WORLD WAR II

Each of the three coins in this series are dated 1991-1995, and commemorate the 50th anniversary of U.S. involvement in World War II, which lasted from 1941 to 1945. Pieces were coined and issued in 1993. The obverse of the clad half dollar was designed by George Klauba. It depicts the faces of three members of the service superimposed upon the "V" for victory symbol. The reverse, by Bill J. Leftwich, portrays a Pacific island battle scene.

	Quan. Issued	MS-65	Proof-65
(1993) 1991-1995P World War II			
Clad Half Dollar..192,968	(290,343)	$11.00	$15.00

U.S. Mint Sculptor/Engraver Thomas D. Rogers, Sr. designed the silver dollar showing an American soldier on the beach at Normandy. The reverse depicts the shoulder sleeve insignia of Supreme Headquarters Allied Expeditionary Force, with a quotation from Dwight D. Eisenhower.

(1993) 1991-1995D World War II		
Silver Dollar 94,708	24.00	
(1993) Same type W mint proof..(322,422)		27.50

Both proof and uncirculated versions of the $5 gold coin were struck at the West Point mint. The obverse, designed by Charles J. Madsen, depicts an American serviceman with rifle raised in victory. The reverse, by Edward Southworth Fisher, features a "V" for victory in the center with Morse code for the letter superimposed.

(1993) 1991-1995W World War II			
Gold $5..23,089	(65,461)	150.00	135.00

MODERN COMMEMORATIVES –
World Cup Soccer
1994 WORLD CUP TOURNAMENT

The 1994 World Cup Tournament was the culmination of soccer games among 141 nations. The United States was selected to host the XV FIFA World Cup play-off, and three commemorative coins were issued to celebrate the event. Each of the coins employs a shared design on the reverse.

The obverse of the clad half dollar depicts a soccer player in action. It was designed by Richard T. LaRoche. The reverse, designed by Dean McMullen, features the official World Cup USA 1994 logo flanked by laurel branches.

	Quan. Issued	MS-65	Proof-65
1994D World Cup Tournament Clad Half Dollar	52,836	$10.50	
1994P Same type P mint proof	(122,412)		$10.50

The obverse of the silver dollar coin features two competing players converging on a soccer ball. It was designed by Dean McMullen who also executed the reverse design, the official logo which is used on all of the World Cup coins.

	Quan. Issued	MS-65	Proof-65
1994D World Cup Tournament Silver Dollar	81,698	26.00	
1994S Same type S mint proof	(576,978)		28.00

Both proof and uncirculated versions of the $5 gold coin were struck at the West Point mint. The obverse, designed by William J. Krawczewicz, depicts the modernistic gold World Cup Trophy. The reverse was designed by Dean McMullen and shows the same logo used on other World Cup coins.

	Quan. Issued		MS-65	Proof-65
1994W World Cup Tournament Gold $5	22,464	(89,619)	150.00	120.00

MODERN COMMEMORATIVES —
Thomas Jefferson, Vietnam, U.S. POWs,
THOMAS JEFFERSON
250th Anniversary Birth of Thomas Jefferson

	Quan. Issued	MS-65	Proof-65
1993 (1994) P Thomas Jefferson Silver Dollar	266,927	$30.00	
1993 (1994) S Same type S mint proof	(332,891)		$25.00

VIETNAM VETERANS MEMORIAL
10th Anniversary of Vietnam Veterans Memorial in Washington, D.C.

1994W Vietnam Veterans Memorial Silver Dollar	57,317	38.00	
1994P Same type P mint proof	(226,262)		40.00

U.S. POWs
Tribute to American Prisoners of War

1994W U.S. POW Silver Dollar	54,790	31.00	
1994P Same type P mint proof	(220,100)		29.00

MODERN COMMEMORATIVES —
Women Veterans, U.S. Capitol , Civil War Battlefields

WOMEN VETERANS
All Women, Past and Present, Who Served in the Armed Forces

	Quan. Issued	MS-65	Proof-65
1994W Women Veterans Silver Dollar	53,054	$24.00	
1994P Same type P mint proof	(213,201)		$26.00

U.S. CAPITOL
The Bicentennial of the U.S. Capitol

1994D U.S. Capitol Silver Dollar	68,352	22.00	
1994S Same type S mint proof	(279,416)		23.00

CIVIL WAR BATTLEFIELDS
Preservation of Historic Battlefields

1995S Civil War Battlefield Preservation Clad Half Dollar	119,510	18.00	
1995S Same type S mint proof	(330,099)		18.00

	Quan. Issued	MS-65	Proof-65
1995P Civil War Battlefield Preservation Silver Dollar 45,866		$26.00	
1995S Same type S mint proof ....(55,246)			$35.00

1995W Civil War Battlefield Preservation Gold $5 12,735		300.00	
1995W Same type W mint proof..(55,246)			200.00

CENTENNIAL OLYMPIC GAMES
Atlanta, Georgia Olympic Games

1995S Olympic Games. Basketball Clad Half Dollar 171,001		23.00	
1995S Same type S mint proof ....(169,655)			17.00
1995S Olympic Games. Baseball Clad Half Dollar...............164,605		23.00	
1995S Same type S mint proof ....(118,087)			14.00
1996S Olympic Games. Swimming Clad Half Dollar 49,533		40.00	
1996S Same type S mint proof ....(114,315)			14.00
1996S Olympic Games. Soccer Clad Half Dollar 52,836		29.00	
1996S Same type S mint proof ....(122,412)			60.00

MODERN COMMEMORATIVES —
Olympic Games, (Cont'd)

	Quan. Issued	MS-65	Proof-65
1995D Olympic Games. Gymnastics Silver Dollar	42,497	$60.00	
1995P Same type P mint proof	(182,676)		$30.00
1995D Olympic Games. Paralympics Silver Dollar	28,649	75.00	
1995P Same type P mint proof	(138,337)		34.00
1995D Olympic Games. Track and Field Silver Dollar	24,796	55.00	
1995P Same type P mint proof	(136,935)		31.00
1995D Olympic Games. Cycling Silver Dollar	19,662	75.00	
1995P Same type P mint proof	(118,795)		34.00
1996D Olympic Games. Tennis Silver Dollar	15,983	125.00	
1996P Same type P mint proof	(92,016)		47.50
1996D Olympic Games. Paralympics Silver Dollar	14,497	175.00	
1996P Same type P mint proof	(84,280)		45.00
1996D Olympic Games. Rowing Silver Dollar	16,258	150.00	
1996P Same type P mint proof	(151,890)		40.00
1996D Olympic Games. High Jump Silver Dollar	15,697	185.00	
1996P Same type P mint proof	(124,502)		36.00

1995W Olympic Games. Torch Runner Gold $5	14,675	200.00	
1995W Same type W mint proof	(57,442)		150.00
1995W Olympic Games. Stadium Gold $5	10,579	250.00	
1995W Same type W mint proof	(43,124)		165.00
1996W Olympic Games. Flag Bearer Gold $5	9,174	270.00	
1996W Same type W mint proof	(32,886)		215.00
1996W Olympic Games. Cauldron Gold $5	9,210	270.00	
1996W Same type W mint proof	(38,555)		215.00

MODERN COMMEMORATIVES —
Special Olympics,
National Community Service, Smithsonian
SPECIAL OLYMPICS GAMES

	Quan. Issued	MS-65	Proof-65
1995W Shriver Silver Dollar	89,301	$30.00	
1995P Same type P mint proof	(351,764)		$17.00

NATIONAL COMMUNITY SERVICE

1996S Community Service Silver Dollar	23,468	200.00	
1996S Same type S mint proof	(100,787)		31.00

SMITHSONIAN INSTITUTION 150TH ANNIVERSARY

1996D Smithsonian Silver Dollar	30,593	80.00	
1996P Same type P mint proof	(126,616)		35.00

	Quan. Issued	MS-65	Proof-65
1996W Smithsonian Gold $5	21,840	$330.00	
1996W Same type W mint proof	(8,948)		$225.00

BOTANIC GARDENS

1997P Botanic Gardens Silver Dollar	57,272	37.00	
1997P Same type P mint proof	(264,528)		37.00

JACKIE ROBINSON

1997S Jackie Robinson Silver Dollar	30,180	45.00	
1997S Same type S mint proof	(110,002)		35.00

1997W Jackie Robinson Gold $5	5,174	835.00	
1997W Same type W mint proof	(24,072)		260.00

FRANKLIN D. ROOSEVELT

	Quan. Issued	MS-65	Proof-65
1997W Franklin D. Roosevelt Gold $5 11,805		$220.00	
1997W Same type W mint proof..(29,233)			$200.00

NATIONAL LAW ENFORCEMENT OFFICERS MEMORIAL

1997P Law Enforcement Silver Dollar......................................28,575		85.00	
1997P Same type P mint proof...(110,428)			90.00

ROBERT F. KENNEDY

1998S Robert F. Kennedy Silver Dollar 106,422		33.00	
1998S Same type S mint proof ....(99,020)			40.00

BLACK REVOLUTIONARY WAR PATRIOTS

1998S Black Patriots Silver Dollar...37,210		75.00	
1998S Same type S mint proof ....(75,070)			70.00

DOLLEY MADISON COMMEMORATIVE

	Quan. Issued	MS-65	Proof-65
1999P Dolley Madison Silver Dollar	89,100	$40.00	
1999P Same type P mint proof	(224,400)		$40.00

GEORGE WASHINGTON COMMEMORATIVE GOLD

1999W George Washington Gold $5	22,511	210.00	
1999W Same type W mint proof	(41,693)		220.00

YELLOWSTONE NATIONAL PARK

1999P Yellowstone Silver Dollar	62,000	35.00	
1999P Same type P mint proof	(144,900)		35.00

LIBRARY OF CONGRESS BICENTENNIAL

2000P Library of Congress Silver Dollar	35.00	
2000P Same type P mint proof		37.50
2000W Library of Congress bimetallic $10	800.00	
2000W Same type W mint proof		500.00

LEIF ERICSON MILLENNIUM

2000P Leif Ericson Silver Dollar	28,100	35.00	
2000P Same type P mint proof	(142,900)		35.00

AMERICAN BUFFALO COMMEMORATIVE

2001D Buffalo / Indian Silver Dollar	90.00	
2001P Same type P mint proof		90.00

CAPITOL VISITOR CENTER

2001P Visitor Center, clad Half Dollar	12.00	
2001P Same type P mint proof		15.00
2001P Visitor Center Silver Dollar	37.50	
2001P Same type P mint proof		42.50
2001W Visitor Center $5	250.00	
2001W Same type W mint proof		250.00

SALT LAKE OLYMPIC GAMES

2002P Salt Lake Olympic Silver Dollar	35.00	
2002P Same type P mint proof		40.00
2002W Salt Lake Olympic $5	210.00	
2002W Same type W mint proof		240.00

MODERN COMMEMORATIVES

MODERN COMMEMORATIVES

MODERN COMMEMORATIVES

GOVERNMENT COMMEMORATIVE SETS

1983-84 OLYMPICS

Date   *Price*

1983 and 1984 proof dollars $20.00

1983 and 1984 6 coin set. One 1983 and one 1984 uncirculated and proof
    dollar. One uncirculated and one proof gold $10. ....390.00

1983 Collector set. 1983 PDS uncirculated dollars..30.00

1984 Collector set. 1984 PDS uncirculated dollars..45.00

1983 and 1984 gold and silver uncirculated set. One 1983
    and one 1984 uncirculated dollar and one 1984 uncirculated gold $10.................225.00

1983 and 1984 gold and silver proof set. One 1983 and one 1984 proof
    dollar and one 1984 proof $10.* 225.00

1986 STATUE OF LIBERTY

1986 2 coin set: proof silver dollar and clad half dollar..............................17.50

1986 3 coin set: proof silver dollar, clad half dollar and gold $5................125.00

1986 2 coin set: uncirculated silver dollar and clad half dollar. 15.00

1986 3 coin set: uncirculated silver dollar, clad half dollar and gold $5. ....135.00

1986 6 coin set: 1 each of proof and uncirculated.* 250.00

1987 CONSTITUTION

1987 2 coin set: uncirculated silver dollar and gold $5. ....120.00

1987 2 coin set: proof silver dollar and gold $5..120.00

1987 4 coin set: 1 each of proof and uncirculated.* 250.00

1988 OLYMPIAD

1988 2 coin set: uncirculated silver dollar and gold $5. ....125.00

1988 2 coin set: proof silver dollar and gold $5..125.00

1988 4 coin set: 1 each of proof and uncirculated.* 250.00

1989 CONGRESS

1989 2 coin set: proof silver dollar and clad half dollar..............................19.00

1989 3 coin set: proof silver dollar, clad half dollar and gold $5................120.00

1989 2 coin set: uncirculated silver dollar and clad half dollar. 20.00

1989 3 coin set: uncirculated silver dollar, clad half dollar and gold $5. ....145.00

1989 6 coin set: 1 each of proof and uncirculated.* 250.00

Packaged in cherrywood box.

GOVERNMENT COMMEMORATIVE SETS
1991 MOUNT RUSHMORE

Date   *Price*
1991 2 coin set: uncirculated half dollar and dollar. $37.00
1991 2 coin set: proof half dollar and silver dollar. 37.00
1991 3 coin set: uncirculated half dollar, silver dollar and gold $5. ....140.00
1991 3 coin set: proof half dollar, silver dollar and gold $5...135.00
1991 6 coin set: 1 each of proof and uncirculated.* 285.00

1992 XXV OLYMPIAD

1992 2 coin set: uncirculated half dollar and dollar. 25.00
1992 2 coin set: proof half dollar and dollar...32.00
1992 3 coin set: uncirculated half dollar, dollar and gold $5 ....160.00
1992 3 coin set: proof half dollar, dollar and gold $5....................................160.00
1992 6 coin set: 1 each of proof and uncirculated.* 300.00

1992 COLUMBUS

1992 2 coin set: uncirculated half dollar and dollar. 33.00
1992 2 coin set: proof half dollar and silver dollar. 37.00
1992 3 coin set: uncirculated half dollar, silver dollar and gold $5. ....160.00
1992 3 coin set: proof half dollar, silver dollar and gold $5....................................140.00
1992 6 coin set: 1 each of proof and uncirculated.* 315.00

1993 BILL OF RIGHTS

1993 2 coin set: uncirculated half dollar and dollar. 27.00
1993 2 coin set: proof half dollar and silver dollar. 27.00
1993 3 coin set: uncirculated half dollar, silver dollar and gold $5. ....150.00
1993 3 coin set: proof half dollar, silver dollar and gold $5....................................145.00
1993 6 coin set: 1 each of proof and uncirculated.* 300.00
1993 "Young Collector" set: silver half dollar. 17.00
1993 "Educational" set: silver half dollar and Madison medal. 12.00

1993 THOMAS JEFFERSON

1993 3 piece set: Jefferson dollar, nickel and $2 note 100.00

1993 WORLD WAR II

1993 2 coin set: uncirculated half dollar and dollar. 27.50
1993 2 coin set: proof half dollar and silver dollar. 34.00
1993 3 coin set: uncirculated half dollar, silver dollar and gold $5. ....150.00
1993 3 coin set: proof half dollar, silver dollar and gold $5....................................150.00
1993 6 coin set: 1 each of proof and uncirculated.* 320.00
1993 "Young Collector" set: clad half dollar...16.00
1993 "Victory" set: silver dollar, French franc...12.00

1994 WORLD CUP SOCCER

1994 2 coin set: uncirculated half dollar and dollar. 29.00
1994 2 coin set: proof half dollar and silver dollar. 31.00
1994 3 coin set: uncirculated half dollar, silver dollar and gold $5. ....160.00
1994 3 coin set: proof half dollar, silver dollar and gold $5....................................150.00
1994 6 coin set: 1 each of proof and uncirculated.* 310.00
1994 "Young Collector" set: uncirculated clad half dollar..10.00
1994 "Special Edition" set: proof clad half dollar and silver dollar. 26.00

1994 U.S. VETERANS

1994 3 coin set: Unc. POW, Vietnam and Women dollar 100.00
1994 3 coin set: proof POW, Vietnam and Women dollar 90.00

Packaged in cherrywood box.

GOVERNMENT COMMEMORATIVE SETS
1995 SPECIAL OLYMPICS

Date   *Price*
1995 2 coin set: proof Schriver dollar, 1995-S Kennedy 50¢ $100.00

1995 CIVIL WAR BATTLEFIELD PRESERVATION
1995 2 coin set: uncirculated half dollar and dollar 45.00
1995 2 coin set: proof half dollar and silver dollar 55.00
1995 3 coin set: uncirculated half dollar, dollar and gold $5 ....320.00
1995 3 coin set: proof half dollar, dollar and gold $5..................................270.00
1995 6 coin set: 1 each of proof and uncirculated.* 600.00
1995 "Young Collector" set: uncirculated half dollar......................................17.00
1995 2 coin "Union Set": half dollar and dollar..50.00
1995 3 coin "Union Set": half dollar, dollar and gold $5..............................275.00

1995-96 CENTENNIAL OLYMPIC GAMES
1995 4 coin set #1: uncirculated 50¢ Basketball,
   $1 Gymnast, $1 Paralympics, $5 Torch 270.00
1995 4 coin set #2: proof 50¢ Basketball, $1 Gymnast,
   $1 Paralympics, $5 Torch 175.00
1995 2 coin set #1: proof $1 Gymnast, $1 Paralympics 65.00
1995 "Young Collector" set: uncirculated Basketball half dollar....................15.00
1995-96 16 coin set: 1 each all uncirculated coins.* 1,275
1995-96 16 coin set: 1 each all proof coins.*...1,100
1995-96 32 coin set: 1 each all uncirculated and proof coins.*....................2,350

1996 NATIONAL COMMUNITY SERVICE
1996 proof silver dollar and Saint-Gaudens stamp 50.00

1996 SMITHSONIAN INSTITUTION 150TH ANNIVERSARY
1996 2 coin set: proof dollar and gold $5 ....225.00
1996 4 coin set: 1 each of proof and uncirculated. * 675.00
1996 "Young Collector" set: proof silver dollar 36.00

1997 BOTANIC GARDENS
1997 Dollar, Jefferson nickel and $1 note..260.00

1997 JACKIE ROBINSON
1997 2 coin set: proof dollar and $5 gold 225.00
1997 4 coin set: 1 each of proof and uncirculated 1,200
1997 3 piece legacy set: Baseball card, pin and $5 gold 300.00

1997 NATIONAL LAW ENFORCEMENT OFFICERS MEMORIAL
1997 Insignia set: dollar, lapel pin and patch..90.00

1998 ROBERT F. KENNEDY
1998 2 coin set: RFK dollar and JFK silver half dollar................................375.00
1998 2 coin set: RFK dollar, proof and uncirculated 70.00

1998 BLACK REVOLUTIONARY WAR PATRIOTS
1998 2 coin set: uncirculated and proof dollar...100.00
1998 "Young Collector" set: uncirculated dollar 70.00
1998 Coin and 4 stamps set 70.00

Packaged in cherrywood box.

GOVERNMENT COMMEMORATIVE SETS

1999 DOLLEY MADISON COMMEMORATIVE

Date   *Price*
1999 2 coin set: proof and uncirculated dollars $67.50

1999 GEORGE WASHINGTON
1999 2 coin set: 1 each proof and uncirculated $5 gold 425.00

1999 YELLOWSTONE NATIONAL PARK
1999 2 coin set: 1 each proof and uncirculated dollars..75.00

2000 LEIF ERICSON MILLENNIUM
2000 2 coin set: proof $1 and Islandic 1,000 kronur...75.00

2001 AMERICAN BUFFALO
2001 2 coin set: proof and uncirculated dollars 180.00
2001 coinage and currency set..110.00

2001 CAPITOL VISITOR CENTER
2001 3 coin proof set...250.00

2002 SALT LAKE OLYMPIC GAMES
2002 2 coin proof set...250.00
2002 4 coin proof and uncirculated set..500.00

BIBLIOGRAPHY

Bowers, Q. David. *Commemorative Coins of the United States: a Complete Encyclopedia.* Wolfeboro, N.H., 1991.
Bullowa, David M. *The Commemorative Coinage of the United States 1892-1938.* New York, 1938.
Mosher, Stuart. *The Commemorative Coinage of the United States 1892-1938.* New York, 1940.
Slabaugh, Arlie. *United States Commemorative Coinage.* Racine, 1975.
Swiatek, Anthony and Breen, Walter. *The Encyclopedia of United States Silver and Gold Commemorative Coins 1892-1954.* New York, 1981.
Taxay, Don. *An Illustrated History of U.S. Commemorative Coinage.* New York, 1967.

PRIVATE OR TERRITORIAL GOLD COINS

The words "Private Gold," used with reference to coins struck outside of the United States Mint, are a general term. In the sense that no state or territory had authority to coin money, private gold simply refers to those interesting necessity pieces of various shapes, denominations and degrees of intrinsic worth that were circulated in isolated areas of our country by individuals, assayers, bankers, etc. Some will use the words "Territorial" and "State" to cover certain issues because they were coined and circulated in a territory or state. While the state of California properly sanctioned the ingots stamped by F. D. Kohler as state assayer, in no instance were any of the gold pieces struck by authority of any of the territorial governments.

The stamped ingots made by Augustus Humbert, the United States assayer of gold, were not recognized at the United States Mint as an official issue of coins, but simply as ingots, though Humbert placed the value and fineness on the pieces as an official agent of the federal government.

Private coins were circulated in most instances because of a shortage of regular coinage. In the western states particularly, money became so scarce that the very commodity that the pioneers had come so far to acquire was converted into a local medium of exchange.

Ephraim Brasher's New York doubloon of 1787 described on page 44 also falls into this class.

BIBLIOGRAPHY

Adams, Edgar H. *Private Gold Coinage of California 1849-1855.* Brooklyn, N.Y., 1913.

Adams, Edgar H. *Official Premium Lists of Private and Territorial Gold Coins.* Brooklyn, N.Y., 1909.

Bowers, Q. David. *The History of United States Coinage as Illustrated by the Garrett Collection.* Los Angeles, Cal., 1979.

Bowers, Q. David. *A California Gold Rush History Featuring Treasure from the S.S. Central America.* Wolfeboro, NH, 2001.

Breen, Walter and Gillio, Ronald. *California Pioneer Fractional Gold.* Santa Barbara, Cal., 1983.

Clifford, Henry H. *Pioneer Gold Coinage in the West- 1848-1861.* Reprint from "The Westerners Brand Book- Book Nine." Los Angeles Corral, 1961.

Doering, David. *California Fractional Gold.* Seal Beach, Cal., 1982.

Griffin, Clarence. *The Bechtlers and Bechtler Coinage and Gold Mining in North Carolina 1814-1830.* Spindale, N.C., 1929.

Kagin Donald H. *Private Gold Coins and Patterns of the United States.* New York, 1981.

Lee, Kenneth W. *California Gold — Dollars, Half Dollars, Quarter Dollars.* Santa Ana, Cal., 1979.

Owens, Dan. *California Coiners and Assayers.* Wolfeboro, NH; and New York City, 2000.

Seymour, Dexter C. *The 1830 Coinage of Templeton Reid.* American Numismatic Society Museum Notes No. 22. New York, 1977.

TEMPLETON REID
Georgia 1830

The first private gold coinage under the Constitution was struck by Templeton Reid, a jeweler and gunsmith, in Milledgeville, Georgia in July, 1830. To be closer to the mines, he moved to Gainesville where most of his coins were made. Although weights were accurate, Reid's assays were not and his coins were slightly short of claimed value. Accordingly, he was severely attacked in the newspapers and soon lost the public's confidence. He closed his mint before the end of October, 1830 and his output amounted only to about 1,600 coins. Denominations struck were $2.50, $5.00 and $10.00.

1830 $2.50	V. Fine	$38,000
1830 $5.00	V. Fine	110,000

TEMPLETON REID — GEORGIA

1830 TEN DOLLARS ....V. Good $125,000
(No date) TEN DOLLARS..V. Good 90,000

TEMPLETON REID
"California Gold 1849"

The enigmatic later issues of Templeton Reid were probably made from California gold. Reid, who never went to California, was then a cotton gin maker in Columbus, Georgia, where he died in 1851. The coins were in denominations of ten and twenty-five dollars. Struck copies of both exist in various metals.

The only specimen known of the $25 piece was stolen from the Cabinet of the U.S. Mint on August 16, 1858. It was never recovered.

1849 TEN DOLLAR CALIFORNIA GOLD (Smithsonian Collection) .... *Unique*
1849 TWENTY-FIVE DOLLARS CALIFORNIA GOLD .... *Unknown*

THE BECHTLERS
Rutherford County, N. C. 1830-1852

Two skilled German metallurgists, Christopher Bechtler and his son August, and later Christopher Bechtler, Junior, a nephew of Christopher the elder, operated a "private" mint at Rutherfordton, North Carolina. Rutherford county in which Rutherfordton is located was the principal source of the nation's gold supply from 1790 to 1840.

The coins minted by the Bechtlers were of only three denominations, but they cover a wide variety of weights and sizes.

The Bechtlers have the distinction of producing the first gold dollar in the United States. The government mint did not release the first regular series until 1849.

The inscription "Aug. 1, 1834" on one variety of the five-dollar piece has a special significance. The Secretary of the Treasury recommended to the Director of the Mint that the gold coins of the reduced weight bear the date "Aug. 1, 1834." Instead of this, however, a new U.S. gold design was used (the motto was omitted). Christopher Bechtler evidently acted on the official recommendation to avoid any difficulty with Treasury authorities.

THE BECHTLERS
CHRISTOPHER BECHTLER

	V. Fine	E. Fine	A. Unc.	Unc.
ONE DOLLAR CAROLINA, 28 gr. N reversed	$1,300	$2,000	$3,100	$4,800
ONE DOLLAR N. CAROLINA, 28 gr. centered, no star	2,700	4,200	7,000	13,000
ONE DOLLAR N. CAROLINA, 28 gr. high, no star	6,000	8,500	12,500	21,000

ONE DOLLAR N. CAROLINA, 30 gr.	1,600	2,800	4,400	10,000
$2.50 CAROLINA, 67 gr. 21 carats	3,750	7,500	8,500	16,000

$2.50 CAROLINA, 70 gr. 20 carats	4,000	7,250	8,500	16,500
$2.50 GEORGIA, 64 gr. 22 carats	4,250	7,250	8,500	16,500
$2.50 GEORGIA, 64 gr. 22 carats — even 22	5,000	8,200	10,000	22,500

Beaded Border   **Serrated Border**

$2.50 NORTH CAROLINA, 75 gr. 20 carats. RUTHERFORD in a circle. Border of lg. beads	8,750	12,000	16,500	28,000
$2.50 NORTH CAROLINA, without 75 G	9,000	12,000	16,000	26,000
$2.50 NORTH CAROLINA, without 75 G, CAROLINA above 250 instead of GOLD				*Unique*
$2.50 NORTH CAROLINA, 20 carats on obv. 75 gr. on rev. Border finely serrated	12,000	16,000	26,000	—

THE BECHTLERS

	V. Fine	E. Fine	A. Unc.	Unc.
5 DOLLARS CAROLINA, RUTHERFORD, 140 gr. 20 carats. AUGUST 1, 1834.				
Plain edge	$4,500	$6,750	$8,750	$16,500
Reeded edge	5,750	9,000	13,000	25,000
BECHTLER without star and C.	—			
5 DOLLARS CAROLINA, 134 gr. 21 carats, with star	4,250	6,500	8,000	15,000
5 DOLLARS CAROLINA, 134 gr. 21 carats, no star, (Reverse of A. Bechtler as shown below)	—	—		
5 DOLLARS GEORGIA, RUTHERFORD, 128 gr. 22 carats	4,600	6,750	8,750	18,500
Similar. Colon before 22 and after 128 G	—	—		

	V. Fine	E. Fine	A. Unc.	Unc.
5 DOLLARS GEORGIA, RUTHERF. 128 gr. 22 carats	4,600	6,750	8,750	18,500
5 DOLLARS CAROLINA, RUTHERF. 140 gr. 20 carats. AUGUST 1, 1834	4,600	6,750	8,750	18,000
Similar. 20 distant from carats	6,500	9,750	13,000	21,000

Without 150 G

Beaded border design

	V. Fine	E. Fine	A. Unc.	Unc.
5 DOLLARS NORTH CAROLINA, 150 gr. 20 carats	6,900	11,000	17,000	33,000
5 DOLLARS. Same as last variety without 150 G	8,500	14,000	18,000	36,000

AUGUST BECHTLER
1842-1852

	V. Fine	E. Fine	A. Unc.	Unc.
1 DOLLAR CAROLINA, 27 gr. 21 carats	$950.00	$1,400	$2,200	$3,700
5 DOLLARS CAROLINA, 134 gr. 21 carats	4,000	5,500	8,000	19,000

THE BECHTLERS

	V. Fine	E. Fine	A. Unc.	Unc.
5 DOLLARS CAROLINA, 128 gr. 22 carats	$7,750	$9,500	$14,500	$24,000
5 DOLLARS CAROLINA, 141 gr. 20 carats	6,500	8,750	12,000	22,500

(Restrikes in "proof" exist from original dies.)

NORRIS, GREGG & NORRIS
San Francisco 1849

Collectors consider this piece the first of the California private gold coins. A newspaper account dated May 31, 1849, described a five-dollar gold coin, struck at Benicia City, though with the imprint San Francisco. It mentioned the private stamp of Norris, Gregg and Norris. The initials N. G. and N. were not identified until 1902 when the coins of Augustus Humbert were sold.

	Fine	V. Fine	E. Fine	A. Unc.	Unc.
1849 HALF EAGLE — Plain edge	$3,000	$4,500	$7,500	$10,000	$21,000
1849 HALF EAGLE — Reeded edge	3,000	4,500	7,500	10,000	21,000
1850 HALF EAGLE with STOCKTON beneath date...					Unique

MOFFAT & CO.
San Francisco 1849-1853

The firm of Moffat and Company was perhaps the most important of the California private coiners. The assay office they conducted was semi-official in character. The successors to this firm, Curtis, Perry and Ward, later established the United States Branch mint of San Francisco.

In June or July, 1849, Moffat & Co. began to issue small rectangular pieces of gold owing to lack of coin in the locality, in values from $9.43 to $264. The $9.43, $14.25 and $16.00 varieties are the only types known today.

The unique specimens of the $9.43 and $14.25 ingots are in the National Coin Collection in the Smithsonian.

MOFFAT & CO.

$9.43 Ingot (*Unique*)...	—
$14.25 Ingot *(Unique)*..	—
$16.00 Ingot	$25,000

The dies for the $10 piece were cut by a Bavarian, Albert Kuner. The words MOFFAT & CO. appear on the coronet of Liberty instead of the word LIBERTY as in regular United States issues.

	Fine	V. Fine	E. Fine	A. Unc.	Unc.
1849 FIVE DOL.(All varieties)	$1,000	$1,500	$3,000	$4,750	$10,000
1850 FIVE DOL. (All varieties)	1,000	1,600	3,100	5,250	10,500
1849 TEN DOL.	2,400	3,500	7,500	11,000	22,000
1849 TEN D.	2,500	3,600	8,000	13,000	25,000

United States Assay Office
AUGUSTUS HUMBERT
U. S. Assayer 1851

Augustus Humbert, a New York watchcase maker, was appointed United States Assayer, and he placed his name and the government stamp on the ingots of gold issued by Moffat & Co. The assay office, a provisional government mint, was a temporary expedient to accommodate the Californians until the establishment of a permanent branch mint.

The fifty-dollar gold piece was accepted as legal tender on a par with standard U.S. gold coins and was known variously as a slug, quintuple eagle or five-eagle piece. It was officially termed an ingot.

LETTERED EDGE VARIETIES

	Fine	V. Fine	E. Fine	A. Unc.	Unc.
1851 50 D C 880 THOUS., no 50 on reverse. Sunk in edge: AUGUSTUS HUMBERT UNITED STATES ASSAYER OF GOLD CALIFORNIA 1851.........................	$7,500	$11,000	$16,000	$24,000	$37,500

MOFFAT — HUMBERT

	Fine	V. Fine	E. Fine	A. Unc	Unc.
1851 50 D C Similar to last variety, but 50 on reverse	$8,500	$15,000	$21,000	$35,000	$47,000
1851 Similar to last variety, but 887 THOUS.	8,200	13,500	18,000	28,000	43,000
1851 50 D C 887 THOUS., no 50 on reverse	—	—	—		
1851 50 D C 880 THOUS. Rev. rays from central star *(Unique)*				—	

REEDED EDGE VARIETIES

	Fine	V. Fine	E. Fine	A. Unc.	Unc.
1851 FIFTY DOLLS 880 THOUS. "Target" reverse	$5,500	$7,750	$12,500	$19,000	$33,000
1851 FIFTY DOLLS 887 THOUS. "Target" reverse	5,500	7,750	12,500	19,000	33,000
1852 FIFTY DOLLS. 887 THOUS.	5,500	7,750	13,000	20,000	35,000

MOFFAT — HUMBERT

A unique proof specimen of the 1851 with 887 THOUS. was sold at the Garrett II auction in 1980 for $500,000.

The withdrawal of the discredited private coins of $5, $10 and $20 denominations as a result of the new U.S. Assay operations caused a new turn of affairs for Californians. Fractional currency coins of almost every nation were pressed into service by the Californians, but the supply was too small to help to any extent. Moffat & Co. proceeded in January, 1852 to issue a new ten-dollar piece bearing the stamp MOFFAT & CO.

Close Date   **Wide Date**

	Fine	V. Fine	E. Fine	A. Unc.	Unc.
1852 TEN D. MOFFAT & CO. (Close date)..	$2,400	$3,800	$7,000	$16,000	—
1852 TEN D. MOFFAT & CO. (Wide date).....	2,400	3,800	7,000	16,000	—

| 1852 TEN DOLS. 1852, 2 over 1 .... | 1,500 | 2,750 | 4,800 | 8,250 | — |
| 1852 TEN DOLS. .... | 1,300 | 2,200 | 3,500 | 6,600 | $14,000 |

| 1852 TWENTY DOLS. 1852, 2 over 1............ | 3,400 | 5,500 | 9,250 | 17,000 | — |

[290]

UNITED STATES ASSAY OFFICE OF GOLD
1852

The firm of Moffat & Co. was dissolved in 1852 and a newly reorganized company known as the United States Assay Office of Gold, took over the contract. Principals were Curtis, Perry and Ward.

	Fine	V. Fine	E. Fine	A. Unc.	Unc.
1852 FIFTY DOLLS. 887 THOUS..................	$5,500	$7,750	$12,500	$19,000	$33,000
1852 FIFTY DOLLS. 900 THOUS..................	5,500	7,750	13,000	20,000	34,000

1852 TEN DOLS 884 THOUS.	1,200	1,850	3,000	5,750	13,000

1853 TEN D. 884 THOUS............................	4,500	7,800	14,000	20,000	—
1853 TEN D. 900 THOUS............................	2,800	4,250	6,750	10,000	15,000

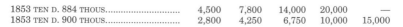

UNITED STATES ASSAY OFFICE

	Fine	V. Fine	E. Fine	A. Unc.	Unc.
1853 TWENTY D. 884 THOUS.	$5,250	$9,000	$13,000	$19,500	$30,000

1853 TWENTY D. 900 THOUS.	1,350	1,800	3,400	5,200	9,500

U. S. ASSAY — MOFFAT

The last Moffat issue was a 1853 twenty dollar piece that is very similar to the U.S. double eagle of that period. It was struck after the retirement of John L. Moffat from the Assay Office.

	Fine	V. Fine	E. Fine	A. Unc.	Unc.
1853 TWENTY D.	$2,500	$3,250	$5,000	$7,750	$16,000

J. H. BOWIE

Joseph H. Bowie joined his cousins in San Francisco in 1849 and possibly produced a limited coinage of gold pieces. A trial piece of the dollar denomination is known in copper, but may never have reached the coinage stage. Little is known about the company or reason for issuing these pieces.

J. H. BOWIE

1849 5 DOLLARS.............. —

CINCINNATI MINING & TRADING CO.

The origin and location of this company are unknown.

	E. Fine	Unc.
1849 FIVE DOLLARS	Unique	
1849 TEN DOLLARS	$225,000	—

(Beware of spurious specimens cast in base metal with word TRACING in place of TRADING.)

MASSACHUSETTS AND CALIFORNIA COMPANY
San Francisco 1849

This company was believed to have been organized in Northampton, Mass. in May, 1849.

	Fine	E. Fine
1849 FIVE D. ...	$50,000	$125,000

MINERS' BANK
San Francisco 1849

The institution of Wright & Co., exchange brokers located in Portsmouth Square, San Francisco, was known as the Miners' Bank.

A ten dollar piece was issued in the autumn of 1849, but the coins were not readily accepted because they were worth less than face value. The firm was dissolved on January 14, 1850. Unlike most California issues, the gold in these coins was alloyed with copper.

Plain border   **Crimped border**

	V. Fine	E. Fine	A. Unc.	Unc.
(1849) TEN. D, plain border.	$7,750	$14,000	$19,000	$42,000
(1849) TEN. D., crimped border	8,500	15,500	21,000	46,000

J. S. ORMSBY
Sacramento 1849

The initials J. S. O., which appear on certain issues of California privately coined gold pieces, represent the firm of J. S. Ormsby & Co. They struck both five and ten dollar denominations, all undated.

	V. Fine
(1849) 5 DOLLS. Plain edge *(Possibly Unique)*	—
(1849) 5 DOLLS. Reeded edge *(Unique-Smithsonian Collection)*	—
(1849) 10 DOLLS. *(4 known)*	$130,000

PACIFIC COMPANY
San Francisco 1849

The origin of the Pacific Co. is very uncertain. All data regarding the firm is based on conjecture.

Edgar H. Adams wrote that he believed that the coins bearing the stamp of the Pacific Company were produced by the coining firm of Broderick and Kohler. The coins were probably handstruck, with the aid of a sledgehammer.

1849 1 DOLLAR .... (unique)
1849 5 DOLLARS
    E. Fine $140,000

1849 10 DOLLARS
    A. Unc.....................$185,000

F. D. KOHLER
California State Assayer 1850

The State Assay Office was authorized April 12, 1850. Governor Burnett appointed F. D. Kohler that year, who thereupon sold his assaying business to Baldwin & Co. He served at both the San Francisco and Sacramento Offices. The State Assay Offices were discontinued at the time the U. S. Assay Office was established Feb. 1, 1851.

Ingots issued ranged from $36.55 to $150. An Ex. F. specimen sold in the Garrett Sale, 1980 for $200,000.

$36.55 Sacramento	—
$37.31 San Francisco	—
$40.07 San Francisco	—
$45.34 San Francisco	—
$50.00 San Francisco	—
$54.09 San Francisco	—

Note: A $40.07 ingot was stolen from the Mint Cabinet in 1858 and never recovered.

DUBOSQ & COMPANY
San Francisco 1850

Theodore Dubosq, a Philadelphia jeweler, took melting and coining machinery to San Francisco in 1849.

	V. Fine
1850 FIVE D.	$50,000
1850 TEN D.	55,000

BALDWIN & COMPANY
San Francisco 1850

George C. Baldwin and Thomas S. Holman were in the jewelry business in San Francisco and were known as Baldwin & Co. They were the successors to F. D. Kohler & Co., taking over its machinery and other equipment in May, 1850.

	Fine	V. Fine	E. Fine	A. Unc.	Unc.
1850 FIVE DOL.	$4,000	$6,750	$12,500	$17,000	$25,000
1850 TEN DOLLARS — Horseman type	17,000	34,000	50,000	70,000	—

	Fine	V. Fine	E. Fine	A. Unc.	Unc.
1851 TEN D.	5,750	10,000	20,000	30,000	—

BALDWIN & COMPANY

The Baldwin & Co. $20 piece was the first of that denomination issued in California. Baldwin coins were believed to have contained about 2 percent copper alloy.

	E. Fine	Unc.
1851 TWENTY D.	$95,000	—

Beware of spurious specimens cast in base metal.

SHULTZ & COMPANY
San Francisco 1851

The firm located in back of Baldwin's establishment operated a brass foundry beginning in 1851. Judge G. W. Shultz and William T. Garratt were partners in the enterprise.

	Fine	V. Fine	E. Fine	A. Unc
1851 FIVE D	$17,000	$33,000	$43,000	$55,000

DUNBAR & COMPANY
San Francisco 1851

Edward E. Dunbar operated the California Bank in San Francisco. Dunbar later returned to New York and organized the famous Continental Bank Note Co.

	E. Fine
1851 FIVE D	$90,000

WASS, MOLITOR & COMPANY
San Francisco 1852-1855

The gold smelting and assaying plant of Wass, Molitor & Co. was operated by two Hungarian patriots, Count S. C. Wass and A. P. Molitor. They maintained an excellent laboratory and complete apparatus for analysis and coinage of gold.

The company struck five, ten, twenty and fifty dollar coins. In 1852 they produced a ten dollar piece similar in design to the five dollar denomination. The difference is in the reverse legend which reads: S.M.V. (Standard Mint Value) CALIFORNIA GOLD TEN D.

No pieces were coined in 1853 or 1854, but they brought out the twenty dollar and fifty dollar pieces in 1855. A considerable number of the fifty dollar coins were made. There was a ten dollar piece issued in 1855 also, with the Liberty head and small close date.

Large Head, Pointed Bust

	Fine	V. Fine	E. Fine	A. Unc.	Unc.
1852 FIVE DOLLARS. Small head with rounded bust	$2,500	$4,750	$9,750	$14,500	$30,000
1852 FIVE DOLLARS. Large head with pointed bust	2,500	4,500	9,500	13,500	26,000

Large Head   **Small Head**

Small Date   **1855**

	Fine	V. Fine	E. Fine	A. Unc.	Unc.
1852 TEN D. Large head	1,700	2,800	5,000	9,000	—
1852 TEN D. Small head	4,000	5,500	12,500	17,000	—
1852 TEN D. Small close date			Rare		
1855 TEN D.	9,500	16,000	22,000	32,000	—

WASS, MOLITOR & COMPANY

Large Head   **Small Head**

	Fine	V.Fine	E. Fine	A. Unc.	Unc.
1855 TWENTY DOL. Large head................		—	$90,000	—	—
1855 TWENTY DOL. Small head................	$7,500	$15,500	25,000	$37,500	—

1855 50 DOLLARS	15,000	19,000	29,000	48,000	$125,000

KELLOGG & COMPANY
San Francisco 1854-1855

John G. Kellogg went to San Francisco October 12, 1849, from Auburn, New York. At first he was employed by Moffat and Company, and remained with that organization when control passed to Curtis, Perry and Ward. When the United States Assay Office was discontinued December 14, 1853, Mr. Kellogg became associated with G. F. Richter, who had been an assayer in the government assay office. These two set up business as Kellogg & Richter December 19, 1853.

When the U. S. Assay Office ceased operations a period ensued during which no private firm was striking gold. The new San Francisco branch mint did not produce coins for some months after Curtis & Perry took the contract for the government (Ward having died). The lack of coin was again keenly felt by businessmen who petitioned Kellogg & Richter to "supply the vacuum" by issuing private coin. Their plea was soon answered, for on February 9, 1854, Kellogg & Co. placed their first twenty-dollar piece in circulation.

The firm dissolved late in 1854 and reorganized as Kellogg & Humbert. The latter partner was Augustus Humbert, for some time identified as U.S. Assayer of Gold in California. Regardless of the fact that the branch mint was

[298]

KELLOGG & COMPANY

then producing coins, Kellogg & Humbert issued $20 coins in 1855 in a quantity greater than before.

	Fine	V. Fine	E. Fine	A. Unc.	Unc.
1854 TWENTY D.	$1,500	$2,100	$3,700	$4,750	$11,000

The 1855 twenty-dollar piece is similar to that dated 1854. The letters on the reverse side are larger and the arrows longer on one 1854 variety. There are several die varieties of both issues.

1855 TWENTY D.	1,500	2,200	3,800	5,000	13,500

In 1855 Ferdinand Grüner cut the dies for a round format $50 gold coin for Kellogg & Co., but coinage seems to have been limited to presentation pieces. Only 10 to 12 pieces are known to exist. A "commemorative restrike" was made in 2001 using transfer dies made from the original and gold recovered from the S.S. Central America. These pieces have the inscription S. S. CENTRAL AMERICA GOLD, C.H.S. on the reverse ribbon.

	Proof
1855 FIFTY DOLLS.	$160,000

OREGON EXCHANGE COMPANY
Oregon City, 1849
THE BEAVER COINS OF OREGON

Upon the discovery of gold in California there was a great exodus of settlers who joined in the hunt for the precious metal. Soon returning gold seekers offered their gold dust, which became the accepted medium of exchange. As in other western areas of that time, the uncertain qualities of the gold and weighing devices tended to irk the tradespeople, and petitions were made to the legislature for a standard gold coin issue.

On February 16, 1849, the legislature passed an act providing for a mint and specified five- and ten-dollar gold coins without alloy. Oregon City, the largest city in the territory with a population of about 1,000, was designated as the location for the mint. At the time this act was passed, Oregon had been brought into the United States as a territory by act of Congress. When the new governor arrived March second, he declared the coinage act unconstitutional.

The public-spirited people, however, continued to work for a convenient medium of exchange and soon took matters into their own hands by starting a private mint. Eight men of affairs whose names were Kilborne, Magruder, Taylor, Abernethy, Willson, Rector, Campbell and Smith set up the Oregon Exchange Company.

The coins struck were of virgin gold as specified in the original act. Ten-dollar dies were made later, and were of finer design and workmanship.

	Fine	V. Fine	E. Fine	A. Unc.	Unc.
1849 5 D..........................(6,000 minted)	$11,000	$19,000	$27,500	$38,500	—

	Fine	V. Fine	E. Fine	A. Unc.	Unc.
1849 TEN D......................(2,850 minted)	27,500	45,000	60,000	87,000	—

MORMON GOLD PIECES
Salt Lake City, Utah 1849-1860

The first name given to the organized Mormon Territory was the "State of Deseret," the last word meaning "honey bee." The beehive, which is shown on the reverse of the five-dollar 1860 piece, was a favorite device of the followers of Joseph Smith and Brigham Young. The clasped hands appear on most Mormon coins and exemplify strength in unity. "Holiness to the Lord" was an inscription frequently used.

MORMON GOLD PIECES

Brigham Young was the instigator of the coinage system and personally supervised the mint which was housed in a little adobe building in Salt Lake City. The mint was inaugurated late in 1849 as a public convenience.

	Fine	V. Fine	E. Fine	A. Unc.	Unc.
1849 TWO AND HALF DO	$6,000	$9,000	$14,000	$21,000	$32,000
1849 FIVE DOLLARS	4,750	8,250	11,500	16,500	27,500

	Fine	V. Fine
1849 TEN DOLLARS	$90,000	$125,000

	Fine	V. Fine	E. Fine
1849 TWENTY DOLLARS	$30,000	$55,000	$80,000

The Mormon twenty-dollar piece was the first of that denomination to be coined in this country.

1850 FIVE DOLLARS	
Fine	$5,250
V. Fine	9,000
Ex. Fine	12,000
A. Unc.	18,000
Unc.	28,000

MORMON GOLD PIECES

1860 5D

Fine	$8,000
V. Fine	15,000
Ex. Fine	20,000
A. Unc.	26,000
Unc.	36,000

COLORADO GOLD PIECES
Clark, Gruber & Co. — Denver 1860-1861

Clark, Gruber and Co. was a well-known private minting firm in Denver, Colorado, in the early sixties.

	Fine	V. Fine	E. Fine	A. Unc.	Unc.
1860 2½ D	$1,100	$1,500	$2,700	$3,700	$9,000
1860 5D	1,300	1,900	2,900	4,000	9,500

1860 TEN D	3,500	5,500	9,000	13,000	23,000
1860 TWENTY D	25,000	40,000	65,000	95,000	—

The $2.50 and five-dollar pieces of 1861 follow closely the designs of the 1860 issues. The main difference is found in the legends. The reverse side now has CLARK GRUBER & CO. DENVER. PIKES PEAK is on the coronet of Liberty.

1861 2½ D	1,000	1,600	3,000	5,000	10,000
1861 FIVE D	1,300	2,000	3,400	5,500	18,000
1861 TEN D	1,400	2,000	3,500	6,500	16,000

COLORADO GOLD PIECES

	Fine	V. Fine	E. Fine	A. Unc.	Unc.
1861 TWENTY D	$5,000	$9,000	$20,000	$35,000	$80,000

JOHN PARSONS & COMPANY
Tarryall Mines — Colorado 1861

Very little is known regarding the mint of John Parsons and Co., although it is reasonably certain that it operated in the South Park section of Park County Colorado near the original town of Tarryall, in the summer of 1861.

PIKES PEAK GOLD

	V. Fine
(1861) Undated $2^1/_2$ D	$85,000
(1861) Undated FIVE D...	100,000

J. J. CONWAY & COMPANY
Georgia Gulch, Colorado, 1861

Records show that the Conway Mint operated for a short while in 1861. As in all gold mining areas the value of gold dust caused disagreement among the merchants and the miners. The firm of J. J. Conway & Co. solved this difficulty by bringing out its gold pieces in August, 1861.

(1861) Undated $2^1/_2$ DOLL'S...	57,500
(1861) Undated FIVE DOLLARS	90,000
(1861) Undated FIVE DOLLARS, Similar.	
Variety without numeral 5 on reverse	55,000

J.J. CONWAY & COMPANY

(1861) Undated
    TEN DOLLARS ....   —

CALIFORNIA SMALL DENOMINATION GOLD

There was a scarcity of small coins during the California gold rush and starting in 1852, quarter, half and dollar pieces were privately minted from native gold to alleviate the shortage. The need and acceptability of these pieces declined after 1856 and they then became popular as souvenirs. Private coinage became illegal with passage of the Act of 1864, but production continued until 1882 before the law was enforced.

The designs of the early issues were similar to those of the larger territorials. Later issues showed greater variety, had lower intrinsic value, and were often struck from highly polished dies giving prooflike surfaces. In contrast to the tokens, which lack the denomination and were often back dated, California small denomination gold was mostly made in the year indicated (1852-1882). Authentic pieces have CENTS, DOLLAR, or an abbreviation thereof on the reverse.

A total of about 10,000 pieces still exist; of these nearly 500 different varieties have been identified, many of them very rare. Although some of the early pieces are machine made with reeded edges, most are hand struck and have crude designs and incomplete features. Many bear the maker's initials: D, DN, GL, DERIB, N, NR, L, H, G, GG, FD, or DERI. Major types are listed below; values are for the commonest varieties of each type. The tokens are generally much less valuable. Modern restrikes and replicas (which often have a bear in the design) have no numismatic value.

Values are only for genuine coins with the denomination on the reverse expressed as: CENTS, DOL., DOLL., *or* DOLLAR.

QUARTER DOLLAR — OCTAGONAL

	EF-40	AU-50	MS-60
Large Liberty Head:			
Value and date in wreath	$130.00	$200.00	$250.00
Value and date in beaded circle	135.00	225.00	300.00
Value and CAL in wreath	115.00	150.00	225.00
Small Liberty Head:			
Value and date in wreath	115.00	150.00	225.00
Value and date in beaded circle	120.00	160.00	235.00
Value in shield, date in wreath	120.00	160.00	250.00
Value and CAL in wreath	120.00	175.00	300.00
Large Indian Head:			
Value in wreath	170.00	225.00	325.00
Value and CAL in wreath	135.00	200.00	300.00
Small Indian Head:			
Value in wreath	160.00	215.00	375.00
Value and CAL in wreath	375.00	475.00	675.00
Washington Head 1872:			
Value and CAL in wreath	400.00	600.00	925.00

CALIFORNIA SMALL DENOMINATION GOLD
QUARTER DOLLAR — ROUND

	EF-40	AU-50	MS-60
Large Liberty Head:			
Value and date in wreath	$120.00	$200.00	$275.00
Value and CAL in wreath	115.00	170.00	250.00
25 CENTS in wreath		Rare	
Small Liberty Head:			
Value and date in wreath	125.00	200.00	300.00
Value in shield, date in wreath	130.00	225.00	375.00
Value and CAL in wreath	125.00	200.00	250.00
Large Indian Head:			
Value in wreath	275.00	400.00	600.00
Value and CAL in wreath	235.00	325.00	475.00
Small Indian Head:			
Value in wreath	125.00	200.00	350.00
Value and CAL in wreath	250.00	375.00	600.00
Washington Head 1872:			
Value and CAL in wreath	450.00	650.00	900.00

HALF DOLLAR — OCTAGONAL

	EF-40	AU-50	MS-60
Large Liberty Head:			
Value and date in wreath	165.00	250.00	400.00
Value and date in beaded circle	110.00	150.00	275.00
Value and CAL in wreath	150.00	275.00	400.00
Legend surrounds wreath	285.00	450.00	650.00
Small Liberty Head:			
Value and date in wreath	135.00	230.00	375.00
Value and CAL in wreath	120.00	210.00	300.00
Small eagle with rays	750.00	950.00	1,650
Large eagle with raised wings	750.00	950.00	1,650
Large Indian Head:			
Value in wreath	150.00	275.00	400.00
Value and CAL in wreath	130.00	250.00	375.00
Small Indian Head:			
Value in wreath	175.00	300.00	450.00
Value and CAL in wreath	335.00	450.00	600.00

HALF DOLLAR — ROUND

	EF-40	AU-50	MS-60
Liberty Head:			
Value and date in wreath	125.00	185.00	300.00
Value and CAL in wreath	140.00	225.00	350.00
CALIFORNIA GOLD around wreath	150.00	235.00	375.00
Large Indian Head:			
Value in wreath	135.00	200.00	325.00
Value and CAL in wreath	120.00	175.00	275.00
Small Indian Head:			
Value in wreath	150.00	225.00	350.00
Value and CAL in wreath	130.00	200.00	300.00

DOLLAR — OCTAGONAL

	EF-40	AU-50	MS-60
Liberty Head:			
Value and date in wreath	300.00	425.00	700.00
Value in beaded circle	325.00	450.00	750.00
Legend around wreath	325.00	500.00	900.00
Large eagle	1,450	2,250	3,400
Large Indian Head:			
Value and date in wreath	425.00	700.00	1,150
Value in wreath	475.00	750.00	1,300
Small Indian Head:			
Value and CAL in wreath	475.00	750.00	1,300

CALIFORNIA SMALL DENOMINATION GOLD
DOLLAR — ROUND

	EF-40	AU-50	MS-60
Liberty Head:			
Value and date in wreath	$1,000	$1,400	$2,400
Date beneath head	1,500	2,000	3,200
Indian Head:			
Date beneath head	1,200	1,700	3,000

See bibliography on page 283.

CALIFORNIA GOLD INGOT BARS

During the Gold Rush era, gold coins, ingots, and "dust" were sent by steamship from San Francisco to other ports, most importantly to New York City and London, where the gold was sold or, in some instances, sent to mints for conversion into coins. The typical procedure in the mid-1850s was to send the gold by steamship from San Francisco to Panama, where it was sent across 48 miles of land on the Panama Railroad, then loaded aboard another ship at the town of Aspinwall on the Atlantic side. On September 12, 1857, the *S.S. Central America*, en route from Aspinwall to New York City with over 475 passengers, over 100 crew members, and an estimated $1.6 million in gold (in an era in which pure gold was valued at $20.67 per ounce) was lost at sea. Miraculously, over 150 people, including all but one of the women and children, were rescued by passing ships. The *Central America* went to the bottom of the Atlantic Ocean off the Carolina coast.

In the 1980s a group of researchers in Ohio formed the Columbus-America Discovery Group and secured financing to search for the long-lost ship. After much study and many explorations, the wreck of the *Central America* was discovered 7,200 feet below the surface. Tommy Thompson, Bob Evans, and others from C-ADG used the robotic *Nemo*, a sophisticated device weighing several tons, to photograph the wreck and to carefully bring to the surface many artifacts. A king's ransom in gold ingots was found along with over 7,500 coins, the last mostly consisting of Mint State 1857-S double eagles.

The over 500 gold ingots furnished a unique opportunity to study specimens that, after conservation, were essentially in the same condition as they were in 1857. These bore the imprints of five different California assayers who operated seven offices. With few exceptions, each ingot bears individual stamps indicating its maker, a serial number, the weight in ounces, the fineness (expressed in thousandths, such as 784 indicating 784/1000th pure gold), and the 1857 value in dollars. The smallest bar found was issued by Blake & Co., weighed 4.95 ounces, was 795 fine, and was stamped with a value of $81.34. The largest ingot, dubbed the "Eureka" bar, bore the imprint of Kellogg & Humbert, and was stamped with a weight of 933.94 ounces, 903 fine, and a value of $17,433.57.

Blake & Co., Sacramento, California: From December 28, 1855, to May 1858, Blake & Co. was operated by Gorham Blake and W.R. Waters. • 34 ingots recovered. Serial numbers in the 5,100 and 5,200 series. Lowest weight and value: 4.95 ounces, $81.34. Highest weight and value: 157.40 ounces, $2,655.05. These bars have beveled or "dressed" edges and may have seen limited use in California commerce.

Harris, Marchand & Co., Sacramento and Marysville: Founded in Sacramento in 1855 by Harvey Harris and Desiré Marchand, with Charles L. Farrington as the "& Co." The Marysville office was opened in January 1856. Serial numbers in the 6,000 series are attributed to Sacramento, comprising 36 bars, and a single bar in the 7,000 series (7095) is attributed to Marysville. The Marchand bars each have a circular coin-style counterstamp on the face. Lowest weight and value (Sacramento): 9.87 ounces, $158.53. Highest weight and value (Sacramento): 295.20 ounces, $5,351.73. • Unique Marysville bar: 174.04 ounces, $3,389.06.

Henry Hentsch, San Francisco: Henstch, a Swiss, was an entrepreneur involved in banking, real estate, assaying, and other ventures. In February 1856, he opened an assay office as an annex to his bank. It is likely that many of his ingots were exported to Europe, where he had extensive banking connections. • 33 ingots recovered. Lowest weight and value: 12.52 ounces, $251.82. Highest weight and value: 238.84 ounces, $4,458.35.

Justh & Hunter, San Francisco and Marysville: Emanuel Justh, a Hungarian, was a lithographer in San Francisco in the early 1850s. In 1854-5 he worked as assistant assayer at the San Francisco Mint. Solomon Hillen Hunter came to California from Baltimore. The Justh & Hunter partnership was announced in May 1855. • Although study is continuing, the 60 ingots in the 4,000 series are tentatively attributed to San Francisco, and the 26 ingots in the 9,000 series are attributed to Marysville. • Lowest weight and value (San Francisco): 5.24 ounces, $92.18. Highest weight and value (San Francisco): 866.19 ounces, $15,971.93. • Lowest weight and value (Marysville): 19.34 ounces, $356.21. Highest weight and value (Marysville): 464.65 ounces, $8,759.90.

Kellogg & Humbert, San Francisco: John Glover Kellogg and Augustus Humbert, two of the most famous names in the minting of California gold coins, formed the partnership of Kellogg & Humbert in spring 1855. The firm was one of the most active of all California assayers during the mid-1850s. • 346 ingots recovered, constituting the majority of those found. • Lowest weight and value: 5.71 ounces, $101.03. Highest weight and value: 933.94 ounces, $17,433.57.

A selection of gold ingots from the S.S. *Central America* treasure (with an 1857-S $20 double eagle shown for scale, near lower left). • 1: In background: Harris, Marchand & Co., Marysville office, serial number 7095, 174.04 ounces, 942 fine, $3,389.06 (all values as stamped in 1857) • 2: Standing, back left: Henry Hentsch, San Francisco, serial number 3120, 61.93 ounces, 886 fine, $1,134.26 • 3: Next to preceding, vertical: Kellogg & Humbert, San Francisco, serial number 215, 944 fine, $1,045.96 • Next to preceding, small and near center: Blake & Co., Sacramento, 19.30 ounces, 946 fine, $297.42 • In front of preceding: Another Blake & Co. ingot, rectangular "Twix Bar" shape, serial number 5216, 915 fine, $266.12 • To right of both Blake ingots: Justh & Hunter, Marysville office, serial number 9440, 41.79 ounces, $761.07 • Far right: Justh & Hunter, San Francisco office, serial number 4243, 51.98 ounces, 916 fine, $984.27 • Lower right foreground: Harris, Marchand & Co., Sacramento office, serial number 6514, 35.33 ounces, 807 fine, $589.38 • Lower right, near $20: Harris, Marchand & Co., Sacramento office, serial number 6486, 12.64 ounces, 950 fine, $245.00.

CIVIL WAR TOKENS — 1861-1864

Civil War Tokens are generally divided into two groups: tradesmen's tokens, and anonymously issued pieces with political or patriotic themes. They came into existence only because of the scarcity of government coins and disappeared as soon as the bronze coins of 1864 met the public demand for small copper change.

From the outset of the Civil War, government cents were insufficient in number, widely hoarded and worth a premium over all other currencies. As a result of this scarcity of cent pieces, private copper coins were issued by many individuals. Their wide circulation was made possible by the scarcity of copper-nickel cents and the public dislike of fractional paper money.

The tradesmen's tokens were issued by various firms to provide change and advertise the dealers' wares. They usually bore an implied or an explicit promise of redemption in goods or money. The second type was simply unauthorized substitutes for government coins, produced at a profit by private manufacturers and put into general circulation through various agencies.

These tokens are of great variety in composition and design. A number were more or less faithful imitations of the copper-nickel cent. A few of this type have the word "NOT" in very small letters above the words "ONE CENT."

Many pieces, especially of the tradesmen token type, were individual in device and size, representing any caprice of design or slogan that appealed to the maker. Some were political or patriotic in character, carrying the likeness of some military leader such as McClellan or bearing such inscriptions as "Millions for contractors, not one cent for the widows." An estimated 50,000,000 or more of these pieces were issued. Approximately 10,000 different varieties have been recorded.

The legal status of the Civil War Tokens was uncertain. Mint Director Pollock thought they were illegal; however, there was no law prohibiting the issue of tradesmen's tokens or of private coins not in imitation of United States coins. A law was passed April 22, 1864 prohibiting the issue of any one or two-cent coins, tokens, or devices for use as money, and on June 8 another law was passed which abolished private coinage of every kind.

Values shown are for the most common tokens in each category.

	Fine	V. Fine	E.Fine	Unc.
Copper or Brass Tokens	$10.00	$11.00	$15.00	$36.00
Nickel or German Silver Tokens	27.50	42.00	60.00	110.00
White Metal Tokens	32.00	50.00	70.00	125.00
Copper-Nickel Tokens	40.00	57.50	80.00	150.00
Silver Tokens	100.00	170.00	225.00	450.00

BIBLIOGRAPHY

Fuld, George and Melvin. *U.S. Civil War Store Cards.* Lawrence, MA, 1975.

CONFEDERATE STATES OF AMERICA
CONFEDERATE 1861 HALF DOLLAR

The half dollar struck by the Confederacy was unknown to collectors until 1879. A specimen of the coin and the Confederate die were found in the possession of Dr. B. F. Taylor of New Orleans. Mr. E. Mason, Jr. of Philadelphia purchased Dr. Taylor's specimen and the reverse die and later sold them to J. W. Scott and Company of New York.

CONFEDERATE STATES OF AMERICA — 1861

Five hundred genuine 1861 half dollars from the New Orleans mint were acquired by J. W. Scott and Company. The reverses were smoothed off and then restamped with the Confederate die. These are known as restrikes, and usually have slightly flattened obverses.

According to records only four originals were struck. These were made on a hand press. Original silver half dollar planchets were used, as well as the original obverse die. One of the coins was given to the Secretary of the Confederacy Memminger who passed it on to President Jefferson Davis for his approval. Another was given to Prof. J. L. Riddell of the University of Louisiana. Dr. E. Ames of New Orleans received a third specimen, the last being kept by Chief Coiner B. F. Taylor, who sold it later as mentioned above.

Lack of bullion prevented the Confederate government from proceeding with any coinage plans that might have been made.

J. W. Scott struck some tokens in white metal using the Confederate reverse die and a special die bearing the inscription:
4 ORIGINALS STRUCK BY ORDER OF C. S. A. IN NEW ORLEANS 1861 ******* REV. SAME AS U.S. (FROM ORIGINAL DIE SCOTT)

	Confederate Reverse	Scott Obverse

	Quan. Minted	V. Fine	E. Fine	Unc.
1861 HALF DOL. (Ex. Rare)	4	—	—	—
1861 HALF DOL. Restrike	500	$3,000	$4,500	$7,000
1861 Scott Token obverse. Confederate reverse	500	1,000	1,600	3,000

THE CONFEDERATE CENT

An order to make cents for the Confederacy was placed with Mr. Robert Lovett Jr., an engraver and die-sinker of Philadelphia, through a jewelry firm of that city. Fearing arrest by the United States government for giving assistance to the enemy, Mr. Lovett decided against delivering the coins to the Confederate government and hid the coins and dies in his cellar.

The original dies were later purchased by Capt. John W. Haseltine who made restrikes from the dies. In 1960 the dies were copied and additional pieces made by Robert Bashlow. These show die cracks and rust marks that distinguish them from earlier copies. They have very little numismatic value.

1861 Cent original (copper-nickel)	Unc.	12	$32,000
1861 Cent restrike (copper)	Proof	55	7,250
1861 Cent restrike (gold)	Proof	7	27,500
1861 Cent restrike (silver)	Proof	12	8,500

LESHER REFERENDUM DOLLARS

Coined by Joseph Lesher in 1900 and 1901 at Victor, Colorado, these private tokens were used in trade to some extent, and stocked by various merchants who redeemed them in goods. Coins were numbered and a blank space left at bottom of 1901 issues, in which were stamped names of businessmen who bought them. All are quite rare; many varieties are extremely rare. Composition is .950 fine silver alloyed with copper.

	Ex. Fine	A. Unc.	Unc.
1900 First type, no business name	$1,350	$1,900	$3,250
1900 A.B. Bumstead, with or without scrolls	900.00	1,250	2,000
1900 Bank type	8,500	—	—
1901 Imprint type, no name	1,000	1,500	2,300
1901 Imprint type, with name (as listed below)			
Boyd Park, Slusher	1,250	1,600	2,500
Mullen	2,100	3,500	4,750
Cohen, Klein	3,000	4,500	—
Alexander	3,750	5,500	—
White	4,500	6,250	—
Goodspeeds, Nelson	5,500	8,000	—
A.W. Clark	(unique)		

FEUCHTWANGER TOKENS

Dr. Lewis Feuchtwanger produced a metal that was really a variety of German silver consisting of nickel, copper and some zinc. He suggested as early as 1837 to Congress that his metal be substituted for copper, and made one-cent and three-cent trial pieces that circulated freely during the coin shortage of 1836-1844.

	Fine	E. Fine	A. Unc.	Unc.
1837 One Cent, Eagle	$75.00	$185.00	$275.00	$385.00
1837 Three-Cent, N.Y. Coat of Arms	300.00	800.00	1,500	2,750
1837 Three-Cent, Eagle	500.00	1,750	3,000	4,800
1864 Three-Cent, Eagle	400.00	1,000	2,200	3,500

COINS AND TOKENS OF HAWAII

There are only five official coins that were issued by the Kingdom of Hawaii. These include the 1847 cent issued by King Kamehameha III and the 1883 silver dimes, quarters, halves and dollars of King Kalakaua I which bear his portrait. The 1883 eighth dollar is a pattern, while the 1881 five cent piece was an unofficial issue. After Hawaii became a U.S. Territory in 1900, the legal tender status of these coins was removed and most were withdrawn and melted. Owing to a lack of small change on the islands, the early tokens were widely accepted and circulated freely.

One Cent 1847   Ten Cents 1883

	Quan. Minted	Fine	V. Fine	E. Fine	MS-60	MS-63	Proof
1847 Cent	100,000	$225.00	$300.00	$500.00	$850.00	$1,950	
1881 Five Cents		2,000	3,500	6,500	9,000	15,000	—
1883 Ten Cents	(26) 250,000	50.00	90.00	225.00	900.00	1,500	$8,000
1883 Eighth Dollar ($12^1/_2$ c)	(20)						35,000
1883 Quarter Dollar	(26) 500,000	45.00	75.00	100.00	200.00	350.00	9,000
1883 Half Dollar	(26) 700,000	80.00	125.00	225.00	900.00	1,800	11,000
1883 Dollar	(26) 500,000	250.00	350.00	650.00	3,500	8,500	15,000

HAWAIIAN TOKENS

Thomas Hobron Token 1879   Haiku Plantation 1882

Wailuku Plantation 1871   Wailuku Plantation 1880

	Fine	V. Fine	E. Fine
Waterhouse Token 1860. Title of Kamehameha IV	$650.00	$1,200	$2,500
Wailuku Plantation Token, $12^1/_2$ (cents) 1871	300.00	500.00	900.00
Wailuku Plantation Token, 1 Real 1880	250.00	400.00	800.00
Wailuku Plantation Token, Half Real 1871 and 1880	500.00	800.00	1,400
Thomas Hobron Token, $12^1/_2$ (cents) 1879	250.00	350.00	500.00
Haiku Plantation Token, One Real 1882	250.00	450.00	650.00

	Fine	V. Fine	E. Fine
Grove Ranch Plantation Token, 12½ (cents) 1886	$450.00	$550.00	$900.00
Grove Ranch Plantation Token, 12½ (cents) 1887	600.00	900.00	1,500
Kahului Railroad Token, 10 cents 1891	500.00	750.00	1,300
Kahului Railroad Token, 15 cents 1891	500.00	750.00	1,300
Kahului Railroad Token, 20 cents 1891	500.00	750.00	1,300
Kahului Railroad Token, 25 cents 1891	500.00	750.00	1,300
Kahului Railroad Token, 35 cents 1891	500.00	750.00	1,300
Kahului Railroad Token, 75 cents 1891	500.00	750.00	1,300

ALASKA RURAL REHABILITATION CORPORATION TOKENS OF 1935

These tokens were issued by the U. S. Government for the use of the colonists of the Matanuska Valley Colonization Project to supply them with much needed Federal aid. They were redeemable only at the ARRC stores. The "Bingles," as they were called, were in use only about six months during 1935-1936 after which they were redeemed for regular U. S. money and destroyed. They were issued on a basis of family dependents. Each token is the size of the corresponding U. S. coin with the exception of the one cent piece which is octagonal. The design is the same on both sides of each denomination.

Aluminum

Quan. Minted	E. Fine	Unc.	Quan. Minted	E. Fine	Unc.
1c 5,000	$25.00	$50.00	25c 3,000	$35.00	$60.00
5c 5,000	25.00	50.00	50c 2,500	50.00	90.00
10c 5,000	25.00	50.00	$1.00 2,500	75.00	140.00

Brass

$5.00 1,000	100.00	175.00	$10.00 1,000	150.00	225.00

UNITED STATES COINAGE FOR THE PHILIPPINES

The Philippine Islands were acquired by the United States in 1899 as part of a treaty with Spain ending the Spanish-American War of the previous year. A military government was replaced with a civil administration in 1901, and one of its first tasks was to sponsor a new coinage that was compatible with the old Spanish issues, yet was also legally exchangeable for American money at the rate of two Philippine pesos to the U.S. dollar.

The resulting coins were introduced in 1903 and bear the identities of both the Philippines (Filipinas in Spanish) and the United States of America. Following Spanish custom, the peso was divided into 100 centavos. A dollar-size coin valued at one peso was the principal issue in this series, but silver fractions were also minted in values of 50, 20 and 10 centavos. Minor coins included the copper-nickel five-cent piece, as well as one-centavo and half-centavo coins of bronze.

A rise in the price of silver forced the reduction of the fineness and weight for each silver denomination beginning in 1907, and subsequent issues are smaller in diameter. The smaller size of the new silver issues led to confusion between the silver 20-centavo piece and the copper-nickel five-centavo piece resulting in a mis-matching of dies for these two denominations in 1918 and again in 1928. A solution was found by reducing the diameter of the five-centavo piece beginning in 1930.

In 1935 the Commonwealth of the Philippines was established by an act of Congress, and a three-piece set of commemorative coins was issued the following year to mark this transition. Despite the popularity of United States commemoratives at that time, these sets sold poorly, and thousands remained within the Philippine Treasury at the onset of World War II. The commonwealth arms was adapted to all circulating issues beginning in 1937.

The advance on the Philippines by Japanese forces in 1942 prompted removal of much of the Treasury's bullion to the United States. More than 15 million pesos worth of silver remained, mostly in the form of one-peso pieces of 1907-1912 and the ill-fated 1936 commemoratives. These coins were hastily crated and dumped into Manila's Caballo Bay to prevent their capture. Partially recovered after the war, these coins were badly corroded from their exposure to salt water, adding further to the scarcity of high grade pre-war silver coins.

The Philippines became became an independent republic on July 4, 1946, ending a historic and colorful chapter in U.S. history and numismatics.

PHILIPPINES UNDER SOVEREIGNTY OF THE U.S.

Bronze Coinage

Half Centavo

	Quan. Minted	V. Fine	E. Fine	MS-60	MS-63
1903	12,084,000	$1.00	$2.25	$12.00	$20.00
1903 Proof	(2,558)			35.00	60.00
1904	5,654,000	1.25	3.00	15.00	30.00
1904 Proof	(1,355)			40.00	75.00
1905 Proof only	(471)		60.00	110.00	200.00
1906 Proof only	(500)		45.00	75.00	150.00
1908 Proof only	(500)		45.00	75.00	150.00

PHILIPPINES UNDER SOVEREIGNTY OF THE U.S.

Philippine coins dated from 1903 to 1919 were struck at the Philadelphia and San Francisco Mints. Those dated after 1920 were made in Manila. During World War II coins of 1944 and 1945 were made at Philadelphia, Denver and San Francisco.

Price Contributors to the Philippine Listings
Lyman Allen, Gary G. Allison, Raymond Czahor, Robert Mish.

Bronze Coinage

One Centavo

	Quan. Minted	V. Fine	E. Fine	MS-60	MS-63
1903	10,790,000	$1.00	$2.50	$15.00	$25.00
1903 Proof	(2,558)			30.00	60.00
1904	17,040,400	1.00	3.00	15.00	25.00
1904 Proof	(1,355)			40.00	70.00
1905	10,000,000	1.50	3.00	20.00	30.00
1905 Proof	(471)		60.00	125.00	200.00
1906 Proof only	(500)		45.00	75.00	150.00
1908 Proof only	(500)		45.00	75.00	150.00
1908S	2,187,000	4.00	8.00	35.00	55.00
1909S	1,737,612	12.50	25.00	90.00	125.00
1910S	2,700,000	4.00	8.00	70.00	125.00
1911S	4,803,000	3.00	6.00	50.00	100.00
1912S	3,001,000	5.00	10.00	60.00	100.00
1913S	5,000,000	2.00	5.00	30.00	45.00
1914S	5,000,500	2.00	5.00	30.00	45.00
1915S	2,500,000	40.00	90.00	225.00	425.00
1916S	4,330,000	10.00	25.00	100.00	150.00
1917S	7,070,000	3.00	10.00	35.00	65.00
1918S	11,660,000	3.00	5.00	25.00	40.00
1918S Large S		100.00	200.00	400.00	700.00
1919S	4,540,000	2.00	5.00	30.00	70.00
1920S	2,500,000	12.00	18.00	100.00	200.00
1920	3,552,259	2.00	9.00	40.00	90.00
1921	7,282,673	2.00	7.00	35.00	60.00
1922	3,519,100	2.00	6.00	35.00	60.00
1925M	9,325,000	2.00	4.00	35.00	50.00
1926M	9,000,000	2.00	4.00	35.00	50.00
1927M	9,270,000	1.50	3.50	25.00	35.00
1928M	9,150,000	1.50	3.00	25.00	35.00
1929M	5,657,161	3.00	7.50	35.00	50.00
1930M	5,577,000	1.50	3.00	25.00	45.00
1931M	5,659,355	1.50	4.00	30.00	50.00
1932M	4,000,000	3.00	6.00	35.00	60.00
1933M	8,392,692	1.50	3.00	25.00	40.00
1934M	3,179,000	1.50	4.00	30.00	50.00
1936M	17,455,463	1.00	3.00	25.00	35.00

PHILIPPINES UNDER SOVEREIGNTY OF THE U.S.
Copper-Nickel Coinage

Large Size Five Centavos
1903-28

Reduced Size Five Centavos
1930-35

	Quan. Minted	V. Fine	E. Fine	MS-60	MS-63
1903	8,910,000	$1.00	$3.00	$18.00	$25.00
1903 Proof	(2,558)			45.00	75.00
1904	1,075,000	2.00	4.00	20.00	35.00
1904 Proof	(1,075)			50.00	100.00
1905 Proof only	(471)		75.00	125.00	200.00
1906 Proof only	(500)		60.00	110.00	175.00
1908 Proof only	(500)		60.00	110.00	175.00
1916S	300,000	50.00	75.00	400.00	600.00
1917S	2,300,000	4.00	10.00	90.00	150.00
1918S	2,780,000	3.00	5.00	50.00	125.00
1918S Mule. Small date reverse of 20 Centavos		400.00	1,000	3,500	5,000
1919S	1,220,000	6.00	15.00	120.00	175.00
1920	1,421,078	6.00	15.00	120.00	175.00
1921	2,131,529	6.00	15.00	100.00	190.00
1925M	1,000,000	20.00	50.00	125.00	200.00
1926M	1,200,000	7.00	15.00	75.00	125.00
1927M	1,000,000	6.00	12.00	60.00	80.00
1928M	1,000,000	6.00	12.00	75.00	125.00
1930M	2,905,182	2.50	5.00	35.00	65.00
1931M	3,476,790	2.50	5.00	45.00	75.00
1932M	3,955,861	2.00	4.00	40.00	65.00
1934M	2,153,729	3.00	5.00	60.00	110.00
1935M	2,754,000	2.50	5.00	65.00	90.00

Silver Coinage

Large Size Ten Centavos
1903-06

Reduced Size Ten Centavos
1907-35

1903	5,102,658	2.25	5.00	30.00	50.00
1903 Proof	(2,558)			50.00	90.00
1903S	1,200,000	12.50	30.00	150.00	275.00
1904	10,000	18.00	30.00	80.00	100.00
1904 Proof	(1,355)			75.00	135.00
1904S	5,040,000	2.25	4.00	40.00	60.00
1905 Proof only	(471)		85.00	140.00	225.00
1906 Proof only	(500)		75.00	110.00	175.00

PHILIPPINES UNDER SOVEREIGNTY OF THE U.S.

	Quan. Minted	V. Fine	E. Fine	MS-60	MS-63
1907	1,500,781	$3.00	$5.00	$45.00	$70.00
1907 S	4,930,000	2.25	3.50	35.00	60.00
1908 Proof only	(500)		75.00	110.00	175.00
1908S	3,363,911	2.00	4.00	45.00	65.00
1909S	312,199	25.00	50.00	300.00	475.00
1911S	1,000,505	4.00	9.00	60.00	100.00
1912S	1,010,000	4.00	9.00	80.00	150.00
1913S	1,360,693	4.00	9.00	70.00	100.00
1914S	1,180,000	8.00	15.00	140.00	200.00
1915S	450,000	15.00	40.00	250.00	425.00
1917S	5,991,148	2.00	3.00	30.00	60.00
1918S	8,420,000	1.50	2.50	25.00	40.00
1919S	1,630,000	2.00	4.00	40.00	75.00
1920	520,000	5.00	12.00	75.00	140.00
1921	3,863,038	1.50	3.00	22.00	40.00
1929M	1,000,000	1.50	3.00	20.00	40.00
1935M	1,280,000	1.50	2.50	20.00	30.00

Large Size Twenty Centavos
1903-06

Reduced Size Twenty Centavos
1907-29

	Quan. Minted	V. Fine	E. Fine	MS-60	MS-63
1903	5,350,231	3.50	6.00	35.00	75.00
1903 Proof	(2,558)		75.00		125.00
1903S	150,080	25.00	50.00	300.00	475.00
1904	10,000	30.00	45.00	90.00	150.00
1904 Proof	(1,355)		80.00		150.00
1904S	2,060,000	4.00	7.00	60.00	110.00
1905 Proof only	(471)		125.00	190.00	300.00
1905S	420,000	12.00	30.00	125.00	175.00
1906 Proof only	(500)		100.00	160.00	225.00
1907	1,250,651	3.00	16.00	80.00	125.00
1907S	3,165,000	3.00	5.00	60.00	75.00
1908 Proof only	(500)		100.00	160.00	225.00
1908S	1,535,000	3.00	5.00	50.00	75.00
1909S	450,000	15.00	45.00	300.00	450.00
1910S	500,259	15.00	45.00	425.00	550.00
1911S	505,000	12.00	30.00	300.00	400.00
1912S	750,000	8.00	20.00	175.00	250.00
1913S	948,565	6.00	15.00	125.00	200.00
1914S	795,000	4.00	12.00	85.00	150.00
1915S	655,000	12.00	45.00	250.00	375.00
1916S	1,435,000	6.00	15.00	90.00	150.00
1917S	3,150,655	3.00	5.00	35.00	60.00
1918S	5,560,000	3.00	4.00	30.00	50.00
1919S	850,000	4.00	6.00	50.00	80.00
1920	1,045,415	4.00	10.00	100.00	150.00
1921	1,842,631	2.00	4.00	40.00	60.00
1928M Mule. Large date rev. of 5 Centavos	100,000	15.00	50.00	300.00	400.00
1929M	1,970,000	2.00	3.50	30.00	40.00

PHILIPPINES UNDER SOVEREIGNTY OF THE U.S.

Large Size Fifty Centavos **1903-06**

	Quan. Minted	V. Fine	E. Fine	MS-60	MS-63
1903	3,099,061	$8.00	$13.00	$50.00	$110.00
1903 Proof	(2,558)			90.00	165.00
1903S			(rare)		
1904	10,000	35.00	45.00	120.00	200.00
1904 Proof	(1,355)			120.00	180.00
1904S	2,160,00	10.00	17.50	100.00	150.00
1905 Proof only	(471)		150.00	275.00	400.00
1905S	852,000	15.00	35.00	250.00	550.00
1906 Proof only	(500)		125.00	250.00	350.00

Reduced Size Fifty Centavos **1907-21**

1907	1,200,625	9.00	20.00	90.00	175.00
1907S	2,112,000	5.00	12.00	75.00	125.00
1908 Proof only	(500)			250.00	350.00
1908S	1,601,000	6.00	12.00	120.00	250.00
1909S	528,000	10.00	30.00	150.00	300.00
1917S	674,369	10.00	25.00	120.00	225.00
1918S	2,202,000	4.50	8.00	60.00	100.00
1919S	1,200,000	5.00	9.00	85.00	125.00
1920	420,000	4.50	8.00	35.00	75.00
1921	2,316,763	3.00	6.00	30.00	55.00

Large Size One Peso **1903-06**

[317]

PHILIPPINES UNDER SOVEREIGNTY OF THE U.S.

	Quan. Minted	V. Fine	E. Fine	MS-60	MS-63
1903	2,788,901	$16.00	$30.00	$150.00	$250.00
1903 Proof	(2,558)			225.00	300.00
1903S	11,361,000	14.00	20.00	120.00	200.00
1904	11,355	75.00	110.00	225.00	300.00
1904 Proof	(1,355)			225.00	350.00
1904S	6,600,000	15.00	25.00	125.00	180.00
1905 Proof only	(471)		300.00	500.00	800.00
1905S	6,056,000	20.00	35.00	150.00	300.00
1906 Proof only	(500)		250.00	400.00	600.00
1906S	201,000	1,000	1,900	6,500	11,000

Reduced Size One Peso
1907-12

1907S	10,278,000	5.00	10.00	75.00	110.00
1908 Proof only	(500)			400.00	600.00
1908S	20,954,944	5.00	10.00	60.00	100.00
1909S	7,578,000	6.00	12.00	65.00	110.00
1910S	3,153,559	8.00	20.00	100.00	225.00
1911S	463,000	20.00	50.00	500.00	750.00
1912S	680,000	20.00	60.00	550.00	850.00

COMMONWEALTH ISSUES OF THE PHILIPPINES

Bronze Coinage

One Centavo

1937M	15,790,492	1.00	2.00	8.00	15.00
1938M	10,000,000	.75	2.00	8.00	12.00
1939M	6,500,000	1.00	2.00	10.00	20.00
1940M	4,000,000	.50	1.50	8.00	12.00
1941M	5,000,000	1.00	2.00	10.00	25.00
1944S	58,000,000	.10	.25	1.00	1.50

COMMONWEALTH ISSUES OF THE PHILIPPINES

Copper-Nickel Coinage

Five Centavos

	Quan. Minted	V. Fine	E. Fine	MS-60	MS-63
1937M	2,493,872	$3.50	$6.00	$35.00	$50.00
1938M	4,000,000	1.00	2.50	20.00	30.00
1941M	2,750,000	3.00	5.00	30.00	50.00

Copper-Nickel-Zinc Alloy

1944	21,198,000	.20	.30	1.25	2.50
1944S	14,040,000	.20	.30	1.00	1.50
1945S	72,796,000	.20	.25	.75	1.50

Silver Coinage

Ten Centavos

1937M	3,500,000	1.25	3.00	20.00	30.00
1938M	3,750,000	1.00	2.00	12.00	15.00
1941M	2,500,000	1.25	2.50	15.00	22.00
1944D	31,592,000	.30	.50	1.50	2.00
1945D	137,208,000	.25	.50	1.00	1.75

Twenty Centavos

1937M	2,665,000	2.00	3.00	20.00	35.00
1938M	3,000,000	1.50	2.00	10.00	15.00
1941M	1,500,000	2.00	2.25	12.50	20.00
1944D	28,596,000	.50	.75	1.75	3.00
1944D, D over S	} 82,804,000	12.50	25.00	60.00	100.00
1945D		.30	.50	1.25	2.50

COMMONWEALTH ISSUES OF THE PHILIPPINES
Silver Coinage

Fifty Centavos

	Quan. Minted	V. Fine	E. Fine	MS-60	MS-63
1944S	19,187,000	$1.00	$2.00	$4.50	$6.00
1945S	18,120,000	1.00	2.00	4.50	6.00

PHILIPPINE COMMEMORATIVE ISSUES
Establishment of the Commonwealth

Silver Fifty Centavos

1936M	20,000	27.00	45.00	70.00	85.00

Silver Pesos
Bust of Murphy and Quezon

1936M	10,000	45.00	65.00	140.00	175.00

PHILIPPINE COMMEMORATIVE ISSUES
Establishment of the Commonwealth

Bust of Roosevelt and Quezon

	Quan. Minted	V. Fine	E. Fine	MS-60	MS-63
1936M..	10,000	$45.00	$65.00	$140.00	$175.00

BIBLIOGRAPHY

Allen, Lyman L., *U.S. Philippine Coins*, Lyman Allen Numismatic Services, Oakland Park, FL, 1998.
Shafer, Neil, *United States Territorial Coinage for The Philippine Islands*, Whitman Publishing Company, Racine, WI, 1961.

CHECKING YOUR COINS FOR AUTHENTICITY

Coin collectors occasionally encounter counterfeit coins, or coins that have been altered or changed so that they appear to be something other than what they really are. Any coin that does not seem to fit the description of similar pieces listed in this catalog should be looked upon with suspicion. Experienced coin dealers can usually tell quickly if a coin is genuine or not, and would never knowingly sell spurious coins to a collector. Coins found in circulation or bought from a non-professional source should be examined carefully.

The risk of purchasing a spurious coin can be minimized through the use of common sense and an elementary knowledge of the techniques used by counterfeiters. It is well to keep in mind that the more popular a coin is among collectors and the public, the more likely it is that counterfeits and replicas will abound. Generally, collector coins valued at under $100 are rarely replicated because of the high cost of making such items. The same is true of counterfeits that are made to deceive the public. In modern times few counterfeit coins have been made because it is more profitable for the fakers to print paper money.

REPLICAS: Reproductions of famous and historical coins have been distributed for decades by marketing firms and souvenir vendors. These pieces are often tucked away by the original recipients as curios, and later are found in old furniture by others who believe they have discovered objects of great value. Most replicas are poorly made by the casting method, and are virtually worthless. They can sometimes be identified by a seam that runs around the edge of the piece where the two halves of the casting mold were joined together. Genuine specimens of extremely rare or valuable coins are almost never found in unlikely places.

COUNTERFEITS: For many centuries counterfeiters have produced base metal forgeries of gold and silver coins to deceive the public in the normal course of trade. These pieces are usually crudely made and easily detected by close examination. Crudely cast counterfeit copies of older coins are the most prevalent. These can usually be detected by the casting bubbles or pimples that can be seen with low power magnification. Pieces struck from hand made dies are more deceptive, but the engravings do not match those of genuine mint products.

CHECKING YOUR COINS FOR AUTHENTICITY

More recently, as coin collecting has gained popularity and rare coin prices have risen, "numismatic" counterfeits have become more common. The majority of these are die-struck gold coin counterfeits that have been mass produced overseas since 1950. Forgeries exist of most U.S. gold coins dated between 1870 and 1933, as well as all issues of the gold dollar and three dollar gold piece. Most of these are very well made, as they were intended to pass the close scrutiny of collectors. Few gold coins of earlier dates have been counterfeited, but false 1799 $10 gold pieces and 1811 $5 coins have been made. Gold coins in less than extremely fine condition are seldom counterfeited.

Silver dollars dated 1804, Lafayette dollars, several of the low-mintage commemorative half dollars and the 1795 half dimes have been forged in quantity. Minor-coin forgeries made in recent years are the 1909-S V.D.B., 1914-D and 1955 doubled die Lincoln cents, as well as 1877 Indian Head cents, 1856 Flying Eagle cents and, on a much smaller scale, a variety of dates of half cents and large cents. Nineteenth century copies of colonial coins are also sometimes encountered. In this catalog a star has been placed adjacent to the colonial coins where deceptive copies exist.

ALTERATIONS: Coins are occasionally altered by adding, removing or changing a design feature (such as a mint mark or date digit) or by polishing, sandblasting, acid etching, toning or plating the surface of a genuine piece. Changes of this sort are usually done to deceive collectors. Among U.S. gold coins, only the 1927-D double eagle is commonly found with an added mint mark. On $2.50 and $5.00 gold coins, 1839 to 1856, New Orleans "O" mint marks have been altered to "C" (for Charlotte, N.C.) in a few instances.

Over a century ago $5.00 gold pieces were imitated by gold plating 1883 Liberty five cent coins without the word CENTS on the reverse. Other coins commonly created fraudulently through alteration include the 1799 large cent,1909-S, 1909-S V.D.B., 1914-D, 1922 "plain" and 1943 "copper" cents. The 1913 Liberty nickel has been extensively replicated by altering 1910 and 1912 nickels. Scarce, high-grade Denver and San Francisco mint Buffalo nickels of the 1920's, 1916-D and 1942 over 1941 dimes, 1918 over 1917-S and 1932-D and S quarters and 1804 silver dollars have all been made by altering genuine coins of other dates or mints.

DETECTION: The best way to detect counterfeit coins is to compare suspected pieces with others of the same issue. Carefully check size, color, luster, weight, edge devices and design details. Replicas generally have less detail than their genuine counterparts when studied under magnification. Modern struck counterfeits made to deceive collectors are an exception to this rule. Any questionable gold coin should be referred to an expert for verification.

Cast forgeries are usually poorly made and of incorrect weight. Base metal is often used in place of gold or silver, and the coins are light weight and often incorrect in color and luster. Deceptive cast pieces have been made using real metal content and modern dental techniques, but these too usually vary in quality and color.

Detection of alterations sometimes involves comparative examination of the suspected areas of a coin (usually mint marks and date digits) at magnification ranging from 10x to 40x. Coins of exceptional rarity or value should never be purchased without a written guarantee of authenticity.

Professional authentication of rare coins for a fee is available through the American Numismatic Association, 818 North Cascade Avenue, Colorado Springs, Colorado 80903, and the International Numismatic Society, P.O. Box 66555, Washington, D.C. 20035. Authentication is also included with the services offered by commercial grading services, and by some independent coin dealers.

MISSTRUCK COINS AND ERROR PIECES

With the production of millions of coins each year, it is natural that a few abnormal pieces escape inspection and are inadvertently released for circulation, usually in original bags or rolls of new coins. These are not considered regular issues because they were not made intentionally. They are all eagerly sought by collectors for the information they shed on minting techniques, and as a variation from normal date and mint series collecting.

Nearly every misstruck or error coin is unique in some way, and prices may vary from coin to coin. They may all be classified in general groups related to the kind of error or manufacturing malfunction involved. Collectors value these pieces according to the scarcity of each kind of error for each type of coin. Non-collectors usually view them as curios, and often believe that they must be worth much more than normal coins because they look so strange. In reality, the value assigned to various types of errors by collectors and dealers reflects both supply and demand, and is based on recurring transactions between willing buyers and sellers.

The following listings show current average values for the most frequently encountered kinds of error coins. In each case the values shown are for coins that are unmarred by serious marks or scratches, and in uncirculated condition for modern issues, and extremely fine condition for obsolete types. Exceptions are valued higher or lower. Error coins of rare date issues generally do not command a premium beyond their normal values. In most cases each of these coins is unique in some respect and must be valued according to its individual appearance, quality, and eye appeal.

There are many other kinds of errors and misstruck coins beyond those listed in this catalog. Some are more valuable, and others less valuable then the most popular pieces that are listed here as examples of what this interesting field contains. The pieces illustrated are general examples of the types described. For additional details and information about these coins the following books are recommended:

Margolis, Arnold. *The Error Coin Encyclopedia.* Second Edition, 1993.

Herbert, Alan. *Official Price Guide to Minting Varieties and Errors.* New York, 1991.

Fivaz, Bill and Stanton, J.T. *The Cherrypickers' Guide to Rare Die Varieties.* Third Edition. Savannah, 1994.

The coins discussed in this section must not be confused with others that have been mutilated or damaged after leaving the mint. Examples of such pieces include coins that have been scratched, hammered, engraved, impressed, acid etched, or plated by individuals to simulate something other than a normal coin. Those pieces have no numismatic value, and can only be considered as altered coins not suitable for a collection.

1. CLIPPED PLANCHET: An incomplete coin, missing 10-25% of the metal. Incomplete planchets result from accidents when the steel rods used to

MISSTRUCK COINS AND ERROR PIECES

punch out blanks from the metal strip overlap a portion of the strip already punched. There are curved, straight, ragged, incomplete and elliptical clips. Values may be greater or less depending on the nature and size of the clip. Coins with more than one clip usually command higher values.

2. MULTIPLE STRIKE: Coin has additional image from being struck again off center. Value increases with number of strikes. These minting errors occur when a finished coin goes back into the press and is struck again with the same dies. The presence or absence of a date will also affect values.

no rim   with rim

3. BLANK or PLANCHET: A blank of metal intended for coinage but not struck with dies. In the process of preparing blanks for coinage the pieces are first punched from a strip of metal and then milled to upset the rim. In most instances first process pieces (blanks without upset rim) are slightly more valuable than the finished planchets. Values shown are for the most common pieces.

4. DEFECTIVE DIE: Coin shows raised metal from a large die crack, or small rim break. Coins that show evidence of light die cracks, polishing or very minor die damage are generally of little or no value. Prices shown here are for coins with very noticeable raised die crack lines, or those where the die breaks away producing an unstruck area known as a cud.

5. OFF CENTER: Coin has been struck out of collar and incorrectly centered with part of the design missing. Values are for coins with approximately 10-20% of design missing from obsolete type coins; 20-60% missing from modern coins. These are misstruck coins that were made when the planchet did not enter the coinage press properly. Coins that are only struck slightly off center, with none of the design missing, are called Broadstrikes (see category 6). Those with nearly all of the impression missing are generally worth more, but those with a readable date and mint are the most valuable.

6. BROADSTRIKE: A coin that was struck outside of the retaining

collar. When coins are struck without being contained in the collar die they spread out larger than a normal piece. All denominations have a plain edge.

7. LAMINATION: A flaw with a fragment of metal peeled off the coin's surface. This defect occurs when a foreign substance such as gas oxides or dirt becomes trapped in the strip as it is rolled out to the proper thickness. Lamination flaws may be missing or still attached to the coin's surface. Minor flaws may only decrease a coin's value, while a clad coin that is missing the full surface of one or both sides is worth more than the values listed here.

MISSTRUCK COINS AND ERROR PIECES

8. BROCKAGE: Mirror image of the design impressed on the opposite side of the same coin. These errors are caused when a struck coin remains on either die after striking, and impresses its image into the next blank planchet as it is struck, leaving a negative or mirror image. Off-center and partial brockage coins are worth less than those with a full impression. Coins with negative impressions on both sides are usually mutilated pieces made outside the mint by pressing coins together.

9. WRONG PLANCHET: A coin struck on a planchet intended for another denomination or of the wrong metal. Examples of these are cents struck on dime planchets, nickels on cent planchets, or quarters on dime planchets. Values vary depending on the type of error involved. Those struck on coins of a different denomination that were previously struck normally, are of much greater value.

	1. CLIPPED PLANCHET	2. MULTIPLE STRIKE	3. BLANK PLANCHET	4. DEFECTIVE DIE	5. OFF CENTER	6. BROADSTRIKE	7. LAMINATION	8. BROCKAGE
	1	2	3	4	5	6	7	8
Large Cent	$50.	$400.	$60.	$15.	$100.	$30.	$15.	$250.
Indian 1c	25.	200.	—	10.	55.	40.	8.	200.
Lincoln 1c (95% Copper)	3.	20.	3.	10.	3.50	6.	1.50	25.
Steel 1c	15.	150.	18.	15.	45.	25.	15.	90.
Lincoln 1c zinc	2.	25.	1.50	10.	3.50	2.50	15.	35.
Liberty 5c	30.	400.	—	30.	70.	70.	18.	300.
Buffalo 5c	20.	500.	—	25.	50.	50.	5.	500.
Jefferson 5c	4.	18.	5.	12.	8.	8.	5.	45.
Wartime 5c	10.	350.	350.	20.	65.	55.	5.	300.
Barber 10c	60.	200.	10.	75.	75.	75.	12.	100.
Mercury 10c	18.	200.	10.	25.	25.	25.	7.	100.
Roosevelt 10c (S)	5.	70.	10.	35.	30.	35.	8.	85.
Roosevelt 10c (C)	3.	20.	3.50	15.	7.	6.	7.	50.
Washington 25c (S)	15.	150.	35.	20.	45.	45.	18.	100.
Washington 25c (C)	4.	50.	4.	10.	17.	15.	10.	55.
Bicentennial 25c	15.	200.	—	50.	50.	45.	25.	200.
Statehood 25c	35.	225.	—	25.	150.	125.	50.	350.
Franklin 50c	50.	700.	18.	100.	300.	125.	30.	500.
Kennedy 50c (S)	18.	400.	18.	55.	200.	125.	24.	400.
Kennedy 50c (C)	15.	150.	20.	24.	50.	40.	15.	300.
Bicentennial 50c	25.	300.	—	75.	100.	75.	20.	—
Silver $1	35.	2000.	450.	600.	700.	1200.	30.	
Eisenhower $1	40.	1200.	50.	500.	550.	175.	40.	1500.
Bicentennial $1	50.	2000.	—	1000.	600.	190.	40.	—
Anthony $1	25.	500.	35.	100.	50.	40.	30.	300.
Sacagawea $1	30.	500.	40.	50.	95.	75.	50.	350.

MISSTRUCK COINS AND ERROR PIECES

9. WRONG METALS

STRUCK ON:	1¢ ZN	1¢ CU	1¢ Steel	5¢	(S) 10¢	(C) 10¢	(S) 25¢	(C) 25¢	(C) 50¢
Indian 1¢	np	—	np	np	600.	np	np	np	np
Lincoln 1¢	—	—	—	np	255.	225.	np	np	np
Buffalo 5¢	np	800.	np	—	900.	np	np	np	np
Jefferson 5¢	70.	60.	np	—	150.	75.	np	np	np
Wartime 5¢	np	550.	800.	—	200.	np	np	np	np
Wash 25¢ (S)	np	145.	950.	60.	85.	—	—	—	np
Wash 25¢ (C)	110.	145.	np	45.	—	90.	—	—	np
1976 25¢	np	200.	np	250.	—	600.	—	—	np
Statehood 25¢	1500.	np	np	350.	np	1200.	np	—	np
Walking 50¢	np	—	1500.	—	—	np	—	np	np
Franklin 50¢	np	650.	np	500.	700.	np	225.	np	np
Kennedy 50¢	250.	300.	np	350.	400.	250.	250.	125.	—
1976 50¢	np	—	np	350.	—	—	—	300.	—
Eisenhower $1	np	1600.	np	1000.	—	1500.	—	1200.	1000.
Anthony $1	1800.	1400.	np	—	np	—	—	600.	np
Sacagawea $1	1500.	np	np	1500.	np	1000.	np	800.	np

The Kennedy 50¢ struck on an Anthony $1 planchet is very rare. Coins struck over other coins of a different denomination are usually valued three to five times higher than these prices. Values for 50-State quarter errors vary with each type and state, and are generally much higher than for other quarters. Coins made from mis-matched dies (Statehood quarter obverse combined with Sacagawea dollar reverse) are extremely rare.

np = not possible

HARD TIMES TOKENS ERA 1832-1844

We are indebted to the following contributors who initially helped bring the first Hard Times token special section together in the 1978 *Guide Book:* Edward Janis, Gil Steinberg, Joseph Levine, and Paul Koppenhaver. Larry Johnson revised the text and updated the valuations to reflect today's token prices.

"The issues commonly called Hard Times tokens mark a period of peculiar interest in the Numismatic history of the United States. They form a group by themselves as distinct as the Colonial Series so-called, or the State Issues which followed the Revolution. Unlike those, they had no semblance of authority behind them, and they combine, therefore, the character of Political pieces with the catch-words of party cries; of Satirical pieces with sarcastic allusions to the sentiments or speeches of the leaders of opposing parties; and in some degree also of Necessity pieces, in a time when, to use one of the phrases of the day, 'money was a cash article,' hard to get for daily needs; and though the dearth of a circulating medium, was not quite so great as it occasionally seems to have been over the border, when even buttons were made to do duty, not alone as is jestingly said, for the contribution-box, yet currency was difficult to obtain for the small change of petty expenses." This quotation is the introduction to Lyman Haynes Low's *Hard Times Tokens*, second edition reference published in 1906. Low's token numbering system of the 183 types of Hard Times tokens known to him has been expanded to nearly 500 different types identified in Russell Rulau's *Standard Catalog of United States Tokens, 1700-1900.*

Prior to Andrew Jackson's election as President of the United States in 1829, the Second Bank of the United States operated under a 20-year charter which granted it complete control over the currency system of the United States. Jackson disliked this bank not only for economic reasons, but also because of political considerations. In 1832 Jackson vetoed a bill rechartering the bank, preferring instead to order the transfer of government deposits to state banks, many of which were owned by political cronies.

HARD TIMES TOKENS ERA 1832-1844

This action unfortunately also took away some stability from an already shaky economy and created a growing climate of mistrust. Jackson's economic policies contributed to a nation-wide financial collapse. By 1837 hundreds of banks and large businesses had closed; the nation was gripped by a severe depression. Specie payments (disbursements in gold and silver) were suspended on May 10th, 1837, in an attempt to stop the outflow of scarce reserves. Even the small change needed for everyday necessities was hoarded, and large cent sized tokens quickly appeared as substitutes for coins to fill this compelling need, circulating freely at the value of one cent. The economic principle of Gresham's Law (bad money drives the good from circulation) was again proven to be reliable.

The primary attraction of Hard Times tokens is the wide variety of styles and themes used to reflect the passions of the day. Many are satirical pieces produced by Jackson's political enemies to lampoon the president's economic policies. Some voice anti-slavery sentiments. Legends on these pieces often made use of popular slogans, such as the most famous battle cry of the United States naval battle with Tripoli, MILLIONS FOR DEFENSE — NOT ONE CENT FOR TRIBUTE. Most are store cards used to promote various enterprises. It must be noted that a token could be produced for as little as a half cent each, which could result in a nice profit when used in place of a cent when making change. It is estimated that 10-20 million tokens were produced during this era. Many common varieties can be found in inexpensive lower grades at most coin shows, while some are quite rare and elusive. The collecting challenge is to find choice examples in any grade; outstanding examples in both color and strike will command large premiums. Many large coin collections also contain examples of Hard Times tokens because of their important role in our monetary history.

HARD TIMES TOKENS

This special section is intended to be an introduction to the series, once described by Neil Carothers as "Quaint and curious relics of our currency history". Store card/political mules, as well as those pieces dedicated entirely to advertising, are omitted because of space limitations. Interested collectors are encouraged to obtain a reprint of Low's reference book as well as the new *Standard Catalog* to gain a better appreciation and understanding of this fascinating series.

	VF	EF	AU
L1. HT1. Andrew Jackson			
Copper	$5,500	$9,000	—

	VF	EF	AU
L5, HT7. Jackson, small head			
Brass	$400.00	$700.00	$900.00

HARD TIMES TOKENS

	VF	EF	AU
L3, HT5. Jackson President			
Brass	$250.00	$600.00	$700.00

	VF	EF	AU
L57, HT76. Van Buren, facing left			
Brass	$2,500	$3,500	$4,500

L4, HT6. Jackson Pres. of U.S.			
Brass	175.00	300.00	550.00

L162, HT77. Van Buren, right			
Copper	400.00	600.00	850.00

L.56, HT75. Van Buren, left			
Copper	85.00	175.00	375.00

L.7, HT15. Whig Victory			
Copper	2,250	3,250	—

L.13, HT26. William Seward			
Brass	200.00	300.00	425.00
L.14, HT27. Glory and Pride			
Brass	300.00	450.00	750.00

L.66, HT24. Agriculture			
Copper	155.00	300.00	500.00

HARD TIMES TOKENS

	VF	EF	AU
L.16. HT30. Gulian Verplanck			
Brass	150.00	$250.00	$350.00

	VF	EF	AU
L.54, HT81. Woman & Sister			
Copper	$85.00	$200.00	$400.00

L.6, HT14. Whigs of N. York
Brass 350.00   550.00   800.00

L.49, HT73. Half Cent 1837
Copper 80.00   140.00   275.00

L.55, HT63. Loco Foco 1838
Copper 38.00   75.00   190.00

L.8, HT9. My Victory/Jackson
Copper 20.00   55.00   100.00

L.37, HT61. Benton Mint Drop
Copper 25.00   60.00   175.00

HARD TIMES TOKENS

	VF	EF	AU

L.12, HT25. A Plain System
Copper $20.00 $65.00 $125.00

L.51, HT70. Roman Firmness
Copper 20.00 40.00 75.00

	VF	EF	AU

L.18, HT32. Executive Experiment
Copper $20.00 $40.00 $75.00

L.40, HT65. Head/May Tenth
Copper 20.00 65.00 100.00
L.47, HT66. Phoenix/May Tenth
Copper 20.00 40.00 75.00

L.21, HT35. Not One Cent
Copper 125.00 300.00 400.00
L.31, HT46. Not One Cent, motto
Copper 20.00 40.00 75.00

L.63, HT21. Ship/No Lightning
Copper 20.00 85.00 150.00

L.45, HT56. Phoenix/Not One Cent
Copper 20.00 40.00 100.00

HARD TIMES TOKENS

	VF	EF	AU
L.44, HT69. Ship/Jackson			
Copper	$20.00	$40.00	$95.00

	VF	EF	AU
L.60, HT18. Ship/Lightning			
Copper	$20.00	$40.00	$95.00

L.58, HT16. Ship/Star border			
Copper	20.00	40.00	85.00

L.65, HT23. Ship/Liberty Head			
Copper	75.00	150.00	200.00

L.59, HT17. Ship/Wreath border			
Copper	20.00	40.00	85.00

BIBLIOGRAPHY

Rulau, Russell. Standard Catalog of United States Tokens 1700-1900. Iola, Wisconsin. 1997.

BULLION PRICE CHARTS
BULLION VALUE OF SILVER COINS

Silver Price Per Ounce	Wartime Nickel .05626 oz.	Dime .07234 oz.	Quarter .18084 oz.	Half Dollar .36169 oz.	Silver Clad Half Dollar .14792 oz.	Silver Dollar .77344 oz.
$3.00	$.17	$.22	$.58	$1.09	$.45	$2.32
3.50	.20	.25	.63	1.27	.52	2.71
4.00	.23	.29	.72	1.45	.59	3.10
4.50	.25	.32	.81	1.63	.66	3.48
5.00	.28	.36	.90	1.81	.74	3.87
5.50	.31	.40	1.00	1.99	.81	4.26
6.00	.34	.44	1.09	2.17	.89	4.64
6.50	.36	.47	1.18	2.35	.96	5.03
7.00	.40	.51	1.27	2.53	1.04	5.42
7.50	.42	.55	1.36	2.72	1.11	5.80
8.00	.45	.58	1.45	2.90	1.19	6.19
8.50	.48	.62	1.54	3.08	1.26	6.58
9.00	.50	.65	1.63	3.26	1.33	6.96

BULLION VALUE OF GOLD COINS

Gold Price Per Ounce	$5.00 Liberty Head 1839-1908 Indian Head 1908-1929 .24187 oz.	$10.00 Liberty Head 1838-1907 Indian Head 1907-1933 .48375 oz.	$20.00 1849-1933 .96750 oz.
$ 200.00	$ 48.37	$ 96.75	$ 193.50
225.00	54.42	108.85	217.69
250.00	60.47	120.94	241.88
275.00	66.52	133.03	266.07
300.00	72.50	145.13	290.25
325.00	78.60	157.22	314.44
350.00	84.65	169.31	338.63
375.00	90.70	181.40	362.81
400.00	96.75	193.50	387.00
425.00	102.80	205.60	411.19
450.00	108.84	217.69	435.38
475.00	114.89	229.78	459.56
500.00	120.94	241.87	483.75

The U.S. bullion coins first issued in 1986 are unlike the older regular issues. They contain the following amounts of pure metal: Silver $1, 1 oz.; Gold $50, 1 oz.; $25, $1/2$ oz.; $10, $1/4$ oz.; $5, $1/10$ oz.

UNITED STATES BULLION COINS
Silver

The silver eagle is a one ounce bullion coin with a face value of one dollar. The obverse has Adolph A. Weinman's Walking Liberty design used on the half dollar coins from 1916 through 1947. His initials are on the hem of the gown. The reverse design is a rendition of a heraldic eagle by John Mercanti.

Designers: Adolph A. Weinman (obverse), John Mercanti (reverse); composition 99.93% silver, .07% copper; weight 31.101 grams; diameter 40.6mm; net weight one oz. fine silver; reeded edge; mints: Philadelphia, San Francisco and West Point.

UNITED STATES BULLION SILVER COINS

	Quan. Minted	Unc.	Proof
$1	1986..........5,393,005	$18.00	
$1	1986S .....(1,446,778)		$27.00
$1	1987.........11,442,335	10.00	
$1	1987S ....(904,732)		26.00
$1	1988..........5,004,646	11.00	
$1	1988S ....(557,370)		110.00
$1	1989..........5,203,327	11.00	
$1	1989S ....(617,694)		34.00
$1	1990..........5,840,210	12.00	
$1	1990S ....(695,510)		30.00
$1	1991..........7,191,066	10.00	
$1	1991S ....(511,925)		62.00
$1	1992..........5,540,068	11.00	
$1	1992S ....(498,654)		40.00
$1	1993..........6,763,762	11.00	
$1	1993P.........(403,625)		100.00
$1	1994..........4,227,319	12.00	
$1	1994P.........(372,168)		100.00

	Quan. Minted	Unc.	Proof
$1	1995..........4,672,051	$12.00	
$1	1995P ....(395,400)		$100.00
$1	1995W..........(30,125)		2,200
$1	1996..........3,603,386	21.00	
$1	1996P ....(473,021)		55.00
$1	1997..........4,295,004	12.00	
$1	1997P ....(429,682)		100.00
$1	1998..........4,847,549	10.00	
$1	1998P ....(452,319)		52.00
$1	1999..........7,408,640	10.00	
$1	1999P ....(549,769)		85.00
$1	2000(W).....9,239,132	10.00	
$1	2000P		35.00
$1	2001(W).....9,001,711	10.00	
$1	2001P		35.00
$1	2002(W).....................	9.00	
$1	2002W		35.00

UNITED STATES BULLION GOLD COINS

The gold American Eagle bullion coins are made in four denominations that contain 1 oz., $1/2$ oz., $1/4$ oz. and $1/10$ oz. of gold. The obverse features a modified rendition of the Augustus Saint-Gaudens design used on U.S. twenty dollar gold pieces from 1907 until 1933. The reverse displays a "family of eagles" motif designed by Mrs. Miley Busiek and engraved by Sherl J. Winter.

Uncirculated American Eagles, unlike their Proof counterparts, are not sold directly to the general public, but to a series of authorized buyers. These buyers obtain the uncirculated bullion coins from the Mint based on the current spot price of the metal plus a small premium. The coins are then sold to secondary distributors for sale to other dealers and the general public. These coins have legal-tender status only for their stated dollar face value.

UNITED STATES BULLION COIN SETS

	Proof
1987 Gold Set. $50.00, 25.00	$700.00
1988 Gold Set. $50.00, 25.00, 10.00, 5.00	900.00
1989 Gold Set. $50.00, 25.00, 10.00, 5.00	900.00
1990 Gold Set. $50.00, 25.00, 10.00, 5.00	900.00
1991 Gold Set. $50.00, 25.00, 10.00, 5.00	900.00
1992 Gold Set. $50.00, 25.00, 10.00, 5.00	900.00
1993 Gold Set. $50.00, 25.00, 10.00, 5.00	900.00
1993 Bicentennial Gold Set. $25.00, 10.00, 5.00, $1 Silver Eagle and medal	450.00
1994 Gold Set. $50.00, 25.00, 10.00, 5.00	900.00
1995 Gold Set. $50.00, 25.00, 10.00, 5.00	925.00
1995 Anniversary Gold Set. $50.00, 25.00, 10.00, 5.00, and $1 Silver Eagle	3,000
1996 Gold Set. $50.00, 25.00, 10.00, 5.00	950.00
1997 Gold Set. $50.00, 25.00, 10.00, 5.00	775.00
1997 Impressions of Liberty Set. $100 platinum, $50 gold, $1 silver	1,600
1998 Gold Set. $50.00, 25.00, 10.00, 5.00	750.00
1999 Gold Set. $50.00, 25.00, 10.00, 5.00	800.00
2000 Gold Set. $50.00, 25.00, 10.00, 5.00	1,200
2001 Gold Set. $50.00, 25.00, 10.00, 5.00	1,100
2002 Gold Set. $50.00, 25.00, 10.00, 5.00	900.00

UNITED STATES BULLION GOLD COINS

TENTH-OUNCE GOLD $5.00

Designers: Augustus Saint-Gaudens (obverse), Miley Busiek (reverse); composition, 91.67% gold, 3% silver, 5.33% copper; reeded edge; mints: Philadelphia, West Point.
$5 diameter 16.5mm; weight 3.393 grams; net weight 1/10 oz. fine gold.

	Quan. Issued	Unc.	Proof
$5 MCMLXXXVI (1986)	912,609	$45.00	
$5 MCMLXXXVII (1987)	580,266	45.00	
$5 MCMLXXXVIII (1988)	159,500	75.00	
$5 MCMLXXXVIII (1988)P	(143,881)		$60.00
$5 MCMLXXXIX (1989)	264,790	70.00	
$5 MCMLXXXIX (1989)P	(84,924)		60.00
$5 MCMXC (1990)	210,210	70.00	
$5 MCMXC (1990)P	(99,349)		65.00
$5 MCMXCI (1991)	165,200	90.00	
$5 MCMXCI (1991)P	(70,334)		65.00
$5 1992	209,300	45.00	
$5 1992P	(64,902)		80.00
$5 1993	210,709	45.00	
$5 1993P	(58,649)		90.00
$5 1994	206,380	45.00	
$5 1994W	(62,100)		65.00
$5 1995	223,025	45.00	
$5 1995W	(48,675)		65.00
$5 1996	401,964	40.00	
$5 1996W	(57,449)		100.00
$5 1997	528,266	50.00	
$5 1997W	(35,164)		120.00
$5 1998	1,344,520	40.00	
$5 1998W	(39,706)		80.00
$5 1999	2,750,338	40.00	
$5 1999W	(19,919)		70.00
$5 1999W, Unc. made from unpolished proof dies		450.00	
$5 2000	569,153	40.00	
$5 2000W			100.00
$5 2001	269,147	38.00	
$5 2001W			80.00
$5 2002		38.00	
$5 2002W			70.00

UNITED STATES BULLION GOLD COINS

Designers: Augustus Saint-Gaudens (obverse), Miley Busiek (reverse); composition, 91.67% gold, 3% silver, 5.33% copper; reeded edge; mints: Philadelphia, West Point.
$10 diameter 22mm; weight 8.483 grams; net weight 1/4 oz. fine gold.

QUARTER-OUNCE GOLD $10.00

	Quan. Issued	Unc.	Proof
$10 MCMLXXXVI (1986)	726,031	$120.00	
$10 MCMLXXXVII (1987)	269,255	100.00	
$10 MCMLXXXVIII (1988)	49,000	100.00	
$10 MCMLXXXVIII (1988)P	(98,028)		$130.00
$10 MCMLXXXIX (1989)	81,789	100.00	
$10 MCMLXXXIX (1989)P	(53,593)		130.00
$10 MCMXC (1990)	41,000	130.00	
$10 MCMXC (1990)P	(62,674)		130.00
$10 MCMXCI (1991)	36,100	200.00	
$10 MCMXCI (1991)P	(50,840)		130.00
$10 1992	59,546	120.00	
$10 1992P	(42,290)		140.00
$10 1993	71,864	110.00	
$10 1993P	(46,271)		140.00
$10 1994	72,650	100.00	
$10 1994W	(47,600)		140.00
$10 1995	83,752	100.00	
$10 1995W	(46,825)		150.00
$10 1996	60,318	100.00	
$10 1996W	(37,755)		150.00
$10 1997	108,805	110.00	
$10 1997W	(29,984)		150.00
$10 1998	309,829	90.00	
$10 1998W	(29,731)		125.00
$10 1999	564,232	80.00	
$10 1999W	(34,410)		150.00
$10 1999W, Unc. made from unpolished proof dies		400.00	
$10 2000	128,964	110.00	
$10 2000W			180.00
$10 2001	71,280	90.00	
$10 2001W			160.00
$10 2002		90.00	
$10 2002W			130.00

UNITED STATES BULLION GOLD COINS

Designers: Augustus Saint-Gaudens (obverse), Miley Busiek (reverse); composition, 91.67% gold, 3% silver, 5.33% copper; reeded edge; mints: Philadelphia, West Point.
$25 diameter 27mm; weight 16.966 grams; net weight 1/2 oz. fine gold.

HALF-OUNCE GOLD $25.00

	Quan. Issued	Unc.	Proof
$25 MCMLXXXVI (1986)	599,566	$250.00	
$25 MCMLXXXVII (1987)	131,255	250.00	
$25 MCMLXXXVII (1987)P	(143,398)		$260.00
$25 MCMLXXXVIII (1988)	45,000	275.00	
$25 MCMLXXXVIII (1988)P	(76,528)		275.00
$25 MCMLXXXIX (1989)	44,829	350.00	
$25 MCMLXXXIX (1989)P	(44,264)		290.00
$25 MCMXC (1990)	31,000	425.00	
$25 MCMXC (1990)P	(51,636)		290.00
$25 MCMXCI (1991)	24,100	450.00	
$25 MCMXCI (1991)P	(53,125)		450.00
$25 1992	54,404	275.00	
$25 1992P	(40,982)		275.00
$25 1993	73,324	200.00	
$25 1993P	(43,319)		250.00
$25 1994	62,400	200.00	
$25 1994W	(44,100)		250.00
$25 1995	53,474	275.00	
$25 1995W	(46,200)		275.00
$25 1996	39,287	300.00	
$25 1996W	(34,769)		250.00
$25 1997	79,605	250.00	
$25 1997W	(26,801)		250.00
$25 1998	169,029	175.00	
$25 1998W	(25,550)		270.00
$25 1999	263,013	175.00	
$25 1999W	(30,452)		270.00
$25 2000	79,287	175.00	
$25 2000W			300.00
$25 2001	48,047	190.00	
$25 2001W			300.00
$25 2002		175.00	
$25 2002W			250.00

UNITED STATES BULLION GOLD COINS

Designers: Augustus Saint-Gaudens (obverse), Miley Busiek (reverse); composition, 91.67% gold, 3% silver, 5.33% copper; reeded edge; mints: Philadelphia, West Point.
$50 diameter 32.7mm; weight 33.931 grams; net weight one oz. fine gold.

ONE OUNCE GOLD $50.00

	Quan. Issued	Unc.	Proof
$50 MCMLXXXVI (1986)	1,362,650	$325.00	
$50 MCMLXXXVI (1986)W	(446,290)		$490.00
$50 MCMLXXXVII (1987)	1,045,500	325.00	
$50 MCMLXXXVII (1987)W	(147,498)		490.00
$50 MCMLXXXVIII (1988)	465,000	325.00	
$50 MCMLXXXVIII (1988)W	(87,133)		490.00
$50 MCMLXXXIX (1989)	415,790	325.00	
$50 MCMLXXXIX (1989)W	(53,960)		475.00
$50 MCMXC (1990)	373,210	325.00	
$50 MCMXC (1990)W	(62,401)		475.00
$50 MCMXCI (1991)	243,100	325.00	
$50 MCMXCI (1991)W	(50,411)		475.00
$50 1992	275,000	325.00	
$50 1992W	(44,835)		475.00
$50 1993	480,192	325.00	
$50 1993W	(34,389)		490.00
$50 1994	221,633	325.00	
$50 1994W	(46,300)		500.00
$50 1995	200,636	325.00	
$50 1995W	(48,075)		525.00
$50 1996	189,148	325.00	
$50 1996W	(36,086)		480.00
$50 1997	664,508	325.00	
$50 1997W	(27,803)		480.00
$50 1998	1,468,530	325.00	
$50 1998W	(26,047)		480.00
$50 1999	1,505,026	325.00	
$50 1999W	(31,446)		490.00
$50 2000	433,319	325.00	
$50 2000W			725.00
$50 2001	143,605	325.00	
$50 2001W			625.00
$50 2002		325.00	
$50 2002W			480.00

UNITED STATES BULLION PLATINUM COINS

American Eagle platinum coins are made in four denominations and sizes that are different from the similar gold coins. The one ounce coin is designated $100.00 and contains one ounce of pure platinum. Fractional denominations containing 1/2 ounce, 1/4 ounce or 1/10 ounce, are called $50, $25 and $10 respectively.

Designers: John M. Mercanti (obverse) and Thomas D. Rogers, Sr. (reverse). Composition, .9995 fine platinum. Mints: Philadelphia, West Point.

ONE OUNCE PLATINUM $100.00

	Quan. Issued	Unc.	Proof
1997	56,000	$525.00	
1997W	(16,000)		$700.00
1998	133,002	525.00	
1998W	(26,047)		700.00
1999	56,707	525.00	
1999W	(12,351)		700.00
2000	10,003	660.00	
2000W			750.00
2001	14,070	530.00	
2001W			700.00
2002		525.00	
2002W			680.00

UNITED STATES BULLION PLATINUM COINS

HALF-OUNCE PLATINUM $50.00

	Quan. Issued	Unc.	Proof
1997	20,500	$375.00	
1997W	(14,637)		$400.00
1998	32,415	325.00	
1998W	(13,919)		400.00
1999	32,309	325.00	
1999W	(11,098)		400.00
2000	18,892	400.00	
2000W			420.00
2001	12,815	400.00	
2001W			410.00
2002		315.00	
2002W			375.00

QUARTER-OUNCE PLATINUM $25.00

1997	27,100	$220.00	
1997W	(18,726)		$200.00
1998	38,887	190.00	
1998W	(14,203)		200.00
1999	39,734	190.00	
1999W	(13,524)		210.00
2000	20,054	260.00	
2000W			225.00
2001	21,815	300.00	
2001W			250.00
2002		175.00	
2002W			200.00

UNITED STATES BULLION PLATINUM COINS
TENTH-OUNCE PLATINUM $10.00

	Quan. Issued	*Unc.*	*Proof*
1997	70,250	$70.00	
1997W	(37,260)		$115.00
1998	39,525	70.00	
1998W	(19,919)		110.00
1999	55,955	75.00	
1999W	(19,123)		120.00
2000	34,027	80.00	
2000W			130.00
2001	52,017	80.00	
2001W			125.00
2002		70.00	
2002W			110.00

UNITED STATES BULLION COIN SETS

1997 Platinum Set. $100.00, 50.00, 25.00, 10.00	$1,600
1998 Platinum Set. $100.00, 50.00, 25.00, 10.00	1,375
1999 Platinum Set. $100.00, 50.00, 25.00, 10.00	1,400
2000 Platinum Set. $100.00, 50.00, 25.00, 10.00	1,500
2001 Platinum Set. $100.00, 50.00, 25.00, 10.00	1,400
2002 Platinum Set. $100.00, 50.00, 25.00, 10.00	1,400

THE GUIDE BOOK AS A COLLECTIBLE

A Guide Book of United States Coins has long held the record for being the longest running annual retail coin price guide. It has now passed its fiftieth anniversary, and collectors seem to be almost as interested in assembling sets of old *Red Books* as of old coins. The reason for this popularity seems to be that collectors have a penchant for completing sets of many things. The demand for old editions of the *Red Book* that are still in existence has created a solid market for them.

Those who save old editions of the *Red Book* seem to do so for many reasons. Some maintain a reference library of all kinds of coin publications. To them having one of each edition is essential, because that is the way old books are collected. Others are speculators who believe that the value of old editions will go up as interest and demand increases. The great majority of people who save old *Red Books* do so to maintain a record of coin prices going back further than any other source.

Following price trends in old *Red Books* is a good indicator of how well coins of any date or denomination are doing in comparison to each other. The price information published in this book each year is an average of what the entire market is paying for each coin. As such it is a valuable benchmark showing how prices have gone up or down over the years. It is information like this that often gives investors an edge in predicting what the future may hold.

Old *Red Books* are also a handy source of information about collecting trends. They show graphically how grading has changed over the years, what new coins have been discovered and added to the listings and which areas are growing in popularity. Studying these old books can be educational as well as nostalgic. It's great fun to see what your favorite coins sold for 15, 25 or more years ago. It can also be a bit frustrating to realize what might have been if we had only bought the right coins at the right time in years past.

Many collectors have asked about the quantities printed of each edition. Unfortunately that information has never been published, and now even the manufacturer has no records of how many were made. The original author, R.S. Yeoman, told inquirers that the first press run on November 1946 was for 9,000 copies. In February 1947 an additional 9,000 copies were printed to satisfy the unexpected demand.

There was a slight difference between the first and second printing. The wording in the first printing, at the bottom of page 135 reads, "which probably accounts for the scarcity of *this date*," That line was changed to "...the scarcity of *1903-O*" in the second printing.

The second edition had a press run of 22,000. The printing of each edition thereafter gradually increased, with the highest number ever being reached with the 18th edition, dated 1965. In that year, at the top of a booming coin market, a whopping 1,200,000 copies were produced. Since that time the numbers have decreased in proportion to the market, but still maintain a record of being the world's largest selling coin publication each year.

In some years a very limited number of *Red Books* were made for use by price contributors. Those were interleaved with blank pages. No more than 50 copies were ever made for any one year. Perhaps fewer than 20 were made in the first few years. Three of these still exist for the first edition, and one of the second edition. They are valued at $1,500 each. Those made in the 1960s sell for around $50 each today.

There are other unusual *Red Books* that command exceptional prices. One of the most popular is the special edition that was made for, and distributed only to, people who attended the 1986 ANA banquet in Milwaukee. Only 500 of those were printed with a special commemorative cover. Copies have sold for $75 to $100 each and are always in demand.

Error books are also popular with collectors. The most common is one with double stamped printing on the cover. The second most frequently seen are those with the cover put on upside down. Probably the best known of the error books is the 1963, 16th edition with a missing page. For some uncanny reason page 239 is duplicated in some of those books, and page 237 is missing. The error was corrected on most of the printing.

Those who collect old *Red Books* find them in the strangest places; everywhere from flea markets to Hospital libraries. Garage sales are the most fruitful source. I have heard many stories of collectors finding first or second editions in a garage sale for 10¢ or 25¢. Others come from book stores at 50¢ or $1, but if you want to collect these books seriously you will probably have to look for them in numismatic book auctions. There you will compete with others, and probably have to pay prices close to those shown in the accompanying chart.

Condition of these old books is just as important as it is for old coins. A "new" book is one that has never been abused and is fresh and clean with no writing or blemishes. These are of course in highest demand. You can also find nice used copies that are still clean and in good shape, but slightly worn from use. Perhaps the gold stamping on the cover is a bit faded, or someone has added their name on the inside cover. These are of course worth less than a new copy, but are still considered collectible. Only the rarest editions are worth a premium in badly worn condition.

VALUATION GUIDE FOR PAST ISSUES OF THE GUIDE BOOK

Year / Edition	Issue Price	V. Good	Fine	V. Fine	New
1947-1st, 1st printing	$1.50	$175.00	$250.00	$400.00	$750.00
1947-1st, 2nd printing	1.50	175.00	225.00	350.00	700.00
1948-2nd	1.50	90.00	100.00	145.00	275.00
1949-3rd	1.50	90.00	100.00	150.00	300.00
1951/52-4th	1.50	70.00	90.00	135.00	200.00
1952/53-5th	1.50	175.00	215.00	375.00	600.00
1953/54-6th	1.50	40.00	50.00	75.00	150.00
1954/55-7th	1.75	40.00	50.00	75.00	150.00
1955-8th	1.75	25.00	35.00	60.00	100.00
1956-9th	1.75	25.00	40.00	50.00	85.00
1957-10th	1.75	20.00	30.00	40.00	65.00
1958-11th	1.75	—	10.00	15.00	35.00
1959-12th	1.75	—	15.00	25.00	35.00
1960-13th	1.75	—	6.00	8.00	18.00
1961-14th	1.75	—	4.00	6.00	15.00
1962-15th	1.75	—	4.00	5.00	8.00
1963-16th	1.75	—	4.00	5.00	8.00
1964-17th	1.75	—	4.00	5.00	7.00
1965-18th	1.75	—	3.00	4.00	6.00
1966-19th	1.75	—	3.00	4.00	6.00
1967-20th	1.75	—	3.00	5.00	8.00
1968-21st	2.00	—	3.00	5.00	10.00
1969-22nd	2.00	—	3.00	5.00	10.00
1970-23rd	2.50	—	3.00	6.00	11.00
1971-24th	2.50	—	3.00	4.00	6.00
1972-25th	2.50	—	6.00	9.00	12.00
1973-26th	2.50	—	4.00	5.00	7.00
1974-27th	2.50	—	2.00	4.00	6.00
1975-28th	3.00	—	—	4.00	5.00
1976-29th	3.95	—	—	4.00	5.00
1977-30th	3.95	—	—	4.00	6.00
1978-31st	3.95	—	—	4.00	5.00
1979-32nd	3.95	—	—	4.00	6.00
1980-33rd	3.95	—	7.00	10.00	19.00
1981-34th	4.95	—	—	2.00	5.00
1982-35th	4.95	—	—	2.00	5.00
1983-36th	5.95	—	—	2.00	5.00
1984-37th	5.95	—	—	2.00	5.00
1985-38th	5.95	—	—	2.00	5.00
1986-39th	5.95	—	—	2.50	5.00
1987-40th, special A.N.A. cover	—	—	10.00	50.00	200.00
1987-40th	6.95	—	—	3.00	6.00
1988-41st	6.95	—	—	3.00	5.00
1989-42nd	6.95	—	—	3.00	8.00
1990-43rd	7.95	—	—	2.00	7.00
1991-44th	8.95	—	—	2.00	5.00
1992-45th	8.95	—	—	2.00	6.00
1992-45th, special A.N.A. cover	—	—	5.00	20.00	150.00
1993-46th, hard bound	9.95	—	—	2.25	7.00
1993-46th, soft bound	6.95	—	—	1.00	5.00
1994-47th, hard bound	9.95	—	—	1.00	4.00
1994-47th, soft bound	7.95	—	—	1.00	4.00
1995-48th, hard bound	10.95	—	—	1.00	4.00

VALUATION GUIDE FOR PAST ISSUES OF THE GUIDE BOOK

Year/Edition	Issue Price	V. Good	Fine	V. Fine	New
1995-48th, soft bound	$7.95	—	—	$1.00	$3.00
1996-49th, hard bound	10.95	—	—	—	4.00
1996-49th, soft bound	7.95	—	—	—	3.00
1997-50th, hard bound	11.95	—	—	—	5.00
1997-50th, coilbound	8.95	—	—	—	5.00
1997-50th, special anniv. cover	24.95	—	—	20.00	120.00
1998-51st, hard board	11.95	—	—	—	2.00
1998-51st, soft bound	8.95	—	—	—	1.50
1999-52nd hard bound	11.95	—	—	—	2.00
1999-52nd coilbound	8.95	—	—	—	1.50
2000-53rd hard bound	12.95	—	—	—	2.00
2000-53rd coilbound	8.95	—	—	—	1.50
2001-54th hard bound	13.95	—	—	—	1.50
2001-54th coilbound	9.95	—	—	—	1.50
2002-55th hard bound	14.95	—	—	—	—
2002-55th coilbound	10.95	—	—	—	—
2002-A.N.A. special edition	100.00	—	—	20.00	125.00
2002 S.S. Central America	—	—	—	25.00	150.00
2003-56th hard bound	15.95	—	—	—	—
2003-56th coilbound	11.95	—	—	—	—
2003-56th soft bound	11.95	—	—	—	—

INDEX

INDEX — *Continued*

INDEX — *Continued*

The following numismatic magazines are obtainable by subscription. They are published monthly or as indicated below. Information or sample copies may be obtained by writing to the individual publisher.

The Numismatist
Published by the American
Numismatic Association
818 North Cascade Ave.
Colorado Springs, CO 80903

Numismatic News (Weekly)
700 E. State Street
Iola, Wisconsin 54990

Coins Magazine
700 E. State Street
Iola, Wisconsin 54990

Coin World (Weekly)
P.O. Box 150
Sidney, Ohio 45365

The Canadian Numismatic Journal
Published by the Canadian
Numismatic Association
P.O. Box 226
Barrie, Ontario, Canada

COINage Magazine
4880 Market Street
Ventura, California 93003

Whitman® Coin Books & Products

Handbook of United States Coins
The Official Blue Book of U.S. Coins
R.S. Yeoman

United States and Canada Coin Collector's
Check List and Record Book
0-307-19099-4

Official A.N.A. Grading Standards
for United States Coins, 5th Edition
0-307-09097-3

Coins: Questions & Answers
Clifford Mishler
0-307-09359-X

Photograde Coin Grading Guide, 18th Edition
James F. Ruddy
0-307-99361-2

Handbook of Ancient Greek and Roman Coins
Zander H. Klowans and K.E. Bresset (Editor)
0-307-09362-X

Guide Book of Untied States Currency, 3rd Edition
Kenneth Bresset
0-307-48003-8

Whitman Guide to Coin Collecting
Kenneth Bresset
0-307-48008-9

Coin folders, albums, starter sets, and a variety of
storage boxes and holders are also available.